Johburg to London

A Journey

By

Jack Chernin

© Copyright 2007 Jack Chernin

The right of Jack Chernin to be identified as author of this work has been asserted by her in accordance with the Copyright, Designs and Patents Act 1988.

All rights reserved.

No reproduction, copy or transmission of this publication may be made without written permission. No paragraph of this publication may be reproduced, copied or transmitted save with the written permission or in accordance with the provisions of the Copyright Act 1956 (as amended).

ISBN 978-1-84753-009-7

Published by Lulu
www.lulu.com

Acknowledgements

I would thank Lisa Chernin (possibly a very distant relative), Ella Harris and Paul Edmondson for their assistance, help, corrections and encouragement.

Dedications

I would like to dedicate this book to my wife Ann and my children Joel, Celia, Rowan and their respective partners, Claire, Pete, and Samantha and not least of all my three grandsons, Billy, Tommy and Jimi.

21 Berea Road Bertrams

Part One

Growing Up

Chapter 1

This is not a conventional autobiography but, rather, a random look back at what has happened to me as far as I can remember. Well, then, who am I? I was born in Vryburg in the North Cape Province of South Africa. My mother was born in Lithuania and travelled to South Africa with her parents when she was five years old. My father was born in Cape Town and his parents originated from what is now Belarus.

My great grandfather lived in a small village known in Yiddish as a shtetel. Apparently the local Jews lived apart from the rest of the community in what can only be described as a ghetto. The Jewish families all had Hebrew names until the male members of the family were drafted into the Czar's army and then given Russian names. My great grandfather and his brothers were given the name Chernin a version of the Russian word "chornin" meaning black. This was due to his dark Mediterranean appearance.

At the turn of the century, during the time of pogroms, the migration of Jews to Western Europe and the Americas was well underway. Some also migrated to the Southern Hemisphere and particularly South Africa. My paternal and maternal grandparents were amongst those. Apart from my paternal grandmother, who was known to my sisters, my cousins and me as our Bobe, I never knew my maternal grandparents.

I grew up mainly in the Johannesburg suburbs of Bertrams and Doornfontien. These were the residential areas where newly arrived Jewish immigrants tended to first settle. After they became established and financially more secure, they moved up to the plusher, more luxurious leafy Northern Suburbs. My family never moved away from Berea Road, Bertrams. Before the war my father, who was a pharmacist, had built his chemist shop and house with the proceeds of my mother's inheritance in Parktown, one of the northern more affluent suburbs of Johannesburg.

My father's business failed and soon after the outbreak of the Second World War, he volunteered. This resulted in my mother and my sisters and me 'living' in a hostel for soldier's families who were serving in East and North Africa. I think we lived there for about a year before my mother, who to say the least was very quarrelsome, managed to find a flat at 21, Berea Road, Bertrams. This was my address until my final year at school when I ran away from home and went to live with elder sisters who were both married by then.

I purposely mentioned my address for the following reasons. It was by Johannesburg standards an old house built at the end of last century and was one of the first double-storey houses to be built in what was then on the outskirts of Johannesburg. As far as I know, it was the property of Cecil Rhodes and the house where the ill-fated Jameson raid was plotted.

[In December 1895 Dr.L.S.Jameson led a group of 500 Chartered Company police from Mafeking into the Transvaal Republic to try to overthrow President Paul Kruger. In early January at the battle of Doornkop Dr Jameson surrendered]

Later it became a hotel and then a boarding house. There were local residents in the Berea Road who still remembered the house as it was. It apparently stood in the middle of an acre site with a tennis court as well as a swimming pool.

We rented most of the upstairs and our share consisted of a very small kitchen, three rooms and a bathroom. Even though there was a corridor the three rooms were also linked to each other by a connecting doorway so that you could get through the flat by walking from one room to another. The kitchen did not have a sink so all water was carried in and wastewater carried out. By the time we moved there the building and the grounds had deteriorated. A block of flats known as Rhodes Court facing onto Rhodes Avenue, parallel to Berea Road was built on the site where the swimming pool had been.

A two-storey block of single rooms constructed on one side of the property and the rest of the grounds including the tennis court were overgrown with veld grass. The main building where we lived showed its age with its dark red brickwork and unpainted wooden window frames and a dark red tin roof. It was known locally as a haunted house and could quite easily be used as a set for a ghost film.

It was always a source of embarrassment to me when people would describe the house as "an old haunted house". Then I would have to confess to living there. They then would look at me with a mixture of astonishment, disgust and pity. Some would actually ask if it is really haunted while others would assume that it was and ask whether or not I was frightened.

The state of the grounds was hidden from the pavement by a wall built of modern bricks. The wall was about 50 yards from the main entrance to the old building and a gravel footpath led up to what remained of the front veranda. To emphasize the pedigree of the building' on the inner wall of the veranda there was a picture made of ceramic tiles of two male ducks apparently duelling and the caption in the corner was 'choice le roi'. That tiled picture was the subject of endless speculation as to whether or not it was the cover to an entrance or a posting box. Often my mother, sisters, various neighbours and I sat on the veranda on hot summer evenings putting the world right and nearly always the picture was part of the conversation. Each new summer attracted more of the local young lads to engage my sisters in conversation with my mother ever present.

Sitting on the wall with our feet dangling on the street side was the alternative to the veranda. As twilight approached we watched the bats flying round and when darkness came we would stare up at the stars and tried to identify various heavenly configurations.

My sisters and me outside our hostel

An elderly Jewish couple owned the property. He was a retired orthodox rabbi and his wife, who wore long dresses, granny boots and a headscarf covering a wig, always looked as if she had just arrived from Eastern Europe. Neither of them really mastered English and spoke Yiddish nearly all the time to each other and everyone else including the black servants. They had three sons; one was a well-known practicing orthodox rabbi who sadly died at a fairly young age. The next son was a bachelor who lived in a single room on the ground floor and never spoke to his father and he was known by his mother's maiden name but remained very religious. The third son suffered from what today would be called scoliosis that left him with a slight hunchback. My mother always claimed that he was very bitter about his physical appearance and stated that, as God was not kind to him why should he believe in God. He was divorced from his first wife and in those days especially among the Jewish community divorce was considered a tragedy. My mother and all of her generation were fluent in Yiddish and she conversed with her parents only in Yiddish. She grew up in the Western Transvaal in a town called Zeerust. Outside the home her first language was

Afrikaans, which in the pre-First World war days was closer to Dutch than modern Afrikaans. English was learnt at school but later became her first language. My father was born in South Africa and bilingual although his language of choice was English, hence both of my parents spoke English with a local South African accent. This was an important factor at the time because most of the parents of my contemporaries had arrived in South Africa either in their teens or as young adults. Their first language was Yiddish and English was acquired and always spoken with a heavy 'Yiddish' accent and never fluently from a grammatical point of view.

Languages were a very important influence on the local street culture. English was the first language of the Jewish youth born in South Africa. We were all taught Afrikaans at school and understood enough Yiddish to be able to converse with our parents and grandparents. All the young boys learnt to read Hebrew for religious purposes. Ever present and all around us were the African languages that regrettably we did not treat as important at the time. We all knew words and even the odd sentence in Zulu or Fanagalo but unfortunately whatever we knew were statements in the imperative. The result was that a stranger would often have difficulties understanding the street language. Although it was basically English with Yiddish, Afrikaans and Zulu words and expressions mixed in.

Many of the immigrants who arrived before the Second World War had managed to ship most of their possessions including furnishings, soft furnishings, pictures, cutlery, crockery and other household goods. So much so that once inside their houses you could easily have thought that you were in a shtetel in a village in Eastern Europe and not in a city built in the middle of the high veld.

My father was mostly absent from home. When we first moved out of the hostel he was still 'up north' which meant either in East or North Africa. He returned home unexpectedly in 1942. I was walking home from school and as I reached within a block of our house our elderly old landlord was waiting for me. He kept saying in his broken English "Come quick Daddy home". I did not really understand what he was on about until I saw my father standing in front of the house. I remember running up to him and jumping into his arms in a state of bewilderment and remained as close as possible to him for the rest of that day. I don't remember how my two elder sisters reacted when they came home from school.

My Father – enjoyed hunting, shooting and fishing

My father soon had to return to camp. He was posted to the military hospital in Kimberly, approximately three hundred miles from Johannesburg, where he was one of the duty pharmacists. For the rest of the war years my father was only home on his weekend leave. So our mother brought up my sisters and me. In the immediate post war years after my father was demobbed he wanted to own his pharmacy and looked for a place where there was potential with very little opposition. He found a small dorp (village), called Evaton, about forty miles south of Johannesburg near the town of Vereeniging, which is on the Transvaal side of the Vaal River.

During the week he stayed in Evaton and came home on Saturday nights. We could not afford a car so he used to travel home either by train or lift or sometimes in an African bus. The train from Vereeniging to Johannesburg was a steam train as were most of the South African railways in those days. The journey took well over an hour with numerous stops before arriving at Park station in the very centre of white Johannesburg. From the station he would catch the C1 tram to Bertrams and then had a ten-minute walk to our flat. This meant that he would arrive home late on a Saturday and depart either late on Sunday or very early on Monday. The result was that we saw far less of him than we actually ever realized.

In those days anyone who was six foot tall was considered big and my father stood an inch short of six foot and on the occasions when he was seen in the neighbourhood his large size and his status as a pharmacist always commanded a certain amount of respect. Although no one ever mentioned it to me directly, we as a family were an enigma. How come a professional man with good earning potential was living with his family in such relatively poor conditions?

It was only a few years ago, when I met up with Stanley, one of my childhood and neighbourhood friends, that I realized how poor we actually were. The cause of our relative poverty was due to the fact that my father was never able to run his pharmacy to make a profit. He always had debts and my mother was always short of cash. This caused endless quarrels and sometimes the rows were very bitter. If a weekend went by without a row I would quietly give thanks and school the following Monday seemed so much better.

Once my sisters married and I had my Bar Mitzvah my father's visits became less frequent. He had made a definite decision to leave my mother and me. By now mother had found herself employment managing a local dry cleaning shop. This meant that she was now tied to shop hours so after school I had to make certain that the basic household goods were always in stock. One of those necessary items was paraffin to fuel the primus stove. Our rather small kitchen did have a little electric cooker that took ages to boil a kettle of water and in the mornings my mother preferred to use the primus stove. To me, this took longer to prime before lighting than the cooker took to boil the water. Needless to say I hated the paraffin smell and the primus stove. In addition, my mother became extremely angry with me if I failed to complete my daily chores and that was frequent.

The reason for my forgetfulness was the remains of a tennis court, situated over the road. With some effort we could actually play tennis there. Most of the winter we played football with a variety of sized balls ranging from tennis balls to a full size football. In summer it was cricket with real bats and real stumps but an imitation cricket ball. Alternatively we used anything that could be made to stand upright that was the width of three cricket stumps. After school the court was the meeting place where we would pick teams; then we played on our Wembley, Lords and Wimbledon.

Together with Stanley, Leib, Alan, Zeve, Abe and the rest of the gang we played, argued and fought with one another. That was our life and we lived every moment to the full. Many a time my post school and vacation afternoons were interrupted. The time passed faster than I calculated. The sudden appearance of my mother, returning from work would cause me to rush over and try to open the door for her, run upstairs grab the paraffin bottle and the shopping list and rush off to the corner shop. On my return I would be lucky if I escaped with only shouting; most of the time a beating followed, especially if I could not prove that I had done my homework. It was as if all my mother's problems were taken out on me; I was her escape valve.

However unpleasant these frequent episodes were they did not override the temptation to join the boys on the court, on the street or at the local swimming baths. Deep down I could not put my heart and soul into any game and let myself go. I always had a nagging feeling that I was letting my mother down while she was working hard for me.

Chapter 2

My final year at junior school was the last that I can recall being relatively successful with a year-end report that was decorated with mainly A's and B's. At the age of twelve I was transferred to the local high school a year younger than most of my contemporaries. The high school was the co-educational Athlone High School named after the Earl of Athlone. The school badge featured Windsor Castle except for the motto "fearless and faithful" which was written in English instead of Latin. The school was located on the outer edge of the suburb of Bez (short for Bezeidenhout) Valley. At the top end of the valley were the moderately affluent areas of Observatory and Yeoville. Further down the valley and moving toward the city, Bertrams and Doornfontien was where many of the new Jewish immigrants lived.

Myself in the 'garden' of Berea Road

Seventy five per cent of the pupils at Athlone High School were Jewish. At the end of my second year the girls were relocated to a separate all girls school and we became Athlone Boys High School. Needless to say that once the girls departed the atmosphere deteriorated and everything became much rougher.

The 'Jewishness' of the school was very apparent on Jewish religious holidays. The handful of non-Jewish pupils had to attend an almost empty school. The school had a high academic standard and boasted an excellent cadet band, but was mediocre at sports by South African standards. It was taken for granted that Athlone would win the inter-school cadet band contest and the school war cry would be shouted over and over again.

Every high school for white boys and girls in South Africa had its own war cry usually composed of hybrid Zulu, Latin and gibberish. At every inter school competition such as the swimming gala the war cry was yelled out after each individual victory and the overall winners carried on shouting the war cry all the way home. The only occasion Athlonians shouted their war cry was at the band competition. The competition was held once a year on a midweek day. The school was given a half day off to attend with special buses laid on.

During my first year at high school the band won an unprecedented seven out of ten trophies and we were all on cloud nine. We boarded the buses for the return journey to school but as we tried to settle, euphoria took over. We all jumped off the bus and lined up behind our band. The band started to play and we proceeded to march toward the city centre. It was building up to the rush hour. However, three hundred excited schoolboys marching behind their victorious band was difficult to stop. The police, mostly white in those days, were tolerant and controlled the traffic, allowing us to march down Eloff Street to the Union Grounds, a parade square, near the city centre. Once we reached them we dispersed more from exhaustion than persuasion from the senior boys. By the time I reached home our exploits were in the late edition of 'The Star'. That night we were on national radio news and by the weekend we were featured on the cinema film newsreels. Our school had its highest profile ever and we all lived on it for many weeks after.

My school career went slowly in the opposite direction. The South African education system was such that at the end of each school year, from your first year at school onwards, you had to pass the annual exams to proceed to the next year. There was no automatic movement upwards with your age. If you failed your exams you had to repeat the whole year. December was the end of the academic year and school reports were posted home with the results. Apart from whether you passed or failed, you were also given your position in the class. On average, there were about 30 pupils per class and those who came 28th onwards normally failed. Ninety five per cent passed but for those who failed it was a terrible time. The parents felt let down and disgraced, the child was shunned into a corner and spent the next year in a class of younger pupils and treated as a sad interloper. In addition the casualty lost touch with immediate contemporaries. In every sense of the word you were branded by all and sundry as a failure.

At the end of the first year of high school I was still within the top fifteen. By the end of the second year I dropped into the late twenties. By the end of the third year I failed.

I was now completely alone with my mother. My sisters were married and my father's departure was permanent with a divorce in the offing. The law as it was then did not give my father a chance. All that my mother would concede to was a legal separation. My father's struggle for a divorce continued long after I had left South Africa and settled in England.

One aspect about growing up during that era and in that part of Johannesburg was that to all intents and purposes we were in a ghetto both physically and mentally. Looking back in almost every house in the locality lived a Jewish family, or so it seemed. We hardly ever mixed socially with anyone else. They were gentile families, probably in greater numbers than we realised at the time. We shut them out of our lives as they lived mainly in the small blocks of maisonettes or in the streets that we never visited.

Strangely enough there was one Christian family, the Berrys, who lived amongst us. They, one way or another, dominated our young lives. Their house fronted onto Gordon Road, but they also owned the tennis court (our playing field). Old Mr. Berry owned two cars. Both were nineteen twenties American Ford convertibles which he only used to fetch and carry Mrs. Berry from church. He always offered whoever was hanging around a ride. We sat in the back seat with the wind in our faces while he drove to the Troyville Catholic Church. After dropping her off outside the church, he always took us for a drive. One of our favourite places that we called the dam stood on the outskirts of Johannesburg. The dam is now part of a large leisure picnic complex with restaurants and walks, and is now known as Galloolies Farm. He always parked near a willow tree that overhung the water and we used the branches to swing out over the dam. We would throw stones into the water and contemplate if there were any fish and occasionally took notice of the bird life.

This was one of the few occasions when my friends actually ventured away from our urban jungle into the veld. I was more fortunate because my father liked fishing and before he finally left us he regularly took me by train to various dams, lakes and rivers. Many were within an hour and a half train ride from Johannesburg Park Station. My father, being South African, was familiar with the veld. Most of my friends' parents were born in Eastern Europe, and knew little of their new country.

The other important contribution the Berrys made to our lives was the fact that they had a workshop, which was never locked. We were allowed to use all but the most expensive of the tools. We learnt to saw, file and bang nails to our hearts content. Between the old tennis court and the Berrys house were two huge Blue Gum trees that stood side by side. It took at least four of us with outstretched arms to measure the base circumference of the trees. They must have been at least 300 feet high and could be seen for miles around a local identifying landmark. The Berrys had four grownup sons; one was killed during the war in North Africa and I remember how we all struggled to stay away from the tools and the tennis court for nearly two weeks so as not to disturb them. Our attitude was conditioned by our Jewish culture where after a family bereavement the family sat in mourning for at least a week (sitting Shiva).

One of the Berry boys, Duggie, after his discharge from the army became a taxi driver. He always worked at night and stayed in bed most of the day. After school when we were not playing games, we would stare through the fly screen window of Duggie's bedroom talking to him. We all thought he was the greatest and wisest. The Berry's house was situated on about a half an acre of land with numerous trees, bushes and even a bamboo bush. Before football and cricket began to dominate our leisure time, the Berry's grounds were our very own adventure playground. We climbed the trees, hung and swung from the branches; we leapt from tree to tree. Tarzan had a lot to answer for. To us, without knowing it, the Berry's was an oasis, a chance for us to become familiar with working class urban white Johannesburg.

About a mile up the road toward central Johannesburg was the suburb of Doornfontein with its local high street called Beit Street. Doornfontein during the war and immediate post-war years was the hub of working class Jewish life; even more so than Bertrams. Along Beit Street the shops were all sorts of oversized delicatessens and kosher butchers. The combined bakery and delicatessen known as Crystals and Goldenbergs, along with the kosher butcher, were the dominating shops. There were dozens of smaller shops ranging from the usual pharmacists, clothing, shoe, stationery, food shops, fish shops, cafes, fish and chip shops and every other type of small retailer associated with any Anglo-Saxon high street. Most important of all were the two local cinemas the 'posher' Apollo and the 'fleapit' Alhambra.

Those two cinemas dominated most of our Saturday afternoons. My sisters regularly dispatched me at half past twelve each Saturday to be first in the queue for bioscope tickets. For my trouble I was rewarded by being allowed to sit with them in one shilling and a penny instead of the sixpenny seats, which would have confined me to the first five front rows. This was where all the rowdy kids sat (two seniors were allowed to invite junior to join them). I was given a pre-decimal ten pence piece, one penny for my tram fare, a sixpence, for my entry ticket to the bioscope and a ticky (three pence) for an ice cream or drink. I was expected to walk home with my friends who had sat in the sixpenny seats.

Siemert Road conveniently split Doornfontein into two halves by intersecting Beit Street at right angles. Trams travelled in an easterly direction from central Johannesburg into the commercial part of Beit Street. On the left hand side, as seen from the up-stairs of the tram, the first large building was the Apollo Bioscope and, next to it, Crystals. Goldenbergs was further down on the right. Greek owned cafes occupied most of the corners on both sides of the road. The Alhambra was on the first block passed Siemert Road. Most of the shops were located on the left side of Beit Street. The only prominent feature on the right hand side was Doornfontein Hebrew School (The Talmud Torah).

The roads leading off from the right side of Siemert Road led to Ellis Park Stadium; at that time the home of rugby, then later cricket. Beit Street ended in a T-junction about a half-mile further on from Siemert Road. At the bottom of Beit Street were the Ellis Park tennis courts and the Ellis Park swimming baths. All these facilities were within walking distance from our homes in Bertrams.

Walking down Beit Street you could be forgiven for thinking that you were in Eastern Europe. Most of the elderly women wore headscarves, long dresses, shawls and boots, while the men, mostly grey bearded wore black suits and hats. The most common street language was Yiddish. All the residential streets crossed Beit Street at right angles and were lined with rows of semi-detached houses and, among them, the occasional bungalow style house all with a front stoep (veranda). Each house was built in a similar style, out of a dark brown brick. Some of the homes had the bricks plastered over and painted (white washed). Inside every house it was customary to have an ornamental samovar standing on the sideboard alongside the compulsory pair of candlesticks and the Menorah (seven branched candlestick). The streets, like almost all of Johannesburg suburban streets, were lined with mature Plain trees. In the summer they created a lovely cool green canopy and in winter their leafless branches allowed the sun in to warm all the houses, especially those facing north.

A few hundred yards from the intersection of Beit Street and Seimert Road on the Berea side of Doornfontein was the Doornfontein Synagogue. Its two famous stone lions guarded the entrance. The synagogue became known as the 'Lions Shul'.

Five hundred yards up Seimert Road stood two more Synagogues, less than one hundred yards apart. The Ponaviser and the Chassidic Synagogue. These two synagogues marked the end of a line of three green islands. Each green was equal in length, and as wide as three houses.

On either side of the greens were roads running in a downward direction fenced in by knee high black chains. Hence their local name the 'Chain Parks'. They served the local youth in the same manner as the Berry's tennis court served my neighbourhood but more so because they were covered in manicured grass. During school hours the local toddlers were let loose then under the supervision of their black nannies. During the evenings, local youths collected and often formed the arena for individual or gang fights.

Further up the road towards Berea, there were two more large synagogues on Saratoga Avenue. The first one was known as the 'Berylla Chagie' named after a Cantor who left to seek his fame in the USA as an opera singer. The one nearest to the city centre was the Great Synagogue also known as Wolmarans Street Synagogue. This was the largest synagogue in Johannesburg and was the seat of the Chief Rabbi.

Every Saturday from about the age of eleven until my Bar Mitzvah I used to walk to the Wolmarans Street Synagogue. During the time the Torah was taken out of the Ark to be read, I used to visit my grandmother (my Bobe) who lived in a nearby block of flats. All her worldly possessions were located in a single room apartment. It was full of family photographs covering the period from her life in Russia and Belarus to my generation. Conversation was always a bit stilted because she only spoke Yiddish and Russian and my Yiddish was very basic but still she managed to coax out of me all the family gossip. Although I would arrive at her house between ten and half past in the morning, she always gave me the impression that she had just got out of bed. My visits usually ended after I had finished my cup of tea and I was given a sixpence for my troubles.

I normally returned to the service in time to hear and see the replacing of the Torah into the ark and the closing of the ark. This always followed by the Chief Rabbi's sermon. He would always begin by quoting from the passage of the Torah that had been read that morning and converting it into some modern day message. The congregation was frequently verbally scolded for not maintaining the highest Talmudic standards. If you happened to be in the synagogue a year later when the same passage was read the sermon always began in a similar fashion and final lesson and rebuke altered slightly to fit some topical event or other.

Two of the many sermons that I sat through stuck in my mind. One was related to kosher dietary laws that I heard during the sixties when I returned to Johannesburg from London for my late father's funeral. The rabbi of the day was disturbed by the fact that the Israeli airline was debating whether or not all food served had to be kosher. The rabbi quoted a Spanish airline that had stated that on Fridays only fish will be served and why did EL AL not follow a similar course. If you fly with a Jewish airline you should only be served kosher food. He finished on a shrill stating that when a Jewish airline has to even think about serving non-kosher food this can only lead to "spiritual indigestion."

The other was about the ancient Israelites who were continuously fighting battles with neighbouring tribes to protect their land. There was a long time when no actual physical battles were fought but the country was in a continuous state of battle readiness. There were endless verbal battles between the Israelites and their neighbours. While the politicians were stating that there was peace one of the prophets who was disturbed by the status quo said yes there is peace, peace and yet there is no peace – 'shalom, shalom ve-ein shalom'. When I think of modern Israel I hear the sad cry from that rabbi on a Saturday morning so many years previously.

The battles of ancient Israel had a profound effect upon me and probably many of my contemporaries. In my case I had to move from a home in a more affluent part of Johannesburg to live in a hostel and then into the old 'haunted house' in Berea Road Bertrams. The break-up of my parents marriage had, even if I was not aware of it, unsettled me. Anti-Semitism was all round us, we were always subject to abuse and attack from the local non-Jewish white and mainly Afrikaaner youth. Post war we all became aware of the Holocaust. Before 1948 when the state of Israel was founded we regarded Palestine as our homeland. Every Jewish home had a blue and white collection box on the sideboard with the bold letters of the JNF (Jewish National Fund) on it. The money was to buy land in Palestine. After 1948 we were to a certain extent preoccupied by the existence of Israel and our thoughts was on "aliya" which meant migration to settle in Israel. My life at the time, along with most of my contemporaries, was like being engulfed in a permanent cultural conflict.

The conflict of our status would emerge when we were quizzed about our nationality. The answer was always that we were Jewish. Being anything else, that is South African, was never considered. However, with regard to sport, we were very South African. If any South African achieved anything in any field that was internationally recognised, we rejoiced in it. When a Jewish sportsman represented the country the whole Jewish community celebrated and when "off the cuff" anti-Semitic remarks were made toward that individual, we all hurt. I only really thought of my self as South African when I left South Africa.

Chapter 3

The one aspect of white South Africa that the Jewish Community adopted almost in total was the attitude toward the black population. As soon as they settled and could afford it they employed a black servant. Black people were referred to politely as the 'natives' and the servant was the native girl or the native boy. In Yiddish black servants were referred to as the 'schochedikes'. They soon learnt to speak to their servants in the imperative and shout at them when they did things wrong. The female servants were referred to as 'the girl' the male servants 'the boy' irrespective of their age. The black women were all given the name Annie and the Black men John or Johannes. Our parents never attempted to change anything even though most of them had actually been on the receiving end of racial insults and many had experienced persecution in various European countries. Their preoccupation was to survive in this 'new' world then to make a success, which nearly always meant becoming wealthy.

Every house built for white occupants, Europeans as they were called then, no matter how small, always had a back yard. At the bottom of the yard was a building detached from the main house. This was the servants' quarters. It consisted of a single room just big enough to contain a bed, cupboard and or a wardrobe and a table. The servants had to have their own toilet; Blacks and whites never used the same facilities. In older houses it was simply a squat toilet, which we called a 'native toilet'. At the time we were conditioned to believe that it was good enough for them, because they were basically 'primitive' and a primitive facility is all that they required. Some outbuildings had a sink with running water or even a shower. Hardly any servants' quarters had electricity; they were given an issue of candles or a paraffin lamp which was their only lighting. Some of the post war houses built for Whites had laid on hot water. The inner walls were crudely plastered or just bare brick. The solitary window was nearly always covered with makeshift curtains. Those were usually the white Madam's throw outs. In wintertime the only heating was from a portable brazier type of fire. The walls always seemed to be stained with smoke and even in the daylight were, to us, dark and dingy. Most whites seldom went into the 'girls' room and never really knew who actually spent the night there.

During the winter months of June and July, Johannesburg, being almost six thousand feet above sea level, experienced cold winter nights. In order to keep their rooms warm, the Africans always lit solid fuel fires. Large four-gallon tin cans with numerous ventilation holes filled with coal were placed on the edge of the street pavements and coaxed alight. They were left in the street until smoke was burnt off and the coals were glowing red. The 'braziers' were then carried into the servant's room and left to smoulder through the night.

Many of the streets of Johannesburg during the hours of five to seven in the evening were covered with a layer of thick smoke. Although annoying to the white residents, they accepted the situation because the alternative was to provide proper heating for their employees. Every year several deaths were reported as a result of carbon monoxide poisoning in non-ventilated servants' rooms.

We were always led to believe that is how black servants lived and did not know any better. We thought they were content with their lot. Looking back they were laughing and smiling, well fed, everything provided for and it was because they were better off than their kin who lived in the townships. Black areas did not have the dignity of being called towns or villages.

My mother never employed a servant 'girl' for both economic reasons and because the flat we lived in was serviced by a flat 'boy'. It was his job to clean our flat every day, dusting, sweeping, emptying the wastewater from our kitchen and polishing our floor. He did this not only in our flat but also the landlord's and the other tenants'. Every Saturday a washerwoman came and collected our dirty washing at the same time returning last week's washing cleaned and ironed.

Weekly rituals, carried out by my sisters, were to make a duplicate laundry list of all that was taken away and check all that was returned. I can never ever remember anything missing. The bundle of dirty washing was carried away on the head of Jesse our washerwoman. She returned the laundry to us all pressed, starched, ironed and neatly folded. The neat packed wash load was carried on her head. It never occurred to me at the time to marvel at how such a task was carried out.

The journey began from our flat in Berea Road, Bertrams. Jesse would walk with the bundle of dirty washing on her head to the bus station near the centre of Johannesburg alongside Joubert Park. The tram and bus route that served our area did not run 'native' trams or buses. She somehow managed to board the green PUTCO bus (for Blacks only) with her bundle and then travelled for an hour to her home in Orlando (now one of the suburbs of Soweto). Her home probably did not have installed tap water and electricity. Water had to be boiled over a coal or wood fire in the equivalent of a copper.

All the washing was done by hand using bars of washing soap. It was dried in the open then ironed with an iron heated over the fire. Everything was returned whiter than white and ironed to perfection. For this she was paid something in the region of ten shillings and was given a cup of tea on her arrival every Saturday morning and perhaps some left over food to take home to her family.

I have a particular reason to be very grateful to Jesse. Shortly after my father had left us Jesse on that occasion delivered the washing on a weekday. Her time of arrival coincided with my mother returning home from work. I as usual had been playing in the Berry's court with the boys and had neglected my duties including my homework. Jesse was sitting, as she usually did, on a small stool drinking a mug of tea and I offered to run out to purchase the bottle of paraffin, bread etc. Instead of letting me go my mother first rebuked me, then enquired about my homework. I replied honestly that I had not yet done it but would do so that evening. My mother was always under some form of stress and my reply enraged her. Apart from shouting at me she grabbed a military type cane, of which we had several in our house, and lashed out at me, beating me on my back. One lashing did not satisfy her anger toward me and she continued to strike out at me but before the fourth strike Jesse jumped up and restrained my mother and pushed her into a corner. A black woman, a native grabbing and restraining her white Madam from beating her son was an unimaginable scene in post-war Johannesburg.

My mother, although now restrained by a small gentle Jesse, grew even angrier and tried to force her way back to me. The windows were open and Jesse called out in Zulu to Piet the flat 'boy' for help and by the time he arrived my mother had calmed down but continued to rebuke me. Although my back was stinging and very painful I refused to cry, grabbed some money and ran out to the corner shop. Jesse waited for my return to feel reassured that there would be no repeat. Then she departed in tears. My mother carried on as if nothing had happened.

All blocks of flats in those days, for whites only, had a team of flat boys who lived in servants' quarters located either in the basement or on the roof garden. They were employed to maintain the property, clean the hallways, corridors, and grounds including the usual ground level parking space. One of the most important duties was to maintain the boilers to provide hot water for all tenants. They were low paid and were often country 'boys'. They had grown up in rural areas and not in the townships and still had strong tribal affiliations. Most were barely literate in their own language, and understood and spoke English with difficulty - so we thought at the time. All black males in domestic type service throughout South Africa wore a standardized uniform. It was made out of a rough gabardine material. The trousers were shapeless three-quarter length, without a fly and tie cord to hold them up. The 'shirts' were short sleeved and collar-less with a single shirt pocket. All the edges were trimmed with a dark red trimming. They were not styled into any reasonable shape. Trouser legs looked like two canvas cylinders and the shirt a shortened smock. This was an all year uniform; no extras were handed out for winter.

Walking through Johannesburg flat land Hillbrow, parts of Berea and Killarney, you could at any time of the day and night see huddles of 'Flat Boys' sitting on the pavements staring, talking or playing various card or board games. Either their daily tasks were completed during the early hours or the work required not much effort so there was no need to work continuously. Wages were poor, labour was cheap and there was plenty of it.

Our flat boy Piet somehow managed not to have to wear that unbecoming uniform and wore ordinary long trousers a shirt and an apron.

Not only did my family and the other tenants know him but he was also known among my street friends. He started his work early in the morning by cleaning out the landlord's coal stove and kitchen. He then came up to our flat to empty our kitchen wastewater before he started on his daily cleaning duties. He always finished most of his tasks by midday like all domestic servants seemed to do. After lunch all male and female domestics washed and changed into a clean uniform and gathered on the pavements in front of their houses. Those in charge of white children, the nannies, would wash, eat, and change while their white charges were having their midday sleep. In the afternoons, the children were taken for a walk to the local parks or simply kept in their pushchairs while their nannies participated in the pavement conversations.

Piet was very flamboyant and had a large collection of smart suits, shirts, bow ties and matching shoes. His weekend began Saturday midday but like all the domestics he never really had a complete day off. They still had to attend to the hot water and bin emptying on Sundays. My friends and I often sat in Piet's 'room' listening to his wind up gramophone playing one of his vast collections of popular African 78 rpm records. We would also stare at his photographs and pictures that decorated the bare brick walls and wondered where he actually kept all his clothes. We would sit there feeling uncomfortable but felt that this was their standard of living and they did not need any better.

On Sunday afternoons Piet would dress up in one of his many light coloured suits with a matching shirt, bow tie, brown and white shoes, a Panama hat and walking stick or cane. The stick was not just for decoration but a weapon to protect him as did most 'Flat Boys' who carried protective sticks or knobkerries as they were called. Township dwellers mostly protected themselves with knives or other pocket weapons. Whenever Piet set off with a large grin and returned with an even larger smile we all interpreted that to be an individual happy with his lot. The thought that this might be an escape for a while under the influence of alcohol did not enter our heads nor did the grown-ups ever mention it at the time.

Conversations between whites and Africans were always very stilted and limited in content. Most verbal exchanges consisted of the whites telling the blacks what to do. It was always in the imperative. Most whites believed that if they spoke in broken English - in other words impersonated the way the blacks spoke English - they would be better understood. The situation was compounded by the fact that Africans nearly always laughed which only encouraged the whites. No one ever thought that they might be laughing out of politeness or at how stupid we sounded. Very few urban whites spoke any of the African languages with any fluency. So while they were laughing they may have actually been cursing their white bosses. This caused amusement to their colleagues and is probably what they were really laughing at.

One thing we took for granted, as part of the street scenery of suburbia, was the cluster of Africans standing or sitting around the streets. Some would be clad in their working clothes; others wore brown or blue boiler suites or overalls. The female domestic uniform was a blue skirt, a white blouse and a white apron and a dark beret or a woolly hat. The female uniforms were spotlessly clean and ironed to perfection as if there was a pride in wearing it. It is surprising with hindsight how it seemed to us that the Blacks appeared to accept what the Whites handed out to keep them as second-class citizens. We grew up accepting their status as the norm.

Johannesburg in the summer months is subject to frequent thunderstorms. In order to contain sudden large volumes of rainwater deep storm gutters were built between the road and the pavement. When these gutters were not full of flowing water they functioned as street benches for the urban blacks to sit on. They sat on the edge of the pavement with their feet dangling in the gutter. Those were the urban gathering places. No doubt these were also places where basic politics was discussed, and as few whites understood their language they could plot to their hearts content.

During our daily travels we took these suburban roadside scenes for granted. The fact that the gutters were where most urban Africans spent a great deal of their time was not only taken for granted by the whites, but expected of them. In the pre-war and immediate post-war years any African who dared to step into the path of any oncoming white person risked not only verbal abuse but also a physical attack. They should know their place or as the Afrikaners put '*die kaffir in sy plek*'.

The only non-whites we encountered at school were the cleaners and the maintenance men. They also lived on the school premises but we never ever saw their quarters let alone went anywhere near to them. Like everywhere else in South Africa we knew that they were people in the background who we needed, but regarded with indifference and disrespect.

Afrikaans was a taught language introduced to us when we reached middle school and no doubt the Afrikaans speaking children had a similar experience with English. We were completely separated from the other two major ethnic groups of the population, namely the Africans and the Afrikaners and were rarely encouraged to mix with them or learn their language.

Chapter 4

During the war years there was a white political group know as the Ossewabrandwag or the OB's. They were pro-German and needless to say strongly anti-Semitic. Even after the war anti-Semitism was ever-present especially in the areas like Doornfontein, Bertrams, Troyville and Bezuidenhout Valley where the working class Jews lived in close proximity to urban working class Afrikaners and English speaking South Africans.

Gangs of young whites would pick on Jewish boys. Fights were frequent and there were also the occasional Jewish gangs who would fight back. There was always an atmosphere of nervous mistrust in all groups and this led to everyone being on the defensive. Most people held definite and decisive views. There was no room for compromise and it was against such a background that an atmosphere of 'hidden' hysteria was ever present among all the white groups.

Wherever we went, be it going to and from school, visiting friends, playing sport or going to the bioscope we always, metaphorically speaking, looked over our shoulders. We were wary of the local Afrikaans boys, who whenever they were in groups, found an excuse to heave anti-Semitic insults at us. If we were not quick enough they would physically attack us. One particular Saturday afternoon we were exiting the local Apollo cinema, when a white gang decided to sort us out. Hymie, our friend, had taken on the two notorious Osborn brothers and given them a good hiding in a fair fight during the previous week after school. The brothers had brought their mob to the bioscope. For some unknown reason they were after Lieb, one of our crowd. As we walked out onto the pavement we all became separated and I was with Lieb. They grabbed Stan instead, the biggest of our lot, and managed to isolate him. Lieb and I walked on thinking that Stan would slip away and be waiting for us further on. When Lieb and I stopped to look for Stan it was too late; they had already given him a good beating. Lieb and I never forgave ourselves. Stan never forgave us either for not going back sooner, but at the same time we knew we could have done nothing about it as we were totally outnumbered and very frightened. Stan's parents eventually had the brothers prosecuted in a criminal court. What we did not know at the time was that he had suffered sustained internal damage, which has plagued him most of his life.

If that was not enough, we were also frightened of being attacked by black gangsters. Street robbery, bag snatching and mugging of whites, particularly at night, was not uncommon as far back as I can remember. All the windows of the white homes had burglar proofing and about one in five homes had a guard dog. There was a constant fear of having your home broken into.

Somehow or other all those fears and concerns were put aside. Nothing ever prevented us from going out at night, especially to Saturday night parties. It is difficult now to conceive that I was prepared to walk alone at night through the streets of Johannesburg while preoccupied with the two main fears that I would either accidentally cross the path of a wandering gang of white thugs or be mugged by black gangsters.

Walking past a building that had its customary black night watchman sitting around the entrance to the buildings he was guarding, with an assegai and a knobkerrie either in one hand or close by his side gave a temporary feeling of security. I always hoped that, if attacked, they would come to my rescue. I always felt a great sense of relief once I had opened my front door and closed it safely behind me. However there was still one obstacle to overcome, my mother. If she was still awake she would almost invariably scold me for being in so late particularly if it was after 11 p.m.

As I mentioned previously the education system was modelled on the pre-war English system. All schools had uniforms that consisted of a blazer, white shirt, school-tie and blue or grey trousers. The trousers could be worn short or long. English speaking high schools frowned upon the wearing of shorts. In the wintertime, you had to wear the special school jersey. The prefects always made certain that you wore the correct uniform; a non-school jersey had to be worn under your shirt. Right through the summer months you still had to wear your blazer, made out of a woollen fabric and a tie until you reached your home. If you were seen walking home in the summer with temperatures in the high seventies and low eighties, carrying your blazer and tie-less, the next day you would be reprimanded and punished. The girls wore gym-slips with a felt hat, shirt, tie and blazer in the winter but in the summer they were allowed to wear cotton dresses and straw hats and no blazers. Most of the Afrikaans High Schools had a summer uniform for the boys as well.

The Afrikaans High School boys wore khaki shorts in the summer, long socks and brown shoes, a form of dress that was retained by many Afrikaner males into adulthood whereas the English speaking white South Africans looked down on that style. This, then, became another cause of fragmentation of the society we were growing up in. We identified ourselves with the white English speaking population yet we thought of ourselves as being Jewish. Our parents and home life never let us forget that. We never actually realised or felt that the white population was actually the minority.

We were in a democracy where there was voting for municipal councils, for provisional councils, and for government of the country. There were the different political parties that we, via our parents, were affiliated to. The fact that the non-white population consisting of the Africans, Indians and Coloureds (people of mixed race) did not have the vote was taken for granted. It was never pointed out to us at school or anywhere else that it was not exactly true democracy. We always puzzled about whether or not the Portuguese community was considered to be white. As for the Chinese we accepted that they did not have a vote and were not white. In our minds the society was split into definite strata. Whether we liked it or not the Afrikaners were at the top of the pecking order, followed by the English, then the Jews and Greeks and at the bottom of the white pile were the Portuguese.

My mother always used the expression 'the lowest of the low.' That structure of our society was taken for granted and manifested itself in many ways. The employees in the civil service, the police, railways and post-office were almost all Afrikaners. The business world, legal and medical professions were almost totally dominated by the English speakers, which included the Jews. The corner cafes were nearly all owned by the Greeks while the fruit and vegetable shop was the domain of the Portuguese. These divisions were not just confined to Johannesburg but to most of the country.

In those days in Johannesburg the only Afrikaners we came across were from the working classes. It was at the end of my school days, after I moved away from Johannesburg that I really, for the first time, came across professional Afrikaners and realised they were not just confined to being bus and tram drivers, railway workers, postmen and policemen.

We lived in a world which, looking back could be classed as a large, mental ghetto. We had our values; anything that was not part of us was inferior. Near my junior school was a cluster of very low quality housing occupied by what we called poor whites. These houses by our standards were only a little better than what we expected to see in the townships. They were badly maintained and permanently in need of major repair. Although these houses were in a 'white' area some of the inhabitants to us were more coloured than white. Many of the children attended our school, which in spite of its name was not a school for Jews only. In the South Africa of those days racial classification was all-important. All South Africans from a very early age can tell whether or not a person has the slightest trace of non-white blood.

While I was still attending junior school it was announced that the Second World War was about to end. We were told that Winston Churchill was going to broadcast over the wireless the moment that peace was signed. The day was going to be called VE Day.

At the back of where we lived in Bertrams were Koppies (hills), which was still a bit of wild veld in the middle of Johannesburg. The Koppies were really a one-sided series of rocky outcrops about 500 feet high. At the top of the Koppies were houses and flats that had a commanding view of most of Johannesburg; hence its name 'Bellevue'. One incomplete building consisted of three walls without windows, doors, and cement. The owners went bankrupt and the building was left to the elements. On the top tier of that structure the Johannesburg municipality erected a large illuminated cross to commemorate the outbreak of peace. On the day of Churchill's speech we were all assembled in the school hall to listen to the speech over a crackling radio. After the speech the headmaster Mr. Arenson said a prayer and all the school sang the hymn 'O God Our Help In Ages Past.'

During the immediate post-war period our local cinemas showed, on the newsreels, the horrific pictures of the Nazi death camps. They were only shown to the evening audiences to, supposedly protect us children from the horrific scenes of heaps mainly Jewish dead bodies. The real horror of the Holocaust definitely influenced the Jewish community's appreciation of the victory celebrations, although we had not experienced firsthand any of the physical side of the war. Most of my generation at that time never really grasped what had happened. There was a sense of "thank God we are living in South Africa and not in Europe." However during the war the South African Jews did experience anti-Semitism from the pro-German group the Broederbond and the Ossewabrandwag.

Although we had not experienced the horrors of the Nazis we were growing up in atmosphere of what can only be described now as multiple ethnic phobia. The English speaking South Africans referred to themselves as English, the Afrikaans speaking Afrikaners and then the rest of the white population referred to themselves according to their ethnic origins such as the Jews, the Greeks and the Portuguese. Then there were all the non-white groups that in the South African vernacular of the day were referred to as Non-Europeans. This group included the Indians, coloureds (mixed race) and the Africans who were composed of different tribal groups such as the Zulus, Xhosas, Basotus and many others from neighbouring countries. In those post-war years the country was crying out for some one to be brave enough to begin the long road to non-racialism. The white leader was then Jan Smuts who was adored by all the whites except the Afrikaners, but did not take the initiative regarding the question of race relations.

The next momentous event of that era was the visit to South Africa by the Royal Family, the King and Queen and the two princesses. From the day HMS Vanguard sailed out of Southampton, we were kept informed of their every movement by the press, the radio and cinema newsreels of the day. The whole country started a huge clean up with vast amounts of money spent on decorations. All the big cities and towns had mock-ups of royal carriages with the Royal Family sitting inside as if it were a state occasion. I remember standing with my mother and countless others in Eloff Street, opposite the OK Bazaars watching the unveiling of a mock-up of the royal carriages being constructed on the balcony. Everyone including, the few blacks that were allowed to stand on the pavement with us, applauded each stage of the operation.

Their ship docked in Cape Town and as the King and his family stepped onto South African soil, they were greeted by the Prime Minister the late General Jan Smuts. The event was broadcast all over the Union, as it was called in those days. From that day onwards and for the next few months the newspapers gave detailed graphic accounts of the visit punctuated with endless photographs of flag waving white crowds.

Pretoria is one of the capitals of South Africa. The Royal Family was scheduled to drive down to Johannesburg from Pretoria for the day. Johannesburg was and still is the biggest city in terms of size, population and economy in Southern Africa. However as Pretoria is the administrative capital of South Africa, the Royal Family were accommodated there. Once they entered the Johannesburg city boundary flag waving school children lined the streets.

I was in the final year of junior school and the part of their route into the city centre was within walking distance of the school. We were all issued with a dress code and anyone who did not comply would not be allowed to stand in the front two rows.

About two hours before they were due to arrive we were marched to our school's allotted pitch. We stood there gradually wilting in the blazing sun for the best part of an hour and a half. When the procession finally arrived they drove past in a Daimler motorcar with the hood down. Although they must have taken less than ten seconds to pass us, I remember seeing the two princesses sitting in front of the King and Queen and I was amazed at how much make-up they all appeared to be wearing. They waved and smiled while we cheered and in the car behind was Jan Smuts. Then it was all over. On our way back to school everyone tried to hide their disappointment.

Although we sat in the same class and played with some of those kids from the slum houses at the back of the school suspicion never left us. On one occasion we met one of our schoolmates from the 'poor houses' with her mother and it was obvious to us that the mother was not pure white. In those days the girls all had to help prepare the school sandwiches. Soon after, that girl's mother was revealed to be Coloured, the whisper in school was not to eat the sandwiches on the days those girls were on 'duty'. This was the attitude in spite of the fact that nearly every white family had a black servant who always helped prepare the food for their employers. During my final year at high school two of the girls from those 'poor houses' were involved in a well-publicised court case about prostitution.

Chapter 5

About once a month my father would take me on a fishing trip. Fishing was a pastime definitely not associated with urban Jews. My father knew every dam, lake and river within a two-hour train ride from Johannesburg Park station. We would set out from our home in Berea Road, Bertrams, for a ten-minute walk to the tram stop. As we walked along we must have been a spectacle for the neighbourhood to stare at. The tram ride into town took about twenty minutes. Often or not our destination was decided by the departure time of the next train.

Somehow or other whatever train we caught we always found ourselves in a carriage alongside either potential fisherman or people who were just curious to know where we were going. Nine out of ten of our fellow travellers, on a Sunday morning, were Afrikaners. My father having grown up in South Africa spoke Afrikaans fluently. Once we had exchanged greetings and told everybody of our destination, the conversation would then be about the best spot for catching this or that type of fish. Usually after a half hour into our journey my father would start recounting his hunting and fishing adventures in East Africa where he was posted during the early years of the war.

The South African army was mostly involved in what was formally known as the East Africa campaign fighting the Italians in Ethiopia (Abyssinia as it was known then) and the remnants of the East Africa German Corp in Tanzania (formerly Tanganyika). My father, as a pharmacist was attached to the Medical Corp and must have had enough spare time to have gone on numerous hunting and fishing expeditions. Luckily for me the stories were nearly always told in Afrikaans and although I understood most of the conversation it was easy for me to switch off and not have to hear the same tale for the nth time. However the listeners were always impressed as most of the tales seemed to revolve around encounters with crocodiles. The story I heard most was the one about how they would set out on boat with dog sitting in the bows. The presence and smell of the dog was supposed to have summoned up those modern demons from the river depths only to have their lives terminated by a rifle bullet. The crocodiles were carved up into bits, including their skin, and converted into all sorts of trophies. Many years later, after my mother had died I found a collection of black and white snapshots taken on a Kodak box camera that confirmed many of his stories.

Chapter 6

From my point of view the train journey provided me with a passing glimpse of the African townships and shantytowns. The majority of whites never went anywhere near the black townships and really knew very little about the true living conditions of the majority of South Africans. A glimpse from a train window passing by the townships was all that most whites ever saw and what they saw never failed to cause a grimace of some kind. What was visible was rough dirt roads with no roadside drainage or pavements. Houses built out of mud or with mud bricks and galvanized tin roofs held down with stones. There were makeshift fences to mark some of the property boundaries. Some houses had glass in the windows others had space for a window which was boarded up at night or when the owners were not there. There were always hordes of children playing in the streets and very mangy looking dogs wandering round the houses. Alongside the brown mud walled houses were the shacks made of almost anything, Hessian, rusting strips of roofing zinc, odd wooden planks and even bits of cardboard. Adjacent to each dwelling was a small outhouse, the toilet with three walls and a door surrounding a hole in the ground and a sort of seat above the hole. The water supply was a communal hand water pump, which was always surrounded by women and children filling water into 4-gallon old paraffin tins. There was plenty of waste ground with scruffy horses and donkeys grazing on what was left of the veld grass.

As the train passed by, the whites would say 'that's typical the way they live... they don't know any better... that's all they need and look how happy they are....' They spoke as if they were talking about some form of inferior species not human beings. Among the housing shambles there were the occasional brick built house with a veranda and perhaps and old motorcar parked alongside the house. That sight was the cue for a series of remarks about look how well they are doing, rising above their stations and no doubt this covered among some whites hidden feelings of fear and jealousy. The only township in those days where Africans lived in houses that matched those of the working class whites was Sophia town. This Sophia town was actually within the municipal boundaries of Johannesburg and was once a white suburb and somehow Africans had managed to acquire the right to buy property in that area. There was a tram service into Sophia town, electricity and telephone lines in some parts, shops and cinemas. The inhabitants were forcibly removed in the late Fifties by the police and re-housed elsewhere after the nationalist government passed the Group Areas Act.

One of the many townships that we passed as the train journeyed toward the West Rand was called Mlamlamkuzi, which our flat boy Piet told me meant "separator of the fighting bulls". I never, ever established whether or not that was the correct translation. A popular destination of ours was the town of Vereeniging about fifty to sixty miles south of Johannesburg, located on the Transvaal side of the Vaal River. The railway line was not yet electrified, so we made the journey by steam train. There were two rail routes to Vereeniging one via Germiston on the East Rand and the other via Krugersdorp on the West Rand where the train turned and headed due south for Vereeniging.

The journey took about an hour and a half, plenty of time for my father to tell his stories to other passengers. Sometimes fellow travellers would persuade him that the dam or lake at so and so en route was far better for fishing than where we were going. This often resulted in us getting off the train before our actual destination in an attempt to find this new fishing 'Shangri-La'. However, eight times out of ten we did end up where we had set out to be. Once we arrived at Vereeniging we would either walk the few miles to the river or occasionally take a taxi.

We were always stared at as we disembarked. Usually we were the only persons wearing khaki helmets and carrying fishing rods. On the days when my father decided to take a taxi it was great relief, as I would be spared the feeling of being very self-conscious as both Blacks and Whites stared at us.

Large wide rivers like those in Central Africa are rare in South Africa. The Vaal River was always a welcome sight. A barrage had been built about twenty miles downstream from Vereeniging. The stored water caused the river to be as much as a quarter mile wide for a long way upstream. The spot we fished from was not far from the road so it was accessible by taxi. The first task was to always set up our rods, bait our hooks, cast into the river and prop our rods up to wait for a bite. Then we would settle down, have a snack and a drink and make our picnic site comfortable. Our bait was always Mealie pap (a type of dry porridge), which was kneaded carefully to surround our hooks and in the hope that fish would find it appetizing. We did not have maggots, worms or any form of live bait.

The river was lined with endless willow trees whose branches hung over the riverbanks, providing marvellous shade and shelter from the sun. Toward midday the temperature rose rapidly but under the trees it was cool and comfortable. After about an hour staring quietly into the river without a bite, I was sent on a sortie to spy on other fisherman and see how they were doing. There were always other fishermen who normally arrived in motorcars. It was a rare sight to see a father and son walking through the streets carrying fishing rods and a box of tackle. When it became really hot it was time for a swim. Both my father and I enjoyed swimming. We normally only swam out twenty to thirty yards from the bank. The river current was never strong enough to inhibit me from swimming halfway across the river.

Every now and again the locals would pass by whilst out for a stroll. On one occasion during the hottest part of the afternoon, we were staring attentively at my rod waiting a bite when a group of young African children suddenly appeared on the river bank about twenty yards from where we were. Of course in those days we called them 'picaninies' and, although not feeling in any way threatened, we kept a watchful eye on them. The ages ranged from about five to twelve. We made no attempt to communicate with them and they totally ignored us. They proceeded to undress. Some had swimming trunks, some in their underpants and the very young stripped completely. We never associated swimming as an African sport or pastime. It was a common sight to see young blacks playing around in shallow dams and rivers but swimming only short distances.

To our complete surprise the oldest one dived into the water and started to swim out into the middle of the river. Gradually they all followed with the very youngest last. They all bundled their clothes into small parcels and tied it to their waists. They swam in a line with the oldest in the front and the very youngest at the back. Swimming styles were a mixture of crawl, breaststroke and a 'dog paddle' and while swimming they were continuously calling out to each other. Slowly they made their way safely to the other side of the river, a distance of about four hundred yards. Once they had reached the other side they disappeared into the bush. About two hours later we saw their heads bobbing up and down in the water as they swam slowly back to our side of the river. Once back they then walked away carrying their bundles of wet clothes.

Just outside the municipal boundary of Vereeniging the Klip River flows into the Vaal at a place called Peacehaven. A road bridge crosses over the Klip River about a mile from where it flows into the Vaal River. A taxi would offload us by the bridge and then we would walk carefully through marshes until we reached the riverbank for our day's fishing. The river was only about thirty yards wide with enough trees to provide shade but not too close to make casting difficult. Although we were in sight of the suburb of Peacehaven and could see the cars crossing the bridge, it was a sanctuary from the city life of Johannesburg to me.

One Saturday afternoon I had a prearranged meeting with an ex-army friend of my father and his son John at Johannesburg Station. We caught the train to Evaton where my father had his pharmacy. Evaton was about fifteen miles from Vereeniging. We arrived at four in the afternoon and my father closed the shop at five p.m. We all bundled into a customer's car who, for the cost of the petrol, drove the four of us to the Klip River. My father had borrowed a piece of canvas from the local railway yard, which we proceeded to convert into a shelter before dark. Then we setup our fishing rods and had them baited and in the water before it became too dark to see without a torch or paraffin lamp.

John collected firewood and before long we had a boiling kettle and prepared our evening meal braaivleis (barbeque) style. After the meal, we settled down to watch our rods as the moon rose higher into the night sky. The night noises had begun with the frog chorus at one end of the scale and the night crickets at the other. The noise seemed to inhibit any conversation. Underneath the trees, just over the water the flying fireflies created flashes of light.

The temperature dropped slowly, and about eleven o'clock I wrapped myself in a blanket under our canvas shelter and in spite of the hardness of the ground I soon fell into a deep sleep. It seemed no sooner had I closed my eyes than I was awake again to see the magnificent red sky that is the hallmark of every African dawn.

My father, his friend Mr. C and John were silhouetted by the early morning light against the riverbank. Once I could see properly, I noticed that my father was holding my bending rod and I could hear the noise of the ratchet on the fishing reel. John was holding a landing net and Mr. C. directed operations. It was another half-hour before we landed the fish that had swallowed my baited hook. The fish turned out to be a sixteen-pound river carp. It was the largest river fish I had ever seen and as far as I can recall the largest fish that I ever saw caught. Once we had safely landed our catch and secured it in a keep-net, we settled down to enjoy a camp breakfast.

We caught nothing more that day but did enjoy showing off our trophy to everyone who came within ten yards of us. At last, the fish that did not get away - it was no tale and it was there for all to see. In fact as the day wore on the news of our catch spread along the river. Fishermen came by all day to admire our trophy. On late Sunday afternoon our 'taxi' came to collect us, drove us to the railway station, and delivered the canvas back to the yard from where we had borrowed it. We carefully wrapped our fish in a wet cloth and took it home with us.

During the journey home we rehearsed over and over again about how we were going to tell the story of our catch. We arrived home at about ten o'clock and my mother and sisters expressed their usual relief at seeing us arriving home safely. Apart from greetings we said nothing. Because we did not tell them the usual tales about the ones we caught and gave away, they started to question us. My father in a round about way told them about our catch, which they listened to with their usual disbelief till eventually I displayed our fish that was still only just alive. My father then killed it.

Somehow or other the whole neighbourhood got to know about our catch and before the fish was disembowelled and prepared for cooking. Everyone seemed to come to our house to see the miracle fish for themselves. I well remember eating carp for near enough the rest of the week.

Not all fishing trips were at ideal riverside locations. Very often, we would end up at some dam or lake, which was nothing more than a shallow depression in the veld that had accumulated rainwater as well as water from natural springs. The local landowner had sometime in the past stocked it with fish or the fish had somehow arrived via local streams. Those places were often treeless; hence there was no escape from the midday sun.

One of these dams was located near a dorp (a village) called Grassmere and to get there you had take the train to Vereeniging via the West Rand. You could travel by train to Vereeniging (south of Johannesburg) by two routes, one via the East Rand and the other via the West Rand. The next stop along the line after Grassmere was called Lens. The line to Vereeniging via the East Rand passed through dorp with a similar sounding name and on more than one occasion we caught the wrong train.

I can never remember catching any fish at the treeless dam near Grassmere. Quite often my attention strayed from my fishing rod to watch long tailed birds that seemed to be able to only fly above the height of the grass. The long tail appeared to weigh it down as it dipped into the grass every thirty to fifty yards. My father called them flops and said by chasing them you could catch them quite easily because they would slow with exhaustion. However, whenever I approached one of them, it took off into the sky and flew well beyond my reach. I never succeeded in ever seeing one actually settling in the grass.

My last memory of Grassmere was when we were fishing with my father, Mr. C and his son John. At about three in the afternoon, not having caught any fish, the heat got the better of us. We decided to call it a day and walked to the small siding at Lens to catch the next train. While standing alongside the rail track a local farmer came by and told us that none of the Sunday afternoon trains stopped at Lens and that we should make our way to Grassmere. The quickest and probably the only way to get there was to walk there. We set about walking alongside the railway track. For most of the way the railway line was level with the surrounding veld but, every now and again, the track dipped into a narrow cutting to a depth of about ten to twenty feet. The walls of the cuttings were pock marked with numerous holes made by birds for use as nests. As we passed by, the birds flew in and out of their nests screaming at us.

While in the narrowest part of a deep cutting, we heard the sound of a steam train approaching and there was no way we could scramble out of the cutting. We all found a crag in the cutting wall in which we lodged ourselves hoping that we were safely out of reach of the approaching locomotive. We were all sprayed with steam as the black locomotive passed by within touching distance. The driver looked at us with absolute astonishment. By the time we reached Grassmere station our clothes had dried off and most of the soot brushed off. Those on the platform waiting to catch the same passenger train looked on with amazement as the four of us appeared from along the railway lines.

The weekend fishing excursions helped me to escape from suburban Johannesburg and provided another view of South Africa. The only experience most of my contemporaries had of the world beyond Johburg was when they went on summer picnics to one of the many picnic spots about an hours drive from the city.

Chapter 7

About year after the Second World War ended my father opened a pharmacy in the village of Evaton. As an ex-soldier he received a government loan to set up his chemist shop. This meant that he had to spend the week away from the family, which was exactly what he had been doing during the war years. His pharmacy was located on the edge of the town on the road to the location where the Africans lived. He believed that most of his trade would be with the Black population. The Whites would travel the mile or so from the dorp centre rather than travel ten to fifteen miles to Vereeniging where the nearest chemist shops were located. The only vacant property was a house that had been converted into a green grocery shop by a Portuguese family. It was a square white building with a central entrance. There were no real shop windows only the remains of bedroom windows on either side of the entrance. The only inner wall was a central partition, which split the 'house' into two large empty spaces. Once through the entrance, you had two choices - left into the green grocery shop or right into the pharmacy. The shop fittings separated the dispensary from the rest of what, to me, seemed a rather empty shop.

Although post-war Evaton was only about forty five miles from Johannesburg and about twelve miles from Vereeniging, in terms of modernity it could have been a thousand miles away. Like all dorps throughout South Africa the roads were sand or dirt. The nearest stretch of tarmac was about six miles away and that was the main road from Johannesburg to Vereeniging. There were no storm gutters or pavements; the garden was simply the remnants of the veld in front of the houses that lined the roads. The dorp was 'planned' in so far as the roads were laid in a large grid type pattern making large blocks. The houses built within these blocks were each constructed individually. Some faced the road while others were set at various angles in the plots. The plots were one-third to an acre in size. Most of the old houses were made mainly out of corrugated zinc while the newer houses were brick built. All the houses had tin roofs and a front veranda with some enclosed in dark gauze to keep the insects out. To get onto the front veranda you had to negotiate at least two red steps. The floor of the veranda was made out of the same red concrete, as were the steps.

There was no electricity at all and most houses had water wells headed by a hand pump. At the rear of the house, were the usual servants' quarters and a small outhouse, the toilet made of corrugated zinc. The toilet seat straddled a black bucket and at the rear of the toilet was a flap for the night time removal and emptying of the bucket.

A small gate opened onto a sand path that led to the front veranda with a larger gate for cars. Apart from some rose bushes and the odd fruit tree, there were no proper gardens; a front lawn would have taken up far too much precious water. Scattered all over the dorp were blue gum trees; otherwise the impression was as if a bit of the veld had been disrupted by houses, sheds and roads.

Evaton was located only on one side of the railway line. From the station, a road passed through rows of tall blue gum trees and was crossed at right angles by the minor roads that made up the grid pattern. About two miles down that road was my father's pharmacy. Occasionally my mother, two sisters, and I would have a Saturday outing to Evaton. We usually arrived mid morning by steam train from Johannesburg and were dressed up more for a city occasion than a visit to dusty dorp. The local men were dressed in Khaki and the women in cotton frocks, stockingless and flat shoes. Speaking English, the four us, my sisters in white high-heeled shoes and me in a jacket and tie and mother with hat and veil and handbag stood out like sore thumbs. All passers by, black and white, stared at us. Occasionally my father arranged for the local taxi or a friend who owned a car to collect us and that saved any embarrassment. We also had to take our own food with us. At closing time a taxi spared us the return walk to the station and we would arrive back at our flat in Johannesburg about ten at night.

These family excursions out of Johburg into Afrikaans South Africa, instead of helping to integrate us, only helped to emphasize the difference. Although as a family we had relatively little money, we dressed as if we were on a shopping expedition to town. We looked and felt affluent compared to what we saw. The lack of public utilities, i.e. electricity, running water and main drainage, the dirt roads and the tin roofs were to us were symbols of a lower standard of living. There was an air of poverty and the Afrikaners were only living to a standard a little better than the natives. However, we had never actually been into any African home. The only African homes we had seen were the rooms of the servants, so our comparison was flawed but no one at the time ever pointed that out to me.

During the winter vacation of my last year at junior school, my father decided that I could spend my vacation in Evaton. My father rented a room in the home of a local Afrikaans family. The house was only about a hundred yards from his chemist shop. He stayed there during the week and travelled back to Johannesburg on Saturday, returning early on Monday morning. The family consisted of a divorced woman who had three children, all younger than me. Also living in the house was her teenage brother. Her father and other members of her family lived 'close' by. They only spoke Afrikaans and at that time of my life I had hardly ever spoken Afrikaans other than at school. So for me there was a communication problem. I could not understand any of them and they could not understand me. The house was on the opposite side of the sand road from the chemist shop and about 100 yards nearer toward the station. Apart from the chemist shop and its accompanying house there were no other dwellings White or Black within a quarter of a mile of the house. Although the highveld appears flat it is an illusion. The land slopes gently up or down and the nearest house seemed to be at the top of the long dusty road situated behind some planted Blue Gum trees.

Without electricity at all in the village, at night the only light was from the stars and the moon. There was no running tap water in the house either. It was hard to believe that less than twenty miles away in Vereeniging they had street lighting, both tap water and sewage systems and electricity power supply to each house. The only houses that had any form of electric lighting in Evaton were those houses that had installed a petrol driven generator of some sort. There were a few wind-driven generators but they were very primitive. Domestic radios powered by batteries had just become available at the time. This was the only form of evening entertainment.

I remember the family sitting around my father's radio carried into the living room, which was lit by a combination of candles and Tilly lamps. It all seemed so dark, primitive and scary. The programs that we listened to were broadcast in Afrikaans, which I did not understand. Most of what they listened to was comedy programmes. It was worse for me as I watched everyone else laughing and I did not know what they were laughing at. It was July, the middle of winter, the evenings and nights were cold. The living rooms and bedrooms had no heating at all. At about nine o'clock my father, holding an oversized torch, led me to our room and undressed and climbed into a very cold bed. It was so dark outside that it made no difference whether or not the curtains were drawn or not.

I usually woke up after my father, got dressed and then joined the rest of the family for breakfast. There was always a strong smell of percolating coffee that bubbled away on the coal stove and the South African version of an Aga cooker. Breakfast nearly always was a bowl of mealie pap (porridge made out of maize meal) followed by a plate of scrambled eggs and fried Boerewors. The African servant girl who referred to me as kleinbass prepared breakfast. Apart from her own African language she only spoke Afrikaans. After breakfast the children and the teenage brother Johan and I were left to entertain ourselves until lunchtime.

I nearly always wore khaki shirt and shorts, a sleeveless pullover and shoes and socks. The children and Johan never wore shoes and walked barefoot. I secretly envied them as it was considered to be 'macho' to be able walk barefoot. Their feet were 'leathered'. My feet were far too soft to be able to walk comfortably for any length of time without shoes. After all they had hardly ever worn shoes and probably found it as difficult to walk with shoes as I did to walk barefoot. My undeclared ambition was return to Johannesburg and be able to walk barefoot without flinching.

City dwellers of my generation referred to the country folk of the type I was now living with as Japies or Plaas (farm) Japies. Although we were less than two hours drive from Johburg most of the White inhabitants of Evaton had probably never been there. Most of my city contemporaries were as equally ignorant of how the country folk lived. We knew them as the people of the platteland and never really associated with or recognized them as our fellow countrymen. This was yet another racial group to add to the already long list.

I was about eleven years old and, like young South Africans of my generation, was acutely conscious of all these divisions. There I was to all intents and purposes a million miles away from my home and the only person who I could feel any affinity with was my father. Just to remind you, my father spoke, apart from English, fluent Afrikaans and Yiddish but somehow had avoided religious teaching. He could not read Hebrew and never attended a synagogue other than for weddings. Apart from his family in his youth he was never surrounded by as much Jewish culture as I was. During the war years there were not many other Jewish soldiers. Now he had opted for living away from us most of the time among the people of the platteland.

I felt as if I was permanently on the sidelines, a spectator not even close to my father, who seemed at times as distant from me as everyone else in the room. However what I did know was that as long as I was away from home and on holiday I had to make the most of my stay even though I felt uneasy.

The house, like many Boer houses was very spartan. The floors were either bare wood or stone. At the most they may have a covering with a strip of lino; carpeting was something out of this world. The furniture was very basic, either pine or a local hardwood with perhaps one item (usually the sideboard) made out of a special Cape hardwood known as 'stinkwood'.

Framed family photographs were everywhere as well as religious pictures and icons. It was the drawings and icons all representing some aspect of Jesus and the resurrection that made a Jewish boy at the beginning of his teens feel so very uncomfortable. After all, I like all my friends in Johburg, was indoctrinated against Christianity. Any symbol of Christianity sent cold feelings through us. It was something we would try and avoid. Nevertheless here I was and here I was going to be for the rest of the school holidays. I would have to accept them in the hope that they would do likewise.

Even at that young age we very aware of the concept of sin. I had sinned without any choice and even worse had enjoyed the fried Boerewors and mealie pap. Once breakfast was over I put to the back of my mind that what I ate was not kosher and that I may have even eaten pork with seemingly my father's knowledge. Apart from non-kosher meat I was drinking milk and eating meat dishes at the same time not milk before meat, as is the kosher tradition. My feeling of sin soon vanished as we went out to play.

We seemed to be preoccupied with trying to kill birds. We made ourselves catapults or catties as we called them. We would spend a long time looking among the few accessible trees for a forked or Y shaped twig. We would skin the bark off and then carve out grooves at two ends. Tie string into the grooves. Then attach to bits of elastic or better still two pieces of rubber cut out of a bicycle or car inner tube. Two more bits of string attached to the loose ends of the rubber. A piece of leather was tied onto the loose ends to hold a small stone, our ultimate weapon. As soon as our catties were completed we collected a pile of suitable stones then set about shooting at targets. As the birds were inaccessible, the targets were usually bottles. We spent many a morning just trying to hit a target and a poor unsuspecting bird that was silly enough to fly within our range. Luckily for the birds, I can't remember ever succeeding. Another homemade weapon was a bow and arrow also made from the local trees and ordinary string. The force generated by the bow was hardly sufficient to propel the arrow to penetrate paper ten yards away.

My father, whose confessed pastime was hunting, shooting, and fishing, took an occasional interest in our activities. He gave us lessons in the use of a cattie but, once again, all the birds escaped. He turned up one morning with a pellet gun that was more like a toy rifle that fired small round pellets with enough force to pierce cardboard at a range of twenty yards. He made us promise that we not would use each other as targets. We were now in position to fire up into the air at flying birds but once again they all survived.

The house was actually surrounded by about six acres of land, some cultivated to produce fresh vegetables. To help grow the crops, a small dam had been constructed in the middle of the plot and was fed by a very slow underground spring. The dam was rectangular in shape, about twenty to thirty yards long and ten yards wide. We cleared out the water channel that fed the dam and managed after a few days, actually to increase the height of the water to about four foot, sufficient to float an old rowboat that we had found on daily walkabouts.

We loaded the boat onto a soapbox cart we had made in one afternoon using wheels from a discarded pram. Immediately after the launching the boat sank. We managed to drag it out and then set about mending the holes with mud from the bottom of the dam which was left in the sun to dry. It turned out to be waterproof for at least a couple of days. The boat was small enough and the dam big enough for us to be able to row up and down endlessly. After a few days of rowing we all had blistered hands to show for our efforts. When I returned to Johburg I proudly showed off my hands to my friends.

I spent most of the day with the three children and Johan. Day by day my ability to communicate in Afrikaans improved. At the same time, Johan did attempt to speak to me in English. While we were active I enjoyed it all but as soon as there was a lull, I felt uneasy as though I did not really belong and was only tolerated because of my father.

On one of our strolls we came across a neighbour who had a donkey, which was just left to graze on their plot of land. I told my father about it and he then arranged for the donkey to be allowed to graze on the part of our plot of land that was not cultivated. We had to keep it tethered to long rope to prevent it from feeding on the vegetable plots. From our point of view the donkey was to be ridden and before long we managed to climb on to its back. A saddle was out of the question; all we had was rope attached to a bridle which we forced into its mouth. The ability to sit on the donkey's back without falling off was quite an achievement. Only with coaxing, shouting, and a certain amount of whipping by someone behind the donkey did it actually move without being pulled forward by the rope that was attached to its head.

The donkey in question!!

During the war years, and in the immediate post-war years, we read comic papers such as Film Fun and Radio Fun. There was hardly an edition that did not feature a donkey being ridden and coaxed along by the rider dangling a carrot in front of its head. As the animal tried to eat the carrot, it had to reach forward. The rider made certain that the carrot was out of reach of the donkey and hence it moved forward. Naturally, we tried that trick without any success. The donkey showed very little interest in carrots or it lunged forward and grabbed the carrot in its mouth and stood still very stubbornly chewing its prize. In desperation, we dangled a piece of bread in front of the donkey's nose and used a much longer stick. This worked and we found ourselves propelled forward very insecurely on an unsaddled donkey. Our activities attracted a lot of attention and nearly always had the audience giggling waiting for one of us to fall off the animal's back.

Diagonally opposite our house in Johannesburg was another large house built at the turn of the century that had survived the developers. The house was single storied but had numerous rooms as well as cellars and belonged to a family named Garlick. One of the young Garlick family, was a member of our gang so we often played in the grounds of that rather large corner house. One of the characteristics of the house was that it had a large sweet chestnut tree in the middle of an unkempt garden. Every late summer we spent many hours knocking chestnuts out of the tree. Old man Garlick bought and sold almost anything, which he stored in the grounds before being sold on. One of their purchases was a mountain of old bottles mostly old medicine bottles made out of blue glass. I remember one day the bottles, being packed into large sacks and loaded onto a lorry and driven off. One of my first surprises of my Evaton holiday was to discover that my father had bought the bottles and they were piled up in a corner of the grounds of the house where I was spending my school vacation.

An old African was employed to wash the bottles and every now and again he would take a wheelbarrow full of newly washed bottles to the back of the chemist shop. In those days, pharmacists still made up all sorts of medicines in the back dispensary. Most were inventions of my father that he had persuaded the local doctors to prescribe.

They were his personal magical cures for every type of ailment. I should imagine a modern bottle collector transported back to that bottle-mountain would have thought that they had won the lottery. From our point of view those bottles provided an endless supply of targets for our catties and my pellet gun. We also discovered that bottles floating on the dam were great targets for our stone missiles. The broken bottles sunk to the bottom and the mud coloured water hid from our view the broken glass. This activity came to a sudden end when Johan, wading barefoot into the dam to free the boat, stood on some glass and ended up with a nasty cut on his foot. Had we been living in a town we would have rushed him to hospital to have the wound stitched up. All that did happen was that my father cleaned the wound, applied some antiseptic and bandaged the cut in such a way that it held together and healed in a matter of days.

My father's pharmacy in Evaton

Three weeks when you are very young seems like an eternity and when I eventually returned to home in Johannesburg I felt that I had to adjust back to city life with all its modern comforts. Although I was now back with electric lights, running water, flush toilets and the radio in English I felt ill at ease. I had just experienced another world or another aspect of South African culture. But at that age one is not aware of cultural differences and differing standards so everything is compared to what you are familiar with. I also felt that a gap was developing between me and my neighbourhood friends and I had now seen and tasted part of the South Africa that was generally looked down upon and even ridiculed by those around and closest to me.

Toward the end of my stay in Evaton one evening just before dark I walked into the bedroom that I shared with my father only to find him standing with his arms around the woman of the house, Johan's sister. She looked sheepish and tried to break away but my father held on, smiled at me as if nothing had happened and then eventually let go. I just looked away feeling both very embarrassed and bewildered and did not know what to make of it all. I never ever told anyone what I had witnessed that evening.

Chapter 8

About one Sunday a month we would have a family gathering. There would be my Aunt Fanny, my mother's elder sister her husband and their two sons and daughter. In addition there were other cousins, my mother's half-brother's son who were at that time permanent boarders in my aunt's house.

They were also almost my parents' age and in fact they had all grown up together in a small town Zeerust in the Western Transvaal close to Mafeking.

My maternal grandfather, who I never knew, came to South Africa from Lithuania via the United States. My mother's mother was his third wife and she died during the 1919 flu epidemic. His previous wives had also all died. My mother was the second youngest of the girls and she had a younger brother. He had two children by wife number two who were born in Philadelphia. After their mother died he returned to Lithuania and married my Grandmother and the four children were born there spoke Russian as well as Yiddish. My grandfather sailed to South Africa on his own and worked as a Smous (a peddler) travelling round the country and for some reason or other settled in Zeerust. He then brought out all the family from Lithuania to join him including the two children born in Philadelphia who were much older. Their children together with my mother, her sisters and brother all grew up together in Zeerust. When my mother started school the official languages were English and a South African version of Dutch, which was well on its way to becoming Afrikaans.

The Jewish community of Zeerust at the time, as far as I know, consisted of my maternal grandfather and his family. Once he had his family settled in the town, he established himself as the miller and moneylender. Photographs show him to have had a very patriarchal appearance, always wearing a black jacket, a waistcoat, and a tie that was worn as a cravat. A large rimmed flat black hat and, of, course a large tidy grey beard with bushy eyebrows completed his image. Apart from his town activities he owned several farms on which he raised cattle. The largest of the farms he shared with his eldest son Mishameyer (from Philadelphia) and his wife who produced for him six sons; the eldest and youngest were twins. Those boys were the nephews of mother but were almost the same age. My mother was in her early teens when her mother died and she and her elder sisters more or less had to fill the role of the woman of the house. This arduous task was made a lot more bearable because of the availability of cheap Black servants.

My grandfather probably arranged for my mother's eldest sister Aunt Fanny to marry my Uncle Louis. They remained in Zeerust and ran the local grocery store. They had three children, two boys and a girl. As to how my father came onto the scene I can only speculate that they were introduced via a shadchan (a matchmaker) and my father was bought. They were both in their early twenties when they got married.

Before the marriage my father lived with his parents in Johannesburg in the suburb of Newlands that bordered onto Sophiatown. Even in those days, Newlands was not the most desirable area for a Jewish family to live and it is probably the reason why my father was totally out of touch with Judaism. He could not read the Hebrew prayers and I doubt if he had had a proper Bar mitzvah. When they first met my father was an apprentice pharmacist. For some reason or other there was some difficulty with regards to completing his studies in South Africa. With the help of my grandfather he was able to travel to the UK and managed to complete his apprenticeship and acquire qualifications that allowed him to practise as both a pharmacist and an optician.

My mother and father spent over a year living in both Glasgow and Edinburgh and my eldest sister was born in Edinburgh. They returned to Johannesburg and, shortly after, my second sister was born. This was followed by a period of my father working as a pharmacist mainly in rural areas of the Transvaal, Orange Free State and the Northern Cape Province. They ended up in 1936 in a town called Vryburg in the far northern most part of the Cape Province where I was born. Once again it was a short stay and they ended up back in Zeerust. It was from my eldest sisters' recollections that I gleamed what life was like in Zeerust with my grandfather.

My cousins, the children of Aunt Fannie and Uncle Louis, who are in the same age group as my elder sister all mention how terrified they were of my grandfather. They never walked past the front of his house except on religious holidays and Friday evenings when they were expected to go and give the traditional greeting. Somehow he did not quite terrify my sister as much and she apparently received favoured treatment that did not go down well with my cousins. Every Friday night he gave them all a penny, which was spent on sweets during the following week. My sister used to ask my father for a penny before the Friday night visit and my grandfather believed that she was saving her money. No doubt that must have pleased him.

After my grandfather's death in 1938 my parents moved back to Johannesburg but the rest of the clan remained in Zeerust. My father worked in a pharmacy in the Turfontein area of Johannesburg where the Johannesburg racecourse was located. I think that both my parents and in particular my father had a passion for gambling. It was while we lived in Turfontein that we met an English immigrant family, the Davises, who remained close to our family for the rest of their lives. In 1939 my father acquired his own pharmacy in Parktown which, in those days was on the very edge of Northwest Johburg. A few doors away we had our own house built with, like the pharmacy, the money my mother had inherited. The Davis family also moved into the area.

My earliest childhood memories are of sitting on the steps of the entrance to the chemist shop and looking up the road, identifying the makes of cars to astonished adults. I also remember being terrified of fireworks and hiding behind the sofa. My eldest sister told me that I had developed a very bad cough and none of my father's nor any doctor's magic potions could cure my ailment. The general consensus was that I should be taken to the seaside, the nearest being at Durban four hundred miles away; the sea air would cure me. Money was short but my mother's faith in gambling came to the rescue. My mother backed a horse called the 'Isle of Capri', which was a rank outsider, but won and the odds were such that she won enough money to pay for the two of us to go to Durban for a holiday. I can still remember leaving the station and seeing the sea at a distance for the first time. I can still see what seemed to be huge grey waves against a dull sky. I also remember a visit to a place called Umhlanga Rocks and seeing a huge stone arch with the sea smashing through it. The hat I was wearing was blown off my head and an African guide tried to retrieve it. I was teased for years to come about the fact that some shark was probably wearing my hat. My next memory is someone from our hotel thinking he was doing me a favour by dragging me screaming into the terrifying waves of the Indian Ocean. War was declared while we were in Durban and next thing I knew we were back at the pharmacy in Parktown.

Many years later Mrs Davis told me that during this period the quarrels between my parents went from bad to worse. Luckily for me, I don't remember any of them. But my eldest sister was old enough to know what was going on and when things got really bad she would walk my sister and me over to the Davis household to seek sanctuary. The pharmacy as a business went steadily down hill and by 1940 the house and the chemist shop was sold and my father joined the army and we then moved to a much smaller rented house. Shortly afterwards my father was posted 'up North' which meant East Africa and we moved to the hostel for soldiers' wives.

On those weekends when peace reigned in our house we would, like most Bertrams and Doornfontien Jewish families, go out on Sunday afternoon. It would be a trip to the Zoo, the Zoo Lake, Joubert Park, Pretoria or window-shopping in central Johannesburg and nearly always ended with listening to a 'palm court orchestra'. We were all given a treat of a parfait or an ice cream. There were the picnics to Florida Lake that was an excuse for my father to go fishing. Whenever it was possible my father and I would go on one of our fishing expeditions. About once a month there were the visits to various aunts, uncles and grown-up cousins scattered not only all over Johburg but along towns of both the East and West Rand. Trips to the latter would mean a train ride.

Either my parents would phone a relative and invite themselves over or they would phone us and actually ask us to visit them. Occasionally, our family would be the hosts by either inviting some relative or they would invite themselves. This system meant that we were occupied almost every Sunday afternoon and kept in touch with the family.

Visits were to my Aunt Fanny's household or to one of my married cousin's who grew up with my mother in Zeerust who was the oldest son of my mother's half brother Mishemayer. His wife was a very attractive Polish Jewess and they had five daughters. Originally, the wedding was arranged so that she could acquire South African citizenship. The plan was that she would leave him. She did not and the marriage lasted for the rest of their lives.

Once the decision had been made to visit my Aunt Fanny's household (either they had invited us or we had invited ourselves), the trek across Johburg began. First of all there was the inevitable period of having to decide what to wear and then being dressed in our Sunday best. Although our house and that of my aunt was located on the East Side of Johannesburg, the public transport was such that all tram and bus routes radiated into the city. So we would walk to the tram stop and catch a tram into the city centre, about a twenty-minute tram ride. Then we would 'traipse' over to the terminus from where the trams departed to Kensington. We travelled right to the end of the line and then there was a ten-minute walk to my aunt's house. I always remember arriving slightly hot and bothered as we were greeted stepping on to the front veranda.

The afternoon followed a regular formula. After the initial greetings, we wandered round the garden; the house was on a half-acre plot. Then the new bits of furniture or additions/repairs to the house would be discussed in detail. I remember that when there was a major addition such as a new three-piece suite or dinning room table, etc., this would have already been described many times over the telephone and now it could be seen in the 'flesh.' Mid-afternoon tea and cakes were served and we were made to eat our fill by our aunt and then scolded by our parents for over-indulging. The gathering fragmented after tea into the men gradually moving toward the inevitable poker game, while the women began the endless analysis about all the members of our extended family. One particular cousin, his wife and five daughters were nearly always the first to be pulled apart.

Another essential topic was Zeerust. My mother's brother, Ben, and his family and her half brother Mishemayer and sister Gita still lived in Zeerust. I was the only family member who had never been to Zeerust so to me this was a magic place that I had to one day visit and to see the graves of my grandparents. Almost every month one of our extended family travelled to Zeerust for a weekend. Both of my sisters had spent school vacations in Zeerust.

Between six and seven in the evening the card game was halted for dinner which was nearly always fish, chicken (which, in those day was still the most expensive form of meat), or scrambled eggs and/or omelettes. The ever presence of a Black domestic servant helped to ease the burden of preparing the meal. No invitations were ever issued if it was the servants' Sunday off. Once the meal was over the card game resumed as soon as possible. It was dark by then so we were dispatched to the living room to listen to records (the old 78s), or the radio. The records were always played on a radiogram with an automatic changer so at least six records could be stacked up. Listening to records was a great treat for my sisters and me because all we had at the time was a very old table-model wireless.

The Bing Crosby record album "The Bells of St.Marys" was all the rage during that era. We first heard all the 'A' sides then the 'B' sides and then a mixture. Slowly we worked through my cousin's record collection. My sisters were now in their middle teens and were taught how to foxtrot and waltz. Normally Sunday was an early to bed night because of school on Monday but on these nights the card game had preference and very often the evening would end close to midnight. I well remember desperately trying to stay awake. Once the card game was finally over whoever had been lucky would distribute some of their winnings to my cousins, my sisters and myself. The older ones would receive more than I did. If I was given a half-crown I knew the rest were given five shillings. One of our older cousins would drive us home in their family car.

Weddings, engagement parties and Bar mitzvah receptions were nearly always held on a Sunday. Those events usually used up at least four Sundays a year and they were all occasions for a Sunday late night. At those occasions the chief topic of conversation was the family and the ups downs of their respective occupations, professions or businesses. Politics was only occasionally discussed but when it did come up, anyone who tried to raise the topic of Black deprivation or Black rights was always in a minority and likely to be ganged up on. If different or radical opinions were brought up, tempers would rise and the worst insult or accusation was to call someone a communist. Any Black who was politically active and any White who showed any concern was branded a communist. Such were the opinions of those who gathered together. The passion and aggression displayed during such political debates really only reflected that of the White society at large. Occasionally the debates were serious and rapidly deteriorated into an argument resulting in insults flying like confetti. Inevitably the protagonists ended up not speaking. I can seldom remember a time when at least one relative was not on speaking terms with another member of the family. Strangely enough the major family celebrations like weddings Bar mitzvahs etc. were the occasions when all previous rows were forgiven.

The welfare of even the most distant cousin was a cause for concern. As predictable events like a Bar mitzvah drew near the family concerned was always a prime target for gossip. I was twelve, my pre-Bar mitzvah year, my first year at high school. The pressure on me was slowly building up and all the relatives were aware, but never said much, that arrangements were not going smoothly. I now know that even my most distant relatives were acutely aware of our family problems. They knew my father for what he was and also my mother's erratic temperament, and how bitter she was about aspects of her married life. She never spoke of my father's aberrant behaviour in front of us children and defended him whenever the need arose.

Chapter 9

In this chapter I have written what I can recall of my Bar mitzvah which took place more than a half a century ago. It is a personal account of my preparation, my ceremony and the effect that this ritual had upon me and my family. My father was not religious and could not read the prayers in Hebrew. It is not a detailed description of the usual preparation for, and the actual Bar mitzvah ceremony. There are numerous texts and books available to those who would like to read a more detailed account of the preparation for, and the actual, Bar mitzvah ceremony.

South African schools all have very distinctive uniforms with their own colorful blazer. Athlone High schools was a rich green with thin yellow and red stripes.

At the end of that year I moved from junior school to high school and that was the last time I remember ever receiving a school report that my family and I were proud of. It was standard practice for all Jewish children particularly boys to attend Hebrew classes in the afternoon after school. During my first year at high school it was even more important for me to attend because, like all Jewish boys most of your twelfth year is spent preparing for your Bar mitzvah. The nearest Saturday to your thirteenth birthday is when you would be called up in the Synagogue to read a portion of the law. After each Jewish New Year the reading of the five books of Moses and the Torah begins and is completed by the end of the year only to be read all over at the start of the next year. The same amount is read each week so it is easy to predict or determine what portion the Bar mitzvah boy has to be prepared for. It was not read but recited or chanted in a very old traditional manner. A particular shaped accent represents each sound. There are specially prepared books which have each portion of the law printed in Hebrew with the musical accents overprinted on each word. In theory once you have learnt the sounds you should be able to chant any portion of the Torah. The Bar mitzvah boy has to spend the first few months of his twelfth year mastering this chant known colloquially as the 'Trop.'

That year, the year of my Bar mitzvah preparation was the beginning of a very traumatic year in both my own and my family life. It was my first year at high school and it was the local Athlone High School. (During the post war years schooling was totally segregated not only into Black and White schools but also into English and Afrikaans speaking schools.) There was a very definite pecking order among the White schools. My sisters were attending Parktown High Schools for girls located in a smart area of Johburg. This was because they had attended the junior feeder school before we had moved to Bertrams. My mother had tried to get me into Parktown High School for Boys but without success, hence I had to attend a school that was both different and inferior to my sisters. The whole neighbourhood knew that my sisters were at Parktown, which had kept them aloof from the locals. The fact that I had not succeeded in going to an equivalent High School implied that I was not as clever as they were. It also had the effect that the only neighbourhood that I really knew was that of Bertrams and surrounding districts. My sisters' friends and social life were mostly located in the Parktown area; hence even within my family there were social differences with me at the bottom in every sense.

The high school day began at about half-past eight with classes actually beginning at nine. There were two breaks and school ended at about 2pm. Organised sport in the form of team games, swimming, tennis, even chess and music, were all extra-curricular activities in the afternoons. For most of the Jewish boys under that age of thirteen this caused problems because of having to attend Hebrew school in the afternoons. Needless to say, sport won out at least once a week. However during the year building up to Bar mitzvah, apart from the normal Hebrew lessons that lasted an hour, there was an extra half-hour or more devoted to learning your 'piece.' My Bar mitzvah coach/teacher decided that my musical ear was not good enough; I could not sing in tune and would never survive the chanting of my 'piece'. Instead he decided unilaterally to only allow me to read the blessings that have to be recited before each reading and a minimal short section that is recited before the true 'portion'. The decision should really have been my father's but this was at the time our family was breaking apart. My father had to all intents and purposes now left my mother and was living all week at Evaton and returning home on occasional weekends. I never actually asked where he spent most weekends. I just imagined that he stayed on at Evaton or I blanked it out my mind. My sisters and possibly the whole neighbourhood knew a great deal more than I did but never said anything to me.

When it comes to religious matters Jewish women are generally second-class citizens who are not consulted. My mother never understood the intricacies of the Bar mitzvah ceremony and did not realise that all was not well. Mainly because she was working full time and having to support, feed and clothe, us she did not really have the time or the energy to probe the matter of my so called tone deafness any further. About six months before the actual date my mother took an afternoon off work. We both went to one of the local synagogues and met with one of the Rabbis to find out how to 'book me in'. He made no comment about the absence of my father, made a note in the appropriate diary and collected a two-pound deposit. I told him what I was being taught and what I was and was not going to recite. He simply shook his head unsympathetically but made no further comment or asked questions.

A Bar mitzvah in a Jewish household is an occasion for a celebration. There is always a reception of some kind either on the Saturday night or on the following Sunday afternoon. A hall, caterers and a band are hired. Invitations are printed and posted to all and sundry requesting the presence of……, at the Synagogue and then at the reception. In addition there is also an invitation to lunch after the Saturday service. As the day nears there is normally constant turmoil in the family. In my case, with my father absent, it seemed like very little was being done.

The birthday of a close school friend was near to mine and his Bar mitzvah was to be on the same Saturday. His father was the proprietor of the largest jewellery manufacturer in Johannesburg. He also happened to be one the cleverest boys in the class, he nearly always came first or second and the only anxiety he seemed to show was what can only be described as stage fright. The service and reception were all a matter of fact and perhaps he sensed or knew that it was almost chaos with me. He and my other school and neighbourhood friends never asked me anything other than in what synagogue was I going to be 'Bar mitzvahed'.

Both of my sisters were courting and were well on their way to becoming officially engaged. So I now had two future brothers-in-laws on the scene and neither of them had a traditional Jewish upbringing. At that time their knowledge of Jewish religious ritual was very poor and neither of them could read prayer book Hebrew. Each afternoon I attended my Bar mitzvah class and the actual day was approaching. Not knowing for certain what arrangements my parents were going to make for the reception just heaped more stress upon the already existing stresses of the time. My non-ability to sing my 'portion' of the law can be recorded as a failure.

The Jewish community, who socially kept very much to themselves and had either fled persecution in Europe or were the descendents of those who had fled from anti-Semitism, had in a very short time adopted the values of the white community. Many, like my paternal grandparents, had arrived at the turn of the century and those before them arrived during the days of the diamond and gold rushes. Those, who like my parents had grown up in South Africa, were as South African as Biltong or Mealie-pap and were very much involved in the running of the country at the local and national political levels. Those who arrived in the immediate pre-war days never lost their 'foreign' accents. There was almost a divide between those Jews who were Yiddish and those who were South African.

My Bar mitzvah lessons were well underway and the synagogue was booked. I don't think that my mother really understood that I was only going to recite a small 'portion' of the prayers but that the actual Haftorah recited by the Bar mitzvah boy was going to be done by one of the Saturday regulars.

There was no question of allowing me to read it as it had to be chanted and, as said before, my musical ear was not considered up to standard. Had my father known, or cared about, what was going on he may have protested but whether that would have helped is only open for speculation: Orthodox Jewry had its rules irrespective of its effects.

The South African school year follows a calendar year and, as my birthday is in January, my approaching Bar mitzvah coincided with the start of my second year at high school (having passed my first year). About three weeks before the event, after one our family gatherings at my aunts, my parents decided to get their act together. Our landlord, old Mr. Gervis, gave permission for a marquee to be erected in the grounds outside of the building and a caterer was booked. So I was going to have reception after all on the following Sunday. The invitations were printed and it was all systems go.

An uncle, my father's brother, provided the money (his present), for a new suit, my Bar mitzvah suit, which was my first pair of long trousers. Another tradition was that at the reception the Bar mitzvah boy has to make a speech, which strangely enough was written for you by the same individual who prepared you for the synagogue ritual. All he did was to glean through a book of speeches and chose the one he decided suited your personality. Luckily for me my sisters got hold of the speech and virtually rewrote it and rehearsed me over and over again until I was word perfect.

I well remember leaving school on Friday afternoon and telling one of my school friends that tomorrow was Solly's big day and mine. He also was going to be 'Bar mitzvahed' on the Saturday but he had no trouble in learning to sing his Haftorah. He caught his bus home in one of the richer parts of the city and I caught mine travelling in the opposite direction to one of, as far as the Jewish community was concerned, the poorest suburbs. It was going to be the beginning of a very long weekend for me.

That evening there was a lot activity in our flat - visitors, endless telephone calls, and relatives helping with food preparations to feed those of the congregation who were to come to our house for the traditional after-service reception. I was obviously the centre of attention but I felt that what ever was happening round me was not really directed to me but to all the grown ups around me. I managed to get my father to try and attempt to read the prayer that he would have to say in Hebrew. He could not read Hebrew so I tried to write it out phonetically for him beneath the Hebrew words. In spite of my efforts they were not successful and he soon turned his attention to all the people that were coming and going around the flat.

In normal times we spent most of our time in the living/dining room of our flat. Thinking back, there was only just enough room to move between chairs, the piano and the couch. In one corner alongside the piano was a small table on which was proudly placed our wireless with its grand cabinet and large dial. The dial, if you believed it, indicated that you could receive broadcasts from all over world but in reality we only picked up the local South African Broadcasting Corporation (SABC) stations. The wireless was our main source of inhouse entertainment. All meals were eaten at the table and when not used for dining it was used as a desk for board games or card games, or for just sitting round uncomfortably talking to visitors. The top of the sideboard was covered with photographs and on the unusually high mantelpiece were the two candlesticks obligatory in every Jewish household. Our flat with the large dinning room table, the piano, the sideboard, and the long studio couch did not exactly provide a great deal of space for visitors. You either sat or stood in what little space remained between the furniture.

The Friday evening before my Bar Mitzvah my mother seemed to be in and out of our small kitchen with cups of teacakes and sandwiches. My sisters too were busy clearing up and just trying to be helpful and my father entertaining. Ten o'clock at night, unless you are playing cards or having a party, was considered to be late and most visitors would leave by then. In what little time remained before bedtime I tried once again to teach my father to read the prayers in Hebrew and attempted without really knowing how, to write the words phonetically, using the Latin alphabet, under the appropriate Hebrew words. One of my difficulties was that Hebrew is written and read right to left across the page. By the time I retired to bed, my confidence in my father's ability to read the Hebrew was not very high.

Saturday morning I was up early and the butterflies in my stomach grew by the moment. I knew that whatever happened I would have to be at synagogue when the service started. My family did not appear to appreciate my anxiety. The synagogue was about a mile and half from our flat and those days the rule about not riding to synagogue was strictly adhered to. I dressed up in my new long trouser suite and new hat and, proudly holding my new Tallis (prayer shawl) in its new velvet bag, I set off alone hoping that the family would soon follow.

When I arrived at the synagogue I walked in alone, to the front seats that were reserved for the day's Bar mitzvah Boy and his male relatives. In an orthodox synagogue the sexes are separate with the women having to sit upstairs. Women are present merely as 'spectators' and they are not compelled to participate in the prayers. There were frowns from the elders as they saw me take my seat alone. Most of the comments were made in Yiddish and although I could not hear them clearly their body language and facial expressions indicated their disapproval.

Saturday services begin with a series of prayers, led by the Chasen (Cantor) with the congregation joining in. In nearly all synagogues the prayer books have an English translation on the opposite page. Almost all of the congregation, male and female can read the prayers in Hebrew but only very few actually understand them. The service flows along at a fairly fast pace. Passages considered to be not of major importance are read through rapidly but nothing is ever left out. Those passages somehow are read through at a faster pace and only slow when it is necessary for the congregation to join in. Many parts of the service have become rather tuneful and easy to sing and it is during those parts that the congregation becomes vocal often led by a choir. There are parts that only the congregation recites and, to accommodate, the Cantor slows down. The pace is such that if you want to keep up with the service, you won't have a chance to read the translation. On odd occasions during a Saturday morning service I would actually read the English. I never read much because I found it to be a series of repetitive praises etc., and not the most exciting of reads. I often wonder what would happen if the Jews who live in the Diaspora could understand the prayers as easily as they can read them whether or not they could continue to recite them.

To my relief and surprise my father arrived about fifteen minutes after me and took his seat alongside of me. My mother and my sisters took their seats upstairs but on the opposite side and we could all see one another.

The service builds up to the opening of the Ark and the removal of the Torah for that day's reading. The reading of the Torah is spread out over a Jewish calendar year and each day another portion is read and, on Saturdays, seven portions are read and the Bar mitzvah boy has the honour to be allowed to read the seventh portion. Normally, each Saturday, members of the congregation are called up to read and honour for which they will make a donation to the synagogue funds. There are special readers who can chant according to the traditional series of tuneful accents. They must read each word and, if they make a mistake they correct it immediately. A blessing has to be recited before the reading of each portion, which is the duty of the person called up. On a Bar mitzvah day the immediate male members of the Bar mitzvah boy's family are called up. The uncles are usually first then the grandfather and then father and finally the Bar mitzvah boy. This all takes place on the central 'Bimah' at the opposite end to the ark where the scrolls are housed. The Bimah is elevated about five feet above the floor of the synagogue and about six-foot square.

Both of my grandfathers had long since been deceased. Two of my uncles were called up and both struggled to read the prayers. The Bar mitzvah boy is on the Bimah while the relatives are called up and will be alongside his father. The time arrived for my father to say the prayers. The elders of the synagogue stand in vigilance on either side of the current readers. In my case there were two grey bearded old men with their rather well worn black Saturday suits and black hats. They muttered loudly their disapproval about the fact that my father could hardly read the Hebrew and struggled but eventually got there. Then it was my turn.

I had no difficulty with reciting the prayer but since my Bar mitzvah tutor had decreed that due to my supposed lack of ability to sing in tune, I was only trained to 'chant' the first part of my portion. The full Bar mitzvah portion takes about twenty minutes to complete. The part that I was allowed only lasted about five minutes. This already met with the disapproval of the two elders who were flanking me. They were muttering very loudly in Yiddish, frequently stroking their beards and almost spitting out the word 'siss' while clearing their throats - the ultimate expression of their disgust. I was standing in a sea of nervousness and almost as soon as I managed to utter the first words I heard from both sides the 'siss' and they directed their disapproving comments to those members of the congregation who were close to the Bimah. I carried on and probably got worse which induced from them louder comments. (What did they achieve and what a manner to an initiation into religious manhood.) As I stepped down from the Bimah one of the regulars of the congregation started to recite the main portion, which should have been the prerogative of the Bar mitzvah boy. I sat down next to my father. Normally as the Bar mitzvah steps down to rejoin his family, although there is no applause, one normally hears loud whispers of congratulation. I sat down next to my father and there was total silence. I looked up to my mother and sisters who actually smiled at me.

Once the Torah had been returned to the ark, I was called to stand in front of the Rabbi who then proceeded to bless the Bar mitzvah boy. This is followed by a series of explanations of what it all meant and that he should continue to study Hebrew and the scriptures and particularly not forget, in order to become a good Jew, to recite the daily and weekly prayers. At the end of the Rabbi's sermon I had to shake hands with him and I'm certain that, although I was only thirteen, neither of us felt that it was a moment of inspiration. Apart from the normal congratulations I don't recall anyone actually commenting on my performance. I walked home with some of my friends and by the time I reached home the food was spread out over the table.

Our flat soon filled up with relatives and friends and, before eating, there was the blessing performed by old Mr Gervis our landlord. It was soon afternoon and the flat seem to empty as quickly as it filled. The only telephone in the house was located downstairs in a corridor outside of the landlord's room. They did not answer the phone on Sabbath. About mid-afternoon the phone rang and usually one of my sisters would belt downstairs to answer the phone but on this occasion I seemed to be the only one available so I dashed downstairs. Are any of the Chernins around? I recognised my Bar mitzvah teacher's voice and as soon as I said yes he immediately asked how it all went at the synagogue. He did not realise who he was talking to and asked if I had managed the ordeal and indirectly asked if I had performed according to his predictions, that is, tunelessly badly. The words choked in my throat but I said no it had all gone well and everybody was complimentary and then said my farewells and never, ever spoke to or saw him again.

My next ordeal was the reception. At the last minute, that is, within the past three weeks my parents had hired a marquee, which was erected in what was once the front garden of Cecil Rhode's Johannesburg house. The garden was now simply overgrown with veld grass leading up to the front door. An outside caterer had also been arranged. On Sunday morning the preparations were well underway while my sisters rehearsed me for my Bar mitzvah speech. My Bar mitzvah teacher had provided me with a speech from a book of Bar mitzvah Boy thank you speeches. The speech did not entirely meet with the approval of my sisters who then using the original framework completely rewrote it and made certain that once I had learnt it off by heart I was not simply to recite it but had to say it with conviction.

The guests all seemed to arrive at once and I was showered with gifts- mainly envelopes containing money but there was also the odd pen, book, and tie pin etc. After the formal prayers and blessings it was my turn to speak. I remember standing at the top table in front of the microphone, the words came out as I was concentrating on when to pause and when to raise my voice, etc., and before I knew it, it was all over. Unlike the day before in the synagogue when I was greeted with sounds of disgust and disapproval from the old men, there was a loud and long and warm applause and I sat down; it was all finally over. Around me there were looks of approval. However the only time I heard any form of actual praise is when I overheard a conversation between one of my aunts and my parents. My aunt said the speech was wonderful but when she realised that I had overheard her and she said to me that I was not supposed to have heard that.

I never ever knew how much money I received. I think the money was used to meet the costs of the reception and, even then, I think my father was summonsed for non-payment of the caterers. On the following Monday I heard from my friend Solly how well his Bar mitzvah had gone and how many hundreds of pounds he had received plus all the gifts in the form of cricket bats, tennis rackets, etc.

My birthday is in January, the beginning of the South African school year so I should have had time to put it all behind me and concentrate on schoolwork. Such a luxury never ever came my way again. The break between my parents was becoming more permanent and my sisters were now married and out of the house and most of the time it was just mother and me.

The time now began, as stated earlier on, when I was expected to be home when my mother arrived back from her work having made certain that all the necessary chores ascribed to me were done such as the one I detested most, the filling of the paraffin bottles.

Looking back at those times, it was a period of emotional numbness. I did not seem to have any form of status or belonging. I would mix with whoever was around. Like all youth at the time I loved sport but was not good enough at that time to play in any school cricket or soccer team. I ran and swam in the school interhouse relay teams and I once came third in a hundred yard race although I felt that swimming was my best sport. I was not allowed to spend the afternoons in the swimming pool training sessions.

I never spoke to anyone about my family problems, maybe because no one ever asked me about them. But I'm certain, now, most knew - including some of my teachers - more than I did and thought that it was better not to mention. Cruel moments never were far away.

I was once summoned from another lesson to see Mr Campbell the geography master. As I walked into his room he dragged me to corner cupboard and shouted that he had told me to put the books away and all I had done was to leave them on a lower shelf. I explained that I could not reach the top shelves and that there were no vacant stools at the time. He then clipped me round the ear, loudly told me to stand on a heap of manure and grow. If that was not enough, the next day I had failed to return a book to one of my classmates. The next day the teacher stormed into my class, grabbed me and stood me in front of the class and walked to back of the room. He then called the class to attention and pointing at me, said 'Look at him. There stands a boy, who, if you give him a chance, will take the vest off your back.'

School was always very competitive and at the ends of each term, there were tests. You would be graded and positioned in the class according to your marks. That year I dropped down steadily from the middle order to near the bottom of the class. Apart from the humiliation from classmates, I would have to face my mother's rebuke when she read my end of term report. At the end of each school year there are exams and, depending on your performance, you are passed or failed. That year, my second at high school, I just managed to gain promotion to the third year. The writing was on the wall that I was having difficulties with my schooling but no one either at school or within my family reacted.

It was the norm at the time that, once you had been 'Bar mitzvahed', you stopped attending afternoon Hebrew classes except for those who were scholarly or for religious reasons carried on studying classical Hebrew. My mother wanted me to carry on which I did for about a year before secretly giving it up to enjoy free afternoons.

Chapter 11

When the house was built at the end of the last century it was one of the first double storeyed houses in the fast growing gold town of Johannesburg. I suppose the original plan was that the upper floor was to be simply a series of bedrooms not a flat for a family of three.

Shortly after my father had returned from 'Up North' sometime in late 1942 or early 1943 and he was still in the army, he happened to be at home that night. I remember being woken up by my sisters who were standing in their pyjamas by the door, that linked our room to my parents room, shouting that there was a fire. I leapt out of bed and in an instant was alongside them. I glanced through the door that linked our room to the living room, and saw flames reaching up to the ceiling. In my half sleep and bewilderment, I noticed that outside it was still dark. I found out later on that I had been woken up at four in the morning.

My father scurried about and my mother shouted instructions. My sister told my father she had learnt at Guides to cover your face with a cloth and to try and crawl under the smoke to the fire. He attempted to do just that. However the German couple, who lived in a small flat alongside ours, were awake by now, whisked my sisters and me into their flat. As we crossed over the landing I saw a fireman coming up the stairs dragging a fire-hose. I can only assume that they must have decided to let me sleep on as long as possible while the rest of the family battled with the fire. I apparently was only woken up when the fire was beginning to get out of control.

The old landlord Mr Gervis had first noticed the fire. On that night either he could not sleep or it was some minor religious festival that necessitated him getting early. For some reason or other he was walking outside in the dark, around the derelict tennis court when on looking up he saw the flames in our living room. Although he was already in his seventies he managed get back into the house to wake my parents up.

The fire had burnt through to the ceiling of the room below us and, by the time it was daylight, we were allowed into the living room and saw a gaping hole in the floor. Our fridge and the rest of our furniture was charred and blackened and with a smell of smouldering wood. Apparently the cause of the fire was due to an electric kettle that had been left on and had boiled dry. It took several weeks before the repairs were completed and we continued to live as normal while the repairs were in operation. It was a while before the electricity was restored and during that period our kitchenette was out of use. All of our cooking was done on a Primus stove or on an open coal fire in the fireplace, which had survived intact.

After the fire, our living/dining room hardly changed until I left home. On top of the piano were numerous ornaments that my Bobe (grand mother), my father's mother, gave to us from time to time. She used go to the salerooms and buy job lots and any ornaments in them were distributed around the families of my father's two sisters and his brother. I felt that we always had first choice because our Bobe lived in a set of rooms in a building built in the grounds of the property we now occupied. Although our Bobe lived close to us during the latter part of the war years we did not see a great deal of her as she and mother seldom could spend time together without a quarrel conducted in Yiddish.

Chapter 12

The state of Israel was still in its infancy. A great majority of Jewish youth belonged to various Zionist youth groups who hoped that one day they would go on Aliyah (emigration to Israel). I joined the Habonim (the builders) which was the Jewish equivalent of the Scouts. All the Baden-Powell type of concepts and objectives were adopted with a Zionist Jewish theme. We used to meet on Friday nights, which puzzled my mother, no end as to how a Jewish group could arrange to meet on the eve of the Jewish Sabbath. But to make things even worse my mother did not want me to go out at night and 10 p.m. was my curfew time.

The evening began with the usual line up and inspection with all commands and instructions given out in Modern Hebrew. Then there would be serious seminars, usually of a left wing Zionist type. This would be followed by games. All my school contemporaries who had joined the Habonim were about a year older than me and hence were in the older groups known as the Shomers. After a few weeks, the leaders allowed me to join in with the older group. This group was mixed and there was far less scouting and much more politicking and 'cultural activation.' The seminars now included South African politics and we became, through a series of discussions guided by our leaders, aware of the injustices all around us.

Although we were sympathetic to the Blacks it was hard to put our thoughts into practice once we left the group. There would also be talks on the arts. It was during those evenings that I learnt to listen to and appreciate classical music. I also learnt about the different art movements and in particular the impressionists. The evening would always end with traditional Jewish and Israeli dancing and singing which included a Negro spiritual. The relevance was always with us, mainly for two reasons. First, I suppose, in the context of the political atmosphere that surrounded us we could feel what they meant and, second as Jews we knew first hand what it felt like to be persecuted.

Having listened to and participated in those seminars and debates, I began to see that I was living in a totally unjust and confused society, which often brought me into conflict with my family. This was the beginning of the South African era when anyone who spoke up for the non-white population was considered to be a communist. Knowing and aware that I was then living and growing up in an unjust society became a permanent part of my thinking. We talked of being 'cultured', which meant that we were appreciative of European classical music, modern art, literature and theatre. The word European had for us a double meaning. It meant white as well as originating from Europe. Although the Zionist youth movements made us aware of the injustice meted out to the Black population it did not introduce us to the rich African culture that was all about us. We had seminars about the North American black population; hence we knew more about slavery, Jazz, the Blues and Negro spirituals than the majority of the inhabitants of South Africa. Europe and the USA is what we saw on the cinema screens, heard about on the radio and read about in the newspapers. Anyone who was rich enough to make a trip 'overseas' was someone to be admired. Any favourable mention of South Africa by the people overseas filled us pride. The richness of the flora and fauna of our surrounding country was, like most of the African arts, never given a second thought. The real history of South Africa passed us by as we debated the origin of the Zionist Movement, the pogroms, the holocaust and the origin of the trade union movement.

After our debates, as mentioned earlier, the evenings ended with singing and folk dancing. Somehow it always ended at ten o'clock mainly because the black caretaker made it clear to us that our time was up and he wanted to lock up. It was our responsibility to walk the girls home. The debates would continue all the way home. I seldom managed to get home before my curfew time but my mother seemed to be easing up on me.

Often if we passed a cafe that was still open, we stopped for a coke and cream bun. But only if it was safe, that is, there were no Afrikaner youths ready to indulge in some Jew baiting. On many occasions on the way home we came across fights between black or white gangs fighting among themselves or whites under the influence of cheap South African brandy indulging in fisticuffs. We always watched from a safe distance or skirted round so as to avoid the fracas all together.

One evening we were waiting at a tram stop to catch a tram to a meeting in Kensington. While waiting we would always try and thumb a lift. Looking back we all took a terrible chance trying to get a lift at night. This particular Friday evening, we were in an area at the bottom end of Seimert Road which was not the most savoury of areas to be in even in daylight. The tram stop was located just across a major intersection. Wherever you went day or night there were always groups of African men and women walking somewhere and talking loudly and occasionally there would be a group led by an individual with a guitar loudly singing a repetitive phrase which all were either walking or running in tune to. On one particular evening a mixed group of males and females were as usual talking loudly but seemed to be in a hurry.

At the crossroads there were traffic lights, or robots as they are called in South Africa, and the group approached. The lights changed to red and two young women in the front seemed unable to stop and ran across the road in the front of the speeding on-coming traffic. Both ran screaming with fright. The one in front, about two yards ahead of her companion, made it to the other side of the road but the second one was hit by an oncoming car travelling at forty miles per hour. We watched with horror as she was struck by the front of the car. She hit the bonnet and then fell in toward the front grill. The speed of the car, which made no attempt to brake, somehow threw her upwards and she landed on the windscreen and was then catapulted upward and crash landed onto the road head first. We saw it all drawn by the sound of the initial screams. Then the first bang, the second bang and finally the sound of the dull thud as her head hit the road. Total silence followed. It seemed to last forever. The car pulled up about fifty yards down the road. In the darkness we then saw the street light reflected in the ever-increasing pool of blood. Her companions stood in total silence and were too frightened to approach the victim. We just looked on from twenty yards away and then a few minutes later a tram arrived.

The tram stopped for us and once on board we tried not to look back and sat in silence. Each time I closed my eyes I could see the poor woman, running, hitting the car, flying through the air and finally the thud. A scene that I still can see as if it was an action replay. I never discovered what my friends were thinking about at the time nor did I ever find out what became of the accident victim.

I also could not help comparing the scene to an accident that I had seen about two months earlier. It was early afternoon in the Beit Street, the high street of Doornfontein. A white woman in her twenties had stepped out in front of a car, was knocked down and lay on the road unconscious. She landed with her dress and petticoat over her head and was lying facing upwards with all her underclothes exposed. Somehow, within minutes, a white policeman appeared and immediately pulled her dress down to restore her dignity. Cushions and blankets emerged from shops. The woman was made as comfortable as possible. The car had stopped and only the presence of the police prevented the driver from being attacked by a gathering crowd who were all white.

Chapter 13

By my third year at high school, my sisters were married and my father, to all intents and purposes, had left home. He only to returned for brief moments to collect his belongings. My mother made it as difficult as possible for him to enter the house and remove what rightfully was his. The white Nationalist Government was becoming more established as the majority ruling party in an all white parliament. The concept of Apartheid was slowly becoming the norm and being introduced by law, the only post-Second World war government to make racial discrimination legal. The South African army under the leadership of Jan Smuts had made a considerable contribution in terms of manpower and resources toward fighting the Nazi regime. In 1948, the whites narrowly voted Smuts out of power and Smuts himself actually lost his parliamentary seat and only returned as leader of the opposition when one of his party gave up his seat. In subsequent general elections, the White population voted for the Nationalist government in an ever-increasing majority. Thus began the rule of the Nationalist Party that lasted until Nelson Mandela took over as president.

The only vocal opposition came from the trade union movement largely dominated by the South African Communist party. Over the next few decades, both movements were silenced and eventually banned in one form or another. One of the leaders of the Garment Workers was the late Solly Sachs. The government was determined to silence them and all sorts of indecent laws were gradually introduced which, to all and intents and purposes banned or imprisoned anyone, Black or White who stood up for Black rights on the grounds that they were communists.

A protest meeting in which Solly Sachs was to be the main speaker was organised to take place on the Town Hall Square in front of the City Hall. The government made it clear that if Solly Sachs spoke he would be arrested and the meeting broken up. The press and radio media at the time gave the meeting a great deal of publicity. I was standing about a hundred yards from the Town Hall steps from where the speeches were being delivered. The people standing closest to the steps were mainly Black men and women. Most of the Whites were scattered throughout the square. After one or two introductory speeches Solly Sachs was introduced, and the applause and cheers rang round the square. With an air of defiance he began his speech which was in praise of the garment workers and began to demand better wages, etc. An attempt was made by the police to arrest him and the crowd became angry and jeered. Then, as if from the bowels of the earth, a large posse of white policemen emerged from within the Town Hall with batons drawn and charged into the crowd. About half of the police were wearing the blue uniforms and the other half were wearing dark green with either flat caps or helmets. The charging mass of blue and green with batons in the air set those at the front into a panic and they turned and ran to get away from the square most running in my direction. Where I was standing the crowd was not that dense and hence there was enough space for those who were running to scatter. The police struck out at whoever was within their reach and stepped over anyone they knocked to the ground. The only sound was that of the police boots, the shoes of those trying run away, the screams of the women running and the yells of the young policemen who swore out loud in Afrikaans at those they managed to strike. In the rush to get away some fell over and those behind tried to avoid them but invariably they were accidentally kicked by those fleeing and often deliberately by the police. As the crowd thinned I saw an African lying on the ground close to the end of the square bleeding and badly hurt and an elderly White man went to try and attend to him. Most of the people where I was standing were Whites, many unsympathetic to the cause, and some even cheered each time they heard or saw a baton land on target. Also, somehow the police managed to avoid us or made no effort to try and disperse us - their targets were the non-whites.

The government of the day was determined to preserve white rule for as long as possible. There were to be no concessions. If anything, they were going to put the native in his place. The Blacks were a problem, but a very useful source of cheap labour. The reality that the Blacks were in the majority was a concept to be put at the back of your mind. Their requirements were different and they needed far less of everything to survive.

Habonim was only one of several Jewish youth movements ranging from religious to the 'right wing.' The South African Zionist Federation was an organization housed in its own multi-storeyed building whose purpose was to promote Zionism but in reality acted like a 'Jewish Parliament.' The Jewish population at that time behaved almost schizophrenically participating in the White Politics of the day but at the same time very much influenced by the activities of the 'Fed'. All the youth movements held their own summer camps. These were all held at seaside sites during the summer month of December. The majority of the Jewish population lived in and around Johannesburg and Cape Town, however, almost every town had a

Jewish Community and a synagogue although some consisted of only a few families. Likewise, the Jewish youth movements were established in almost every community.

Summer holiday camps were organised on a national level. This provided an opportunity for those who lived inland, who were in the majority, an opportunity to visit the sea and those from the smaller communities to meet up with the city types. Most of the campsites were located in the Cape Province near cities such as East London, Port Elizabeth and Muizenberg on the outskirts of Cape Town, all conveniently reached by rail.

Habonim held their annual jamboree at a site close to East London which was a twenty four-hour rail away from Johannesburg. It required a special reserved train to transport the several hundred youths and their leaders from Johannesburg to East London. The morning of departure converted a platform on Johburg Park Station into a Jewish Jamboree. As it was an overnight journey, all the train coaches had compartments with sleeping bunks for six. The organisers had to allot each person to a compartment and lists were posted on the outside of each compartment. Although we were told in advance which coach we were assigned to it seemed as if no one knew as parents and offspring surged up and down the platform in a state of almost desperation. Once the carriage and compartment had been found, suitcases, rucksacks, blanket roles, etc., were bundled in through the windows and heads were soon leaning out for endless farewell hugs.

This was still the days of steam trains and once the signal to depart was given, the mighty engine released huge columns of smoke and the release, with a great hiss, of steam set the arms of everybody on the platform into a waving motion. Heads were rapidly drawn into the carriage with a last wave to parents and off we set on the long journey to the coast. My mother, at that time, was managing a dry cleaning shop and was not able to see me off.

My luggage was brought to the station in the box of a three-wheel shop delivery bicycle. As almost everybody else had arrived by car, the arrival of my luggage caused a few tut-tuts as well as pitiful looks. Once the journey began my being seen off by a Black shop boy was soon forgotten and in, a state of excitement, I settled down in our compartment. The camp leaders soon did their rounds peering into each compartment along each carriage double-checking that all who should be there were there.

We all had to wear our uniforms but once the train pulled out, we were allowed to change. These camps were mixed and it did not take long for the more forward lads and lassies to seek out each other while the rest looked on in envy. It took at least twenty-four hours to reach our destination and the rest of the train journey provided an opportunity for youthful fun as well as bonding.

An advance guard had left a few days before our departure and their tasks were to erect the tents, install the kitchens, the showers the toilets, etc., hence when we arrived at the camp site all we had to do was find our tents. For those who had never been to camp before it was a time for learning to be independent of parents. Even more impacting was the absence of a Black servant to care for one's needs. Although the Habonim movement was a scout movement, it was based on socialist principles and preparation for Aliyah (immigration to Israel). To be true to those principles and in preparation for a life in Israel the camp did not employ any servants. The campers from the leaders to youngest camper had to all fend for themselves. This meant that we had to prepare and make our beds, clean our tents and had to do various duties such as the cooking, cleaning the kitchen and toilet areas and guard duties. We were also responsible for washing our own clothes.

There were six of us per bell tent and group. Four tents were each day nominated for duties. We were unlucky enough to be chosen for kitchen duties on the day after our arrival. It was our duty to prepare the breakfast, midday meal and evening meal for one day. One of the leaders who was supposed to know what to do was to supervise us and we were to report to him.

Outside of our tent

In order to make the breakfast we had to be up at six am. The cooking was done in large pots heated over open fires. Our first task was to collect the firewood and the coal and light a fire, something we had watched the servants doing daily. We never thought that going to camp for a holiday would involve us in getting our hands covered in coal dust and having to chop wood. We had to fill the huge cooking drums with water from a water tank and keep the water boiling. The breakfast menu was porridge made from mealie meal with bread and jam followed by a fried egg, sausage and baked beans.

Our leader/supervisor was supposed to instruct us as how prepare the food but he had like us been brought up with servants and had probably only ever prepared food when he had been to his first camp. The cooking fire was built up from bricks with iron bars to place the cooking pots over the fire. Several such cooking fires had to be built.

We had to slice the bread and place it on the tables together with the jam. Somehow we had managed to add the right amount of raw oats to the water boiling in one of the large cooking pots. We stirred it with a large stick all the time getting covered in steam and smoke. The tins of beans were heated while the sausages fried. Once the porridge was ready we rang the gong and the silent camp became alive with campers queuing up for their porridge. Once they started to eat we began to fry the eggs. The product of our efforts was only appetizing and edible to the very hungry.

After breakfast we had to clean up and then begin to prepare the midday meal. All the cooking utensils were covered in black soot and smoke and most of the inside was burnt. We were then made to scrub and clean the cooking parts and whatever else we had used. Not one of us had ever washed up in our own homes. After a short break we started to prepare the midday meal. Our first task was to peel the potatoes and prepare the vegetables; needless to say, there was great deal of wastage until we mastered our tasks. The menu for one day was a meat stew. We were given large chunks of stewing beef and proceeded to cut it into small squares. Once all the meat was cut up it was dropped into boiling water and left to stew. From time to time we were told by the leader to add various ingredients such as salt, thickening flour, etc. We also prepared a giant cauldron of rice for pudding. The camp cooking was, to say the least, not the best but food poisoning was not an issue simply because the food was always overcooked. The only cold food that was eaten was cold smoked beef served on Saturday as no fires were to be lit on the Sabbath.

The toilet for the males consisted of a trough for urine. No one seemed to know where the urine (plus a steady trickle of water from an overhead tank) disappeared to. The two large multiple toilet seats were positioned over two large trenches with no partitions (the female toilets did have hessian partitions without doors). For the males, sitting on the toilet was a communal and social event; noises and odours were always a source of jokes. The only privacy was the surrounding wall made up of galvanized zinc; there was no roof and if you overdid your stay certain parts of the body not normally exposed got sunburnt.

The normal camp day began with breakfast followed by an inspection, parade in uniform and various scouting activities. In addition, there was sometimes a seminar on Judaism, Zionism, socialism and sometimes South African politics. We also learned Modern Hebrew songs and dances. Once the morning activities were over it was time for our midday meal. Nearly every afternoon was spent on the beach along a stretch of white sand interrupted by rocky outcrops.

The waves from the vast Indian Ocean with its warm Benguela current scoured the beach. Swimming in such seas was both exciting and dangerous. We were always confined to a roped off area. The leaders held the ropes in place and, like kitchen duties, we all had to take a turn. The strong waves also created an under-current and we had to be vigilant to make certain that no one was suddenly dragged under and swept out to sea beneath the protecting rope.

Evenings were always spent round the beach campfire. There were no lights of any sort in the vicinity. Lying on the beach looking up at cloudless skies and marvelling at the stars of the Milky Way, trying identify heavenly formations made a deep impression on all of us. We also sang songs and listened to readings while sitting on the sand staring at the fire.

The evening campfires also served another purpose and that was to get close to members of the opposite sex. A date was to invite someone of the opposite sex to the campfire. The evening would begin by you either collecting her from her tent or meeting at an appointed place on the beach. Those who were not paired off usually sat close to the front of the fire and the 'dates' sat toward the rear. The bold and the brave usually had a date from the first night onwards whereas the more timid took at least a week before they acquired both the courage and the know-how to ask a girl for a date. I belonged to the latter category and tent mates teased me. They advised me to simply ask someone I fancied.

Irene, a girl with blond curly hair and blue eyes, had attracted the attention of just about every male (including me) on the campsite. It just so happened that her tent had to carry out kitchen duty at the same time as my tent, hence I had an easy introduction to her. I had long thought about how and what I was going to say when I eventually met someone I wanted to ask to the campfire. Here I was working and talking with the belle of the camp and without thinking about it or any hesitation I asked her if I could take her to the campfire. To my amazement and surprise she said yes before I had actually finished asking her. From that moment on I was on cloud nine, desperately trying to behave in a matter of fact way not wanting to reveal that it was to be my first date ever.

That evening as we all got ready to go down to the beach the boys from my tent waited for me to join them. It was then that I told them about my date. At first they did not believe me but after secretly watching as I went over to collect Irene to escort her they realized that I had really scored.

I managed to find my way back to my tent after spending most of the evening with my arm around her shoulder and that first ever kiss. All I remember is that my tent mates had actually unrolled my sleeping bag for me. Whether it was out of consideration or to avoid me disturbing them I never found out. The next day drifted by in a dream and that night was more of the same. At that time the song 'Good night Irene' was just released and to this day that song reminds me of her. However, on the third day after the date I crashed back to earth as she calmly walked in front of me to campfire holding another admirer's hand. I dated a few other girls before the end of camp but none had the magic of Irene.

To return to my first week of camp while I was on kitchen duty, I injured a finger that, in spite of the regular attention of the camp doctor, did not heal and was slowly becoming more painful. One night after the beach singsong, my hand was swelling and the pain more intense. I went to the hospital tent and without further ado, the doctor and his girlfriend ordered me into his car and without saying anything to me drove to the hospital in East London. We arrived there at about eleven at night and all I remember was being given an injection and then taken to a ward and given a set of hospital pyjamas. Apart from being woken up to have my finger dressed, injected and given medication I must have slept for the first twenty-four hours. It was only on the morning of the third day I did become really aware of where I was. Then came the realization that I was suffering from a combination of a very bad infection, exhaustion and possibly, although I was not aware of it at the time, the emotional trauma of my home life. Once I began to interact with my hospital surroundings the fact that no one from the camp had been to visit me did not exactly make me feel that I was missed. I was aware that it was our group's turn to visit East London for a day out. I had hoped that, at least, my tent mates would make the effort to visit me but waited in vain.

During one visiting hour I was staring up at the ceiling trying not to think it mattered whether or not I was visited when an attractive dark-haired girl with large brown eyes suddenly interrupted my view of the ceiling. She introduced herself and sat talking to me for the next hour. She was the daughter of a patient two beds away from me and they noticed how I had been neglected. She sat at my bedside at every visiting time from then on until I was discharged.

After four days of treatment which included regular injections, finger dressing and bandaging, the duty doctor declared that I was fit enough to return to the camp. I was delivered to the hospital at night with no money nor did I know exactly where I was in relation to the camp. The ward sister said that she would phone the camp and ask them to collect me. As there was only one camp type telephone on the site I wondered if the message would ever get to the person. She assured me that she had left the message to collect me at 10 a.m. and that I was to get dressed and be ready for them. It was to be a very long day as they only collected me at about 10p.m. By the time we arrived back at the camp, the campfire session was over and everybody was returning to their tents. My tent mates greeted me as if I had been away for an awayday and they seemed to vaguely recollect that they had been told that I was hospitalised. The following morning I met some of the girls who belonged to the same Johannesburg group as I did and they said they had noticed me missing and had enquired about me. They told me that they knew I was in hospital but were not given in any details. It was as if the authorities did not want it known that one of the campers had contracted an infection that they could not treat. There was still another week to go before the camp ended but it all seemed to fade out.

The two following years I was alone with my mother and there was no possibility that she could afford to pay for me to attend the summer camp. The solution was that I would miss the first week, but in order to get there, I would have to hitchhike the eight hundred miles to East London. I found a willing partner who had friends who would give us a lift to Pietermaritzburg the capital of Natal and from there would make our way down through southern Natal and the Eastern Cape. We were duly delivered to Pietermaritzburg in the early hours of the morning. From there via a series of short lifts we made our way into Pondoland, which was then a Native territory but part of South Africa. We reached Kokstad, the area capital that night and found our way to the police station and without much ceremony they allowed us to sleep in one of the cells. We were given a hard straw mattress and blankets and they conveniently left the self-locking door open. It was a cold, noisy night and neither us of had much sleep. The next morning, after a series of short lifts we found ourselves stuck by a high pass alongside a small hotel. We had a commanding view of the road and could see an approaching car for about twenty minutes before it reached us. We would get up and adopt a pose, which invariably ended in failure as most cars were loaded with holidaymakers and had no room for us. About midday a husband, wife and daughter stopped at the hotel for lunch. They must have been watching us as without us approaching them, they asked us where we were going then offered us a lift. Our luggage was tied between the front wheel mudguard and the bonnet and what did not fit we sat with on our knees. Off we set on journey that was to last another eight hours. They dropped us at ten p.m. about a mile from the campsite. After a few days in the camp my colleague had to return to work but I remained behind as I was offered a place on the train back to Johannesburg. I felt bad as my feelings were that I had let him down. We never saw each other again. The blond Irene was not at the camp

The camp holiday finally ended when we arrived back at Johannesburg Park Station. Once off the train I went to look for my Mother's 'shop boy' who was to take my luggage home for me. I was tapped on my shoulder and on turning around I looked directly at Irene, even more beautiful than when I first met her. Before I could say anything she asked me if still remembered her. After that brief meeting, I have never seen her again.

Chapter 13

During the latter part of the Second World War, I would only see my father on weekends. On Sundays, if we did not go fishing or visiting relatives, we would look to be going out somewhere such as the Zoo or the Zoo-lake or even to a Palm Court type tea-room in the city centre. Train journeys to a lake such as Florida or Germiston or Benoni were another form of Sunday entertainment. One Sunday when I was ten we caught the train to Pretoria - an hour plus journey. This was exciting as I had never been there before and we all knew a great deal about the place as it was the administrative Capital of South Africa.

The exit from Pretoria station was very different from that of Johannesburg where once out of the station you walked into Eloff Street, the main shopping street. From the main exit out of Pretoria station you walked down a series of imposing steps into Station Square. In the centre of the square was a statue of the Boer leader Paul Kruger. (A few years later the statue was moved down the road to Church Square.) Unlike Johburg, the roads of Pretoria were broad and lined with Jacaranda trees. In the distance, Magaliesberg Mountains were visible and the city had a sense of having been planned and had space and dignity - something desperately lacking in Johannesburg. Paul Kruger stared out over the country that he once ruled but had been taken from him. At the base of the statue were four sitting Boer soldiers each with soft hat, a jacket, and a bullet belt worn diagonally across their shoulders. They were holding their guns skyward and each had a sad look of desperation. At least that is how I interpreted the scene.

The Boer War and its aftermath was something we were taught about as soon as we were considered old enough to be introduced to History as a subject. My mother who had grown up in the Western Transvaal, a dominantly Afrikaner area, knew many people whose parents had fought in the Boer War. Likewise men who fought on both sides had taught my father who was predominantly a city boy. The Boer War was generally considered a sad event. An army of untrained soldiers had pushed the British Army to its limits until the mightier forces of the Empire prevailed and the Boer army was eventually overwhelmed.

Unlike Johannesburg, Pretoria has long avenues not frequently intercepted by cross streets. We walked down from the station-square past the Transvaal Museum to Church Square. Surrounding the square is the old Raadsaal and the old Synagogue, which many years later was converted to a courtroom where the notorious treason trials were held. We caught a trolley bus that took us through the city toward the Union Buildings, the seat of government. A very impressive building by any standards it sat on a hill looking down over acres of parkland. The bus dropped us at the bottom of the gardens and we started the long stroll toward the buildings.

I had a fascination for ornamental ponds and they were even more exciting if there were large fish swimming around. We seemed to be passing no end of ponds, shelters and monuments most of them commemorating some aspect or other of the Boer War. To me it felt as though any moment we were going to come across a Boer soldier just waiting to continue the fight. My sisters must have read my thoughts as they laughingly reassured me that the Boer War had ended some forty years ago.

In those days you could walk into the buildings and even have a drink in one of the cafeterias (something that I was able to do again as late as 1973) and wander around the many ponds and fountains. From the base of the building there is a commanding view of the city, as well as a view across the valley in the direction of Johannesburg. Situated on a hilltop on the Southern outskirts of the city is the large Voortrekker Monument. A building was started in 1939 and completed at the end of the Forties and unveiled in the early Fifties. The unveiling involved the re-enactment of the Great Trek when disillusioned Boers set out from the Cape in 1836 toward the hinterland in search of the Promised Land. Many of the trekkers settled in Orange Free State and the Traansvaal, which eventually became the two Boer Republics. Somehow the way we were taught South African history, whether you were English or Afrikaans speaking, managed to engender a silent sympathy for the Boer fighters. We knew all about the White concentration camps but were never told that there were also Black concentration camps and that Black soldiers had fought on both sides. We were told unsympathetically that Blacks fighting for the British who were captured by the Boers were brutally dealt with.

In the centre of Johannesburg behind the city hall is the central library and above the library there is a museum most of which is devoted to the discovery of gold and the founding of the cities along the Witwatersrand. The museum also housed many photographs and documents relating to the Boer War. I remember in my early teens, while wandering around the museum for the nth time, we discovered a reference to the fact that during the early part of the war a Jewish Lads brigade was formed to fight on the side of the Boers. There was a photograph of the group with their own version of the Republic flag which they later presented to Paul Kruger. Apparently he was reported as having been rather indifferent to the Brigade probably because one of the causes of the Boer War was the discrimination against the Uitlanders (the foreigners). The Jews were recent immigrants from Eastern Europe and very prominent in the gold and diamonds dealings. However, later on I found that many of the 'Lads' then migrated to Cape Town and became one of the many 'joiners' the name given to those who abandoned the Boer cause and enrolled as volunteers to fight on the British side.

I remember sitting with my family, glued to the radio, and listening to the 1948 election results. As the night wore on it became very obvious that the ruling United Party led by General Jan Smuts was going to be defeated by the Nationalist Party led by Dr. Malan. The real shock came with the announcement that Jan Smuts had lost his seat. The next day at school there was an atmosphere of doom and gloom and a stunned silence prevailed except for among the very few Nationalist supporters. We noticed that one of them had tied a Nationalist flag to the front frame of his bicycle and that one of our Science teachers Mr Lindeque, who came to work riding on a motor bike with a side car was supporting a Nationalist flag. Later he made it clear to us that his people had now won and were taking over. We felt from the way he spoke to us that the Boer Commandos had returned and would soon be parading alongside their ox-wagons through the streets. Life was now about to return to where the pioneers, the Voortrekkers left off. He lectured to us to remember the fact that we were all South Africans, and that anyone who told us we were not we should beat up. We never ever questioned whether or not he included the majority Black population, and we knew that the new prevailing philosophy was to be the *"Die Kaffir in sy plek en die Coolie uit die land"* (The Kaffir in his place and the Asians out of the land).

I discussed the new political situation with our flat boy Piet and tried to discover whether or not he had any sympathy for Jan Smuts, and was surprised to hear his indifference. The election took place before I had joined the Habonim movement. At school none of us in our debates ever brought up the subject about the disenfranchised majority. Although in the past and in the future years many of the outspoken Whites were Jewish, the average Jew just accepted the concept of Apartheid without much protest. However the establishment of the State of Israel was very reassuring and the Zionist movement in South Africa took on a new meaning. A Jewish community was now developing which, on the surface, was disapproving of the governments' policies but in fact enjoyed the privileges that came with them and began to live with dual loyalties.

In 1949, the first post-war New Zealand (the All Blacks) rugby team toured South Africa. Tours in those days lasted almost as long as the season. The team arrived by sea from New Zealand and travelled around the country by road and by train. Two matches per week were played against provincial teams and university teams. Five test matches were played. The main rugby stadium in Johannesburg was Ellis Park. That also was the home of cricket after the demolition of the original Wanderers Ground in the centre of the city. Three big matches were to be in Johannesburg, two against Transvaal and one test match.

Ellis Park had two side stands but most of the ground was taken up with a grass terrace. For most matches including the Curry Cup inter-provincial matches if you were not on a stand you sat on the grass verge. The authorities, anticipating a large crowd, decided to turn the terraces into standing only by installing crash barriers. To obtain tickets for the matches you either had to purchase them through a club or agent or queue up at the ground on an appointed day. We lived only ten minutes from the stadium and the sale day occurred during one of the school vacations. I went to the ground at five in the morning and spent half the day queuing. Apart from buying tickets for myself, I bought tickets for relatives. One of my cousins kept two for himself and auctioned two, the proceeds donated to a charity. My uncle and cousin bought the test match tickets off me and they sat next to me on a stand specially erected for the matches.

The first match that I saw was the All Blacks against a Transvaal XV a team made up mainly of up and coming players who nearly beat the All Blacks. The main feature of the match was the outstanding performances of both fullbacks - the New Zealander Bob Scott, who graced their team for many years after and the young Transvaal fullback who eventually became a Springbok. The next match, the Transvaal fielded a full strength team and the All Blacks as a gesture in response to the first match put out a midweek team and they still managed to beat the home team. The eagerly awaited first test match was played at Newlands in Cape Town. Those who were not at the match were glued to their radios listening to the match commentary. The All Blacks were playing the better rugby and scored two tries but the Springboks won the match thanks to the kicking ability of a front row forward. His name was Okey Geffin, a Jewish boy from Johannesburg whose inclusion in the Springbok team was not exactly popular with die hard Afrikaners. After his outstanding performance with the boot, the objections were toned down and the press hailed him as a hero. In ordinary conversation he was still referred to as the Jew Boy. The second test was played at Ellis Park and this time the Springboks won by scoring tries, a drop goal as well as penalties from the boot of Geffin. A crowd of 72,000 watched the match, the largest ever recorded in South Africa. I can remember reading in a Sunday paper that one out of every 72 South Africans were at the stadium. The article did not say that they were only referring to White South Africans. There was a small stand reserved for non-Whites (Africans, Asians and Coloureds) and they all cheered for the All Blacks.

Tickets for the test match were a valuable commodity and farmers from the platteland were offering up to one hundred pounds for a ticket, an enormous amount of money in those days. My determination to see the match was such that I did not even consider selling my ticket at any price. Another memorable moment was when the person who sat next to me stood up to shout for the Springboks and lost his false teeth.

Although at the time rugby and cricket were dominant sports among the Whites soccer was also very popular in the urban areas. Those days the main soccer teams were amateur and were Whites only, the Blacks had their own teams and leagues. White football was played at the Wanderers Ground, which was then situated at the back of Park Station. In the late Forties the railway took over the grounds which were then demolished to make way for an enlarged station. Football then moved to Balfour Park until the Rand Stadium was built.

I was about ten when the elder brother of one of my local street mates took me to watch a match at the Wanderers. Every time the ball went out of play a nearby spectator shouted 'good old white line'. It was my first time at a proper soccer match and I did not understand the subtleties of the game and not thinking asked 'who does white line play for'. After much chuckling I was never told the answer but was teased about my ignorance for many years. As juniors we were able to buy a season ticket for a very modest price and until the stadium was demolished watched soccer nearly every Saturday afternoon.

Club rugby was also played every Saturday at Ellis Park stadium but hardly anyone ever watched club rugby (yet inter-provincial games used to attract crowds of 40,000 plus). The only Saturdays that I missed watching soccer was when I went to Ellis Park.

At the start and end of the season touring teams from what was then called Lorenço Marques (now Maputo) the capital of Mozambique (which we also called Portuguese East Africa) and from Luanda in Angola (Portuguese West Africa) used to play against a Southern Transvaal team. Most of the market gardens and green grocer shops used to be owned and run by Portuguese. Most of them lived in small houses on their small-holdings, or so it seemed to us. They did not live in the type of homes we considered to be normally associated with whites. In addition most of them were typically Mediterranean in appearance and my contemporaries and I never knew whether the Portuguese were considered to be White or not. Every time I asked my parents that question I was never given a straight answer. It did not occur to us the fact that they were allowed to play against White teams in a Whites only stadium meant that they must be classed as White.

A few years later after the completion of the Rand Stadium I went to watch a team from Luanda in Mozambique playing against a Southern Transvaal team. I had seen the line up of the visiting players in the local press. One of the player's surnames was Ben. (I forget the rest of his name) which to me was a Hebrew name and it pleased me to think that one of the visiting team of Portuguese Whites was possibly Jewish. Once the visitors took to the field I was even more surprised to find out that the player concerned was Black. Now there was much reason for head scratching. Firstly how had the authorities allowed the visitors to choose a Non-White player? Was that an oversight or had the visiting team insisted on him playing? Or was one of the football authorities trying to convey a message. The next anguish: Was he a Black Jew or did he just happen to have a Jewish name? Lastly, if he was a regular member was there no racial discrimination in Mozambique? Once the game was underway as usual the excitement of the events on the pitch took over and my questions were put to the back of my mind. It was a close game. I do not remember who won but one aspect that I do recall is that Ben turned out to be one of their star players. It did not occur to me then that for a Black to be picked to play in an all white team he had to be very good.

Once the match was over I got a bus to the centre of the City. I sat upstairs and no sooner had the journey begun when the usual post-match analysis began. I joined in and mentioned the contribution that Ben had made and was it not a pity that we could not select Black players. It was as if I had just lit a fire. All the upstairs passengers at first went silent then, one at a time tried to turn discreetly to see who was this talking about the unmentionable. Who was this potential Kaffirboetie (kaffir brother). We don't need people like him. The first person who actually spoke to me tried to reason with me to make me realise that I was simply an idealist who did not live in the real world. I did not give ground but simply restated my case that there were potentially plenty of footballers that we ignored and, if included in the selection process, may help to produce winning teams. I could here loud whispers 'Communist' and slowly the tone became more aggressive 'people like you who cause trouble' and so on. One man walking down the aisle to get off the bus spat on the floor as he passed by my seat. I felt that I had entered a human cauldron and that I was about to be boiled alive or lynched. Luckily those closest to me, although angry, did not threaten me physically. I could see one or two sitting out of reach of me silently winding themselves up to throw a punch. As the verbal abuse increased, I continued to express my views but mindful of the fact that I might be attacked at any moment. Perhaps because I was alone they must have decided that beating me up would be too simple and that frightening me would be more effective. One or two actually stood up and pointed fingers and fists in my direction. The bus reached the city centre and we all stood up to get off. I somehow managed not show any fear and kept my head and once off the bus walked away, whereas they all rushed off to catch their connections.

Chapter 14

The end of my third year at high school my world crashed down around me. My father had now left for good, both of my sisters were married and I was living alone with my mother. At that time, she was working in a dry cleaning shop in Biet Street Doornfontein and I was expected, as mentioned previously, to be at home when she returned having done all the 'shopping'. I was terrified on her arrival home, not knowing what mood she would be in and what I had forgotten to do. More often than not I would be out playing in the street when she arrived home. Although I was supposed to first do my school homework I could never settle down as I had to prepare my own meal when I came in and then had to wash up. Most of my friends were allowed to do their homework in the evenings. Hence if they were not at organised school sport that took place after school they would be playing either cricket or football in Berrys old tennis court across the road from where we lived. I could hear what was going on even in my bedroom and the temptation to join was, in most cases, too great.

I would spend the evening with my mother either listening, to the radio, reading the paper, or doing schoolwork. As the year moved onward and the end of year exams came and went everything in my world seemed to be overcast.

From as far back as I can remember my hands always perspired. As soon as I felt hot due to the air temperature or activity or anxiety my hands began to sweat. I had almost permanently what most people hate and dread - that is sweaty palms. My parents were anxious about it and were forever looking for a cure. It was always a conversation piece among relatives and friends and I was nearly always greeted by "so your hands still sweat…. " My father for a short period was the dispenser at the main city hospital. The chief neurologist examined me and told us that the only treatment or cure was to sever one of the nerves that regulates the perspiration. The operation was considered to be too drastic and it never took place. After my father left us my mother wrote to the surgeon who attended to General Smuts at Groote Schur Hospital in Cape Town for his advice. He replied that we should either follow the surgeon's advice or our own judgement.

Apart from the social effect, the main problem was writing. With almost permanently wet hands the pages were wet and all my work was either smudged or very untidy. I used to keep (and still do) a handkerchief in my palms to protect the paper but that soon became saturated and however many a handkerchiefs I had on me, before long they were all wet in my pockets. How I had coped and passed exams I still don't know. In my third year at high school as the term moved along life got worse. Try as I might, my written efforts deteriorated and when it came to end of session exams I failed and was held back to repeat the year. I managed to get hold of my school report which would announce to my mother that I had failed and hid it from her but I did eventually tell her the bad news. I was verbally scolded and when the news leaked out to relatives and friends everyone made it clear to me that I was a disgrace. No one offered any words of advice of even consolation. All I could hope for was that if I worked very hard during the first months of the new year, they might promote me.

The first school term begins in mid January and on the first day, all those I had regarded as friends were now in the fourth form but the two classmates and myself were back in the third form among boys who had just been promoted. The first few days were devastating, because we were abandoned by our former class mates who had been promoted. It was a long, tedious, boring year and about the only success I had is that I became regular member of one of the school rugby teams. I again did not do very well examwise. I felt that I was going backwards and at the end of the final term, it was touch and go whether or not I would be allowed to proceed to the fourth year.

In Johannesburg at the time there were few small private colleges and one of them was Damelin College located near the city centre in an office block. After enquiries, my mother decided that she could just afford the fees. I was enrolled and the principal allowed me to proceed straight into the fifth form -the final matriculation year where I would have been had I not failed at Athlone High School. I was with completely new set of classmates from different backgrounds and many of them had also experienced school setbacks. The teaching was designed to help those who had to catch up like myself. Coeducational, no school uniform, no prefects and the only discipline was to turn up on time and learn. Also in our class was a Chinese boy, which was the first time that the rest of us had close contact with a Non-Caucasian. At that time the Chinese were classed as Non-Whites. In those days Whites were called Europeans and every other racial group were Non-Europeans. Strangely enough Afrikaans has always used the words Blankes (Whites) and Nie-Blankes (non-Whites). The College also enrolled Asians but they were taught in separate classes.

Toward the end of January and in February all the inter High School Swimming Galas were held at Ellis Park Swimming Pool, only ten minutes walk from where we lived. Even if your school was not participating the galas were always occasions to attend. The boys' high schools held their gala one week and the girls schools took place a week or two later. I was no longer attending a state school but I still felt that it was an event not to be missed. The galas were held on Saturday afternoons. For some reason or other my mother would not give me any money for my entrance fee. In fact, she did not want to let me go to the gala. My sister who had just returned with her husband from Israel was visiting us at the time. It was the first time my sister saw how angry and aggressive my mother could be toward me. She opened her purse gave me money and the two of us left the house having to endure a hail of anger.

All the schools sat in groups on the main grand stand high above the pool. The neutral spectators sat on the opposite side of the pool on a lower stand much closer to the water. I was among a crowd of local Jewish lads and a few of my Habonim friends. (At the particular gala for the first time Rhodean a private (public) had entered and in terms of pupil numbers was less than half the size of state schools.) Halfway through the gala, it became obvious to most that Rhodean was way ahead of the rest of the competition. I don't know what prompted me but I suddenly found myself saying loudly enough to be heard by a large number of people seated near me. "Ech mere a school, they hardly have enough to make a make a Minion and yet they are winning the gala." Those close to me burst into laughter and as it was repeated so did most of the stand. 'Ech mere' is a Yiddish expression similar but stronger than 'blow me.' A Minion is ten males above the age of thirteen, the quorum number required for Jewish religious service. It was the first time that I said something original in front of crowds of peers that had attracted so much attention and latent praise. The laughter had put my home troubles temporarily out of my mind. I walked home in a much better mood than when I had left.

Needless to say my mother's greeting on my return was not friendly. She carried on where she had left off and then went on to blame my sister for leading me astray. The relationship between my mother and myself deteriorated from that day onwards. During the evenings, I found myself besieged. I was supposedly under bad influences and heading for disaster. Her relationship with my eldest sister at that time was also at a low and they were hardly speaking to each other so, naturally, she insisted that I was listening to my sister and not to her. One Monday evening soon after the gala episode her tirade toward me reached a point that I could no longer bear. I tried talking and even shouting back at her but it was hopeless. Without thinking I started to pack all my schoolbooks into my school bag and as many clothes as I could into a rucksack. I walked to the front entrance of our flat but she blocked my way. Without a moment's hesitation I turned and walked to her bedroom and opened the window and climbed out onto the roof of the downstairs kitchen and walked across and climbed down the drainpipe to the ground. I then ran round to the front door, which I opened with my key and grabbed my bicycle that was kept in an alcove at the bottom of the stairs. While I was tying my school bag to the back carrier my mother managed to get to the front door once again blocking my way. On this occasion nothing was going to stop me and I simply pushed her out of the way while she shouted at me and pounded her fists into my back. Mrs. Gervis the landlady heard the commotion and called out to my mother and me in Yiddish to stop but we were oblivious to her cries and I simply pushed passed, lifted my bike down the stairs that led up to the front door, and then rode off. As I peddled for all that I was worth, I felt that I should be crying but the tears that did flow were more in anger about having to take such drastic action. I cycled to my sister's (the one who had been present at the gala incident) flat in Troyville about fifteen minutes away. I left for good, and apart from a short stay of two weeks many years later, I never returned to my mother's house.

My sister was not completely surprised to see me; she had been half expecting me to turn up sooner or later. A logistical problem now ensued the flat had only one bedroom and I had to sleep on the settee in the living room, but I was prepared to put up with anything. The next morning I cycled off to school. I did not tell anyone that the night before I had run away from home and tried to get through the day as if it were just anther school day. By the end of the week, my two sisters and their respective husbands had got together to decide what to do with me. My eldest sister, who at the time still hardly spoke to my mother, and her husband were now renting a three-bedroom house in Orange Grove, a suburb in the north of Johannesburg. They agreed among themselves, without consulting me that I should go and stay with them in Orange Grove. I stayed there until I finished my final school year at Damelin.

I had just turned sixteen and suddenly I found myself in a completely different atmosphere. I was now almost free to come and go as I pleased. The servant did washing and ironing, woke me up in the morning with a cup of tea and cooked my breakfast, prepared my sandwiches and cooked a meal on my return from school. I had a bedroom to myself with a desk so I could retreat to do my homework, etc. The pace of life altered considerably. My afternoons were no longer preoccupied with concern about what I had not done. No more evenings alone with my mother who would either be listening to the radio or reading the evening newspaper from cover to cover when talking on the telephone. Apart from speaking to relatives, there was the occasional call to a family friend Mrs Davis.

The Davis family consisted of a Mr & Mrs and their daughter, Mrs Davis parents and their spinster daughter Miss Hibson (Mrs Davis' sister). They came into our lives before the war. They had migrated from South

Wales to start a new life in South Africa. Their first home was a rented house in Turfontein, a suburb in the southern part of the city. My father at that time was running a pharmacy. Not long after they had arrived a bee stung their daughter and they came to my father for assistance. He helped as best as he could. He always fancied his chances at first aid and used to put the letters ADF (after doctors fail) behind his proper qualifications. That episode led to a lifelong friendship.

After the death of my maternal grandfather, my mother used her inheritance to help my father open his own pharmacy in Parkhurst, a suburb on the North West of Johannesburg. In those days it was on the outer limits of the city. Miss Hibson, a ladies' hairdresser, opened a salon in Parktown North Stores that was at the terminal for one of the many city tramways. Miss Hibson and her parents lived in a flat above the salon. The rest of the Davis family moved into a newly built house about a mile away from my father's pharmacy.

Apart from the opening of the Parkhurst Pharmacy my mother used her money to build a house alongside the chemist shop which was situated on a corner. This was my mother's dream home and for the rest of her life she always referred back to that house. My father was very partial to gambling and women. This all happened before I was old enough to understand what was going on around me. My mother, my two elder sisters, relatives but mostly many years later Mrs Davies, told me much of what I do know in bits. I still don't really know all the events nor all of my father's misdemeanours.

The business only lasted a year or two but they were very troubled times especially for my sisters who were now attending junior school. Whenever the quarrels between my parents became unbearable my eldest sister would walk us to Mrs Davies where we would be looked after until fetched by one of our parents. Very soon after the outbreak of war the business and house had to be sold and we then moved into rented accommodation. All the rest of my growing up years appeared to me as if in the sad shadow of the days past. Every time I saw an English war film about families being bombed out of their homes or long trails of refugees fleeing the advances of the Nazi army I associated it with the loss of our home. The events from then on were related in the early chapters.

The friendship between Mrs Davis' and my mother lasted for the rest of their lives. Before Mr & Mrs Davis returned to England, they talked to each other every night on the telephone.

Chapter 15

Not having the immediate problems of my parents on top of me seemed to give me breathing space. I moved from an 'enclosed' environment to what seemed at the time to be freedom. Apart from telling my sister and my brother-in-law where I was going and getting their token approval, I was free to come and go as I pleased. However my freedom was curtailed by my lack of money. To begin, I was given token pocket money by my sisters. Somehow they managed to contact my father and told him of my flight. For the remainder of my school days I met him about once a month at a flat in central Johannesburg, which belonged to his 'girl friend', and he gave me money to pay my school fees, my bus fairs and a small amount of pocket money. When I needed clothes he took me to a shop where he had an account but most of my clothes were brother-in-law cast-offs.

Most of my school companions came from middle class families and were never short of money. Some already had their own motorbikes and use of family cars. Although when asked I told everyone that I lived with my sister, I never actually told anyone about my running away from home. Whether or not they knew I never ever found out. Although I was pleased to have moved to a private school, the one thing that I did miss was sport, especially rugby and swimming; the two sports in which I began to make some headway. However the fact that I was in my final school year and that I caught up with my peers was more than enough to compensate.

I was still very active in Habonim. We met every Friday night. I was now an established member of the older group known as The Shomers - the guardsmen. Outside of school, Habonim was my only social activity. By now Friday evenings were steeped in Zionism, socialism and culture. Culture meant listening to classical music, real jazz, fine art and literature. We were lectured on all aspects of modern art, the theatre, the revolutions and trade unionism.

The school year was divided into four terms and at the end of the first term we had an examination. Although far from being top I did obtain reasonable marks in the top half for a change. However most of my classmates were like me having to catch up on a lost year.

I was almost independent but still felt responsible to my sister and her husband in so far as I always told them where I was going and my whereabouts.

Habonim now began to take on a more serious note as it was slowly preparing us for Aliya (migration to Israel). The ideal was to go and join a kibbutz, a life which we had been told about but were totally unprepared for.

In order to rectify and prepare the various Zionist youth movements, the Zionist Federation and other organisations had a created a training kibbutz known as Hachshara for all the Zionist Youth movements. The first one that I became aware of was about eighty miles North West of Johannesburg near the small town of Brits close to the Magaliesburg Mountains. The Hachshara was a moderate sized tobacco farm located along one of the irrigation canals fed by the nearby dam on the Crocodile River called the Hartebeespoort Dam. The farm was a working farm with a farm manager who lived in one bungalow with his family. In the main bungalow lived those on Hachshara who had volunteered to migrate to Israel.

The main purpose was to first prepare urban Jewish youth for an agricultural way of life. More important it made South African Jewish youth aware that life backed up by servants was not the norm in most of the world. One of the teachings of the Zionist movement was based on social equality and now on the Hachshara was an opportunity to practise what you preached. Every household chore had to be done and the farm had to be worked.

My first visit to Brits (that is what we called the Hachshara farm) was during the spring vacation of my last year at the government high school. This first trip was more in keeping with the scouting side of Habonim. We were delivered to the farm on the back of a truck. Once we arrived at the farm we were introduced to a very tough looking Israeli who had been seconded to South Africa by the Zionist Federation. He was what we all pictured a true pioneer looked like. Six foot, suntanned with black curly hair, thick set wearing a short sleeved blue shirt, khaki shorts with tough walking sandals. His name was Zvi. He had an air of self confidence and 'enjoyable' suffering having been taken from his homeland to prepare those in the Diaspora to return with him. However, in reality, he probably thought how lucky he was to get away from the then pioneer state of Israel to indulge in the material comforts of the South African Jewry.

Soon after our arrival at the Brits we were told that we going on a two day hike to the Hartebeespoort dam. We were first instructed on footwear and how to avoid blisters, etc., and then do and don'ts and, finally, on observations of the countryside. We all had to take with us our own supply of water and travel food but our tents and sleeping gear were going to be delivered to our overnight stop. We set off about midday and followed the path alongside the irrigation canal. As we walked, Zvi made a point of talking to each group and wherever possible, pointing out to us something he thought that we should be aware of.

The area we were in was generally known as the Middleveld. About fifty miles north of where we were is known as the Bushveld which covers most of the Transvaal. The area is naturally covered with low flat-topped trees and almost all the trees have very unfriendly thorns. The tree cover is dense and where there are no agricultural clearings, the visibility into the bush is limited to about fifty yards. Unless there is a path, it is almost impossible to walk through the bush except where there were no trees. The grass was shoulder high and without the tree covering seemed to retain the heat. So unless you concentrated on a landmark you saw nothing but the trees and grass.

As midday approached the dry heat increased and after our lunch stop our water supply began to run out. In the middle afternoon, one of the leaders sent me, along with two other lads to find some drinking water. We took as many empty water bottles as we could carry and followed the path into the bush. After ten minutes, we found a clear stream and soon were lying on our stomachs drinking the cool water. While we were drinking, we spotted a small snake crawling out of the grass into the stream to swim slowly past us. Normally we would have stood up and either run away in panic or grabbed a stick and attempted to kill it. Our thirst was more important and, with one eye on the snake, we simply carried on drinking. We filled the water bottles and then watched curiously as the snake wandered on away from us. We felt relieved that we had not panicked and that deep down inside the live and let live feeling prevailed. It was probably the first time that each of us had seen a snake in the wild without someone spotting it for us. When we told our story to Zvi he simply replied that he had never seen so many wild snakes before while walking but had decided not to point them out to us to avoid creating either fear or panic.

We reached the dam in the late afternoon and the truck duly arrived with our camping gear. We pitched our tents only discover that we were one tent short. Some of us were going to sleep in the open. The girls in our group were all given preference and then the boys drew lots and I with three other boys ended up having to sleep beneath the stars. While I was preparing my bed roll, one my fellow travellers discovered that his sleeping bag had not arrived. The leader told us that he would have to share my bed. My blankets were too narrow for us lie alongside each other so we had to sleep 'head to tail'. Neither he nor I had much sleep as we kept pulling the blankets off one another.

Once the sun rose up from behind one of the surrounding mountains we were all made to get up, wash and prepare breakfast. The truck came and collected our camping gear and we set off to climb one of the mountains on the side of the gorge through which the river flowed. (The dam was created by a huge concrete wall stretching from the mountain we were about to climb to a mountain on the other side of the gorge)

In the cool of the morning, we walked toward the wall. Looking up, the route chosen looked steep and formidable, and some of the girls in the group needed some persuasion to begin the ascent. We scrambled up the first few hundred feet and then followed what seemed a well-trodden path. After a rest the route up became steeper. I was near the tail end of the trail and suddenly, we all bunched. The path now crossed a crack in the mountainside. It was as if the mountain had been split open. All that was required to cross over the crack was a large footstep. A leader stood on either side of the opening to help us across. I waited patiently at the back of the line until it came to my turn. One of the lads, called Mike, who was at the head of the queue, was almost in tears. He made it clear to one and all that no way was he going step across. Myself and a colleague, the one I had shared my sleeping roll with were going to be the last to cross but the leader made us wait while he tried to encourage the lad to step across. The two of us decided on a solution and that was to push him from behind. We reasoned that he would automatically step over the deep crag. The leader realised what we were about to do and prevented us from carrying out our plan. After a discussion it was decided that as my sleeping friend (Sam) and I were the last in the line we should take Mike back down and make our way back to the farm. Sam and I did our best to hide our disappointment at not been allowed to reach the top of the mountain. We looked down and could see a road alongside the irrigation canal and were told that if we took that road it would only take us about three hours to reach the farm. Looking down, no one realised then that there were two canals and that we could only see one of them. In our haste to depart, the leaders forgot to give us a water bottle or some food or even check whether or not we had any money.

Only the noise of the gravel moving beneath our feet broke the silence as the three of us descended without pausing to look up at what we were not allowed to achieve. We walked across the dam wall only pausing to look at the water on one side and the steep slope on the opposite side. Once we reached a road alongside the canal, we started to walk silently in a single file toward the farm. Some time later our growing thirst forced us into conversation. We came across a family who, for some reason or other, had stopped their car and were picnicking on the only grass that we had seen since leaving the dam. They enquired as to where we were heading and only after consulting their map did we realise that the dam fed two irrigation canals and that we were following the wrong one. The map showed us that if we left the road and headed due North through the bush we would come across the Crocodile River which we had to cross, and that should lead us to our road.

Luckily we were wearing long khaki trousers, boots and shirts with sleeves which we rolled down and set off into the bush. We found a footpath that we reckoned was going in our direction and walked, again, in a silent single file. About an hour later, we emerged from the bush into dense shoulder high grass. Intense heat emanated from the veld, which increased our thirst but we plodded on in silence. The grass gave way to sharp, broad-leafed reeds as we approached the river. The reed leaves were sharp enough to cut into our shirtsleeves. We were relieved to reach the riverbank. The river was about fifty yards wide at that point and flowed at a moderate pace over what seemed to be a rocky bed. We were all confident swimmers so did not hesitate to start crossing. Luckily we had arrived at a point where the river was only about two feet deep and the current was not strong enough to prevent us wading through. We wet our faces but did not drink the water and reached the opposite bank without any mishaps.

Once we were clear of the reeds we emerged into grass that had been grazed and after emptying our boots of the accumulated water started out again. We suddenly found ourselves facing a pack of barking dogs and we realised that we were walking toward a private farm. As we walked, the dogs continued making a terrible din but retreated as we approached. The relief of not walking through long grass or thorn covered trees was such that as long as the dogs stayed some distance from us we were not particularly bothered. A farm soon loomed up on the horizon as we walked to a field of newly planted tobacco.

A group of African farm workers were sitting at the far end of the field having their lunch break. As we approached the dogs ran off toward the farmhouse and the workers seemed amazed at the sight of three English speaking white youths emerging from the river. We greeted them and they replied with, what seemed to us, a typical blank look; a look that we came to regard as the norm. As we did not understand their language it never occurred to us that they may be mocking us. They silenced the dogs temporarily by throwing a few stones at them.

The farmhouse that we approached was a square building with a north-facing veranda covered with anti-mosquito gauze, which made the entrance seem dark. The outer walls were painted a yellowish white and the roof was made up of corrugated zinc painted red. There was no garden of any sort and the ground around the house was trampled dark red soil. Some fruit trees created shaded areas in front of the house. There was some garden furniture under the trees and relaxing there was the farmer and his wife. Although they were obviously surprised to see us they made no effort to get up to greet us other than a hand wave. We greeted them in Afrikaans and they replied without asking us where we had come from or where we were going. It was as if seeing three white Jewish teenagers who had just emerged from a river crossing happened regularly. We asked if we could have a drink and they shouted to the Black maid to bring us water and fizzy lemonade. We told them that we were looking for the irrigation canal and managed to explain that when we had come down from the mountain we had followed the wrong canal road. It turned out that the road we were looking for was only a few hundred yards away from the front of the farm.

Once our thirst was quenched we set off again, and reached our destination after an hour's brisk walk. We arrived back at the Brits farm shortly after the rest of the party had returned by truck. We were expecting to be greeted as reluctant heroes. Instead one leader asked if we were alright but showed very little interest in the fact that we had taken the wrong road and had to walk through the bush and cross a river to get back. They took it for granted that we would get back safely. It was as if we were selected to take Mike down the mountain and escort him back because they knew that whatever happened, we would be able to cope.

After that visit and all the talks that we had every Friday night about Kibbutz life, I decided that I wanted to spend the rest of my life working on the land but it had to be abroad. It did not seem to me that there was a future for a young, Jewish, White male who wanted to do the work himself without having to use what was then cheap Black labour. I wanted to do as much of the work as possible - myself. I wanted to work the land and to be close to the soil. On the Hachshara farm, there was an opportunity to actually join in with the 'inmates.' I wanted to farm and felt that I would eventually end up in Israel, but I felt that I needed to see Europe and North America before settling down. I decided that, after my Matric, I would go to University to study Agriculture. The nearest University that provided such a course was Pretoria University which was an Afrikaans speaking University but that did not bother me at the time.

Chapter 16

The mid-winter academic vacation in South Africa occurs in the month of July. I persuaded Benje, a class mate of mine, to come with me to Brits. During the first week of July, we set out to hitchhike to the Hachshara farm via Pretoria. Our first lift took us straight to Pretoria. In order to reach the road to Brits, we had to pass by Paul Kruger's old house which was now a museum. We decided to look round the house. Everything was arranged as if the old President himself was just out on a visit and would be returning soon. As we walked round in silence looking at all the artefacts, there was an atmosphere of silent sadness.

We walked to the outskirts of Pretoria before we started to hitch and, this time it took us about an hour before an elderly Afrikaans couple in an old American car picked us up. They drove slowly and it was not long before the car began to overheat and our drinking water bottles that we had meticulously filled before leaving Johannesburg now became very useful. Once we were on our way again the small talk drifted into politics. Even though we respected our hosts and were grateful for the lift we were in no mood to be told how well the Nationalist government was doing and how the Communists and Blacks would ruin the country if they were allowed any political rights. We listened politely at first but slowly began to disagree and, within the next twenty miles, they turned on us saying that our views were communistic and no good would come out of being a 'Kaffir bother.' The 'temperature' began to rise and then suddenly the car stopped and we were told to get out and that they regretted having given us a lift.

We were not on the road ten minutes before a farmer with an open truck stopped and let us climb onto the back, and dropped us almost at the door of our destination. The 'inmates' of the Hachshara were always glad to have help and we were provided with free board and lodging.

Apart from the Cape Peninsula, the rain in South Africa falls in the summer months, which makes most of the country unsuitable for growing wheat and other such cereal crops. Maize is the exception and generally thrives in most of the country where the rainfall is adequate. The rainfall is sporadic and where possible crops are grown under irrigation. The Hartebeespoort dam provides water for farming for huge areas. The local climate favoured growing winter wheat using the water from the dam and in the summer, tobacco.

The land farmed by those on Hachshara was on the side of the canal that sloped down into a shallow valley. The slope was too great to simply allow the water to flood over the land. The water had to be guided over terraces until it reached the last valley furrow that drained directly out of the canal. Our first job was to help prepare each terrace so that water flooded gently over it from the main furrow. When that terrace was saturated, the entrance to the next lower terrace would be opened. It was simply a matter of building miniature earthen dam walls and then breaking them open at the appropriate time. It took us a few days to prepare the first field. The first nights we lay in our beds with our bodies aching and tending to our sore blistered hands. Before the sowing could be done, the fields had to first be watered mainly to test how the water would flow. By the third day, we were joined by Sam, another member of the Habonim group that I belonged to.

The three of us were each allocated a vertical series of terraces to look after. As the water from the canal flowed into a shallow dyke that ran across the top of the field, a wall opened which let the water flow into the first terrace and then it would be blocked off to flow along to the next section and so on. One of the regular inmates controlled the main water flow while we made certain that water flowed evenly over the terrace and, when that terrace was almost flooded, we would block off the water flow and tend to the next lower terrace, and so on. This proved that the flow was not too great and that there was no break in any of the mini dams, so all was well. The ground was dry and it soaked up a lot of water but, once it was saturated, it turned into thick red mud. Every now and again our Wellingtons would stick as if we were being sucked down. The flow of the water dictated the pace of work. There rarely was time to catch one's breath and we were not used to labouring. And as the day wore on, we struggled not to flag or give up.

About mid-morning, I looked over toward Sam but could not see him. I thought nothing of it assuming that he may have gone to relieve himself. About five minutes later, I looked for him again but still could not see him. I waited for a break in the water flow and called out to find out if Sam was still around. There was no reply but I noticed the handle of his hoe sticking out of the wet soil. I decided to investigate and ran over to the terrace which was busy flooding. Once I reached where he was working, I found him lying face down in the wet soil and the water running over him. My first reaction was to turn him over to get his face out of the water. He had rolled back and he was breathing very heavy and foaming at the mouth. I shouted over to Benje who came running over as fast as he could through the muddy, wet soil. We managed to half lift and half drag him to a dry patch and then called over to the Hachsharanik Joe who was in charge of us. By the time he reached us we had managed to move Sam out of the midday sun into the shade of some thorn trees at the side of the field. The sluice gate was still open and the water was now rushing uncontrolled over the terraces down to the bottom of the field. Once Joe saw what was happening he asked me to run back to the farmhouse to summon help.

Luckily a tractor and trailer happened to be at the house when I arrived and soon I was on the trailer with the others and the tractor driver was doing his best to drive through the mud to reach Sam. To get as close as possible to Sam we had to detach the trailer and push it the last few yards. Then we lifted him onto the trailer and manhandled the trailer back to the tractor. Sam, by now, was beginning to breathe more normally but was still unconscious. The tractor was in position to hitch onto the trailer. Joe stood with his back up against the trailer waiting to drop the steel peg into position. The rear wheels of the tractor were in thick mud and the driver was having trouble getting the tractor to move. He revved up the engine and let out the clutch a bit too fiercely. The tractor suddenly shot back and the driver's seat now pinned Joe to the back of the trailer and he screamed out in pain. The driver, as quickly as he could moved the trailer forward and Joe collapsed into the mud. In silence, Benje, the driver and I lifted him onto the trailer lay him next to Sam. Somehow or other we managed to hitch the trailer to the tractor and raced back to the farmhouse. With more help we transferred both casualties onto the back of the farm truck and they were driven off to the nearest hospital in the town of Brits about six miles away.

Joe ended up with a few fractured ribs and Sam was diagnosed as having a stress panic attack. The rest of our stay was not as eventful and two weeks later we left to return home. On arrival at my sister's house I discovered that my other sister had given birth to a girl. I now had two nieces from each of my sisters.

In that August I began my last two terms at school. My final matriculation exams were in December. I spent many a day in my room with my books 'swatting' and few days before my exams the 'servant girl' asked me why I spent my days alone just sitting at a desk. I tried to explain to someone who could just about read and write that I was studying. The exams came and went and we had a farewell party. As we left, the Head of School shook hands with each one of us and his farewell words were a Shakespearean quote 'I can't see you fare.'

Chapter 17

It was now December, midsummer, and the peak of the White holiday season when the Whites that can travel to the coast for a vacation. Although the nearest seaside to Johannesburg is Durban, the surrounding coastline is referred to for by some as the South Coast. During the summer months, Muizenberg near to Cape Town is where most of the Johannesburg Jewish population used to hope to go. Those who could not make the thousand-mile journey ended up in Durban. During my latter years at school, I never went on a family holiday. I nearly always found myself over the Christmas weekend watching a cricket match series at Ellis Park which used to be the main cricket venue after the original Wanderers ground made way for the expanding railway station. However a few days before that Christmas a close friend Norman, who had never (apart from Habonim camps) had a summer family holiday, told me that his cousin plus a friend were motoring down to Durban and planned to stay there for a long weekend, and there was space for the two of us in the car. I had managed to save some money out of my monthly allowance that I received from my father which was enough to pay for my and Norman's share of the petrol. I would still have enough left over for pocket money.

The plan was to leave early on Thursday morning, and I went to spend the night at Norman's house. In those days no one thought twice about two lads sharing a bed. As Norman had six sisters, the place for me to sleep was in Norman's room and there was only one bed in the room. We were collected at about six in the morning and the four of us set out on the four hundred mile journey in a two-door Ford Popular. If we were lucky the car reached a speed of sixty miles per hour and took us almost a half a day to reach Northern Natal; the temperature was in the high eighties. We stopped every now again by the roadside and I well remember being almost consumed by the roadside heat and deafened by the screaming of the Cicada beetles. Once we had reached Pietermaritzburg, the capital of Natal, we still had about seventy miles to go. The last stretch of our journey was through the Drakensburg Mountains and our small three speed car had taken its time up and down through some spectacular scenery including the Valley of a Thousand Hills.

We reached Durban in the late afternoon. The city was so very different to what we were familiar with. The first thing that struck me was how green and lush the vegetation in and around the city appeared, in particular an area called the Bluff on the opposite side of the harbour. As we drove toward the seafront it looked as if we were passing through an English city that I had seen in the cinema.

No one had any pre-booked accommodation and the general consensus was that we were going to have to sleep rough. Norman's cousin and his companion decided that, at worst, they would sleep in the car and Norman and I would have to fend for ourselves. I knew the name of the hotel where my cousin who had driven down from Johannesburg and his family were staying. Norman and I were dropped outside of the hotel with our two small bags and we arranged to meet up again in the early hours of Monday morning to start our return journey.

I found my cousin, who had just returned from the beach in the hotel lounge. Norman had left me once I had met up with my cousin and we arranged a time and place to meet. After overcoming his surprise at seeing me he asked where were we staying. I made it clear that we could not afford any form of accommodation and then persuaded him to park his car on the sea front near to some public toilets and to let us sleep in it. He reluctantly parted with his spare car keys and told me that he would move the car for us after ten in the evening. I must have looked hungry and unkempt as they invited me to their room to have a shower etc., and then ordered me a huge plate of sandwiches.

I met Norman at the appointed time and place. He had run into three blokes whom we both knew who had driven down the week before and were staying in a hotel just off the sea front. They generously offered to let us sleep on the floor of their room and had arranged to meet Norman outside of the hotel to take our bags in for us in order not attract the attention of the hotel receptionist. After we had changed, our hosts went down to eat their evening meal and Norman and I went out to find a cheap café. Only after we had ordered our meal did I discover that Norman had no money with him and that I was going to have pay for everything (Luckily I had brought my post-office savings book with me). We both ordered a mixed grill and half way through the meal we noticed that hamburgers were 'off'. After complaining to the management we were both given another complete meal and a voucher for another.

My cousin was greatly relieved when I returned his car keys to him and told him that we had found somewhere to stay. After that Norman and I wandered round the many amusement arcades before returning to the hotel. The hotel service included morning coffee or tea delivered at about 8 am. The knock on the door woke us up and Norman and I had to get up and grab all our belongings and hide in the bathroom before the door was opened to room service.

Our first full day was a Saturday and I had to find a post-office to draw out some money. During that era in most of South Africa all the government Afrikaans speaking whites manned services, public transport and utilities offices, etc. The only exception was in Natal, especially Durban. It felt very strange for me to be in a post-office and listening to the counter staff speaking to each other in English and addressing the customers in a South African English accent. Another major difference was the number of people of Asian (mainly Indian) origin to be seen everywhere. The Indians in the Transvaal tended be shopkeepers and in very specific types of business. You never saw an Asian manual labourer. In Durban it appeared to me as if there were more Asians than Africans and all were working alongside the Africans in all sorts of jobs. To complete the feeling that I was in a different world the atmosphere was hot and humid in contrast to the dry atmosphere of the Highveld.

I made my way back to the beach where I met Norman and our 'roommates.' In those days the beaches were segregated and full of white bodies trying their best to acquire a sun tan. After about a half an hour it soon became obvious that half of Johannesburg's Jewish youth was in Durban and, in all probability, the other half was in Muizenberg.

The warm Indian Ocean provides an endless progression of waves large enough to satisfy the surfers and makes bathing fun. By midday the beach sand is hot enough to burn the soles of your feet and, between frequent dips, we spent the day playing cricket and football and chatting to the girls. While sitting on the beach we were introduced to a medical hypnotist. After chatting to him about his work he then agreed to give us a demonstration and I volunteered. I remember him talking to me and telling me do simple tasks which, apparently, I did. I felt as if I was in a semi-dream like state and vaguely was aware of him telling me what to do. Then I woke up, stood up, but felt as if had returned to a dream.

Later that afternoon we clambered into a car belonging to one of the lads, in whose room we were staying. The car belonged to his father and in those pre-seatbelt days three were squashed into the front of the car and four into the back. I found myself in the back with Natasha (who I had only just met) sitting almost on my lap. I felt quite shy about the situation and very self-conscious about where to put my hands. Natasha did not seem to be bothered at all and after about ten minutes relaxed, sat back, and put her arms around me. Apart from feeling embarrassed I began to feel very hot and my hands started to perspire and I had to struggle to get my handkerchiefs out of my trouser pocket.

We drove north to see the sugar cane fields and then further up the coastline. The atmosphere in the car was jolly and frivolous. I hardly participated in the conversation and only spoke when spoken to. Natasha seemed very pleased with herself and was very much part of the car chat. We stopped at a roadside café and I then discovered that I had hardly any money on me. This meant that neither Norman nor I could order anything nor could I buy Natasha a drink. In those days you always paid for the girls.

Once out of the car, I drifted off and sat by myself much to everyone's surprise. The lads could not understand why I was not clinging to Natasha. The whole group approached me to find out what was up with me. I then had to confess that I hadn't any money on me. I was dragged into the café and all was paid for (by whom I never found out). We all climbed back into the car for the return journey and Natasha made certain that she was sitting on my lap again. This time she immediately sat back with arms rapped around me. By the time we reached the hotel she managed to kiss me - the first time I had kissed a girl in public. We arrived back quite late so there was no time to arrange an evening date. I was teased endlessly that night and took a long time to fall asleep.

The next morning we all met on the beach. Natasha did not show the same amount of interest in me as she had done in the car and I tried not to show my disappointment. After lunch we all caught a bus to the Bluff and, much to my relief, Natasha sat next to me. We all walked along the breakwater and after about five minutes I plucked up the courage to hold her hand which she squeezed tightly and I walked on air.

At the end of the breakwater we all stopped to watch a group of white males with rifles shooting at sharks. Those days any wild life such as snakes, crocodiles and sharks were thought of as threatening and had to be killed. In spite of the fact that there was a shark net to protect the bathers, the 'hunters' believed they were doing everyone a good service. I could not help feeling that it was all 'killing for the sake of killing' and the hunting stories my father had told me suddenly turned sour. However, the touch of Natasha's hand soon took me back into the clouds. We found a bench and then I indulged in my first public necking. The song 'Walking My Baby Back Home' sung by Nat King Cole was oozing out of a radio in a nearby refreshment kiosk. That afternoon lasted forever and I arranged to meet the lads back at the hotel as I had plucked up the courage to walk her back to her hotel. Outside her hotel we said our final goodbye but she was very reluctant to give me her phone number or to arrange to meet again.

I met with the lads again and I asked if anyone knew where she lived and then they told me that she was the steady girlfriend of a medical student who was three years older than I was. However my ego was lifted when I discovered that he was a prefect in my last year at Athlone High School. He had won the Victor Lodorum trophy for both swimming and athletics and played in the first rugby and cricket teams. I knew that I would never see her again. To this day when I hear the song 'Walking My Baby...' I find myself on the Bluff.

Norman and I met up with his cousin and friend just after midnight and we began our journey back to Johannesburg. Once we left Durban and headed into the mountains, we drove into a low cloud with very restricted visibility. It was the first time that I had ever experienced such conditions and was fascinated by the cats' eyes in the middle of the road. The steep mountain roads and the weather slowed us down and by midday we had only reached Northern Natal. I kept dozing off and each time I closed my eyes I was with Natasha. The day temperature rocketed up into the eighties. The car engine started to overheat and we had to stop every now and again. The pump that keeps the petrol flowing into the carburettor began to malfunction but lasted until we reached a garage in the town Volksrust. While the car was being mended I fell into a deep sleep and the next thing I knew we were on the outskirts of Johannesburg.

New Year's day in Johannesburg was spent either picnicking or wandering around the streets watching the groups of Black revellers parading round the streets in a simple band usually consisting of a homemade guitar, mouth organs, whistle, and a percussion instrument - often no more than a simple drum. In most cases the performers were fired up by alcohol and had at least one person sober enough to pass the hat around. The mini-parades lasted until dark and then all went quiet and all the Whites retreated to houses and sat on the front veranda enjoying the cool of the night.

Chapter 18

My other sister by now had bought a house in the suburb of Parkhurst and I decided to stay with them until I knew my matriculation results before deciding what I was going to do with myself. I still had ideas of studying for a degree in Agriculture. My brother-in-law's father lived nearby and he ran a furniture shop on the outskirts of what was then Sophiatown, the Black Township within the city boundary of Johannesburg where the Blacks could actually own property. I took up a temporary job in the shop helping to move furniture and to look after a storeroom. To reach work every morning I would walk round to my boss's house for lift in a Fifties green Austin with flap-out levers for indicators. While driving a great deal of energy was spent banging on the door pillar to get the flaps out.

All the shop assistants were Black or Coloured (mixed race) so for the first time, I spent all day in contact with Non-Whites, that is, apart from the odd customer. The shop was set back from the road with a small, sandy parking area. A high fence topped with barbed wire surrounded the whole complex. The back of the property formed the boundary between Newlands a White suburb, and Sophiatown. The rear of the building that I was working in actually was a mini-part of the boundary. The inner wall was criss-crossed with live wires to keep the would-be burglars out. The mission school and church run by Father Trevor Huddleston was close to the rear of the shop.

In those days the public transport in Johannesburg used electric trams on rails, electric trolley buses and ordinary diesel buses. The tramlines were either in the middle of the road or ran alongside of the pavement. Outside of the shop fence was a short kerb and then a pair of tramlines adjacent to the road. The transport was totally segregated with 'White transport' coloured cream and red and the transport for Non-Whites or Non-Europeans as they used to be called in those days was painted grey. Interestingly the driver and the conductor of the grey transport were both White. There used to be a line into Sophiatown for grey trams only.

Most of the customers at the shop were Black and all goods purchased had to be delivered, even into the heart to Sophiatown. We had two methods of delivery. The lighter goods were loaded onto a small trailer and pulled by a three wheel bicycle which was powered by Moses, one of the African workers who had been with the firm for many years. The heavy furniture was loaded onto a larger trailer towed by the boss's car and Moses would always accompany the boss on deliveries. Every time Moses set out pedalling it always seemed very comical and he enjoyed the attention because he made certain that everyone knew that he was about to depart.

During the day I had time to talk to one of the Black workers and our conversations included politics. He became more relaxed when he realised that I believed in political rights for all Non-Whites and that I was as much against the current Government as he was. After a few conversations I realised that he was studying part-time for his matric, an exam that I had just completed and was waiting for my results. I promised to give him my notes if I passed my exams.

One of the questions that I put to him was how he would, and the Black population in general, react to Whites when eventually they achieved political equality. I was left under no illusion that the average Black hated the Whites and many of his generation would deal ruthlessly if and when a revolution came about. I asked how they would treat me. His reply was that he knew that I was sympathetic and would spread the word as far as he could but there would be those whom the message never reached and to them I would be just another White person. The job ended a few weeks later when the boss decided that he no longer needed me.

After a visit to the college to find out when my results would be available, I found myself working in the college office. One morning the deputy principal asked me to go with him to Pretoria to collect some papers. What I didn't know was that he went to collect the results before they were posted. On the way back to Johannesburg we chatted away and it was only when we reached the office back in Johannesburg he told me he had the results. He had already looked at them and I had passed, but I would have to resit my maths in order to get a higher grade for university entrance. There were resit exams within six weeks and if I wanted, he would enter me right away. Also that I could enroll for extra tuition and, instead of being paid for the work I had done, I would not have to pay tuition fees.

A distant relative travelled to Pretoria every Thursday in a van to deliver pickled cucumbers to delicatessen shops in Pretoria. I sat in the front seat and the African assistant sat in the back of the van on one of the sealed drums containing the cucumbers. The journey took just over an hour and, by the time we reached Pretoria, my clothes had absorbed the smell of a jar of pickles. I made my way to the University and as I walked to the office to enroll, I had to pass through the gauntlet of second year students ready to bait the freshers.

My spoken Afrikaans was limited to basic conversation and by replying to any questions directed at me from the 'gauntlet' in English they thought that I was simply visiting and not a potential student. However, my deception was short lived as I was spotted in the queue for new students and was overheard speaking in Afrikaans in the office. I was accepted for the course that I was interested in provided that I achieved a higher grade in my Maths resit. As I left the office to leave the campus I was dragged and made to sit on the floor surrounded by a group of male students who, tongue in cheek interrogated me. In Afrikaans the word for I is Ek and for pardon is ekskus. However I was not allowed to refer to myself as Ek but dit which means 'it' and had to say 'ditsksus' not ekskus and so it went on. I was also continuously asked why I smelt of vinegar. After about fifteen minutes of being told how I was to behave during the first term I was allowed to leave. I met up with my lift in a small café and had some lunch, and then we departed back to Johannesburg.

The University term did not start until February and, by that time I would have almost completed my resit. Apart from concentrating on my studies, my main worry was now how I was to pay my University fees. I did the round of various Jewish charities and received a series of indifferent replies, mostly to wait and see until I received my resit results. One organisation, the Ort Oze (pronounced ortozey) was a worldwide Jewish organisation set up mainly to help Jews who wanted to learn various crafts and trades which included farming. They said that they would help me provided I worked for a year on their training farm in the Eastern Transvaal near the town of Witbank. The Monday after I sat my resit, I packed up what belongings I could take in a suitcase and my brother-in-law took me to Johannesburg Station. He shook hands with me and wished me luck and made it clear to me that this was now the start of my working life.

Chapter 19

In those days most of the South African railway was steam driven and with a mighty jerk and hiss the dinosaur of an engine gradually pulled me away from a waving brother-in-law. I settled back and contemplated what I had let myself in for and wondered if I would I ever return to city life. I was leaving behind my family and my family life with all of its squabbles, turmoil and upheavals. I was now on my own, having to determine my future and, whatever happened, it had been my choice and I would have to succeed. I felt a calm tingling sensation percolate through me as I sunk back into the seat.

The first part of the journey was due east across the East-Rand and the train did not stop until it reached the end of the electrification. The train turned North-East and the yellow sand of the gold mine dumps which pepper both East and West Rand were now beginning to recede and the train travelled though the flat farmland of the Highveld. I was entering the world where I had hoped to spend most of my life. After about an hour and a half, we reached the first stop - a small town called Delmos and although only an hour away from the metropolis of Johannesburg, it seemed to be a half a century behind. The station buildings were probably originally dating back to the time when the railroad was first constructed. They were made out of corrugated zinc with wooden window frames and were badly in need of a coat of paint. On the platform was a folding table and on it were set out cups and trays of sweets and biscuits and in the middle was a hot water urn to make either coffee or tea. Once the train stopped, all the doors opened and most of the passengers disembarked and made straight for the tea table. A fellow passenger told me that this was a regular tea break stop and assured me that if I wanted to get out for refreshment the train would not depart without me. I indulged in a fresh cream bun and a cup of coffee. The train guard then walked the length of the platform making certain that we first finished our drinks then coaxed us back onto the train.

The train then stopped at every little siding picking up milk urns and African women with bundles on their heads who seemed to be always standing at the wrong spot and as soon as the train stopped ran to the third class departments. Blacks were not allowed to travel in either first class or second compartments. Those were reserved strictly for Whites. If a White was travelling with servants, the servants would first help their masters or mistresses onto the train then run down the platform to the back of the train where the third class carriages were located.

After about half an hour of slow travel, I reached my destination - a dorp (village) called Oogies, which means little eyes. Once off the train, the farm manager and a young trainee and the customary Black servant, whose immediate task was to carry my luggage, met me. As I looked around, I could see in the middle of the platform one small old 'tin' building which housed the ticket office, the waiting room, the station masters office and the signal box. Standing on the platform, which was raised above the surroundings you could see a clear dusty patch where one or two cars, a few pickup trucks and number of horse drawn buggies stood. The car park opened onto a sand road running parallel to the rail track. Between the track and the road was veld grass. All the white males were wearing the traditional khaki trousers and shirts with broad rimmed hats and the women wore dresses made out of flower patterned material. Most of the Blacks, as was common in those days, were dressed in either overalls or shabby old clothes either bought cheaply at the Indian shops or from White held jumble sales. Although this was the first time I had been to Oogies the setting looked strangely familiar and it was only later that I realised how much the scene resembled what I had seen many times in American films.

As I walked to the truck I felt very conspicuous, as if the whole world was gazing at this city boy. I felt uncomfortable as they were wearing the farm khakis and I had a sports jacket, a white shirt with tie, and grey flannels. The farm manager Mr. Skuy, Sam the trainee and myself climbed into the front of the pickup and the African placed my luggage on the back and then climbed onto the open back of the pickup. We drove out of the station car park, turned left, drove for a few hundred yards, then crossed over the railway line at a level crossing and then drove toward the dorp. Running parallel to the railway line was the main Johannesburg to Witbank road, which was tarred. We drove over the main road into the village. Oogies then looked like every small Highveld dorp and much less developed than Evaton, the dorp that I once stayed in during a school holiday.

The sand road, at a right angle to the main tar road, seemed very wide mainly because on either side was a shallow storm trench which separated the road from the veld. On the left hand side were numerous tall-planted Blue Gum (Eucalyptus) trees growing out of the grass. The grass was dry and about three feet high; in among the trees were houses. Many were still built in the old pioneer style of green corrugated zinc with a low flat stoep with a stone floor. There were also some relatively modern brick built houses with red tin roofs.

On the right-hand side were the shops. Each one was a square detached building with a central entrance and two large windows halfway between the entrance and the end of the building. Needless to say, the windows were covered with heavy burglar-proof iron bars. The roof of the building like the houses was peaked and the slope continued over the front stoep. Lingering on the stoep, some sitting, others standing, were numerous Africans. The young males dressed in long trousers standing or leaning and the older males and women sitting. The older women looked very overdressed with long skirts heavy blouses and turbans. There was an atmosphere of a gathering that happened regularly and no one was ever in a hurry. We stopped at a shop and Mr Skuy walked straight in almost as if he parted the Blacks with his stare of disapproval at their presence. It was then that I noticed that he limped. One leg was slightly shorter than the other and he walked on the toes of the shorter leg. Apart from wearing the customary khaki longs he wore a colonial type of khaki coloured pith helmet. Sam and I remained in the cab and we then engaged in small talk while dozens of pairs of eyes stared at us and probably all knew immediately that I was new to the area.

Our next stop was fifty-yards further to the post office. Once again Mr Skuy walked straight into the Whites only area to collect the farm mail and then we began the drive to the farm. The post office was the last brick building on the left and alongside was a series of sheds with old farm machinery and old farm vehicles littered all around. One of the sheds housed the local building merchant and the other sold general farm merchandise. On the other side of the road there were houses, an old hotel, and a furniture store. Each of the sheds/stores had their complement of Black men and women hanging around the front.

After about five hundred yards the roadside verge merged into the veld. From the elevated position in the cab of the pickup could be seen where the large stretches of the veld had been ploughed up and on the cultivated fields were rows upon rows of ripe mealies (maize) beginning to dry off. The sand road dipped down slightly and crossed over a dry stream, and then we turned right. Sam pointed out to me a row of Blue Gum trees in the distance, which broke the flatness of the landscape, and told me that they formed one of the boundaries of the farm. Any vehicle driving along those sand roads created a dust storm and every time we overtook cyclists, who were nearly all Black, they would become covered in a sand cloud. The grass on either side of the road was tall enough to almost hide the fields from view. We drove along for about four miles and then turned right onto farm track only wide enough for the truck to avoid the grass brushing the side of the vehicle. We drove for about mile before we reached the farmhouse. It was a white square house with a green tin corrugated zinc roof with the usual veranda covered with fine meshed 'fly' wire facing due west. Alongside the house was a huge oak tree about twice as high as the house. It must have been planted by the original settlers, and provided a large area of welcome shade.

Mrs Skuy came out of the back door to greet us. She was a relatively large woman who greeted and then shook hands with me. She spoke with (as I now know) what remained of her Yorkshire accent. Sam then showed me to my room, which was a Rondavel, (a round thatched house) built alongside the farmhouse in the front garden. There were single beds and we were to share the building. Although Sam was friendly to me I could not help picking up signals that he had been alone there for a while and was top dog.

No sooner had I unpacked and changed into my brand new khakis we were summoned to lunch. Mr Skuy sat at the head of the table and Sam and I opposite to Mrs Skuy. Once we sat down, a bell was rung and in came a young African about 16 years old wearing a clean ironed khaki shirt and shorts with a white apron which reached down to his knees. The Skuys addressed him as Picanin. They never bothered to find out his real name that I found out later to be Mavimbella. As the farm was owned by a Jewish organisation who were the employers of the Skuys and Sam and I were both Jewish, grace was not said before the meal. After the meal I followed Sam's example - before we stood up to leave we thanked them for the meal and then returned to our Rondavel. The rest of the afternoon I followed Sam round as he diligently showed me what was what - the sheds and barns and the implements etc., and the dos and don'ts.

About five hundred yards away from the farmhouse was a brand new oblong building, which now housed the Hachshara. The building was originally built to house young Jewish trainee farmers sponsored by the Ort Oze however the number of trainees had dropped off to only one in the last few years. The Hachshara farm at Brits had been closed down because the various youth movement and the Zionist federation had decided that the farm at Brits was too uneconomical to maintain. The Ort Oze then offered the use of the hostel and some land and, besides, there was Mr Skuy to help act as adviser or consultant. However by the time that I had arrived the relationship between the Hachsharaniks and Mr. Skuy had cooled to the extent that they were hardly speaking to one another. As I knew most of them sooner, or later, I would have to go across to speak to them. The sole ambition of the Hachsharaniks was to settle on a Kibbutz in Israel. In Israel they would have to do everything as there was no cheap labour and besides it was against their socialist principles to employ cheap labour.

Here were about a dozen white middle class Jewish youth aged between 20 and 30 trying to work the land as well as look after themselves. Like all South African Jewish youth even having to wash up after meal (let alone having to cook the meal) was new experience. Then there was the washing and ironing and (something as alien to them as being on the moon) having to sweep, wash the floors, make the beds etc., and keep the boiler alight for hot water. After the novelty had worn off came the reality that these jobs were not just for one or two weeks but forever and some had to be done every day of the week. Another reality they faced for the first time was that jobs were to be shared out equally with no sexism and it did not matter whether or not you had a professional qualification.

That afternoon they drove past me in their pickup truck and waved. From a distance you could tell that they were having problems. Allowing for the fact that they were wearing their working clothes they looked very untidy. Mr & Mrs Skuy like all South Africans with the help of the servants, were naturally very tidy with nothing out of place. It was beyond their comprehension how young Whites could let themselves go like that.

The next morning at six a.m. Mavimbella woke us up with a cup of tea. (The other African workers would have died of disbelief had I called him then Mavimabella). We would have to do at least two hours work before breakfast.

Sam was older than me and could drive and had passed his driving test. I sat in the front of an old Ford lorry and drove out to one of the fields to collect some recently cut grass that would be stored in the silo for winter feed. The workers all duly climbed onto the back of the lorry as we drove out to the field. Although I had dressed to work I felt redundant standing around not participating in pitch forking the grass onto the truck. Sam stood around and he and the Boss boy gave orders and when I picked up an implement and tried to join in the loading process I was actively discouraged from doing so by Sam and the Boss boy.

After breakfast Mr Skuy, sensing that I wanted to do some actual work, set Sam and me the task of cutting up some old railway sleepers. The sleepers had been bought as a job lot and when sliced in half they would make excellent fencing posts. Under the shade of the oak tree we propped each sleeper up vertically and, using a large two handed saw, we began to cut the sleepers down the middle. We sawed on and off until Friday and I acquired my first blisters and all of me ached.

My first day also introduced me to a daily ritual in which I was not invited to participate. Each morning about 10.30 am Mr & Mrs Skuy would drive in the pickup into Oogies. They would always visit two of the stores, the butcher and the Post-office. In the one of the stores Mrs Skuy would be entertained with a cup of tea while ordering the daily groceries. If anything that was needed for the farm had to be collected, she would remain on her chair while Mr Skuy drove off to wherever he had to. The local gossip, national politics and information would be exchanged in the store. They somehow always returned in time for elevenses for which Sam and I were invited to join them.

On my second day Sam received a letter and informed us all that he would have to go home that weekend. For the rest of the week Sam taught me to drive a tractor and also guided me through my first attempts at driving the old farm truck. He left on the Friday morning and took with him as much of his personal belongings as he could carry but insisted that it was just a weekend visit. However on the Monday while I was sawing a sleeper on my own, Sam arrived driving his mother's car. He packed all that he had left behind into the boot of the car. He then shook hands with me and Mr & Mrs Skuy and then drove off I never saw him again and I never found out the reason for his sudden departure. I did not find out why he had given up the training course nor did I find out whether or not he had taken up farming as a career.

I remained on the farm as the only trainee for the next ten months. Maybe because the pace of life compared to the city life I had just left behind was so much slower, it seemed to take place over a longer period of time. Once I was on my own the first instruction from Mr Skuy was that I must be able to drive any farm vehicle as soon as possible. As all the roads on the farm were private roads, I would not need to have a driving licence. Without the problem of driving among traffic, I mastered with the help of the African drivers within few days the physical process of driving a vehicle.

My stay on the farm was strange as I wanted to participate in and do as much of the work as possible alongside the Black farm workers. On my visits to the Brits Hachshara I had learned to hand milk cows, clean out the cowshed, prepare the milk for the market and keep the records. When I mentioned to Mr Skuy that I was expecting to have to do my share of work in the dairy he hardly looked at me and frowned. I soon learnt that our entire dairy herd consisted of only six cows of which only three were actually producing milk. The person in charge was a young late teen African whose name I never found out.

The whole dairy was not more than a glorified open shed. The basic construction was wooden poles covered with rusty corrugated zinc. At one end there was a concrete trough with chains to put round the cows' necks while they were being milked. It had several partitions so that the cows were separated from one another. I could not understand how such a primitive set up was used for the training of future farmers. The young lad in charge of the cows would drive them in, tie them up and then proceed to milk them in total silence. He stood looking at me in absolute disbelief when, after washing my hands, I picked up a pail and started to milk one of the cows. The cow kept turning as if to see who this stranger was. As soon as I thought that I was finished he politely stepped in front of me and proceeded to check that I actually drained the cow of its daily supply of milk. All the milk was then taken to a small room next to the farmhouse where all the milk from that milking was filtered and what was not needed for the household was then put aside for separation into cream and skimmed milk. The separating machine, a mixture of a centrifuge and a series of elaborate filters, was hand driven. When the appropriate speed was reached a bell would ring. The skimmed milk was used for animal feed and the cream kept for butter making.

Once the second week began, and I was on my own, I established a series of rituals with regard to my role and behaviour, as far as the Skuys were concerned. Each morning, Mavimbella knocking at the door of rondavel woke me up with a cup of tea. I washed using an old jug and washbowl and cold water. Then I would go out to start the day's work and I had to sense which job I was supposed to do. I was never given clear instructions as to what my task for the day or the morning was, and had to learn by observation. Invariably I would have to take the lorry or tractor and trailer loaded with workers out to one of the fields some of which were a mile or two from the farmhouse. At eight o' clock I would return for breakfast, which consisted of a bowl of hot porridge followed by a fried or scrambled egg and a sausage and finished with two pieces of toast and marmalade and coffee. At eleven a.m., it was coffee plus a biscuit. One o' clock was a cooked lunch and hour's rest. Between three and four afternoon tea, like morning coffee, served on the veranda. The day's work ended when the sun went down or six-o-clock. I would return to my rondavel for a cold shower in a shower cubicle attached to my rondavel. I would then lie on my bed either listening to my battery-operated radio (then still a novelty) or reading until Mavimbella rang the bell for the evening meal. I would enter the dining room and, as soon as either Mr or Mrs Skuy appeared, my first words were "Good evening" and I never sat down before they did. Mr Skuy believed that a healthy diet was one that, when you left the table, you felt that you could eat some more - a feeling that I experienced for the rest of the stay on the farm. Once the meal was over, I would always thank them and asked to be excused. This mealtime ritual continued for the duration of my stay on the farm.

Apart from not always being told what job I was supposed do, in the evenings I had to sit through the meal never knowing if what I had done was correct or satisfactory. The only comments that came my way were about what I had not done or done wrong. It was always a relief to leave the table without having negative signals sent my way.

I joined the farm in March at a time when the crops are ripening off and there is lull before the harvest. The rainfall on the Highveld occurs in summer mainly in the form of heavy showers and then, by April, it rained very irregularly until the next spring. The nights were cool to cold, particularly in the early hours before the sun rises. As the autumn wore on, the various crops were harvested and I found myself driving either the truck or a tractor and trailer to bring in the crop. I did my best not just to sit in the cab but helped in the loading or offloading. My body soon adapted to lifting and I became quite fit. In spite of my limited diet, I actually put on weight in the form of muscle.

Most evenings after the evening meal I returned to my room between 7.30 and 8 o'clock then read or listened to the radio and was usually asleep before ten o'clock. Occasionally I would go over and chat to the Hachsharaniks. However, the relationship between them and the Skuys was, to say the least, mildly hostile. Although their attitude spilled over toward me the chance of company overcame my own reluctance. Generally speaking, contact between them and me was either during the weekends or accidental.

The working week ended officially on Saturday at midday. I now had, apart from mealtimes, time to myself. I found that in the Oogies there was a tennis club and they would welcome new members. Oogies was about six miles away and the only way I could get there was to cycle. Saturday afternoons I changed into my tennis gear and tied my old tennis racket to the bike and then cycled off to a tennis afternoon.

Cycling on sand roads is not the most pleasurable way of moving across the Highveld. Although the terrain appears flat, once you are on a bike, it is anything but flat. The roads slope gently upwards or downwards. The sand roads are hard and corrugated in the centre and with nothing but troughs of loose sand on the edges which seem to bury that part of the wheel that is presently touching the ground. If you then tried to ride too near the centre where there is no loose sand, it was like travelling on a permanent boneshaker. Then the art of cycling was to find a bit of road about a third of the way from the edges. Each time a car passed by, you were covered in cloud red dust that entered your lungs and stung your eyes. Luckily on Saturday afternoons, most of the vehicles that would use that road were put to rest for the weekend.

There were about a dozen members of the club who regularly turned up for an afternoon's tennis. Among the players was the local police sergeant, the post-mistress and a few bank employees. All the conversation was in Afrikaans and they mostly supported the Nationalist government hence I had to bite my tongue on more than one occasion. There were times that I would express my anti-apartheid views and waited for an expulsion notice which somehow never arrived. There was only one court so we nearly always played mixed doubles and sat out every alternate game. I had to leave before five in order to be sure that I arrived back at the farm before dark otherwise it would mean cycling along a pitch dark road and to be late for the evening meal was an unforgivable crime.

About three months into my stay on the farm I rode out for my usual Saturday game of tennis. About mid-afternoon, while we were drinking afternoon tea, a meeting was convened. The treasurer informed us that we needed funds to have the court resurfaced. Although we did not own the court, the club was apparently responsible for the upkeep of the court. We decided to organise a dance in three weeks time in the local village hall. A local band was hired and though we were not allowed to sell alcohol, we could sell food and soft drinks. On the day of the dance I dressed in my best jacket and Mr Skuy gave me a lift to the hall. I arrived about an hour before the official start to help with the decorations. We had sold more tickets than we expected so our hopes were high. From the way we all carried on, it became obvious that none of us had ever been involved in organising such a function before. The band consisted of a drummer, a piano accordion, a banjo and a saxophone. They arrived on time and they looked as if they had been plucked straight out of a Cowboy film.

At seven o'clock I was asked to open the door and, to my surprise, there was a queue of people waiting. Within a half-hour the dance hall was full and nearly everybody was dancing. Those who wanted alcohol slipped out into the hotel bar next door to the hall. The dances were a mixture of Afrikaans folk dances, square dances, English country dances and the usual foxtrots, tangos, sambas, etc. Every-body participated as if this was their first and possibly their last dance. We were sold out of everything and made a large profit.

It all ended by midnight and there was no question of the Skuys coming out to fetch me. One of the club members had to drive past the farm gate. They offered me lift but to my horror dropped me at half past midnight at the farm gate and left me to walk the two miles to the farmhouse in the dead of night. It was a dark moonless night and I could hardly make out the narrow road which was slightly lower than the surrounding fields. All I could see were the fence posts. About halfway home, when my initial fear was beginning to subside, I saw on the top of a distant post a shape that looked like a large bird. I was about five yards from the post when I heard hooting and what I thought was a bird turned out to be a big owl which spread its wings and flew straight at me. I ducked then picked myself off the ground and ran to the farmhouse.

Chapter 20

On occasional Saturday evenings I would stroll across and spend and hour or two with the Hachsharaniks. However, this often was as much an endurance test as having to listen to the tennis club politics as they could not contain their anti-Skuy outbursts. No matter what I said I was, in their eyes, entrenched in the Skuy camp and very often I would have to leave and swear to myself that I would not go back. But after a week or two my need for company would make me go back for more. The difficulty that I always faced was the fact that at that time, deep down I was as much a Zionist as they were and had intended to settle in Israel but I was not ready to migrate and was still hoping to attend an agricultural college.

The Hachsharaniks were trying their best to live as they would have to in Israel. Saturday was a non-working day and they worked on Sundays, which upset the locals including the Skuys. They did all their own work and did not employ any African labourers. Apart from those who were on kitchen duty, they all rested as much as they could. Me turning up on Saturday evening having spent the afternoon playing tennis was probably a reminder of what they were giving up.

Sunday morning breakfast was served a half-hour later to make it seem as though Mavimbella was also enjoying a rest day. Some Sunday mornings I was invited to go with Mr Skuy to Oogies to fetch the Sunday papers. On one occasion on our return journey, about three miles from the farm, we saw about a hundred yards in front of us a large black snake. In those days, the sight of a snake provoked the worst in us. Our immediate reactions were drive toward it and kill it by driving over it. As we approached within twenty yards of the snake it reared up and spread its white collar in a defiant pose. We hit the snake full on and pulled up immediately then looked back but there was no sign of the animal. We reversed to the spot where we collided and cautiously got out of the truck. There was no sign of the snake but even more strangely was that there were no signs of any blood or marks on the front of our truck. We decided not look in the surrounding grass for fear that we might meet up with an angry beast.

On most Sundays, after breakfast it was matter of what to do with myself. We had an old police horse on the farm that was kept in a paddock and allowed to graze with the cows. It was there to be used if necessary to round up the oxen used for ploughing, or pulling where the tractors or truck could not be used. Mr Skuy encouraged me to learn to ride the horse. First, it was matter of catching the horse to saddle it up. The only way that could be done was to tempt him into a narrow enclosure with some food. The first Sunday that I actually managed to put a bridle on the horse one of the farm workers who happened to be around showed me how to saddle up the horse and helped me to climb on. He also showed me how to dismount without falling off or ending up under the horse's feet. It was a Cowboy type saddle and the only riding instruction that I received from Mr Skuy was to sit back and balance myself by standing in the stirrups. The first time I walked the horse round a field. Eventually I encouraged the horse to trot and gradually became more confident. I dug my heels into the horse's stomach like I had seen the Cowboys do and, to my surprise, he broke into a slow gallop. Once I got used to that movement, I dug my heels in harder and he suddenly took off and galloped at about twice our previous speed. I now hung on for dear life as the horse raced toward a fence with me struggling to keep my balance. I pulled as hard as I could on the reins but he seemed to have the bridle in his teeth. The fence rapidly approached and I was fully expecting him to attempt to jump over the fence but instead he suddenly stopped and I ended up on his neck. Somehow I managed to scramble back into the saddle and he walked along parallel to the fence and slowly I took control again. This all happened quite a distance away from the farm and I was not certain who had seen me. The only other occasion that I came close to falling off was when, a few weeks later, I managed to get the horse to gallop at full pace and probably due to lack of proper horsemanship the horse tripped and fell forward, and I landed on his neck. The horse stood and immediately began to continue his gallop and I recovered my riding position.

After my third weekend, we had some visitors from Johannesburg and one of them was the daughter of my old Biology teacher. She informed me that the results of the resit exams were out and as far as she knew I had passed my Maths. I was fully matriculated and could now go to University if I so desired.

Whenever I could, I used the horse to explore the farm, which covered about seven hundred morgan (about 1,800 acres). On horseback I was able to reach the extreme boundaries, most of which were out of sight of the farmhouse. Only about half the land was actually cultivated; the rest was used to graze the oxen and the milk cows. In addition, there was about twenty acres of woodland composed mainly of Eucalyptus and Mimosa trees. The woodland was at the back of the Hachshara hostel and so it was an area I kept away from. The western boundary was at the bottom of a gentle slope. To get there would mean riding past the Hachshara hostel and then about five hundred yards further was another hostel where most of the male African farm workers lived. This was a bleak barn-like building with a large hall filled with iron beds and, next to each bed, a primitive locker. I only ever stood at the entrance and never went inside so did not find out whether or not there was a kitchen and what kind of washing and toilet facilities there were. As I rode past at a distance of about fifty yards there was nearly always a group sitting on makeshift stools round a coal brazier. Some would greet me but most never seemed to even look up in my direction.

Once past the hostel, the open veld rolled gently down and the terrain dipped down toward a shallow bowl in the land. A small earthen dam about three quarters of the way down the slope had been constructed. It must have been fed by a spring, as even in the depth of the dry season there was water in the dam the size of a tennis court. There were reeds and other water plants, which were well established which suggested that the dam had been built a long time back and it no longer was needed for whatever it was built for. Further down toward the dip was a group of houses built out of mud bricks with no windows, some had tin roofs but the others had thatched roofs. There were about twenty dwellings arranged in a traditional African style around a series of small courtyards. As I rode by the first time one or two of the women came out to greet me and one elderly man came out to inquire whether or not anything was wrong, otherwise why would a young White take the trouble to come out to them on a Sunday.

As the autumn wore on, we gradually harvested all the beans, sunflowers and mealies. My role nearly always was to drive the farm truck or tractor with a trailer to collect the produce and then bring it in for thrashing. We used an old thrashing machine made mostly out of wood and powered by a belt from one of the tractors, an old Fordson. The sunflowers and maize were hand picked and put into sacks, and then loaded onto the trailer or lorry. When full the load was driven to the thrashing machine and the vehicle would return to the field with the empty sacks. Whenever I could I helped with lifting and especially the sacks that were filled with the corn from the thrashing machine. The beans had to be pitch forked on the truck then fed into the thrasher. We also cut grass for winter feed which had to be stacked or placed into silos.

The harvesting continued until the end of May and, by then, I had become toughened up put on weight, and had a healthy outdoor appearance. I always wore a hat and never took my shirt off so I had lines on my arms and forehead where the sun had not reached. About six weeks after I had begun I decided to spend a weekend in Johannesburg. I did not receive any wages; all I received was free board and lodging. (There was nothing to spend any money on and what money I had brought with me but that did not add up to very much). On the Friday morning I dressed up in my best trousers, white shirt and tie, and my best jacket and brown suede shoes and a packed a weekend bag. I went into Oogies with the Skuys who dropped me on the main road that would lead to the Rand and then on to Johannesburg. At about eleven in the morning I started to hitchhike. I eventually reached the centre of Johannesburg in the middle of the afternoon. Although I had only been away for six weeks, at the age of seventeen it was if I been away for a lifetime. The noise and the pace hit me and although I was in very familiar surroundings and wearing town clothes, I felt like a nervous country yokel. There were even new models of cars that I had not seen before. However, I made way to the bus stop in Eloff Street and caught the trolley-bus that would take me to my sister's house in Orange Grove where I had lived during my last year at school.

I still had a front door key and the servant girl was still the same one when I was living in the house. I was welcomed and, without much ado, a meal was prepared for me. Sam, my Durban companion, together with his family had moved into the house next door to my sister. He and I spent Friday night finding out where the all the Saturday night parties were going to be held. In the mid Fifties in Johannesburg there was no question of meeting your mates down at the pub and then embarking on a pub-crawl. Saturday entertainment for Jewish youth was hoping to be invited to a party or finding out where the parties that you were not invited to were being held. Sam made a few phone calls and we managed to get invited to a few parties.

At one of the parties I met some of my old pals from my Bertram days and to my surprise, one of the lads who had teased and verbally tormented me was there. More important, he had not grown since I last saw him and I was now a few inches taller and a lot broader and my continuous exposure to the sun had provided me with a permanent sun tan. It was a new experience for me to be spoken up to by one of the lads I had looked up to.

During the month I spent preparing for the resit examination I met two girls both of whose families were among the richest Jewish families in Johannesburg. One of them, Linda, lived in a house on a two-acre stand in Houghton, the richest suburb of Johannesburg. Apart from the huge mansion of a house, they had a swimming pool, tennis court and lots of garden. In those days only the very wealthy had one or the other, let alone both. Before I left for the farm I was invited for the odd game of tennis as well as a swim and a meal. I wrote to Linda during my second week and received a reply, which I read over and over again.

On the Sunday after the party I phoned Linda who invited me round for a game of tennis and, once again, my outdoor appearance was the main topic of conversation. During the course of the day I met a few girls with whom I became quite friendly.

On Monday morning I caught the early train back to Oogies with a few more pounds in my pocket given to me by my sisters. I also took with me some more of my old clothes that I had left behind as I had discovered that there was a ready market for second hand clothes among the African farm workers and it would provide me with a source of pocket money.

Chapter 21

As the year moved toward winter the early mornings became cooler with often a thin layer of frost. The frost disappeared as soon the sun rose up into the sky. The winter months are rainless in most of South Africa except for the South West Cape which boasts of a Mediterranean climate. The skies tend to be cloudless for the months of June and July. The setting sun was easily observed, and each day the sun dipped in a spot slightly more North Westerly than the previous day. Mr Skuy pointed out to me a clump of trees on the horizon and said that when the sun reached that point it would be the shortest day and the sun would then begin to move back. Never an evening went by without me observing the sunset and marking the sun's position on the horizon.

One Sunday afternoon after lunch I walked down to the dam that I found while on horseback. I sat on the wall staring into the water and the reeds and watched the occasional bird wade in for drink or a bath. In the sky above, several large heron type birds seemed to be flying effortlessly round in circles. As I lay on my back watching them with the sun on my face I somehow felt relaxed, alone and at peace. The words of a poem by the Afrikaans poet Eugene Marais kept recurring in my thoughts. "*Ek slaap in die rus van die eue gesus ongesien ongestoord, Dof en loom in my sonder droom…*" (I sleep and rest in eternal peace unseen and unheard and thus I wander in my sun dream…). I must have dozed off and the sound of drums must have woken me up. It took me a while to gather my thoughts and realise where I was.

As I sat up I heard the sound of a splash come from the middle of the dam. I looked up and saw some movement in the reeds but could not see what it was moving. I guess it must have been either a fish or some large amphibian but, whatever it was, I never found out. Once I got over staring at the water I heard the drums again and realised that the drumming was coming from the nearby houses that I had previously ridden by.

I walked over to the house and, as I approached, I heard not only the sound of the drums but also a male voice chanting and every now and again there would be a chorus of mixed voices. Following the sound, I found myself in a small courtyard type of enclosure and saw a group of men and women of all ages and some children sitting on the floor. They all had their backs against the walls of the house or the low walls, which extended out from the sides walls of the buildings. My appearance at the entrance did not create a distraction, as if they knew I was coming and that it was only a matter of when would I arrive. I only recognised two or three of the men who half greeted me. Their attention was focused on the elderly man who was doing the chanting.

I sat down and after about ten minutes asked one of the men that I knew what was he saying. I only got a vague reply and I gathered that it was a family type 'religious' ceremony. It was distinctly African in all aspects except the clothes. They were all dressed in shabby western type clothes. The older women wore long dresses with shawls and all the women had some headscarf or beret. Very few African women then went about without their heads covered. The small drum was made out of a hollowed tree trunk covered with animal skin and was held on the lap of one of the men.

The only time that I had seen, other than on films, any form of African tribal dancing or ceremonies were those put on for the Whites on Sundays at the Gold mine recreation ground. All that I knew about African culture was from textbooks and museums. It was quite common in Johannesburg to see a line of African males who had been brought in from all over Southern Africa to work on the mines. Towns' people referred to them as 'raw blacks'. They were shepherded through the streets of Johannesburg to mine compounds. Most of them wore long trousers and with a blanket wrapped round them and behaved and looked as if they were terrified. At the age of fourteen I had seen an African made film called Zonke which is the Zulu word for "each and everyone". The film was an all-African variety show and all the acts were about Africans dancing and singing in a Western style and left me with the impression that African culture was slowly being westernised.

Looking around and listening to the proceedings at first created some confusion in me. Had I at last stumbled upon what was the closest I had ever been to the real African rural culture? As I was beckoned to sit down, which I duly did, and as the ceremony proceeded I felt more and more privileged to be present at a real tribal event. The only African language that I vaguely understood was Zulu and a hybrid language called Fanagalo. After careful listening I realised that the proceedings were in the local African language and here I was participating in a ritual that few Whites had ever attended or even knew about. I stayed for about an hour and a half and then slowly walked back to my rondavel with my head full of the sights and sounds that I had just witnessed. For once I had seen an aspect of Southern Africa that did not involve or suggest violence. I walked home wishing that I had understood what had gone on.

Most of my previous experience with African culture had some aspect of violence associated with it. All the dances performed on Sundays at the mines were based on war dances; most of them had their origins in the Zulu Impis of last century. Street fights involving Black male against Black male, Black female against Black female, Black male against Black female and fights between White males were not uncommon sights on the streets of Johannesburg. There were gangs of young Whites, mainly Afrikaners, whose sole purpose was to fight among themselves or first to hurl insults at Jewish boys and then provoke fights. Many of the older African males carried around a 'knobkerrie' - a stout stick with a round knob on the end. These were used for defence and in any disagreement with another, in particular a younger male, they would wield the stick fast and furiously and it always ended with a split bleeding head.

I once witnessed how ferocity and antagonism could reach a fever pitch in a very short space of time. I was fourteen and I was still living in Bertrams. I had finished my lunch and was settling down to some homework when I heard shouting outside. Alongside the old building where we lived was another block of flats and at ground level were the servants quarters as well as the boiler room that supplied hot water for the flats. A coal merchant's lorry had just delivered a supply of coal. It was very common for any form of delivery to have at least four to six workers who would offload and empty the sacks into the coal store. One of the delivering 'boys' said something to one of the women who worked as a domestic for one of the White flat occupants. Whatever was said, or maybe it was the reply, by the time I looked out of the window stones and pieces of coal were flying in all directions. On one side there were the flat 'boys' and domestics and on the other side, the delivery 'boys' who now retreated to their lorry. How no one was hurt or property damaged I will never know but what I did see was terrifying.

On the first payday I was present on the farm I witnessed how quickly debts were settled. One of the African farm workers waited for one of his co-workers to collect his pay and then demanded the shilling that was owed to him. The request was refused and before anything else could be said a fight over the shilling began. The rest of the workers just stood around and watched as blows rained down in all directions. Eventually, Mr Skuy, with a revolver in his pocket, put an end to the violence. Whether or not the debt was settled I never found out. After that episode I got to know more about the farm workers and learnt that there were small cohorts and there was no love lost between them.

Soon all the crops were harvested and then the preparation of the ground for the next season's crops began. I spent many a day on the tractor ploughing. My greatest concern was to make certain that the furrows were straight. Every now and again, Mr Skuy would drive out to where I was working and check on the accuracy of my steering. I never tired of seeing the soil being turned over and the fresh earth being exposed. There nearly always were one or two heron-type birds in attendance ready gulp down any form of wildlife the plough unravelled.

In fields that had not been cultivated for a few years or where the soil was very dry our tractors were not capable of ploughing. The oxen were used on such fields. A span of oxen generated more and the right type of power than a tractor. There were at least fourteen oxen in a span and driving them was a very skilled task. Each farm always employed a driver who knew all the oxen by name and they in turn were all trained to obey his commands. The only part that I could play was to help with the spanning in of the oxen. The animals would be driven against a fence and somehow they would line up in pairs, always with the same partner. With their back to fence they would lower their heads so a leather rope could be placed round their heads. They were all red Afrikaner cattle and all had long horns and all they had to do was suddenly lift their heads and you would have a horn sticking into you. Hence you watched the animal's eyes for any movement. Your only weapon was your boot to kick the ox on the nose if it should try to lift its head before you secured the rope and the yolk. However, every now and again one of the animals would get its revenge.

One afternoon the oxen were pulling a wagon and the fifth from the front pair became very restless and refused to move. The driver went round with his long whip to sort things out which usually meant shouting and whip cracking. The driver did not notice that one of the pair had become detached from its yolk and its head was almost free. As he walked up to the ox to whip it back into the line it turned and lifted his head and caught the driver in the stomach and tossed him into the air. Unfortunately he landed on the head of another ox. When we rushed over to lift him off we discovered that one of the horns was embedded into the groin of the driver. We got him to hospital where he was stitched up and returned to work a week later.

A few weeks after that incident the oxen were pulling a wagon past the farmhouse. I was on a tractor a few hundred yards from the homestead. I heard a very loud bellowing and, looking up, I saw the wagon had come to a standstill. I could see that a pair of oxen was standing at right angles to the rest of team and that the bellowing was coming from those two oxen. Their yolks had become dislodged and the head ropes were tight round their necks. The driver ran up to them shouting and whipping the continuously. The animals started to struggle and pulling sideways. The whole team then became restless. The driver seemed to lose control of not only the animals but himself as well. He ran backwards and forwards cracking the whip and shouting. By the time I got to the scene Mr Skuy and about a dozen workers had intervened and brought some order and calmed the animals. The driver smelt of alcohol and Mr Skuy ordered him onto the back of the truck and told me that he was going take the driver to the Oogies police station. The driver broke down in tears and pleaded saying that he was a "man and did not want to go to jail." Mr. Skuy ignored his pleas and drove off in a hurry.

The driver was released on bail and the case came up in the local magistrate's court about three weeks later. For some reason or other, Mr Skuy managed not be around on the day of the hearing and I had to attend in his absence. The only other time that I had been in a courtroom was during my parents divorce proceedings and that was only for about ten minutes. The usher drew the judge's attention to my presence and I was ordered out. The Oogies magistrate's court was a plain brick building at the back of the police station. Everything was very plain and drab compared to courtroom in Johannesburg. The bench was elevated at one end of the barn like building. In front of the bench were tables at which various court officials sat. One side of the bench was where the accused was penned and the opposite side was a place for the witness. Almost half the building was filled with chairs for spectators, interested parties, etc.

At that time all public buildings had two entrances one for Whites and one for Blacks but this building had only one entrance. On entering the court building, apart from the magistrate and one of the court clerks, I was the only other white present. I presumed that that courtroom was used for Blacks only or the White hearings were held on separate days. I found myself a space on a side bench and across from me were the lines of accused persons. The proceedings moved at production line pace. A large well-dressed African stood in front of the bench. He was the official interpreter and spoke at a phenomenally fast pace while the magistrate hardly looked up and pronounced his sentences in a very matter of fact way.

Our driver was brought forward into the accused box and the interpreter looked over to me as if to say this is your case. For my benefit the proceedings were first conducted in English and then translated into the local African language. To my surprise I was called into the witness box after the charge was read out. I said that the driver had whipped the oxen endlessly. The magistrate asked me if I saw any whip marks on the animals to which I replied yes. I looked around the courtroom and saw the driver's wife staring at me but showed no emotion. I was sent back to my seat and then heard the magistrate announcing the verdict, guilty of cruelty to animals and he fined the driver five pounds; this was more than a months wages. I looked over to the driver's wife who was already untying a small purse in which she kept her money. Once I left the court, to my surprise there was Mr Skuy sitting in the pickup ready to take the driver, his family, and me back to the farm.

Chapter 22

In front of the farmhouse was an acre of orchard. Between the rows of trees were vegetable beds. Mr Skuy showed me how to prune trees and to prepare the beds for next seasons crops of vegetables. My job was first to turn over the soil by digging, then slowly break up all the large lumps and gradually level out the beds so that the irrigation water from a round storage dam ran gently over the beds. When I was not driving the truck or tractor I was working in the orchard. To the annoyance of Mr Skuy, the Hachsharaniks decided to extend their side of the orchard by planting more trees. However he did consent to help them plan the extension to the orchard and show them how to plant young trees.

Among the tasks that I was involved in was the erecting of barbed wire fences round virgin plots of land. The sleepers that I spent many hours sawing in half were used as fencing posts. The corner posts were first firmly implanted at corners of the field. A single strand of wire was then stretched between two posts and this then acted as a straight-line marker. Posts were then implanted at about ten-yard intervals from corner to corner and the strand wire was then attached to the posts. Two more strands of wire were then stretched across from corner to corner.

The Hachsharaniks acquired a small dog, a cross bred terrier, as a pet. At the same time, on our side, we had new brood of turkey and chicken chicks. These were generally allowed to range round our side of the farm. At dusk they would be enticed back into their pens with food. On occasions the dog strayed over to our side and chased the birds but did not do any damage. That evening I was duly dispatched over to the hostel to give out a warning that if the dog strayed over to our side again and threatened any of the poultry it would be shot. After I delivered my message a series of dares and threats were shouted at me and I was booed back to my rondavel.

About a week later I was returning in the late afternoon from a day's fencing when I heard a gun shot. Looking up in the direction of the sound I saw Mr. Skuy walking away from the Hachshara back toward the farmhouse. A cold feeling crept over me as I suspected that the threat to shoot the dog had been carried out. The path that I was walking along passed at a distance of about fifty yards from the hostel. Some of the Hachsharaniks saw me and shouted at me. Not knowing what had exactly happened I walked over to them. As soon as I was close enough they shouted at me, "The bastard boss of yours has shot our dog!" and when I got even closer I was told "to, bugger off you are not welcome here." I did not say anything and turned to walk away toward the farmhouse. As I was walking away with my back to the angry Hachsharaniks one them rushed at me jumped on me from behind knocking me face down. He landed on my back and started punching me in the back and on the head. I managed to shrug him off and fought my way back on to my feet. It was one of their newest and youngest members and he stood back from me and challenged me to fight. We stood eyeball to eyeball and I prepared myself for another physical attack. A verbal onslaught then started and I remained quiet as within me, my sympathies were with them and I thought that Mr Skuy had acted far too hastily and unnecessarily. I stood there for few minutes as the physical side of the attack seemed to have receded, I picked up my hat from the ground and started walk away while verbal abuse continued.

I had decided not to mention to the Skuys what happened to me as I felt sick inside, sorry for the dog and mused over the rights and wrongs of the afternoon's events. Also I was deeply disturbed about whether or not I should have continued the fight or whether my action once I had fended off my attacker was the right one. However my brawl had been witnessed by some of the African workers who told Mr Skuy. At dinner that evening he mentioned briefly that he heard that I had been attacked but never asked if I had been hurt or even barely suggested an apology. After all it was due to his behaviour that I been attacked from the rear and knocked to the ground.

Unknown to me at the time, although two shots were fired at the dog, only one actually hit the dog and it was not killed, only wounded. While I was being assaulted they took the dog in their truck to a neighbouring farmer who was a bit of an amateur vet; the nearest real vet was nearly thirty miles away. The farmer was able to extract the bullet and then kept the dog and nursed it back to health over the next week. However they decided to let the farmer keep the dog for its own safety. The after-effect of taking the dog to a neighbour was that news of the event spread round the whole district. Although most farmers talk of shooting rogue dogs they never actually shot a pet dog hence the sympathies were all with the Hachsharaniks. Because they had set on me I was considered to have had my punishment but the Skuys were treated like many people who overreact with a certain amount of disdain.

Apart from agriculture, the other occupation of the area was coal mining. The big mine companies owned all the mining rights although the farms were owned privately. The coal was not very deep but there was no open cast mine in the vicinity at the time. All the farms in the district used coal for heating. To purchase a supply of coal you simply drove a truck to the nearest mine and paid in the office for so many tons and then drove your vehicle under a shoot and it was loaded straight from the underground processing plants. One of the main committee members of the Ort Oze was a director of a coal mining company and that is probably why the farm was located in that area.

Although I had not yet passed my driving test Mr Skuy used to get me to drive the farm truck to collect coal. On one occasion before the dog episode, two of the Hachsharaniks came with me to find out where the mine was and see the procedure. There was nearly always a queue of a variety of different sized vehicles and some were horse drawn. With about six vehicles to go, the conveyer belt stopped and we were told that there was a breakdown and it would take at least two hours to repair. We decide that it was not worth going back so we decided to wait. We started to talk to one of the White foremen and as we talked to him there was a shift change. He then asked us if we would like to see the mine. We were each given a helmet and a miner's lamp. The actual mining operation was only about fifty feet below ground and we walked down a cavernous tunnel into the darkness. The tunnel was actually carved out of the coalface. There was coal above, below and to the sides of us as we walked down, only the beam of the lamps was visible. As we walked along, the tunnel narrowed but we could still remain upright and soon the tunnel bifurcated. Along the walls white lines were painted and we were told that if you are lost in the mine simply follow a white line. We were taken right to where they were drilling and blasting. The miner then took us to an area he had marked off and then asked us if we believed that coal originated from trees. Then he showed what he had marked and preserved. He shone his lamp on the wall and there was the perfect outline of a tree trunk with some branches still intact and on the bottom were the remains of roots. After we stood there and admired the sight he then said that any disbeliever should see this and then they would be convinced about the origins of coal. We drove the vehicle away from the shoot and drove back to the farm. The next day I drove the lorry back to the mine to fetch the rest of our coal.

Although most of the South African Jewish population was urban and lived in the main cities, there was a sizable minority who lived in the country areas. So much so that almost every small town through out the country had a synagogue. Even a small dorp like Oogies had a few Jewish families, but the nearest synagogue was in Witbank some twenty-five miles away. Most rural Jews ran trading stations and the rest were farmers some of whom owned huge estates and employed hundreds of local African workers and a few Whites as managers. Over the previous decade those farmers used the Ort Oze as a recruiting centre. They would wait until they had at least ten to twelve months training and then come round to invite the lad over to their farm for a weekend and then invariably make an offer that was difficult to refuse.

One of the Hachshara residents was in his thirties and had worked for one of the rich bachelor Jewish farmers. Why he left I never found out, however, he had worked on and off for various Jewish farmers for the past five years. The stories he told made me cringe. Some of the Jewish farmers that he had met were as ruthless, if not worse, to their Black workers than the White Afrikaners. They used imported labour from Malawi (then Nyasaland) and Mozambique who were kept in almost slavelike conditions. After that I had decided that if any offers came my way from those sorts my answer would be no.

Chapter 23

About a month after the dog episode, which occurred near the end of July, I was invited out by a Jewish farmer to spend the day with him. He turned out to be the manager and not the owner and he had recently married a local Afrikaans nurse. The farm was owned by a consortium of Johannesburg Jewish businessmen. Many of the rich Jewish merchants at the time were using their excess wealth to purchase large farms. The Government of the day provided subsidies for White farmers that made large-scale farming quite profitable.

My host Ronnie had, like me, been brought up in Johannesburg in a more middle class northern suburb compared to Bertrams of my early youth. I had heard about him via the bush telegraph in particular the fact that he had been living with the nurse Sandra for a number years and they only recently got married after she had been granted a divorce from her first husband. She had a little girl of three and was expecting another baby. Ronnie was in his late twenties and I felt at the time at ease in his company. To reach the farm we drove about six miles north of Oogies and then turned off the main road and drove for another two miles until we reached the railway line. The main railway line from Johannesburg bisected the farm. The farm was located on an old coalmine. The steel structures that housed all the machinery associated with the mineshaft that brought the coal to the surface and loaded it on to the railway trucks was still in place.

It did not look like a traditional farm as the farm buildings, barns, workers hostels and houses etc. were once part of the mine. All this was on one side of the railway line and two houses one of which was used by Ronnie were on the other side of the railway line. There was even a small station called Minaar, which was also the name of the farm. The station presumably was placed there to serve the mine as there was a rail spur to mine shafts. It all seemed so different with no obvious grain silos or cattle sheds, but there were the usual farm implements lying around in the grass. Planted Eucalyptus trees lined field boundaries and the back of the house was a poultry pen that housed chickens, turkeys and ducks.

I was taken to his house and Ronnie, Sandra and their little girl entertained me on the veranda. Our discussion centred mainly on farming practices and, to me, he seemed to be knowledgeable and aware of the various farming methods. However, what did emerge was Ronnie's indifference to Mr Skuy and his farming methods. Not only that, but according to Ronnie Mr Skuy did not enjoy the confidence of most of the farming community. He wondered how no matter what time of the year it was Mr Skuy always managed his morning visit to Oogies. During the course of the afternoon I was quizzed about my future intentions and my wages etc.

I was taken on a tour of the farm which was about three times the size of the Ort farm, very spread out and took in a railway line, and the mine. One border was a main road and it did not have the appearance of a typical Highveld farm.

About two weeks later I received another visit from Ronnie. This time he made me an offer and, if I accepted, I could start at the end of the month. I told my family and none of them were very enthusiastic about me moving, and the Ort management said that I had a contract with them. The Skuys were indifferent and said that it was up to me. I felt that they were thinking more of their impending retirement than of me, or anything else. I eventually accepted and agreed to leave at the end of the month. The rest of my stay at the Ort farm was in near silence.

The Minaar farm had several houses considered to be suitable houses for Whites to live in. Alongside Ronnie's house was a house that I was to inhabit on my own and on the other side of the railway line were several houses occupied by the White foreman, the White mechanic and other White families who were simply tenants. There was another slightly run down White style house but occupied by the Black Clerk, a retired schoolteacher.

On the last day of October Ronnie came over to collect my belongings and me. On my first weekend I got a lift to Johburg with a middle-aged Jewish bachelor who, during the week, managed one of the Jewish owned trading stores and returned to Johannesburg every weekend. I spent most of the weekend trying to explain to my family what I was about and why I had decided not to continue on the Ort farm. The reason I put forward was that I would learn more about modern and business farming and I was going to be paid a wage of twenty pounds a month with free board and lodging. I did not tell them, but I doubt if I realised it myself, I had had enough of the atmosphere with the Skuys and the continuous conflict with the Hachsharaniks.

The main produce of Minaar was potatoes, mealies, sunflowers and, to a far lesser extent, cattle. During the late winter and early spring the potatoes were still being harvested and two or three mornings a week the big farm truck would make the journey driven by an African who was one of the local tribal chiefs to the Johannesburg market.

The potato truck usually completed its delivery by eight in the morning. The road out of Johannesburg passed nearby to where my eldest sister lived and where the rest of my belongings were including my bicycle. I arranged for the truck to collect me and, to my surprise Ronnie was driving. I never found out why he decided on that particular day to deliver the potatoes himself. I loaded my bicycle on the back which was covered with a canvas canopy supported by a light metal frame. The two African workers climbed into the back and sat with their backs to the driver's cab. My suitcases and bicycle were placed alongside them.

Ronnie's elderly parents lived in Oogies in an old Boer styled house. The walls and roof were made of corrugated zinc and had a large veranda. The inner walls of the house were wooden lined and had been covered with endless layers of varnish. We called there first and I was introduced to his parents. Ronnie's elderly father had arrived in Johannesburg from Eastern Europe in his late teens. He was one member of a Jewish Lads Brigade that volunteered to fight on the Boer side then later fought on the British side. His first language was Yiddish and he still spoke English or Afrikaans with a heavy accent. After having a cup of coffee we then drove onto Minaar.

As we approached the railway line Ronnie decided to first attend to something in the compound. (The compound was what the African workers' living quarters were called). To get there we had drive through the old coal mine loading shafts of which there were two. When we got to the compound, Ronnie found some things not to his liking and became irritated in the tractors shed he found that one of the tractors had broken down and was not working and the White mechanic was not around. Ronnie jumped into the cab, drove off in a hurry under the inner shaft. No sooner had the cab of the lorry passed through when there was mighty crashing sound and the back of the lorry shuddered as the sound of crashing metal continued, then a second of silence and then a scream. Ronnie braked hard and then shouted, "Shit! I forgot about the canopy." We jumped out of the cab and saw parts of the shaft on top of the lorry. We saw that the sharp end of the shaft, from where the coal falls, was resting on the floor of lorry facing the driver's cab. There was a further heap of metal on the crushed canvas. From under the mass of steel one of the Africans crawled out but we could not see the other person, though we could hear his screams. There was no way we could get to him without shifting the steel debris. Ronnie told me to go back to the compound and get help.

The workers who were working in the potato-sorting shed had heard the sound of the crash and as I ran toward the shed they all came running out I shouted, "*Buyanii, boya, boya*!"(Hurry, come quick). They followed in total silence and when they saw what had happened, all somehow knew what to do and with the minimum of instructions set about lifting the metal. The trapped person then became silent and we all feared the worst. I can still see the deep look of concern on all the faces of the men who rushed to the scene of the accident. There were at least fifty men and so it was not long before bits of the metal were lifted skilfully and gently off the truck. The problem was how much more of the shaft was going to fall down. Once we could get into the back of the lorry safely, we saw that the bottom end of the shaft had hit the floor of the truck and slid toward the cab pinning Simon against the cab. The end of the shaft was lodged partly in his chest and partly under his armpit. My bicycle was crushed against his legs. They managed to lift the shaft sufficiently to ease Simon without causing him any more injury. Once the lorry and everybody was at safe distance the rest of the shaft was pulled down with the aid of some rope. In the meantime Ronnie, who had realised that it was his haste and temper that had caused the accident, immediately went to collect his own car and drove Simon off to hospital.

A few days later Ronnie sent me to visit Simon in the hospital. He had sustained a broken collar bone and needed lots of stitches. The hospitals were totally segregated and it was the first time that I had been into hospital for Non-Whites. The Hospital was situated outside of the town of Witbank, whereas the hospital for whites was conveniently located near the centre of the town. The hospital was a single storey red brick building with open verandas. Once inside, I immediately noticed how basic and sparse everything seemed compared to that of the White hospital that I had visited in Johannesburg. I felt very self-conscious as, apart from the odd doctor, I was the only white face about. Once inside Simon's ward, I felt dozens of pairs of eyes staring at me and that the patients were all talking about me. The walls of the ward were painted brick, the steel-framed beds had very thin mattresses and all the blankets were grey or brown. Some of the beds did not appear to have sheets on. All the patients were wearing long pyjama style nightdresses. I went up to Simon's bed and spoke to him. I was not sure whether or not he was pleased or embarrassed at my presence. After a few minutes of small talk the ward nurse told us that he could go home in few days time. As I walked over to the car park, I once again felt that everyone was looking at me.

After my first week at Minaar my romance with farming began to waver. The Ort Farm had a calm, slow atmosphere that I had associated with farming, Minaar seemed busy and impersonal. The house that I lived in was only about a hundred yards from the railway line and all day and most of night the sound of steam engines could be heard. In the early hours of the morning the first engine at a nearby shunting yard could be heard firing up. Lorries and cars kept going backwards and forwards to the local station as well as the comings and goings of the tenants and the Africans who live in the Hostels and compounds. The types of building such as barns, sheds, and dairy and animal pens were not located centrally and were visible or within easy reach of the house. My house would have been more at home in a Johannesburg suburb than on the Highveld.

The days when I could sit on a tractor and plough were now over as there were tractor drivers employed to do that. I was taken out in the farm pickup truck to whichever land was been worked and my job, at that time, was to stand all day in the field and supervise the work force. I stood most days in the field with Tekwan (the nickname given to the White Afrikaans foreman who was tall and thin and always wore a broad brimmed felt hat). Right from the beginning, to Tekwan, I was someone who would be soon gone, and Ronnie the boss who paid his wages. I stood many hours in the hot sun in conversation with Tekwan. One thing that I learnt from him was that someone who drove a steam engine could consider himself to be a real man.

If I did not go out to the field with the truck I would go out on horseback. My horse was brought to me all saddled and ready. The African workers were driven out to the field either on a trailer pulled by a tractor or at the back of the farm lorry when it was not being used to deliver farm produce. Often the trailer would be hitched to the back of the lorry, and the trailer and back of the lorry would be jam-packed with workers so as to avoid more than one journey. Occasionally I would drive the truck then offload the workers and return the empty truck to the compound and then ride out on my horse.

Once all the potatoes had been harvested fields were being prepared for next year's crop and the maize was being planted. Once the first spring rains had fallen, the maize seedlings grew up rather quickly and no sooner had the rows of green seedlings become obvious than myriad indigenous plants commonly referred to as weeds challenged the growth of the maize seedlings. The tractor with a mechanical hoe could remove the weeds in spaces between the rows of seedlings. The weeds that grew in the actual rows had to be removed by hand hoeing. No chemical herbicides were used on the Highveld farms in those days. If herbicides had been used the huge 'cheap' labour force would have been rendered unemployed. The average wage in those days was nine pence (pre-decimal) a day. The workday began at six in the morning and ended at six in the evening. There was a break for breakfast and an hour lunch break. Food was brought out which consisted of dry mealie pap (porridge) some form of vegetable stew and on three days meat (mostly offal) was included. A very cheap brand of coffee was provided. In addition, there was a large drum of drinking water. The only toilet facilities were the bush; the older women who wore long dresses would simply squat down and spread their dresses round them. I would ride back to the farm house for my breakfast or it would be brought out to me, but I always went back for a sit down midday meal.

Tekwan, the Black foremen (known as Bossboys) and I had to walk behind the workers and see that all the weeds were removed and make certain that they were working all the time. In some of the fields the rows were almost a quarter of a mile long. The work was piecework. They were paid per row and one of the Bossboys kept note of the number of rows they completed. I was supposed to check that the Bossboys were not cheating. This was not the type of farming that I had dreamed of. As midsummer approached and the daytime temperature increased, my disillusionment increased but I had made the choice against the advice of others so I had to bear it.

About mid-morning and mid-afternoon a steam driven passenger train from Johannesburg on the way to the eastern Transvaal would pass through the farm. As the railway line bisected the farm if the train could not be seen, it could be heard. At the first sound of the train all workers stopped, cheered and waved. It was a means of knowing what time of day it was. They all yelled "humba ma bomba" (go train) and I wondered what other meanings they associated with the train.

An old man, who any in other society would have been enjoying his retirement always wore an old leather jacket and a big black hat. He had a big round face with a small greybeard and very blood shot eyes. I was standing near him when the morning train passed and after all the usual cheers had subsided he looked up leaned on his hoe and in a deep quiet voice waved and said "humba ma bomba". Those were the only words I ever heard him say.

At the beginning of December Ronnie and his family went to Johannesburg and when he returned on Monday he behaved very differently. He was extremely restless and verbally aggressive. Tekwan assured me that every now and again he had sudden bouts of what he called 'madness' and you had to keep out of his way and your head low till it wore off. During those spells nothing would be right. It was a side of Ronnie that I had not expected and it set alarm bells ringing about my future.

About ten days before Christmas Ronnie went to Johannesburg for a doctor's appointment. He phoned that night and asked me to send, the next day, a live turkey to Johannesburg which would be collected at the station. He said to put it in sealed cardboard box and to make certain that there were breathing holes, and label it live poultry. I was told to put it on the morning train but to make certain that I personally gave it to train guard. I went to the station with the package and showed the stationmaster what I had done, and he approved and I paid the freight charges. Once the train arrived I handed my parcel to the White Afrikaans guard and told him what was in the box and that it would be collected at Johannesburg. I phoned Ronnie and told him that the turkey was on its way.

At seven o'clock that evening Ronnie phoned. I expected to hear that I had chosen a nice fat turkey etc. instead I had my ear holes blasted to kingdom come. Apparently the guard had placed my parcel with the live turkey in an ice-cooled box and when it arrived it was placed in a fridge on Johannesburg station. By the time the person arrived to collect it, one of station officials had somehow found the box, read the label 'live poultry' and opened it to find a half frozen dying turkey in the box. He immediately called the SPCA and a huge inquiry was set in motion and we were being threatened with prosecution. Ronnie called me everything under the sun and I spent the rest of the night reliving the whole episode and wondering what I had done wrong and what effect it would have upon my future.

Three days before Christmas we had had a heavy thunderstorm during the night and the all the soil was wet and muddy. Once the farm roads were wet, the lorry and tractor wheels either slipped over the surface or became bogged down. I was driving the lorry and trailer loaded with workers. The approach to the field was on a slight slope but I had to take a sharp bend before reaching the field. As the lorry moved down, I felt the back wheels sliding and the slightest touch of the brakes initiated a skid. Somehow when I reached the bend the lorry obeyed the steering wheel. The trailer just swung round after us but also stayed on the road. There were squeals and yells mainly from the female passengers as I brought the vehicle to a halt. As they all climbed off the back some looked at me as if I had deliberately frightened them.

They finished hoeing the field in the early afternoon and Ronnie had told me to let them have the afternoon off in preparation for Christmas. I was sent out with the lorry and trailer to collect all the workers. The idea of a free afternoon and the closeness to Christmas had generated an almost carnival atmosphere. As soon as I stopped they all rushed to climb on the lorry and trailer. No one wanted to wait for the second collection. Everyone somehow clambered on and they stood on the trailer and lorry to make as much room for each other as possible. There were three in the cab, and at least two standing on each running board holding on to the doors.

The vehicle strained to move but I eventually began to drive up toward the farmhouse, which was on the highest part of the estate. When we passed by the house they all cheered and I turned to cross over the railway line. The road sloped down toward the railway track and the lorry began to pick up speed. It was an unmanned level crossing and nothing to indicate an approaching train. There was still two hundred yards to go before reaching the railway track. I looked up and I could see a speeding steam engine pulling a goods train. My instinct was to put my foot on the breaks but the pedal simply went down without any resistance and no effect. I started to pump the breaks but still no effect. I also knew that the hand break had not been functional for quite some time. One cab passenger said to me in Afrikaans " *Baas daar kom die trein*" (Boss there comes the train). I managed to drop a gear but pressing the clutch pedal increased our speed and I did not dare do that again. I now realised that we would reach the level crossing exactly the same time as the train. I think the train driver also realised that and blew his whistle as loud as he could. Once more there were cries from in the cab about the train. There was no way I could stop the lorry and we were seconds away from a collision. It must have been out of a pure survival instinct that I stayed calm and kept thinking what to do. Running parallel to the railway and our left was a soft sand track with a slight slope up to the rail track. I turned the lorry left into the sand and miraculously the trailer followed the line of the lorry. The sand slowed us right down as the train sped past us with the driver leaning out of the cab cursing and shaking his fist at us. Once we were on the sand with the lorry stopped, I heard the yells of fear from the passengers who then all jumped off. Those in the cab had grasped what had happened and, like me, sat in silence, then thanked me. After about twenty seconds of calm I jumped out of the cab to check that all was well. All I saw was numerous smiling faces who decided to walk the remaining few hundred yards to the drop off point. Once outside after a drained feeling of relief, a mixture of anger and fear crept over me and I began to curse Ronnie and the mechanic for having let me drive a vehicle which they knew had no hand brake and now all the brakes had failed. I walked away and began to tremble with fear and anger at the thought of what might have happened and that I was nearly responsible for a disaster. Neither Ronnie nor the mechanic was about so I was never able to let off steam at them. About fifteen minutes later I returned to the lorry and drove it off the shed. That night and for many nights afterwards I was haunted by the sight of the approaching locomotive.

Christmas was quiet and still and a chance for me to relax. Ronnie had decided to visit relatives in Johannesburg and I had the place to myself. In the cool of the evening I sat on the stoep and could hear the sounds of celebrations coming from the compound and the African living quarters. No doubt they were drinking native beer, which we considered something very distasteful. They referred to the drink as 'kaffir beer.' On Boxing Day one of my sisters and mother came out to see me and actually spent a night in my house. I felt that they, like me, were disappointed in the non-farm like appearance of Minaar and kept asking where was the milking shed, the barns, the tractor sheds, etc.

The farm started to work again two days after Christmas. I received a phone call the night before the return to work that Ronnie was going to stay in Johburg until after New Years Day. The telephone was a party line and all those on the line had a special ring. Whenever you wanted to make a call you turned a handle and the ring, apart from being heard in the exchange, was also heard by everyone else on the line. Likewise when you phoned, everybody could hear the ring of your phone and if they were so inclined could actually listen to your conversation. Somehow your coded ring became imprinted in your brain so that once the phone rang you only heard your ring. During the night only your ring ever woke you up. It was about ten at night and I had just climbed into bed when Ronnie phoned to say that he was not well. He did not give me instructions and took it for granted that everyone knew what to do. Luckily, at that time of year the main farming activity was weeding. There were some fields that still had to be ploughed to be ready for the planting of grass for cattle feed and all the usual mechanical maintenance.

Somehow the farm seemed to be part of a great big living organism that knew what it was doing. I just drove to where the workers assembled and they and the transport were all waiting with everything in its place and no questions were asked, and no one even noticed that Ronnie was not around. I drove round the farm before breakfast to see that what should be happening was. Later about mid-morning Tekwan casually asked if Ronnie would be back after New Years Day. It had all happened before. By the end of the day there were no problems.

At about eleven pm on New Years Day the phone woke me up and it was Ronnie's wife telling me that he was ill and would not be back for at least a week. The next morning I found everyone waiting for instructions and they were all expecting to see Ronnie. Once I informed them that he would not be there that day, they waited for instructions from me. One of the senior boss boys told me which field they had last worked was now finished and he suggested to me what to do next which I immediately implemented.

After breakfast, the reality of being in charge of a medium sized farm with a few hundred workers came to me with a suddenness that I had not expected. As I walked out of the back door, there was a queue of people telling me that they needed this and that or wanting information or that their child was ill and so on. I drove into Oogies with a list and in every establishment that I went into from the butcher to the supplier of agricultural bits and pieces knew what I had come for and also showed no surprise about the fact that Ronnie was ill. Once back on the farm, I drove round to check on all the activities. It seemed a bit of a relief not be standing in a field with Tekwan. Being the end of the month, it was also payday and the next day two of the White directors of the Farm Company came from Johannesburg with a bag full of cash. The Black accountant known as Mebalion (the one who counts) and who used to be a schoolteacher duly arrived at the house with all the paperwork and the two directors took charge of the proceedings. The directors then hinted that they thought that Ronnie was going to be away at least a few weeks. I now had to face up to the fact that there I was approaching my eighteenth birthday and had been thrown into the deep end.

Ronnie rang me up that evening with a list of instructions. Each morning I had to deal with various demands and I found myself driving round the farm and backwards and forwards to Oogies. On that Saturday everything stopped at one-o-clock and the atmosphere changed from what to me was manic state to complete calmness. Everything seemed to be put to rest. After lunch I sat on the stoep and simply stared out at the veld and longed to walk to the dam on the Ort farm to once again indulge in that peacefulness.

Sunday morning was a chance to sleep late and not be disturbed so I thought. At seven in the morning there was loud knock on the back door. In a dream stance I opened the back door and there was one of the elderly African workers. He asked me to go with him as there was trouble in the compound. I dressed quickly, got out the pickup and we drove down to toward the compound. As we approached, it seemed as if the whole community was awake and were gathered into a large circle. I guessed that there must have been a fight as there was not much shouting but a lot of staring. If the fight were still in progress there would have been a lot of noise. I made way through to the centre and sitting in the middle was a young woman with a man on her lap who was only just conscious. I asked what was wrong and she moved his shirt back and revealed a three-inch stab wound in the upper left part of his chest. For a few moments I was speechless and then two thoughts crossed my mind. One was to call the police and the other to call an ambulance. It was early Sunday morning so both of those services were inaccessible, especially for Blacks. I decided then to call the police as they could probably arouse the ambulance service. Telephoning for the police would have meant going back to the house and then trying to contact the exchange, and the only one open early Sunday morning was at Witbank, twenty-five miles away. I turned to the person who had roused me and told him that I was going to Oogies to see if could fetch the police. I drove the two miles to the main road and then on to Oogies. About a mile down that road I noticed the police sergeant, the one I used to play tennis with, approaching on his motorbike with a sidecar attachment. In the sidecar was a Black constable. We both pulled up and then reversed toward each other. Before I could say anything he made it clear that he knew about the stabbing and was on his way. The bush telegraph seemed more efficient than the telephone service.

  Once back at the scene of the crime he walked up to victim looked at his wound and then shouted out in Afrikaans "Who did this?" Surprisingly, a stocky black woman in her middle thirties stepped out and said that she had. Before anything more was said the police sergeant slapped her face with such force that she took off and landed on her back. She got to her feet holding her bleeding mouth and then he asked her why she did it. She replied that she was the victim's wife and that she had caught him with the woman who was nursing him. There was an eerie silence that lasted for about half a minute and the sergeant went over to have another look at the wound. He turned to me and said that if I called an ambulance it would probably take the best part an hour to reach us if we were lucky, and he may not live that long. The best thing was for me to take him to hospital and then he would see to all that needed to be done. A group of onlookers helped the stabbed man, who was conscious, into the cab and his woman friend got in and sat next to him comforting him. Before we drove off the sergeant said to him in Afrikaans, "If you live then when you come out of hospital come to the station to make a statement."

Any sound or movement that he made while I was driving made me turn cold thinking that any moment I might have a dead person in the cab with me. Also, every time I glanced his way I could see the open wound revealing the inner flesh. We reached the Witbank Hospital for Non-Europeans, which in those days was what places for Blacks only were called, in about three- quarters of an hour. It was a relatively small cottage type of hospital, which seemed to be totally deserted. I wandered around the building and then found a Black male nurse who produced a wheelchair and we both helped the wounded man out of the cab and we wheeled him into casualty. The nurse then left, saying that he would try and rouse a doctor. Five minutes later a young, White male doctor appeared, had a quick look at the wound and said that he would have to take him to a theatre. He asked me, but not the girlfriend, to follow him.

Once he reached theatre, I was told that as no anaesthetist was available I was needed to help. The patient was lifted onto the operating table and tightly strapped down. The doctor, the nurse and I put on surgical aprons gloves and masks. The doctor said to me that if any time I felt ill or dizzy I was to go out and get some fresh air, then return as soon as possible as my assistance was needed. The nurse produced a set of sterile instruments and the doctor then using forceps, looked into the wound. As he lifted the serrated skin, a fountain of blood shot into the air. I ran straight out of the theatre onto the open veranda and, once I caught my breath again, I went back into the theatre. The doctor looked at me and said that it was not too bad as the knife had gone vertically between the skin and the ribs. The rib cage had not been pierced and it was simply a matter of stitching up the wound. All was done without any form of general or local anaesthetic and that is why the patient was strapped down. The procedure took about a half an hour and the doctor then invited me to join him in a morning cup of coffee. I was then told that the victim would be kept in hospital for few days providing no complications developed. I know that he made a full recovery but whether or not he went to the police station to make a statement I never found out.

That evening I received a telephone call from Ronnie's wife telling me that he was no better and that he would not be back for another week or two. The next morning once I reached the compound everyone was waiting for me to tell them what to do. With the help of one of the Boss boys I gave out instructions that no one queried and the farm set itself in motion. Tekwan stood back in a cynical silence and made no attempt to advise me. All he said was Ronnie got that madness again, which was overheard by some of the Boss boys who simply burst into laughter. I found out some time later that Ronnie had had a nervous breakdown before I arrived and that they all presumed that it had happened again.

Ronnie was away for two weeks and, during that time, I rushed about, backwards and forwards to Oogies and Witbank, around the farm and taking various workers to the local doctor for which I was later reprimanded. The directors of the company that owned the farm came out again to pay the workers. They were all on piecework and if they worked hard they could earn as much as two shillings a day. (The average was about nine pence) When a sixteen-year-old boy who had averaged about two shillings a day collected his month's wages, one of the directors turned to me asking how come he was allowed to earn so much.

After wage payout I took them on a tour of the farm. One of the tractor drivers had ploughed the wrong field and when I reprimanded him I was told by the director that I was not forceful enough. I should have shouted and even threatened to hit him in spite of the fact that he was about ten years older than me.

My days centred on being told about this and that problem. I would have to rush out to try and rectify the problem. On one occasion while driving across a patch of short grass I bent the front of the truck round a tree stump hidden by the grass. The mechanic and the blacksmith straightened out the bumper for me knowing that Ronnie would not be pleased. For the next two weeks, a day did not pass without a major or minor mishap. However, I managed to keep things going and any outsider would have thought that all was running like clockwork.

Ronnie's wife came back on her own for a few days, and somehow or other every person in the district knew. She did not want to be alone in her house, so I slept in the spare room. The next day, when I went to collect supplies, the men who worked in the butchery who were all bachelors made suggestive and teasing remarks about Ronnie's wife and me, who was seven months pregnant. I felt both annoyed and embarrassed. At that time, apart from my holiday at the Habonim camp, I had hardly even kissed a girl.

One evening there was a knock at my back door and there was one of the Afrikaners who rented one of our properties. He told me that he needed to go urgently to Oogies to collect something or other and that it would take him too long to cycle there. Without questioning him further, and much to the disgust of the kitchen 'girl' I got out the pick-up truck and was about to put his bike onto the back. He told me that it would not be necessary as he would only be about fifteen minutes and then would I bring him back. I agreed and drove to Oogies. Once we reached the village I expected him to direct me to a house. Instead he directed me to the only bar in the village, and invited me in for drink. I was furious at the thought that I had been tricked. He climbed out of the cab and with a big smile asked me again and then went straight into the bar, which was an old corrugated tin building, turning to grin at me. I drove back to the farm, furious with both him and myself for being tricked. By the time I reached the farm, I began to worry about how he was going to get back. Once back at the farm, I picked up his bike put it on the back of the pickup and drove back to Oogies, drove up to the bar, threw his bike on the steps and drove off. I felt as though the whole village was staring and laughing at me. Back at the farm, the servants did not speak but the looks on their faces loudly said "You will learn".

A week later, Ronnie arrived back at about midmorning. I drove to the farmhouse to greet him. I was looking forward to seeing him and handing back control to him. His first words to me were a string of questions about what was going on and why had I allowed this and that to happen, and a then string of criticisms and rebukes. I felt totally deflated and drove off to a field that was being weeded on that day. Tekwan sensed what had happened and said 'nothing changes'.

On my eighteenth birthday, I drove off in the farm truck to Witbank to take my driving test. I passed and was now in possession of a heavy vehicle driving licence. However, it did not impress Ronnie who, a few days later, dispatched one of the Africans to take his test. He failed because, although his driving was adequate, he could not read and write.

The atmosphere between Ronnie and myself slowly deteriorated and hardly a day went by without me receiving a rebuke. At least once a week a commercial representative would call at the farm trying to sell something or other, and they usually had a meal with us. One evening, after dinner, Ronnie called me into his office to tell me of his dissatisfaction with my work. Once the rebuke was over, I asked when could I leave and his reply was, "now." I agreed and he wrote out a cheque for my wages, I walked back to the dining room and asked the rep if he would give me a lift to Johannesburg. I then packed what belongings I could into a suitcase and then left, never to return again.

Chapter 24

Over the next few days, I was preoccupied with explaining my point of view to my family. Although they never said it to me they assumed that I had been sacked. They all now thought that I was on slippery slope career wise, thoughts that never left them for the next twenty years.

I vacillated between each sister's house, spending a few nights at a time while desperately writing off for jobs. After two weeks, with no replies and no offers, I began to worry. Although my family uttered no comments to me, I felt increasingly close to the scrap heap. I had time to think and I decided that I wanted to travel abroad, work my way round England, Europe and perhaps even North America. I visited the offices of the Union Castle Shipping Line Company and found out that the cheapest fare from Cape Town to Southampton was sixty pounds. They told me that a five-pound deposit would reserve me a place on the Carnarvon Castle sailing to England in September of that year. I could pay monthly provided that the full fare was paid at least four weeks before the date of departure. I went to the nearest post office and drew out five pounds. Apart from the next few months my future was now mapped out. I had to find a job for the next seven months; the departure date seemed ages away. Strangely enough, at that time, the one person who was totally supportive of me going abroad was my mother.

I bought a copy of the 'Farmers Weekly', read the advertisements, and then applied for jobs. In my best handwriting I carefully wrote applications in a format that I had been taught at school. After series of negative or no replies, I got nervous about my future prospects. I began to look through the advertisements in the Johannesburg 'Evening Star'. After a few phone calls, one company invited me to an interview for a post as an 'Office Junior.' They asked me about my previous job. I then spent about ten minutes telling them about my love for farming and that I wanted to eventually study agriculture. They listened politely and then shook hands with me, admiring my enthusiasm and honesty, and then told me that they did not have a job for me.

I received a message via an intermediary that Mr Bornstein, one of the directors of the Ort farm, wanted to see me. I had to phone him and make an appointment at his Johannesburg Office. He was the owner of a company called E-Trading - a wholesale textile company in the middle of Johannesburg. On my way to the appointment I thought that I was going to be told off about my attitude and lack of gratitude to the Ort Oze, etc.

The E-Trading was housed in an opulent building, with an imposing entrance guarded by two concrete elephant heads. Once up the steps and through the entrance you entered a large hall with a large wooden counter that stretched round the perimeter of the hall. Behind the counter there were miles and miles of rolled fabric. As I entered I saw Mr Bornstein without a jacket, wearing a white shirt was leaning on the counter. He greeted me and introduced me to a group of men who were standing by, then he called me aside and we moved away from the group. He told me that he knew that I was unemployed and he also had heard that I planned to go abroad. I was amazed at how quickly the news got around. He asked me what I planned to do for the next seven months, and was I interested in a job if he offered me one. I expected the job offer to be as a temporary office boy in his company. I made my mind up that if the wages offered were reasonable I would accept.

To my surprise, he asked if I would like to work on a farm. He told me that he lived on a smallholding of about ten acres on outskirts of Johannesburg, and that the farm was his wife's hobby and she needed some help. If I was interested he would arrange for me to see the place. I said that I might be and he immediately phoned his wife and arranged for her to collect me that afternoon.

Mr and Mrs Bornstein were both born in Russia and had arrived in South Africa as refugees during the thirties. They spoke English with mild but noticeable East European accents. They were now very wealthy by any standards and definitely were part of the White Jewish upper class. Mrs Bornstein, whose name was Clorina, had the airs of someone indulged in 'culture.' To the Whites, culture meant assuming knowledge and appreciation of European music, art and literature and knowing about the origins of the Impressionists and an appreciation of modern art. The only aspect of indigenous art appreciated by the Whites was the Bushman cave paintings and native woodcarvings.

Clorina collected me in her latest Citroen saloon, the first of the generation of Citroens that had a 'boot' and was definitely 'non-you.' As soon I was in the car she started to speak to me as if she had always known me and, more important, knew a lot about me. I did not feel relaxed, a feeling that remained with me throughout the rest of the time that I dealt with her. We drove due North down Oxford Road, a broad highway that passed through the rich White suburbs of Houghton Rosebank and Dunkeld. We drove down that road way beyond where I had ever been before. Once you passed the trolley-bus terminus, the municipal boundaries of Johannesburg ended. The houses were now fewer and more spread out. Most had a third of an acre of ground. Gradually there were more and more open fields and fewer houses.

We were now in Inanda, the home of the Polo set. We passed by large mansions surrounded by large gardens and also Marist Bothers' Inanda - a large rich Roman Catholic Boys' school. Once we passed the school, we turned and drove down a sand road for about a hundred yards and passed through some very grand gates. Written into the wrought iron arch above the gates were the words Tavrig, the name of the Estate. As we drove in, immediately on our left were poultry sheds and on our right tall pine trees masking some other sheds. Once past the poultry sheds, the drive led up to the garage and the back entrance to the mansion. However we continued along the drive, which appeared to bisect the property, to a parking bay. Once I stepped out of the car, the full sight of the estate made me breathless. The property sloped gently down from the main road toward a shallow valley. Above the car park the grounds were terraced, and on the top terrace was a two-storey white mansion built in the Cape Dutch style with a gable above a grand entrance.

Most of the houses in Johannesburg were bungalow style and had only one storey, only the rich lived in a two-storey house. The upper room, below the gable, opened onto a large balcony. Underneath the balcony there was a playroom with large windows that opened onto a patio. Lawns, flowerbeds and ponds were all round the front and one side. On the opposite side of the mansion the drive led to the garage and servants quarters and a small flat.

Once I stepped out of the car three Collies greeted us. The largest was a young black and white male dog called Pookie. His mother and his limping grandmother, both with brown sable coats, followed him. Pookie leaped up on me, placed his front paws on my shoulders and began to lick my face, a greeting that I did not appreciate. Once the dogs had calmed down we walked up the terrace toward the house. Apart from the main front entrance there were two side entrances, one leading into the spacious living room and the other into the dining area.

Out of a side entrance emerged a Black housemaid wearing the standard light blue frock covered with a spotless white apron. Mrs Bornstein greeted her then inquired if all was well. Next came the waiter/butler wearing a white linen-type suit. He greeted us with a broad smile and wanted to know if we wanted tea and where to serve it. Before we went into the house I was shown the two-bedroom flat built at the back of the mansion. I was told, with regret, that a bachelor friend of the family, short of accommodation, had moved in on a temporary basis but was now thinking of making it a permanent home. The result was that, with regret, if I was to take up the job offer that flat was not available to me. There was a possibility that a room attached to the flat that was used to groom the dogs could be converted into a living accommodation for me.

I was taken on a tour of the house, shown the spacious downstairs with its large lounge, dinning room, playroom, bar and cocktail room, and small library. Apart from the expensive furnishings, the walls were covered with original contemporary paintings and in every nook and cranny were various sized sculptures. On the upper floor were Mrs Bornstein's en-suite bedroom and the bedrooms belonging to each of their two sons with a bathroom between them. A guestroom was occupied by a friend of the family, Peter, who had remained permanently after a 'temporary' visit.

Then I was shown a large landing with an opening onto the fire escape. Leading off from the landing was a shower and toilet. There was room for a single bed and a wardrobe, and it could be partitioned off and made into a small bedroom. I was not shown that there was still another bedroom, which was just kept for visitors. She regretted very much but at present the landing space was all the living-in accommodation she could offer until the outside room was redecorated. That room was at present occupied by the dogs.

The walls of the stairs and the corridors were all lined with paintings and photographs. I followed around in silence, as this was the first time that I had ever been in such a large, luxurious, modern mansion. I could not help thinking about the flat at the top of the old house in Berea Road Bertrams where I had spent most of my school life and where my mother still lived.

A bell rang calling us to tea served on the terrace. In those days, tea in any White household meant an afternoon cup of tea and cakes served on plates with cake forks, etc. We sat on the terrace that apart from the roof of the mansion was the highest point of the estate. Mrs Bornstein began to point out various aspects of the estate to me. The opulence overwhelmed me and I only half listened to Mrs Bornstein's commentary.

Below the car park a central footpath led down into the shallow valley. On the right side of the path was the tennis court and below the tennis court the swimming pool, much larger than the average domestic pool. Below the pool, an orchard, then stables and further down leading down into the shallow valley two fields sown with hay. Along the left-hand side of the footpath were a series of terraced flower and vegetable beds reaching down to the lower fields.

Mrs Bornstein asked about my future plans and mentioned, in an understatement, that she knew that I had been 'fired' from my previous job. She then questioned me about my training on the Ort farm and told me that she was aware that I had planned to go abroad. The subject was treated like a dream that would never come true. She also knew about my background, that my father had walked out on my mother and me, and that I had left home and lived with a sister. She also hinted that she knew about the various misdemeanours my father had been involved in. I felt as if apart from being interviewed, I was also attending a therapy session. She was full of explanations and advice.

During the Fifties the Johannesburg Jews that regarded themselves as being cultured all claimed to have read Freud and Jung. Words like *gestalt* and ego were part of all analytical conversations. In most cases, they had only read paperback editions of psychoanalysis. Mrs Bornstein was no exception, and soon she was telling me about what had gone wrong in my life, and that I was not really to blame but that I had to know about it in order to progress. Finally she brought up the subject of employment. I was needed to help her manage the farm for which I would receive a small wage and free board and lodging, and I would live as part of the family. The room next to the flat would eventually be made available to me. If I was interested I could move in the over the weekend and then start work on the following Monday. Considering that I only really wanted it for the next six months, I decided that it was better than nothing. On the way back to Johannesburg, Mrs Bornstein told me that it was her ambition to try and grow mushrooms to add to her production of eggs, poultry and milk.

My family did not know what to think when I told them about my job offer. The fact that I was going to be living with one of the richest Johannesburg families impressed them, but there were no comments with regard to the nature of the work. I packed a suitcase full of clothes and some books, and on the Saturday morning Mrs Bornstein in her Citroen collected me.

The Bornstein family consisted of Mr and Mrs and their two sons Isaac and Sashi. A Rex Harrison look alike, John Hunter who had only recently migrated from England and worked as a financial journalist, occupied the flat. There was also Peter, the guest who had become a permanent lodger. He worked in the male fashion industry. Each family member had his or her own car as well as the motors belonging to John H and Peter. Mr Bornstein had a large American Packard Car, Sashi a Singer sports, Isaac a Peugeot and of course there was Mrs Bornsteins's Citroen.

Isaac and Sashi both had Bachelor of Commerce degrees from Witwatersrand (Wits) University. Isaac now worked in the family business but Sashi stayed on at University studying for a law degree. Sashi was in his early twenties. He was what I imagined a rich boy to be a good looking, suave and an all over air of self-confidence. More often than not he wore a blazer with a posh university badge, an open neck shirt with a neck cravat, and had an air of cultivated casualness about him. Isaac, during the week always wore a suit and behaved as if the future of the family fortune depended upon him.

After lunch, on my first Saturday, I was invited to sit on the terrace with the family, then introduced to each guest as they arrived. It was a hot, late February afternoon and, as always, my hands were perspiring and I tried my best to dry my hands before greeting each guest. I could see, as I had seen many times before, and I still see today, the look of almost disgust when they felt my sweaty hands. Their expressions made me want to take a step back and apologise. Inwardly I felt guilty for making them feel disgusted. I did not join in the conversation; I did not really know any of them.

Besides, what did I have in common with them? After all, this was a sample of Johannesburg's young high society. Mrs Bornstein sat among all, shiningly healthy like a Hollywood matriarch, whereas Mr Bornstein sat back elegantly grey and looking as if he would rather be somewhere else and hardly ever joined in the conversation.

During that afternoon the car park gradually filled up with young men and women most of them friends of the boys. Each of the two sons' girlfriends arrived in her own car.

It became obvious that, at weekends, Tavrig was an open house for an elite set or select circle. I was encouraged to join in and be part of the group. I was only eighteen at the time whereas most of those present, apart from the two girlfriends, were in their mid-twenties. They were nearly all newly qualified accountants, architects, lawyers, dentists, or they ran their own businesses. There were no scientists or university type academics. They all had, at some time or other, been overseas and had toured round Western Europe and stayed at ski resorts. The conversations centred round have you seen, have you heard, have you read, have you bought and have you heard about so and so. Frequently there were references to a trip overseas and they spoke about London, Paris, Rome and the main ski resorts with an enviable familiarity.

Every one had an opinion about human behaviour and on that subject Mrs Bornstein expressed some very forthright Freudian and Jungian type views. Often a long and, sometimes, heated debate followed. Every now and again some of those gathered would drift off for a game of tennis, or a swim, or a game of snooker and all the while the servants were providing sandwiches, cakes and non-alcoholic refreshments. Sashi and Isaac kept the alcohol flowing - those were long before the days of the Breathalyser.

All afternoon cars kept arriving and departing, some only staying for a short while. It was if everybody had to put in an appearance, pay their respects, and find out the latest social news and where those who mattered were going to spend that evening. The cinema (or bioscope as it was called in Johannesburg in those days) and dinner dance type nightclubs were the main form of entertainment. If the local symphony orchestra featuring a visiting soloist was performing, that was an occasion that you had to have a very good excuse not to attend.

Sunday followed the same pattern except that they began arriving at about eleven in the morning and kept on until well into the evening. Throughout both days, I waited to be invited into any conversation or to participate in a game of snooker or billiards but, once again, my sweaty hands showed me up. After every shot that I played I left behind on the green cloth damp fingerprints. Those who noticed it for the first time remarked but those who had already met me said nothing. I noticed that everybody looked rather apprehensive hoping that no damage was being done to the precious cloth.

Everyone spoke in what my friends and family would have described as a posh accent. I had just spent the best part of a year on the Highveld speaking either in Afrikaans or English to people whose first language was either Afrikaans or in a version of one of the African languages. I did my best to avoid eye contact with Mrs Bornstein who, I felt, was keeping a watchful eye on me and always ready to correct me. I was intimidated which shrunk my confidence. If any remark was directed to me that sounded like praise, it sent me into a state of a temporary high. On the surface everybody was very patronizing but I knew I had to mind myself. It was as if the time I spent with the Skuys on the Ort farm was a good preparation.

On my first Monday I found myself up at six a.m. as I had always done on both previous farms, and set about finding out what had to be done. I wandered around the estate but all the workers knew exactly what to do. I followed Willie, the Black foreman, around. The poultry was cared for, the Jersey cows were being milked, the four mules were fed and then put out to graze. Most of those tasks were accomplished before breakfast. The workers went off to their breakfast of mealie pap, bread, and coffee.

Johannes, a waiter dressed in white, summoned me by ringing a gong, to breakfast in the dining room. The Bornstein family (but not Clorina), John from the flat and Peter the permanent guest arrived at different times, and sat down at the dining table to be served. It was a breakfast served as if we were in a hotel - fruit juice, cereal, fried or boiled eggs, followed by either fried kippers or a fish kedri, or sausages and sometimes even a light steak. Always available were toast or bagels and coffee.

After breakfast I wandered around, again looking for what I should be doing next. Mrs Bornstein finally emerged about midmorning to tell me what she would like done. During our walk about, it also became clear to me that, as she told the servants and workers what to do, I had to oversee all the jobs. There were certain chores which we she and I were going to share such as delivering milk, eggs and flowers to a handful of customers that she had accumulated over the years.

Once she left me and returned indoors, I had a good look at the lower terraces. The skills I had learnt at Ort farm could now be put to good use. The beds planted with flowers desperately needed weeding. I decided to prepare some more beds for both vegetables and more flowers. The orchard needed pruning, and some of the old trees removed and replanted. The lower field used for growing hay and cattle feed was in the firm control of Willie. However, I encouraged him use the mules to plough over some of the fields so that fresh grass could be sown.

A mid-morning gong summoned me to morning coffee and sandwiches on the terrace with Mrs. Bornstein. I told her of my plans and ideas, but she reminded me of her desire to grow mushrooms. While drinking coffee, I listened to gossip and tales about the various weekend visitors (to whom I was not to say anything under any circumstances) and so on. Once we finished our coffee, Mrs Bornstein changed from very casual, into smart casual clothes and drove off to deliver our produce and do some of the shopping.

I set about digging up the terraces and could feel all the workers and servants watching me. There before their eyes was a young, White Jewish male actually digging without a Black worker at his side. There were no lorries, trucks or tractors to drive and no watching over workers, weeding, or harvesting. No people coming at me from all angles asking me for this and that or having to make decisions about which fields to send the tractors and so on. Everything was so laid back compared to what I experienced at Minaar. Life seemed almost horizontal. However, I knew that I could not drop my guard with Mrs Bornstein for one moment, as I was aware that I was totally under her control.

At midday I was called to lunch and at the table was Mrs Bornstein and a friend whom she had collected on her morning social calls. My afternoon work was interrupted by a call to afternoon tea on the terrace and my day finally ended between half five and six o'clock. After a shower and a change of clothes I joined the family for dinner. Apart from the occasional delivery or errand that day set the pattern for the remainder of my working days at Tavrig.

I was told that providing Sashi was not using his sports car, I could use it. Most evenings and weekends Sashi tended to use his mother's Citroen. The novelty of the sports car had worn off, hence there was nearly always a vehicle for me to use. Mrs Bornstein made it clear to me that going out more than once on weekday evenings was not good.

An evening seldom went by without a visitor and I was often called upon to make a foursome at snooker. The household had the latest type of radiogram that played the, then new, vinyl long playing records that spun at thirty-three and a third rpm. They had a large collection of both classical and jazz records, as well as all the recordings of the latest London and New York musicals. As nearly everyone who came to the house had visited England or America at some time or other, they often referred to a show or play or concert they had attended while overseas. If you returned home without visiting almost every West End theatre you could not consider yourself as having been abroad. In addition, you had to know precisely when you had visited all the famous tourist attractions. A photograph of yourself on a ski slope and feeding the pigeons in Trafalgar Square was almost as important as your passport.

Chapter 25

During those early months at Tavrig the fact that I had booked a passage to England was still in the realms of dreamland. In the early days at Tavrig, I did my best to look after the estate but I never felt that I had established any form of control. At the back of mind was the mushroom project. I visited all the local riding schools to try and obtain straw and horse manure only to discover that others had gotten there before me. That was the excuse I used for never actually growing mushrooms.

I also found myself doing what I had done at Minaar that is constantly going on shopping sprees to buy various goods necessary for the everyday running of the estate.

Three times a week a local physiotherapist would call to give Mrs Bornstein her morning massage. She always emerged in a slightly aggressive and bewildered mood. I would be told off for not doing this or that. During morning coffee, I would often be reprimanded for speaking out of turn at last night's social gathering. As the weeks went by I would tense up in her company.

Every six weeks or so, the members of the family would go away for long weekends or trips to their large estate in what was then Rhodesia (now Zimbabwe). Once Mrs Bornstein was out of the way, I could relax and enjoy both my work and the social scene.

Tavrig was on the outskirts of Johannesburg so I was able to re-establish contacts with old friends, particularly Simon and Lorna, the girl I had met while I was retaking my maths. Through her, I met up with Rhona whose father controlled one of the largest women's underwear factories in South Africa. I invited Rhona for a Sunday afternoon drive in Sashi's sports car. We were driving with the roof down on one of the north Johannesburg highways when the car broke down. While investigating the problem, with my head in the engine I could hear the mocking laughter of the passing motorists as they slowed down to avoid us. Rhona made me feel even more uncomfortable as she seemed to have joined in with the teasing. I managed to get the car going again and drove straight back to Tavrig. That weekend, with everyone away, I had the keys of more than one car at my disposal; hence I continued my afternoon drive in a Wolesley.

In her final matriculation year at school, Rhona invited me to her end of year school dance and after the dance, to accompany her to a twenty-first party at the very posh RAC club. I borrowed my brother-in-law's white tuxedo for the occasion and collected her in Sashi's car. While dancing with her in the school hall I felt that Rhona was not with me. After the dance we then drove off to the RAC club. At the club I met up with Lorna and Moira (another school friend). They were as pleased to see me as I was them. As the night wore on, I saw less and less of Rhona and eventually she called me aside and delivered a mental body blow. She told me that she did not want to be with me any more. She had been told that the only reason that I was friendly with her was because of her money, and I need not bother to see her home. I sat back in a state of sick anger, shock and hurt. After all, it was now only a matter of weeks before I was to leave the country. I kept wondering where and how and who had planted such an idea into her head.

Lorna and Moira saw me sitting by myself and came over. They did not have their own transport and were glad at my offer of a lift home. During the journey I told them what Rhona had said to me. Their reaction was one of disbelief. Knowing that the parents of both Lorna and Moira were millionaires, and that they shared my feelings, was very reassuring. They both new Rhona well and, unknown to me a few days later confronted her and insisted that she apologise to me. I never gave her the chance as I managed never to make contact with her again.

I was also able to see more of my family, particularly my mother. Although I never returned to stay with her at 21 Berea Road, Bertrams, the home I had left one evening only eighteen months ago. Every now and again, I would collect my mother in Sashi's car and take her to the pictures. I spent most of the time in her company with gritted teeth trying to avoid having a row with her. However, one aspect of my life she and I were in agreement on was my proposed trip overseas. She was very encouraging, even paid off the last three instalments of my ticket and bought me some new clothes. Nearly every member of my family and most of my friends did not hide a cautious attitude to the idea of me going abroad. As time moved on I acquired a passport, collected my travel documents and bought a single rail ticket from Johannesburg to Cape Town.

As those months went by, I met more and more of the up and coming rich Johannesburg Jewish set. Nearly all had been abroad, and had buckets full of advice about where to stay and what to do. However the old friend of the family, Mrs Davis, who had migrated from England to live in South Africa before the war gave me some of the best advice. She gave me the address of a government agency that dealt with farm camps in England. I wrote to the agency and they sent me addresses of various camps and booking forms which I carefully filled in and felt a little more reassured knowing, that within a week of my proposed arrival in London, I had a job to go to.

I arranged to continue working at Tavrig until the day of my departure. As time went, by I had established some vegetable beds, tidied up the flowerbeds, pruned the orchard and erected a few fences. My relationship with all of the Bornstein Household became very close, but it still did not stop me from watching my every step as far as Mrs Bornstein was concerned. Sometimes, I did actually feel part of the household if not the family.

The exception was Peter who hardly spoke to me and when he did it was as if I was a non-entity. One Sunday morning I had asked him to do something or other and he replied very abruptly, "I do not take orders from the servants," and stormed away. I was left breathless and went upstairs to my room fuming. I could not control myself and, about five minutes later, went downstairs and saw Peter standing in the living room talking to Mrs Bornstein, Sashi and friends. I was in such a rage I walked over to Peter and swung a punch at him calling out, "Who do you think you are calling a servant?" He retaliated and a fight started. All joined in to separate us and, eventually, we were both held apart each with a few facial bruises. Mrs Bornstein, to my surprise turned on Peter, yelled at him and immediately ordered him out of the room. As he rushed upstairs Peter shouted out, "Really Clorina, I expect better of you." They all held on to me until Peter was well out of reach and then calmed me down and offered me a brandy. As I calmed down I apologised to Mrs Bornstein and everyone else for my outburst. As the morning wore on, most who were present at the time agreed with me although they did not approve of brawling in a living room of a posh mansion. Peter was not seen again that day, and for the rest of my stay at Tavrig we managed to avoid each other's company. Someone always contrived to make certain that we were never left alone together in the building.

It was shortly after that episode that I collected my passport and my travel documents and bought my rail ticket from Johannesburg to Cape Town. I looked through those documents many times checking that I had the times and date correct. One thing that I did know about my future was that I did not have much money. I decided to call on a rich aunt and uncle on the pretence that I had come to say goodbye. My aunt who, herself, had never been abroad was half envious and half indifferent. The afternoon ended with her and me going around car show rooms. I had to listen to her trying to persuade the salesman to let her jump the queue to purchase a new car. At the end of the afternoon I reminded her that I had come to say goodbye and it might be a long time before we met again. Just before we parted she opened her handbag and gave me a pound note.

The visit to another uncle at his sewing machine shop a few days later not only produced no money but a polite rebuke. He told me in no uncertain terms that he would never allow either of his children to go abroad except on vacation. The conversation became political. I said that, as the matters stood, sooner or later there would have to be changes. He interrupted me over and over again and saying, "What do you mean the Blacks? Never in my lifetime! No, I can't see that. There is nothing to worry about. They will never take over… It is those like you, the 'communists,' who cause trouble." I left after a very subdued farewell, no richer than when I entered his shop.

My sister and her husband temporarily moved in with my elder sister. I was invited over to a farewell dinner on the last Saturday before my departure. The evening started well but half-way through the meal, my eldest sister and her husband (my brother-in-law) started sending out signals of disapproval about me going away. I was extremely hyped up facing my last few days in South Africa and any adverse comments stung me. As the evening wore on my self-control snapped and I stormed out of the meal.

At last, Wednesday, 5th September 1954 dawned. Mr and Mrs Bornstein were away on a vacation, and they had said their farewells before they left. Sashi had offered to take me and my luggage (two suitcases) to the station in time for my 8.00 pm departure. I tried to treat the day as a normal working day. However while making deliveries, the vehicle I was using broke down. After a few desperate phone calls I eventually got back to Tavrig. One of our Jersey cows managed to get into the vegetable beds and almost destroyed months of hard work. About an hour before Sashi arrived with his girlfriend to take me to the station Willie, informed me that the mules had escaped. It was now almost dark and finding them was not going to be easy. Just as Willie left the room the phone rang. It was an angry neighbour informing me that the mules were slowly destroying her front garden.

Sashi arrived to collect me and assured me that there was nothing more that I could do and, whatever the consequences of that day's event were, they were no longer my problems. I tried my best to hide my anxiety, constantly going over in my mind whether or not I had done everything, and kept thinking about the mules and what Mrs Bornstein was going to say when she returned.

The train journey to Cape Town would take two nights and a day; hence it was necessary to have reserved your seat in advance so as to be certain to have a compartment with a sleeping bunk. On the outside of each carriage was posted a list of the names of the passengers and in what compartment each passenger had been allocated. The train was already in the station when we arrived. Finding my compartment was made easy by the fact that my mother and my cousin who had brought her were standing on the platform alongside the compartment where my name was posted.

Once I had packed my luggage safely into the compartment, I stepped out back onto the platform. By that time, on the platform were one of my sister's and her husband, Isaac Bornstein and his girlfriend and several Tavrig regulars.

I tried to mix with everyone, at the same time staying close to my mother and sister. I first went round and shook hands with everyone and said my farewells and, finally, mother who for the first time gave me long hug and was reluctant, much to my embarrassment, to let go. She could not hold back the tears as I stepped on board the train and went into the compartment to deposit the gifts that I had received. I leaned out of the window and my cousin was standing alongside my mother who held my hand and only let go once the train started moving. The waving continued until we were all out of sight. I sat down in the compartment and introduced myself to the three individuals with whom I was to share the space until the early hours of Friday morning.

It was dark as the train pulled out of Johannesburg. I reflected back on the last time I had been on such a train journey- to Habonim camp. I thought about the number of times I had travelled with my father on trains to fishing trips. A calm feeling came over me as if all the nervous energy of the last month drained away and I could feel my toes and fingertips tingle with relief.

The train stopped at Kimberly about six the next morning. I anxiously looked out the window onto the platform hoping that my Kimberly relatives had made the effort to come to see me, but alas not. Once the train left Kimberly the whole of that day's journey was through the Karroo, a semi-desert. Although an interesting and inspiring landscape, it did not seem to change. If you read or dozed off and looked out again you had to convince yourself that train had actually moved.

The train pulled into Cape Town station at about seven in the morning. As we approached the station, one of my fellow passengers pointed out to me the castle built by the early Dutch settlers. I had read about it and seen many pictures but now seeing the real thing was great. It was the first time that I had seen a real historical castle. In that early morning hour Cape Town was covered in cloud. I was not due on board the ship until about two that afternoon and now had time to kill. I left my luggage at the station and wandered out into the main street of Cape Town and found a café to have some breakfast.

I found the bus station and caught a bus to Sea Point, a bus ride recommended by one of my fellow rail companions. As the bus drove along, I was amazed at the sight of all the houses that crept up the lower slope of Table Mountain all facing the sea. The rows of streets that ran up vertically and ended where the mountain began captivated me. The clouds began to disperse and I saw, for the first time the full beauty of the mountain with its lush green slopes. I never had before seen grass so green nor had I seen such a high mountain. I kept looking at the sea, then the city, and trying my best to absorb it all hoping that I would not forget them. At the bus terminal, I sat on a bench for about half an hour staring at the waves and the rough sea, contemplating the fact that soon I would be sailing over it.

I kept checking on the time and soon returned to city centre, but it was still only about ten. I went to the main square and saw park squirrels for the first time, passed by the parliament building and then visited the museum. I remembered how one of my Afrikaans teachers had praised the museum and told us about the exhibits of the reconstruction of Hottentot and Bushman early life. The very life-like models had prompted him to tell us that we must, at sometime or other, see the 'stuffed Bushman and Hottentots' and as far as I can recall he really believed that they were once real humans.

I arrived at the docks by taxi about three hours before we were due to sail. In the dock was the Canarvon Castle waiting to receive its passengers - my home for the next two weeks. I showed my ticket to a steward at the bottom of the gangplank and, once on board the ship, the crew greeted me and addressed me as Mister and/or Sir. That was the first time that I had been addressed in such a manner and I felt both important and embarrassed. I was guided to my cabin in the depths of the ship. It was a cabin for four and all three of my cabin mates were already stretched out on their bunks very relaxed and indifferent as they had been through this all before. I unpacked some of my belongings and then found my way through a multitude of corridors to the upper deck.

I stood looking, from what seemed to be a great height, down on to the dockside. A crowd was slowly gathering to bid farewell to loved ones, relatives and friends. I kept looking, hoping that my cousins who lived in Cape Town had come to the dockside. As the time of departure approached more and more people assembled on the deck, greeting and waving to those they left behind on the dockside. I noticed that among all the white passengers was one black man. At last; now I could look forward to the end of Apartheid, or so I thought. I could not but wonder how he was feeling suddenly finding himself to be in a minority among people who, in their lives, had been indoctrinated to regard the non-Whites as second-class citizens.

It was now the afternoon of Friday, the 7th September 1954. Standing next to me, leaning on the rails, was young coloured (mixed race) lad who was probably my age. He looked down silently toward the dockside. I plucked up courage and asked him whether he knew anyone looking up at the ship. He replied that his whole family were down there and pointed them out to me. There they were, in the true South African tradition of that era, standing on the side and slightly apart from the rest of the White crowd. I thought carefully about what I said, worrying and hoping that I was not indicating my unease about being in a position where a Non-White was my equal.

About fifteen minutes before sailing, a band on the dockside started to play and that was a signal for streamers to be thrown down by the passengers onto the dockside. The gangplank was drawn up and the ship's sirens and horns let out a series of loud blasts. The tugs replied, and then there was a flurry of activity both on board and on the dockside. Mooring ropes were untied and the gap between the ship and the quayside started to grow as the ship was eased out into the harbour.

I looked up and saw the top of Table Mountain slowly being covered by clouds which the locals called the 'Table Cloth.' I was slowly leaving South Africa and now starting a journey to a New World. Mrs Bornstein had said to me that the moment I leave I will be starting a new life. Like the moments when the train began to pull out of Johannesburg station I felt calm and a state of relaxation crept over me. I stared out toward the magnificent scenery and hoped that I had absorbed it all and would always remember it.

As the ship was making its way out of the harbour, the new passengers started to move around and many of them strolled about with confidence. I was still at the rails and I noticed the African man dressed in his smart suit standing by himself. I turned to the coloured lad next to me and, by now, we were talking to each other. I drew his attention to the lonely black male whom I referred to as an African. He snapped back at me and said, "Are you talking about that Kaffir?"

Part 2

Living In London during the Fifties

Chapter 1

I arrived at Southampton in September 1954 after a two-week voyage from Cape Town. I was aged eighteen. A steam train delivered my fellow passengers and me to Waterloo station about mid morning. I deposited my cases in the left luggage and walked to the main station exit. In my mind I was still at Park Station Johannesburg, where once you left the main exit you stepped out into Eloff Street, the main street of central Johannesburg. From that point you could travel to anywhere in the city. I thought that, once out of the station, it would be an easy walk to South Africa House, which I knew was located at Trafalgar Square.

What a shock! In front an endless line of black taxis, further out the Thames, a bridge, noise - nothing I could relate to. One deep gasp and I turned straight back into the station concourse. Near the left luggage counter I bumped into a fellow passenger, a male nurse, who I had become quite friendly with during the latter part of the sea voyage. He, like me, was on his way to South Africa House. After an enquiry we caught the Bakerloo Line to Trafalgar Square and went to register at South Africa House. While we were looking at a notice board for lodgings, the doorman slid up to our side. He whispered to us that he knew of a very nice place in Clapham. He gave us the phone number and English pennies to make the appropriate phone call, then informed us on how to use the public phone, that is, when to press button A or B.

My friend made the call and was given the instructions on how to get to our newly acquired lodgings. We went back to Waterloo station to collect our luggage then returned to Trafalgar Square to start our bus journey to Clapham. After about five minutes, the bus conductor approached us for our fare. When we told him where we were going he informed us, very loudly, that we were travelling in the wrong direction. Hot, bothered, embarrassed and red-faced we scrambled off with our luggage and duly crossed the road to the nearest bus stop. This time, before boarding, we asked the conductor if we were on the correct route. After two bus changes we arrived at our digs, an address facing Clapham Common.

Sitting on the upper deck of the bus looking out onto a foreign landscape was an amazing feeling. My first time abroad, travelling along streets that were so totally different to what I knew, yet it was also strangely familiar via British films. We could read all the signs on shops, buildings, and street vans. Here we were looking out at a semi-foreign country that was both familiar and unfamiliar. After all we had been brought up in an Anglo-Saxon environment.

There were taxis, commercial vehicles and lots of small to medium sized black cars. Tankers delivering beer from the breweries, coal trucks and peculiar three-wheeled, articulated lorries belonging to British Railways and British Road Services. Once the bus crossed the river we passed through what seemed to us to be Dickensian Battersea. We saw lots of two and three storeyed buildings, houses all blackened by decades of deposits from coal fires, rows of houses with their front doors opening straight onto the streets. Did any house have a garden, and if so, where were they? It did not occur to us that there might be some gardens at the back of the houses.

Many of the road surfaces in that part of South London were still made up of tar blocks and cobbles. A program of road resurfacing was in progress. We saw, much to our amazement, people using old prams or any type of handcart, desperately collecting tar blocks as many and as quickly as possible. It reminded us of what we had, on the odd occasion, seen in the black townships outside of Johannesburg.

My first week in London

At our digs our landlady politely showed us to our room and, for the first of many times to come, recited to us the rules and regulations of the house, the times of breakfast and at what time visitors were to depart. No female visitors after ten! We nervously unpacked, changed, and left for the nearest high street.

Like all white South Africans of that era, we had been pumped full of propaganda of what England and the English were like. At that time white South Africans had not experienced any real deprivation during, and immediately after, the Second World War. On average we had a very high standard of living compared to the post-war British. Our buildings were relatively modern, and we were more familiar with certain domestic goods such as a refrigerators, washing machines and vacuum cleaners. Wages in general (except my own) were higher; hence, prices in the shops seemed to us to be much cheaper. It was strange to see food and green-groceries still priced to the nearest farthing.

We were also programmed regarding the supposed influence the trade unions had on British working life. We could all recite that bricklayers were only allowed to lay so many bricks per day, hence, you would always see English workmen standing around having cups of tea. We never ever mentioned that our relatively higher standard of life was in the main due to an abundance of cheap Black labour.

As we walked down the high street looking for a place to eat, we behaved true to form remarking about the prices of goods and people standing around chatting. After a meal in a Lyons Tea-Room, our first experience in a self-service restaurant, we made our way back to the West End and began a walk, around tourist London which lasted about ten days.

As I walked about, the strangeness of the surroundings seemed to have an air of freshness that helped to maintain a dream-like atmosphere. It took a few days for the reality of actually been in England after the months of mental preparation to sink in. I had to stop pinching myself each time I visited a world-famous landmark. Walking through Green Park I was amazed to see how green-green the grass and leaves were. I had left the Highveld in the middle of winter and even in summer I had never, apart from a morning in Cape Town, ever seen such a rich natural green. We wandered along via bus, tube and foot to art galleries, to museums, to parks, to cathedrals and drifted around Soho. In those days, apart from the presence of street prostitutes, no shop windows had displays of pornography, etc.

We walked along Oxford Street down Regent Street to Piccadilly Circus, then down Piccadilly to Buckingham Palace, back to Piccadilly and then down the Haymarket to Trafalgar Square and on to the river. These were places we had read about, seen pictures of, or had seen in the movies and now we were actually standing in and on the real thing. We also kept bumping into people we had met on the sea voyage from Cape Town.

Almost every second day we made a pilgrimage to South Africa House where I kept bumping into people I knew from back home. They were all a few years older than myself and had completed their studies and training, and had started on their careers. I, apart from eighteen months farming, had no skills and far less money. My generation was still studying and training.

The other most notable aspect of London in those days, especially at night, were the number of American soldiers (GIs) about. After dark, Piccadilly was taken over by American troops that were stationed in England. They were looking for women and a good time, and at the same time there were women who were looking for them.

My friend and I could not help commenting every time we saw a Black person. It surprised us both to see even the odd one.

During my last weeks in Johannesburg I had been given names and addresses of people to look up in London. The first contact that I phoned arranged to meet me in a photographic shop in Oxford Street. She turned out to be the proprietor's daughter.

After about ten minutes of embarrassing conversation, we were invited to a gathering of her 'committee.' All the London Jewish youth of the Fifties seemed to belong to a committee - another way of saying a Jewish youth club. That night I went along to the White House to hear a talk given by the then editor of the *Jewish Chronicle*. The next gathering was on the following Saturday evening at a large house in Golders Green.

I found my way to a house, which almost matched the size of some of the homes of the rich Jewish merchants that I had visited during my last months in Johannesburg. Everyone had to bring an item for an auction, the proceeds of which were to be given to a Zionist Charity. I had bought some small, tourist-type of trinket from a stall in the West End and had it wrapped up.

The front door was open. I walked through and saw a pile of large parcels, which I presumed to be the contributions to the raffle and hoping that I was not being watched, rapidly dumped my miniature contribution on top of the pile. Then I bumped into the girl from the photographic shop. She introduced me to a nearby group who I remembered seeing at the lecture. As the evening wore on, I gave up trying to hold my own in conversation and I felt that, although there was a familiarity about the gathering, I was amidst a strange new culture.

Later in the evening, I happened to be standing near the pile of gifts, which were being readied for auction. A large cigar-smoking character picked my meagre contribution and asked out loudly who the hell had bought that insulting rubbish. Needless to say, I remained silent.

I enquired about times of last trains to a group who were in deep discussion. From this gathering emerged the chap who had mocked my gift and asked me where I was staying. When I told him that it was in South London one side of his mouth dropped but then he immediately offered to take me to my digs. I pretended not to accept his offer but it did not take too much persuasion to change my mind. I was now able to stay on until the end of the party.

I was driven back to my lodgings in a brand new Armstrong-Sidely. Driving through London, I felt for a few moments as if I was back among the rich Jewish community among whom I had lived in my last months in Johannesburg.

Another person on my list that I phoned was Julie, the sister of a couple who lived in the flat at Tavrig. She arranged to meet in the City during her lunch break. I was shepherded to a small restaurant and in addition to being treated to a light meal, I was quizzed about her sister. She arranged to meet me on the next afternoon. We boarded a boat at Westminster pier and sailed down river to Greenwich. The thought of a river trip flashed me back to trips downs the Vaal River passing through uninhabited, wild, willow-lined banks. I was soon brought back to reality sailing under the bridges, passing by warehouses and docks that lined the River Thames.

It was a lovely, warm afternoon and after visiting the Cutty Sark and the Maritime Museum we strolled through Greenwich Park and sat on a bench near the meridian line. We had a wonderful view of the river. Julie was very attractive and about four years older than me. Much to both my surprise and embarrassment she sat arm in arm very close to me. I had never sat that close in a public place to any female before and about ten minutes later she put her arms around me and kissed me. She then stretched herself out on the bench and rested her head in my lap. I felt very self-conscious and looking around, I imagined that everyone was sniggering at us. When we wandered back to the boat I was walking on air and in a state of total disbelief but, at the same time, felt as if I were being teased and played with.

I had arranged to meet my travel companion that evening and Julie came with me. As we approached him at our prearranged rendezvous, Julie and I walked arm in arm. He smothered his surprise and we went off to a pub. That was the first time that either he or I had been in a pub. Neither he nor I knew anything about the varieties of ales available and simply ordered three pints of beer. The barman politely requested that we order more precisely. Julie stepped in and explained to us the differences between bitter and mild ales and suggested to us what to order.

After a meal we parted with Julie at a Tube station after being persuaded that, in England, there was no need to see a woman home. It was quite normal for a woman to go out at night on her own.

Our first two weeks were nearly over and on our second Friday in London, my friend parted for Shoreditch Hospital where he had arranged a job before he had left Johannesburg. That was the last time I saw him.

Chapter 2

A few months before I left Johannesburg I had been told about farm camps for students in England. These were mainly for students who were paid to gather in the harvests. I had written off to an address in Whitehall and they had sent all the necessary information and booking forms. I had arranged to go to camp at Fridaybridge near Wisbech two weeks post arrival in London. On Sunday Julie came to see me depart from Liverpool Street station. A steam train took me to Cambridge where I changed trains for Ely, and then another change finally took me to March where a truck was waiting to collect the other new temporary farm labourers.

The camp buildings were a series of old army Nissan huts. There must have been at least forty occupants to a hut. A bed, a mattress, old army blankets and a wooden cupboard was all that you could claim to be yours. After claiming a patch I dumped my luggage, a suitcase (I had left one of my cases at the digs in Battersea) and a rucksack that I had bought in London, almost all of my worldly belongings.

Most of the other inmates were either German or Scandinavian. However there was one young English lad, Joe, who had just finished his National Service and who happened to be occupying the bed alongside mine. He had already been there for a few weeks and knew his way round. Once I settled down and did some unpacking, Joe took me for a tour round the campsite.

A gong rang inviting us to the dinning room for an evening meal. The price of a weeks rent included full board and lodging. Joe told me not to expect much from the kitchen. I had just had two weeks of tourist class ship's food as well as a fortnight of meagre café meals in London so my first camp meal made me feel as if I had at last returned to the land of real food.

The first Monday morning we were awakened at six and, after an early breakfast, we lined up to be chosen by prospective employers. On my first morning I was taken on a horse cart to an apple orchard. It was the first time I had seen a draught Shire horse. I sat on the cart in a state of amazement at the size of the animal and kept thinking about the draft oxen and mules that I once worked with on Highveld farms.

That day and the next few days, I spent climbing up and down ladders picking apples and getting to know some of the campers.

On Wednesday a local farmer arrived with a small open pick up truck and chose me and a group of about six German students to work on his farm. It was the first time I had ever been among young Germans. As I listened to them speaking German, I discovered that I could understand a great deal of what they were saying. My knowledge of Afrikaans and Yiddish helped me a great deal. To me, Yiddish was a language I associated with the older generation of South African Jews, and when they spoke English we called it 'broken' English. To my generation they were figures of ridicule and when I heard young Germans speaking what sounded to me like Yiddish, I felt very confused. Nevertheless, I never let on that I could understand them. I still felt contempt for Germans and Germany in general. After all the war had only ended nine years ago. They all spoke to me in English.

We were driven to a farm about twenty minutes away from the camp right in the heart of the fens. The totally flat landscape with fields separated by water filled ditches was quite alien to me. Our jobs were to help harvest the potato crop. It was only a matter of about eight months ago that I was supervising gangs of African labourers lifting potatoes. I had just stood around and never actually lifted any potatoes off the ground. Now I found myself facing a role reversal. I had always wanted to work on farm and actually do all the manual work now I was to face the most backbreaking task of all - potato picking.

We stood at one corner of the field looking down the rows of furrows separated by a ridge. The potatoes lay beneath the ridges. There were several two-wheeled horse-drawn carts, a tractor, a mountain of baskets and some farm workers. I was amazed at the clothes the men were wearing. Not standard working clothes such as dungarees or overalls, but jackets, waistcoats, woollen trousers, a flat cap and either a collarless shirt or a shirt with a collar and old tie. It was if they were wearing well-worn office clothes. However, they all wore either Wellingtons or heavy-duty boots.

My companions had done this work the week before and all immediately went over to pick up some baskets. The tractor started up and drove down along the furrows and an implement, which looked like a two-pronged plough, began to open up the ridges exposing the potatoes. Once the first row was opened we walked down and stood about twenty yards apart, then started picking up the potatoes and placing them in a basket. A full basket was left beside the furrow. The tractor now proceeded to open the next row and, when all the potatoes in the first row had been lifted, we moved sideways to the next row, this time working in the opposite direction.

One of the horse-drawn carts moved up the row of the filled baskets. One person sat on the front of the cart and a second walked alongside holding onto a metal bracket at the back of the cart with one hand. As the cart moved forward, the other hand grabbed a filled basket and swung it up to the seated person who promptly emptied the potatoes and threw the empty basket toward the row that was now being picked. Once the cart was full, one of the farm workers would lead the horse toward one end of the field where the potatoes were being stacked and covered with earth for storage.

The two cart operators would swap roles after every few rows while the others would continue to fill the baskets. The swinging of the baskets created a great deal of stress on the shoulder muscles, whereas picking and filling up the baskets in crouched or bent over position with legs apart led to backache and the backward leaning 'potato walk'. Whichever job you did on the potato field was tiring, exhausting and backbreaking. During lunch break you would have to find a way of sitting/lying in the field that would not make the pain feel worse when you restarted work.

On the next Monday morning, the German team that I was working with decided to ask the farmer before we started how much he was going to pay us. He quoted a price, which they discussed among themselves and decided that it was not enough but did not know exactly how to set about the negotiation. I then asked them in German how much they wanted then proceeded with all the negotiations. I actually asked for a higher hourly rate than what they wanted. The farmer agreed to it. The Germans were pleasantly surprised. In my best German I explained to them that they had not asked enough. They listened to me in silence but all had a surprised look. I thought that I had upset them. Later on, during the morning break, they told me that their silence was caused by how much German I understood and how good my German pronunciation was. They also were concerned about how much of their conversation I had understood.

The year was 1954 and it was only nine years since the war had ended. Deep within me, like many persons during that era, I still harboured anti-German feelings. The group I worked with were all a few years older than I was. They had actually lived through the war years in Nazi Germany. Apart from Hans, who was about twenty-four, most of them were from those parts of Germany where they did not experience the direct effects of the military conflict. Hans was from Berlin. He told me that he was drafted into the Hitler Youth and had been trained to operate a machine gun and an anti-aircraft gun. His was posted on the outskirts of Berlin to defend the city against the Russian advance. Hitler had visited his unit before they were sent to the front, and had spoken to them individually about the need and importance of defending their fatherland.

Hans told me that his platoon was in a bunker and they had to keep firing their guns at the advancing Russians. They continued until they fell asleep from exhaustion. After several days they disappeared into the countryside and, by the time he managed to find his way home, the war was over. I listened in silence as Hans related the events that he had experienced. He kept emphasizing that, in spite of the danger, he was so exhausted that he actually fell asleep on a table.

My silence must have conveyed my inner feelings, which were that I was both astounded and horrified that I was in the company of, and associated with, a person who had connections with the Nazis. I wanted to ask how he felt now and what he would say if he knew that I was Jewish but I never got up the nerve to ask him that question.

During one of our tea breaks we were sitting on a grass patch and enjoying the afternoon sun. Hans produced from his pocket a tin of Nivea cream and, using only his forefinger, spread the cream over his face. I had never ever seen any male do that before. It was 'light years' before after-shave and deodorants became the norm. While watching him I noticed that he had a Lawrence Olivier Henry V haircut and only then realized how effeminate he actually was.

The owner of the farm was nearly always working in the field among us. He always tidied up behind the workers. His daughter drove one of the tractors and would often come and sit with us during breaks. The Germans found her difficult to understand and I became the interpreter.

On weekday evenings in the camp, after showering and eating, we would sit around talking but most nights we were so tired that we were all asleep at about 10pm. Wednesday and Friday nights were dance nights, dancing to records. The camp manager played the records (predating disc jockeys) and charged us two and six entry fee. I had learnt to dance foxtrot style on board ship but had not yet acquired any jiving skills or, as it was known then, the 'Teddy Boy' shuffle. It was also the days of dancing only in pairs and you actually went over to ask a girl for a dance. The Scandinavian blonde girls were the most frequently asked. They always danced close 'cheek to cheek' and I looked on enviously.

The 'party culture' that I had grown up with, in Johannesburg, was such that if the girl liked you or vice versa, you would ask to her dance again and again. As the evening wore on you slowly get closer and toward the later part of the evening, if you were still together, and you were brave enough, you would dance cheek to cheek. From then on it was improper to dance with anyone else.

There I was watching very attractive young blonde girls dancing close to their partners after only one dance. Then to both my surprise, and horror, they would break away and dance up close to the next person who asked them. When I eventually asked a blonde Swede to dance, I felt her breadth against me and for a moment I thought that she was mine for the night. I managed to hold on to her for another two or three dances before she broke away to embrace another partner. After feeling rejected, I soon learnt that it would be all right to dance close with my next partner and so on.

On my first Sunday there was a coach trip to Hunstanton, a seaside town. I had lived most of my life four hundred miles from the nearest seaside. Apart from the two-week sea voyage to England, I had only twice before spent any time at the seaside. The sea that I was familiar with was the Indian Ocean. There were always waves breaking over sandy beaches with rocky outcrops. Sitting on the coach, memories of Durban kept flashing by.

It was a calm autumn day and our first stop was Sandringham where we all stepped out of the coach and stared at the gates of the Queen's summer palace. After peeping through the railings at large manicured woodlands, we climbed back onto the coach. Shortly afterwards a very still, calm sea came into view. I had to be convinced that it was really the sea. Tom, who was sitting beside me told me that we were not really looking at the sea but at the Wash. Without a map, I could not fathom it all out and kept thinking that we were looking out over some vast lake. After all, how could there be sea without waves? Luckily for me the tide was in, otherwise, I would have been in a state of total confusion.

The coach off-loaded us in the centre of Hunstanton. We spent the rest of the day wandering around. Walking on the sandy beach convinced me that we were actually at the seaside. The sea air and all the walking and the week's hard work was soon to have its effect. The journey back started with a singsong but ended with everybody asleep.

Fridaybridge farm workcamp

Chapter 3

During my second week, two South African lads arrived at the camp and, like myself, found themselves assigned to a team of potato pickers. We would meet up in the evenings after dinner comparing our aches and pains in the machine-less laundry. It was a new experience for the three of us having to wash our own clothes. Sympathy for the African servant girls we had taken for granted crept into our thoughts. However we managed to spruce ourselves up for the midweek and Friday night dances.

At the end of my second week, the farmer's daughter turned up at the dance having driven to the camp in her father's car. I danced with her most of the evening. However, at that stage of my life, I was still on a learning curve as far as the opposite sex was concerned. At the end of the evening I had not kissed her and, although I wanted to see more of her I did not know how ask her. The next time I saw her was on the following Monday morning driving a tractor and I thought that her father gave me the type of glance that said, "Leave my daughter alone."

After about four weeks my two South African companions, John and Piet, and I were suffering. The potato-walk had got to us. We walked leaning back with our toes pointing outwards and very stiff at the hips. We could not take much more. We had saved most of our wages and decided to go back to London. The camp manager charged us on a daily rate for our board and lodging so we were able to leave midweek.

We caught a bus to March and then a train to Cambridge and, from there, another train to Liverpool Street Station. Once in London we made our way to Earls Court. The youth hostel was full but they sent us to a private, but approved Bed and Breakfast. John and I booked in for two nights and Piet booked in a B&B a few doors down the road. That evening, after a meal in a café, we planned a trip to Scotland. Through the grapevine we had learned that we had to catch the underground to Barnet to where the A1, the road to Scotland, started. We planned to depart in two days time. John and I would have to get to Barnet as early as possible and hopefully meet Piet outside Barnet station. The next morning we asked the landlady if we could have our breakfast at six am.

I phoned Julie and we arranged to meet her on the following day after she finished work. She met me in the West End and took me to Swiss Cottage where she lived with an aunt. After an evening meal with her relatives, she and I went to the local pub. At about 10 pm we returned to her house. Her room was on the third floor and I crept up the stairs as quietly as I could. Time flew by and suddenly it was 2am and I had to creep out of the house as quietly as possible. Once safely out in the street beneath the streetlights, I walked on air in a state of spent ecstasy. I hailed a cab. About a mile from my destination the cab fare reached ten shillings. I asked the driver to stop, paid him, and walked the rest of the way. It was well after 3am when I crept into bed in the Earls Court B & B.

Next thing I knew there was knock on the door and it was the landlord waking us up. I called over to Piet who sleepily told me that plans had changed and there was no need for an early start. He turned over and so did I. In a deep sleep we were woken up by the irate landlord in our room telling us that we were a pair of louts for getting his wife up so early. We were told, in no uncertain terms, to get the hell out within the next ten minutes. Luckily we did not have any packing to do and left unwashed without breakfast. The door was slammed behind us and, from an open window, the landlord continued to curse us.

For some reason or other, John and Piet could not make an early start and our meeting was delayed for two hours. John and I made our way with our rucksacks via the underground to Barnet. We found a café and while eating breakfast our guilt feelings slowly wore off, and the tale of how we were thrown out of our digs in Earls Court began to take root.

At about ten o'clock Piet arrived at our rendezvous point. The three of us caught a bus that dropped us off a few miles up the A1. We found a spot where we thought it would be easy for cars to stop and raised our thumbs at the passing traffic. Ten minutes later a car stopped which took us up the A1 and dropped us off at Luton. Having got away from the built up areas we now sat on a grass verge with the feeling that, at last, we were away from London.

It was at least an hour before our next lift. A light delivery van stopped and John climbed into the front seat and Piet and I climbed into the back and made ourselves comfortable on top of a pile of flattened cardboard boxes. We looked out of the back window at the disappearing road. In those days most of the A1 was a twisting single carriageway road and progress along it was relatively slow. After about two hours, Piet and I dosed off. The driver suddenly braked and sent us crashing onto the floor of the van. I looked up and across to Piet who, like me, was shaken but at the same time in a state of disbelief at the fact that neither of us was hurt. The driver stopped, and he told us that he had to brake to avoid an out-of-control car.

It was dark by the time we reached Bawtry in Yorkshire, where we were dropped off. We made our way to the youth hostel and booked in for the night. Sharing the hostel with us was a party of fourteen-year old school boys who were on a hike across the moors. In the main lounge a group of locals were indulging in an evening of folk dancing. The master in charge of the boys looked like a middle-aged Billy Bunter and he wore a pair of long shorts just held up by a belt that drooped round his rotund waistline. He joined in the dances. During one of the dances his enthusiasm got the better of him and, while skipping and hopping to the music, he was unaware that his shorts were slipping. He continued dancing until his shorts, now around his ankles, tripped him up. By this time all of his class were lying on the floor crying with laughter, and then to add to the comedy, one of the boys helped him up onto his feet. Two other boys immediately hoisted up his trousers and offered him a pair of braces.

The next morning we were on our way. We had decided the night before to make our way to Glasgow and if we got separated we would meet up in the central youth hostel. A lorry driver offered only one of us a lift, which Piet took up. A car picked up John and me and took us to Bradford. We were dropped outside a large cloth mill. As we walked past, the women factory workers leaned out of the windows and waved and whistled at us inviting us to join them.

Our next lift, in a car, took us all the way to central Glasgow and we met up with Piet as planned. It was the beginning of November and the temperature was dropping each day. The three of us had not experienced such cold before. We had to wear almost all our warm clothing. We walked into the town centre at about one o'clock. We could not find a café for a meal and ended up in a restaurant - the type that catered to office workers rather than a trio of rough-clad hitchhikers. Once inside, we decided to brave it out and, to our surprise, a waitress came over to us and directed us to a table for three and handed us each a menu. The prices were more than we budgeted for but we went ahead and ordered. Once our food arrived the rest of the patrons abandoned their frowning glances in our direction.

That afternoon we caught a tram and ended up right in the middle of the district that was then known as the Gorbals. We wandered down the main street staring curiously at the rows of tenement houses. The locals all stared back at us. After an hour of walking we began to feel uneasy and threatened, and when a tram stopped close by we jumped on it. The conductor understood our plight and suggested that we travel along another three or four stops, then get off and catch a tram back to the city centre.

The next day we caught a bus to Loch Lomond and made our way to a youth hostel, a refurbished small castle. After booking in and buying ourselves dehydrated food for our evening meal, we went for a stroll along the shores of the Loch. We passed by a field of ripe potatoes and, without much thought, climbed over a stone wall and dug up enough potatoes to add to our evening meal. That evening in the kitchen there was the usual sprinkling of New Zealanders, Australians and continentals. Everyone, including the warden, wondered about our potatoes. We did our best to reassure all that we had brought them with us from Glasgow.

Later, during the evening we decided on our next moves. I wanted to remain in Scotland and try and find work in a forestry camp while Piet and John decided to return to London. The next morning, after breakfast, we travelled back to Glasgow. We said our farewells and I never saw either of them again.

Chapter 4

I made my way to the Labour Exchange, who then directed me to the recruitment office of the Forestry Commission. They offered me work near a village called Lochgoilhead on the shores of Loch Goil north west of Glasgow which I accepted. They gave me a rail and bus ticket and I was told to catch the afternoon train. I left Glasgow central station at 2.00. A massive steam engine pulled the train into the Highlands. An hour later I had to change trains and after another hour of slow travelling, reached the end of the line. There, the station guard directed me onto a bus.

I finally reached the small village of Lochgoilhead and had to walk about a half a mile to the forestry camp. A very tough looking Scot, Sam, aged about forty, greeted me. He'd been told of my impending arrival. Once inside, I was looked over by all the inmates and I felt that I had just walked into some foreign legion outpost. There were about twenty men; three were in their early twenties and the rest seemed to me to be forty plus.

The wooden hut consisted of a large dormitory, a lounge/dinning room, showers and toilets, and a kitchen. In the dormitory there was a central coal stove that heated both the dormitory and the lounge. The whole building felt very warm and comfortable. Sam showed me to my bed, right next to a stove. On it was a pile of blankets and next to it a locker for all my belongings. Sam introduced me to all the inmates who all spoke with broad Scottish accents, which I struggled to understand. He then called me into his 'office' and I was told of the codes that governed the hut.

I was to pay him so much a week for board, which included breakfast, a packed lunch and an evening meal. He then gave a large mug and asked me to give him my thermos flask; he would fill it for me each morning. It became obvious to me not to step out of line as these were not people to cross. At the same time they would look after you.

I joined in the evening meal of soup, a main course with vegetables, a pudding and a mug of tea. Once the meal was over and the washing up completed, we sat around talking and then retreated to the main dormitory. The fire was stoked up and the temperature crept up well into the seventies (Fahrenheit). The conversation centred round male-type small talk. About ten o'clock everyone prepared for bed. I noticed that some of them had a knife or a small weapon close to their pillow. I was told to cover myself with all the blankets provided. Once in bed, being next to the stove, I began to roast under my covers. However, once the lights were turned off I managed to fall asleep. The fire soon died down and the wooden hut cooled down as rapidly as it heated up, hence all the blankets.

Sam woke us up at six a.m. Stepping out of a warm bed into a cold room took some persuasion. The bathroom was even colder. At breakfast Sam filled our mugs with very hot tea and we all sat down to huge plates of porridge followed by bacon, sausage, eggs and beans, and thick slices of toast. After washing our plates, Sam handed out filled flasks and packets of sandwiches known as a 'piece.'

I was issued with a pair of Wellington boots and a thick, waterproof jacket and trousers. Underneath the rainwear I wore a thick anorak, thick sweater, thick shirt and warm underwear. We then set off in a line, along a footpath that led up through a pine forest up the mountain. Once above the tree line, we stopped and collected our digging implements from a hut. Our task was to dig draining trenches that vaguely followed the contour of the mountain. The trenches were about a foot deep and eighteen inches wide. Each trench was ten yards above or below a parallel trench. The foreman paired me off with one of the older men, and explained to me what had to be done and how to do it. One person would cut down into the soil and the other would remove the piece of turf and place it alongside the trench.

We started in earnest at a fairly fast pace. I thought that it was so that we could warm up, and then we would slow down. The pace never altered. When the morning mist cleared we paused for a few minutes to remove our waterproofs but soon continued to work at the same pace. Although I began to sweat the temperature was only just above freezing so I did not remove any more outer layers of clothes. We stopped for morning break at about ten. I sat down exhausted on a patch of wet grass and, during the break, listened to general conversation. It was then that I realised that we were paid at piecework rates, hence the fast pace of the work.

At midday we paused for a three-quarter hour lunch break and ate our sandwiches in the hut. Not much was said, probably due to the fact we were just too exhausted to carry on any form of conversation. We sat looking out toward the Loch in which a submarine was carrying out training exercises. It would submerge and surface at regular intervals throughout the day and, occasionally, there was a loud booming sound we understood to be the firing off of a torpedo. The scenery was quite spectacular. The entrance to the Loch was relatively narrow guarded by mountains that dropped down right to the waters edge. The slopes of the hills were all wooded and autumn colours were still in abundance. Throughout the day, when there was a chance, I would pause to look around to admire the surroundings the like of which I had never seen before.

At the end of my first day, as we walked down the hillside, my feet were numb, I felt as though I was walking on my ankles. Once inside of the hut we showered, changed, and waited for the call to eat. Our evening meal started with a large slice of thick bread followed by a meat course with a mountain of potatoes and vegetables. The pudding was a soup bowl of custard and fruit pie. Second helpings were available for each course and, needless to say, all the older members had two helpings and then licked the plates clean with bread. Two cups of tea was the finale to our meal. After washing up, we retired to the main dormitory and sat around the fire. As the evening wore on some read others went to the local pub and the conversation nearly always ended up in something anti-English.

A few evenings later, I strolled down to the village hall and met some of the locals who were very curious about me and what had led to working in a forestry camp in Lochgoilhead. During the evening, I joined in a game of Badminton and finished off the evening in the local pub. At the end of my first week I received my first wage packet with which I opened a savings account in the local post office. I was issued a post office bankbook clearly marked Lochgoilhead which, in the years to come, was to cause both surprise and amusement when using post offices in the London area.

At the end of November my body could take no more punishment and, during the lunch break, I told the foreman that I had had enough. He was not at all bothered and said that he had been expecting me to pack it in and was surprised that I had lasted as long as I did. That evening I collected what remained of my wages and my 'cards.' I went into the village to deposit some money and they all seemed to be quite relieved that I was leaving the 'camp' as they regarded most of the inhabitants as company too rough for the likes of me.

While standing at the bus stop I started to thumb a lift. My luck was in, as I was picked up in a pre-war convertible Rolls Royce. My host spoke with a very posh English accent but assured me that he was Scots. As we drove round the shores of Loch Goil he commented on local landmarks while listening to classical music on the radio. We drove at a leisurely pace and when we reached the northern end of Loch Lomond he delivered me to a Youth Hostel, which had four hundred beds spread over several floors. The only other visitor that night was a thirty-year-old Spaniard named Carlos who was hoping to get work in Glasgow.

The rooms were large, each with dozens of beds, and they all seemed equally cold and uninviting. We chose a relatively small room on the second floor. That evening we ate our meal with the Warden, his family and staff that included a number of shepherds who hardly said a word all evening. We were invited to sit around the fire after the meal. At about nine we were politely dispatched off to our room.

Compared to the living room, the bedroom was freezing. We could hear the wind howling all round us. As we walked along, the wooden floorboards creaked and groaned. We each gathered three beds worth of blankets as there was no heating whatsoever in the room. Although I fell asleep rather quickly I kept waking up through the night to hear the wind all round, the floor creaking and doors banging. By morning I had managed to convince myself that there was no such thing as ghosts.

To reach the bathroom, in the morning we had to cross the room and walk down several corridors only to find that the water was freezing cold. The first time I felt warm was after I had drunk a mug full of coffee. After a substantial breakfast, Carlos and I caught the bus to Glasgow.

We booked into the central Youth Hostel and then wandered off round Glasgow. The Dancing Years by Ivor Novello was being performed at the Alhambra theatre. I persuaded Carlos to accompany me that evening. We sat in the front row of the 'gods.' Only when the show began did I realise that it was to be performed on ice. Carlos politely said nothing. While the actors skated they mimed the songs sung by out of sight vocalists. At the beginning of the last act, a spotlight shone onto one of the boxes where a large woman wearing an even larger hat was loudly applauded. She raised her arms and turned toward the stage then began to sing into a microphone with a very loud concert type of voice. Carlos whispered to me that in Spain no soprano would ever use a microphone. At the end of her song more applause, an encore and then the show on ice continued.

The next morning I said goodbye to Carlos and caught a bus to Edinburgh. I sat upstairs and the conductor looked surprised when I asked for a ticket to Edinburgh but he did not tell me that I was on a slow-stopping bus. The bus wound its way through every town and village stopping frequently. I reached Edinburgh about midday and found my way to Kingsknowe where the Youth Hostel was located. After off-loading my rucksack, I walked down to the bus stop and felt quite at home as there was a sign that said 'To Town.' That is how many of the bus and tram stops were marked in Johannesburg.

I climbed to the top of the Scott Memorial, walked up to the castle, down the Grass Market, up and down Princess Street and admired all the buildings. I still think that Edinburgh is one of the most beautiful cities in the world. It was the beginning of December and apart from the early darkness which I was still to get used to, it became a bit too cold for me to hang around the streets so I returned to the hostel where I was able to purchase a cooked meal. The next morning I made my way to the A1, the road to London, which began at the eastern end of Princess Street. I stood on the pavement and watched an endless variety of vehicles pass me by. Numerous pedestrians stared at me with my rucksack on my back and thumb in the air. They probably thought that the last thing any motorist would want to do was to stop and offer me a lift. I decided that the distinctly urban environment was not the best place to stand around waiting for a car to stop so I decided walk along the gutter with my thumb in the air and, half looking in front of me, keeping an eye on the on coming traffic. After ten minutes a car stopped and dropped me about twenty miles down the A1. I was now in open country and felt more at ease.

The next lift took me all the way down to Doncaster. The car was a current model, large Austin and the driver was very dapper and well spoken. As we drove along, he asked the usual questions about me such as where do I come from and what do intend to do with myself, etc. My reply was nearly always that I was a student and that I hoped to study agriculture. As the miles slowly drifted by, it became my turn to inquire about him. He first told me that he worked in theatre but not as an actor. Later he revealed that he used to act but he was now a theatrical agent but only had one client at present. When I asked whom, he told me that it was Gracie Fields. She had just finished a show or shows somewhere in Scotland and was now on her way to one of the Yorkshire cities. Well, why was he not with her? As always he arranged her transport, made certain that she was comfortable, booked a sleeper and had driven off a few hours before her train departed. The objective was to meet at her destination and to make certain all was well. The responses to my questions about Gracie Fields were only vaguely answered. I was not certain whether it was due to his diplomacy or whether he was bluffing. He dropped me off on the outskirts of Doncaster.

I was not on the road for more than ten minutes when a large box shaped post war Austin picked me up. I sat in the front next to rather large, well-spoken man in his early twenties. His hairstyle was short back and sides with a crisp parting. He wore a Harris Tweed jacket, grey flannels and very polished brown shoes. Once we settled into our journey, and after the usual enquiry's about myself, which lasted about ten minutes, I slowly swung the conversation round to him. He turned out be a National Service officer making his way home which was somewhere in Southern England for a short leave. He had been to a public school and had studied music at Oxford, and had concentrated on the organ and hoped to become a professional organist. As we drove south, a thick mist began to cover the road and he had to concentrate on his driving, which slowed down the conversation. However, he did begin to show concern about where I was going to stay in London. I told him that I had the address and phone number of the B & B that I had stayed at when I first arrived. Without saying much, he pulled over at the public telephone box and helped me phone the landlady to make a reservation. Once that formality was over I began to feel hungry.

In those days there were not many bypasses and the A1 travelled through the centre of most cities, towns and villages. While passing through the next village I noticed a sign for a Fish and Chip shop and suggested that he stop. I bought two packets of cod and chips wrapped in newspaper. As we sat in the car eating he first remarked on what a wonderful practical meal it was, then how good it tasted. Next came a lengthy justification of our take away meal rather than having stopped at a roadside restaurant. I had been dreading such a stop mainly because the cost would have been well above my budget. Once we were on our way he confessed that it was the first time that he had actually bought and eaten fish and chips.

Once we reached the outskirts of London the streetlights helped our visibility. Without giving me any reason he asked me the address of my digs and drove right through the centre of London, made his way to Clapham Common and dropped me at the door of my B & B at about nine that night. We did not exchange identities and, unfortunately, I have never met that young gentleman again.

Chapter 5

The next morning, I travelled across to Swiss Cottage and found a newsagent adjacent to the tube station. I wrote down several telephone numbers of potential digs that were advertised in the shop window. I changed a two and sixpenny piece (a half crown) into thirty pennies and made my way to a phone box on the forecourt of the tube station. The third number that I rang had a vacancy and the woman who answered invited me round to a house in Fellows Road. I was shown a room, which had two beds but she was prepared to let me have it as a single room provided if someone else came along, I would share it. I accepted and paid a small deposit. As I left she said that she could tell on the phone that I was not a coloured foreigner otherwise I would have been told on the phone that there were no vacancies. She gave me a set of keys and I told her that I had to go and collect the rest of my luggage from Clapham. As I walked back to the tube station I looked more carefully at the many large multi-storeyed houses which let rooms and noticed that on some of the front windows there were notices saying 'No Coloureds' or even 'No Blacks.' I thought had I left South Africa behind.

Apart from basic furnishings my newly rented room had a gas ring and a kettle. A kettle, frying pan, saucepan, cutlery and crockery were provided. Hence I could prepare a hot drink and even a light snack. There was also a radio, which I had to pay an extra two shillings a week for. That evening, after a meal in a local café, I sat in the room listening to the BBC third program and looked at the employment columns in the *Evening Standard*.

The next morning, I went to Leyton's Wine restaurant behind Selfridges following up on an advertisement for a student to help in the kitchen and to pack wines for postage. The proprietor did not ask any questions about what I was studying. In fact apart from offering me the job without much fuss, he didn't ask anything, other than if I could start immediately.

The kitchen and wine stores and cellar were in the basement and in order to reach the restaurant you had to step up very steep slippery stone stairs. The food was sent up to the dining room via a dumb waiter. My workbench was under the pavement, a converted coal cellar. The cook was a very earthy Irishwoman who immediately decided that I needed looking after. As soon as I began she presented me with a plate of sandwiches and a cup of coffee. She whispered to me that if I wanted anything in the way of food or drink all I had to do was to ask.

Having spent most of the time since my arrival in England working on farms and in the forestry camp, I was fit and strong, which soon came to the notice of the proprietors. If there was lifting of wine crates, baskets, or anything heavy, I was called on. I was also sent on local errands. I was very shy about venturing into the restaurant, perhaps, because I thought of myself in the South African context as the equivalent of a Black worker and had to know my place.

In spite of some packages being returned with the contents dripping out and also breaking a very expensive bottle of wine, the restaurant owners kept me on until Christmas Eve. I enjoyed the work and the Christmas hustle and bustle of Oxford Street. There was a staff party on Christmas Eve and, after a meal and wine, I was given my final pay packet and a couple of bottles of wine to take back to my digs.

My landlord invited me to join them for Christmas lunch but my Jewish background made me hesitate and I did not want to intrude on a family occasion. I gave them my bottles of wine but declined their invitation.

Christmas mornings were like Sunday mornings in the Fifties. The newsagents and continental delicatessens, of which there were many in Swiss Cottage and Finchley Road, were open for business. On Christmas morning the buses ran until midday and the underground became operative at two o'clock in the afternoon.

The price of food seemed expensive to me by comparison to what I knew of food prices in South Africa. I purchased most of my food after work and Sunday mornings, and what I did not realise was that shops that opened evenings and Sundays charged more than the regular weekday stores. I remember buying the smallest tin of instant coffee available, which was the same price as a week's bus fare.

At about eleven on Christmas morning, I caught a bus to Oxford Circus and began to stroll around a rather deserted West End. I wandered down Regent Street toward Trafalgar Square. As I walked up the Strand I read a notice outside a Lyons's Corner House stating that it would be opening at three in the afternoon. With the knowledge that I would be able to purchase an affordable meal, I wandered down to the river and spent a few hours walking along a quiet embankment. I made my way back to Corner House and joined the queue waiting for the opening.

There was no self-service. I sat alone at a table for two and, as I was the only person on my own, the other seat remained empty, which I don't think, pleased the management. After about a half-hour, a small Palm Court type of orchestra appeared. The musicians were dressed formally except for paper Christmas hats. It was not a licensed restaurant but it was during the afternoon closing time and many of the customers had arrived from the emptied pubs. Many looked a bit the worse for wear with either paper streamers draped round them or wearing Christmas hats at odd angles.

Up till then Christmas to me had been just another baking hot public holiday and an excuse for a picnic, or a barbeque, or sunbathing round a swimming pool. It was also an excuse for some of the black population to wander round the streets of Johannesburg in groups singing and dancing. I was now experiencing a winter Christmas for the first time.

I could not help but think of religious festivals – the Jewish holy days - as a family occasion. Sitting in the restaurant, although not missing my own family, I certainly felt an inner sadness about the fact that I hardly knew a soul and that the only way I would have any company was to meet someone accidentally. It took me many years to learn about English pub culture and, besides, I could not really afford to drink. After my meal I wandered round the West End and, as the evening wore on more groups appeared on the streets full of Christmas spirit.

Italian style coffee bars were just beginning to invade London. A frothy cup of coffee (a cappuccino) cost 9d (old pence) compared to 4d for a coffee in a corner house and the food, mainly spaghetti and risotto, was out of my price range.

I spent the rest of the week up till New Year's Eve wandering around the West End and tourist resorts. I spent New Year's Eve in Trafalgar Square joined hands with a multitude singing Auld Lang Syne and then walked back to Swiss Cottage kissing numerous strangers on the way.

On January 2nd I woke up to my first real taste of urban snow. The first fall was so white and clean and all the buildings and trees were transformed from being drab under the grey skies, to picturesque. It was a great feeling trudging along the road to Swiss Cottage tube station, on fresh snow and leaving footprints behind you.

In Northumberland Avenue, near to both Trafalgar Square and South Africa House, was a coffee shop frequented by newly arrived young South Africans as well as the so called 'arty types' or Bohemians. The walls of the coffee house were used as an art gallery. The tables projected out from either wall. There was a central corridor leading to the serving counter. Around each table were sets of high barstools on which the seated clientele always seemed to be indulging in some deep, pseudo-philosophical discussion. Occasionally there would be someone with a guitar singing either folk or protest songs. If there were any South Africans I would try and sit as close to them as possible and hope that they would invite me to join them. More often than not I would slowly get talking to any group who were sitting at the same table as myself. I often sat there for an hour or two having purchased only one cup of coffee.

I had not yet learned that the real place to meet people in England is in a pub, particularly your local. I still saw a pub as a bar or a rough beer hall, which was not a place a nice Jewish boy frequented. However, in those days of limited pub opening hours, coffee bars did also serve as meeting places. It nearly always had a feeling of anti-climax when the group that I had joined departed, as I was now alone again in the big city. A couple of hour's chat would sustain me for a few days.

On most evenings, there were crowds of people wandering around Piccadilly, Leicester Square, Regent Street, Oxford Street and Soho. Piccadilly Circus and Leicester Square always appeared to be overrun by American GI's, and most were in uniform. In Piccadilly Circus, under the neon Coca-Cola sign, there was Forts Café Bar also known as Rainbow Corner which was the GI's meeting place.

Many of the cinemas were in Leicester Square and the theatres spread out all across the West End. From early afternoon until early evening, outside the cinemas and some of the theatres, there were queues. There was no booking for the cinema, hence the need to queue. Although all seats in the theatres could be reserved it was nearly always possible to get a seat or a place to stand in the upper tiers (known as the Gods) by queuing. The pavements of the West End, particularly around Leicester Square were nearly always cluttered with queues waiting to go into the cinema.

Slow moving queues were manna for street entertainers. There were individual singers, groups of singers, jugglers, magicians, escapologists, performing dogs and even a flock of trained budgies. They moved around the different queues. They had their own rules about where and how long to perform. No sooner had an act finished when they would come round with their moneybags while the next act prepared their stage.

In addition to the acts there were characters who would just wander around wearing eccentric clothing. One particular man in his late forties or early fifties always wore an evening tail-coat and white shirt with a butterfly collar and grey spats over his shiny black shoes. His most distinguishing feature was his shoulder length hair which, in the days when every male had a short back and sides or a ducks tail, made him an object of staring. He always held a cane and walked very fast on the edge of the kerb, and sometimes in the gutter, and just seemed to walk from one crowd of people to another never making eye contact with anyone.

There was one particular busking duo, a singer and piano accordionist, who both stood in the middle of Leicester Square. The singer sang out in a tenor voice and could always be heard above the traffic noise. He sang well-known arias and popular concert songs. When he stopped he always received a round of applause from whoever was either in the square or passing through at the time.

As the evening wore on, from about ten until the last tube left, the pavement around Piccadilly, Leicester Square and Oxford Street became more and more congested. As I wandered along among the endless lines of people, I always kept a look out hoping that I might see a familiar face. More often than not I would catch a bus or tube back to Swiss Cottage.

Chapter 6

While drinking in the coffee bar in Northumberland Avenue I noticed a poster advertising for staff in a new coffee house about to be opened in the Haymarket opposite the Haymarket Theatre. I walked over to locate exactly where it was. What I found was a doorway and pinned onto it was a notice advertising that a coffeehouse was about to open on the site. The next morning I found the door open and I wandered down a long corridor that opened into a large room. In the middle was a large stained glass stack-type of sculpture that reached up to the ceiling, the base of which was firmly planted into an irregular small pond. At the end directly opposite the corridor was a serving counter with a modern type of coffee machine and behind that a dumb waiter alongside a staircase leading down to the kitchen. All the rest of the room was filled with easel shaped tables and chairs. The walls were basically dark brown with slabs of coloured shapes giving the impression of a cubist painting.

I was directed downstairs to the manageress's office. It was only a short interview and I was offered a job. She explained to me that they were going to open in few days time and she would like me to start to work immediately which I did.

In the kitchen there was a huge dishwashing machine. As soon as I hung my jacket up and put on an apron and a white coat, I was being instructed by an agent of the machine's manufacturer on how to use it. All the new crockery and cutlery had to be unpacked, washed then sent up to the main restaurant via the dumb waiter. There was an intercom between the two floors. The rules of operation had not yet been established and, within the first hour of operation, someone almost had their arm removed. A signal of certain numbers of rings was soon created and notices hurriedly placed over all of the appropriate buttons.

There were two professional cooks and kitchen assistants. The rest of the counter staff, floor staff and 'washerups' like myself, just beginning their careers, were a mixture of students, artists, and actors. Each time a new person started they had to be instructed on how to use the dishwasher. On one occasion, when I thought that none of proprietors were about, I took it upon myself to teach the newcomers. When I finished I noticed that a boss had been listening to me. I was expecting a reprimand but instead, he came over to congratulate me on a very clear precise delivery. Little did I know at the time that I was to spend most of my working life either teaching or lecturing.

After a week of preparations the official opening of the coffee house took place. A few celebrities, plus numerous business and social acquaintances of the owners, filled the restaurant. After a few speeches, there was the ceremonial starting of the fountain and the lighting up of the central sculpture. The staff then mingled among the guests carrying trays of wine, sherry and schnapps. All the staff, except me, also indulged whenever they could. After about an hour coffee was served up. I was the only person completely sober so, by default, I took charge of this operation and found myself running round organising almost everything. I saw to the working of the machines, collecting the empties, and running up and down the stairs keeping the dishwasher going so that we did not run out of crockery and cutlery. The last guest did not leave until quite late and, by that time, I was quite exhausted and finally sat and had something to eat and a cup of coffee. All around me everyone was smiling and giggling. One of the bosses called me aside and thanked me, and said how he and most of the guests had noticed how my efforts had saved the evening from becoming totally disorganised.

The next day the coffee bar opened to the public and shortly became a popular venue. As the days wore on, with the exception of the cooking personnel, the rest of the staff came and went as the actors, artists and writers all obtained more appropriate employment.

During this period I first came up against, without actually realising it, the subtle subcultures that exist within English society. Although I spoke the same language and understood the overall social rules, I was not brought up or schooled in England I did not know of or understand the unwritten signals and small print of social behaviour. I frequently found myself upsetting some young well-spoken actor or actress who would call me aside and tell me off about something or other and often they told me in no uncertain terms that I was conceited and arrogant. Often when I asked them to do something for a customer they would frequently reply, "I'm not your Black, you know." After each incident I would apologise and retreat into a state of silent self-rebuke but, no matter how I tried, a few days later I would find myself in a similar situation.

One fellow worker who I somehow never managed to upset was a Goanese artist. He had already held an exhibition of his paintings of children, which had been well received. Apparently, he held Portuguese nationality and needed to do either domestic, hospital or catering work for so many months in order to get a permanent work permit. He actually gave me two of his paintings. One of them was a coloured, cubist-type of abstract, which, a few years later I gave away, in a weak moment, to a girlfriend (Ada referred to later). The other picture was a black and white nightmare, which I still have. During quieter periods we would indulge in long conversations about almost every topic.

I normally finished work at about five in the afternoon and then the evening staff would take over. Occasionally I would have to work an extra hour or two. One of the evening workers, Colin, was a tall thin twenty two years old. He wore national health glasses that were patched up with Elastoplasts. He had fair straight hair parted on one side and he looked very much like an overgrown public school boy wearing a well-worn fawn sports jacket, brown trousers and heavy shoes. He spoke with a very posh accent.

Colin told all that during the day he sat and worked in the reading room of the British Library researching for a book he was in the process of writing. During our many discussions he was very dismissive of Shakespeare and tended to praise Bernard Shaw. He claimed to have been married at sixteen and had a child but was separated and had no permanent address. He implied that he had slept rough but now was living in room in Baker Street. At closing time, he would take home any leftover food, mainly sandwiches, that could not be kept until the next day.

[The next time I met Colin Wilson was the day before his book 'The Outsider' was published. The book became a best seller].

Throughout the day, especially during mid-morning and mid-afternoon, local characters such as theatre and cinema doormen, porters, the occasional street entertainer and street photographers would drop in for a coffee. It soon became obvious that the theatre and cinema doormen did not expect to have to pay but, in return, they would help us whenever they could.

Trafalgar Square, was at the bottom of the Haymarket where, throughout the day, there were always tourists. A photographer would approach someone feeding the pigeons and pretend to take a photograph and then would offer to send them a copy of the photo for a fee. Once the money and addresses were exchanged the photographer would then take a real picture with his 35 mm camera. A few days after my arrival in England I gave in and asked for the picture to be posted to South Africa House and, sure enough, on my return from Scotland the snapshot was waiting for me.

One morning, two photographers came in for their morning coffee. They recognised my accent and began to ask questions about the politics of South Africa and predicted before long that there was going to be a blood bath. Then without asking me why I had left they said to each other, after discovering that I am Jewish, here is the first of the new wave of refugees. For many years after, I met people who in principle condemned the Apartheid regime. But when it came to action such as boycotts and marches, they soon shied away. Even some politicians found every excuse not to be too harsh on the white South African government.

Chapter 7

The Lyceum Theatre in the Strand was at that time converted into a dance hall. To me, these were great places. To be able to go to a dance without a partner was something that had never existed in Johannesburg. I was very nervous and self-conscious on my first visit to the Lyceum. Having paid my entrance and cloakroom fee I wandered into the vast ballroom, the former stalls auditorium. There was a huge orchestra led by Oscar Rabin with a vocalist and a compere. After about a half-hour the floor filled up with dancers. You had to have a partner in order to dance. Sitting around the perimeter of the dance floor were groups of girls waiting for a fellow to ask them for a dance. Scattered around hall were the males either in clusters or some, like myself, alone. Once the music started up, the lads would walk across the floor to invite a girl they had selected to dance with them. The girls who were not chosen would pretend to look indifferent and would remain seated or standing. Some would dance with each other. To see two girls dancing together was another novel experience for me. When I eventually plucked up enough courage to ask a girl to dance, the first two refused but I eventually found a willing partner.

The mid-Fifties was the age of the Teddy Boys who wore black or grey jackets with waistcoats that had a very fine black and white check pattern, and white shirts with a neck 'bootlace' or fine thin black tie. Their grey trousers were stovepipe style, tapering from the thighs to very narrow round their ankles. Those who were not Teddy Boys, like myself, wore a sports jacket with a conventional shirt and straight trousers with turnups. The 'Teds' seemed to have no trouble finding a dancing partner and they would always jive except when dancing close up. Those who could not jive did a version of the foxtrot. However, throughout the evening, the compere would invite everyone to do the Tango, Paso Doble or Samba or a new dance called the Mambo.

My main problem when dancing was my perspiring hands. Even constantly holding a handkerchief in my hands did not help. Hence, at the end of each dance, I would be politely thanked and my dancing partner would walk abruptly away from me. I soon learnt to sense a girl who was prepared to tolerate my wet hands and I would end up dancing with her most of the evening.

On the odd occasion I managed to extract a telephone number and make a date. I nearly always, for the first date, met the girl at Piccadilly or Oxford Circus tube station on a Sunday afternoon. We would just walk down to the Embankment, cross over Hungerford footbridge to the Festival Hall gardens and sit on a bench overlooking the river. Sometimes from there we would go on to visit a gallery or museum. My wages were less than five pounds per week. After paying my rent and fares and the trips to the dance halls, I did not have much left. If it were not for the fact that I had meals at work, I would have had no spare money at all. Fortunately most of the girls I dated always offered to pay for themselves which meant that we could have a light snack while resting during an afternoon hike round the West End.

Work at the coffee house must have begun to get the better of me although I was not really aware of it at the time. I began to become critical of the management and, at first, I had my protests and demands listened to. Eventually, I overstepped the mark and the manageress tried to placate me but I was full of it and the result was that I had to either comply or go. I chose to go.

Unemployed again, I was back to perusing the work vacancy columns in the evening papers. One morning while wandering around Earl's Court I saw a sign in a window advertising a vacancy. I passed the shop a few times and eventually plucked up the courage to go in and enquire. The man behind the counter was round faced with a handlebar moustache. I told him that I needed a job and would be willing to consider what he had on offer. He looked at me and said that he knew of a more suitable job in a coffee bar kitchen - would I be interested? On my reply, he phoned the coffee bar which was opposite South Kensington station, and made an appointment for me I went there immediately.

The job was for a kitchen porter, which I accepted without asking any questions. I started at eight am the next morning. I had to leave my digs in Swiss Cottage before seven. In those days, if you bought a return ticket before 7.30am, the price was only a little over half the normal fare. It was known as the Workman's ticket. The early morning tubes were never crowded and most of the travellers were men in their work clothing. Once I had begun to work, I discovered that I had to work seven days a week. On Sundays I only needed to be at work at ten in the morning and worked until midday. Normally I finished at three in the afternoon; hence, I was expected to make up for a shorter day by working a few hours on a Sunday. The tubes started later on Sunday and there was no workman's fare.

A woman who ran the business as a hobby owned the coffee bar. There was a chef, a waitress, a Gaggia coffee machine operator who doubled as the manager and me, the kitchen porter. The day began with my washing up from the previous night and cleaning the kitchen floor, and then I was at the beck and call of the Chef. During the morning it was peaceful and everything seemed to proceed at an even pace. After noon the lunchtime trade began and the pace hotted up in every sense. By one o'clock it was as if all hell was let loose. The waitress was bringing in the orders, the clients were complaining to her about delays and she, in turn, relayed the complaints to the Chef. The demands on me for clean crockery, cutlery, pots and pans increased rapidly. All gas rings on the hob were flaming, the ovens were working overtime and the temperature increased to the extent that both the chef and I were perspiring. Tempers were high and often a pan or pot was flung at me for immediate attention. No one spoke to anyone. Once the last lunch customer had been served everything began to cool down and, by half past two, we all began to speak to each other and the Chef prepared our meals for us.

During the morning most of the customers were foreign students from a nearby private college. Once, while passing through the restaurant on return from an errand, I noticed some of the students doing their maths prep work. Looking over their shoulders, I realised that I had already passed a higher level exam and my immediate thoughts were that I should try and start to look for more appropriate employment.

The Chef let me eat whatever I wanted and often craftily placed a wrapped up food package in my jacket pocket for my evening meal.

I continued to visit the Lyceum whenever I could. Once, in a different dance hall in Charing Cross road, a fight broke out between Black and White males. Within seconds all the Blacks joined in. However, to my amazement, the manager went in and single handily stopped the brawl, throwing out most of those involved from both sides. In those days there were many African students from Ghana and Nigeria and the first wave of West Indian migrants. In any situation the whites were in the majority, however, the majority did not get involved in any inter-racial fights. I never witnessed a brawl in the Lyceum.

One of my dates wanted to see a film showing at a cinema in the Haymarket next to my ex-coffee house. I stood in the queue for the cheapest tickets. As soon as I had purchased them, the doorman, who I regularly gave free coffee and cakes to, recognised me and ushered my partner and myself into the most expensive seats.

Chapter 8

That winter, my first in England, the days seemed to be much longer, darker and colder than I had experienced. Each evening I would buy a copy of the *Evening Standard* and look through the vacancy columns. Eventually I found an advert for a laboratory assistant at St. Bartholmew's Hospital Medical School. I wrote out a letter of application in the manner that I had been taught at High School in Johannesburg. I carefully listed the exams I had passed as well as pointing out that I had university entrance, a South African Matriculation Certificate, and that I could produce a reference if need be. There were no such things as photocopiers and sending an original reference was too risky. Within a few days I received an invitation for an interview.

I had to take time off my kitchen work. My interviewers were the Professor of - and the Reader in - Physiology. The reader was a short, portly man whose name was Dr. Donald Macdonald. I had misunderstood the advert which was really only for someone to tidy up the labs and do the washing up. Once that was explained to me I told them that I was still interested. In spite of the post being the most junior in the department, it seemed as if I was being interviewed for a lectureship. During the interview the Professor read my letter again and asked to see my reference. They were both impressed by the fact that my postal address was NW3. The interview lasted about a half-hour and then I was told that they would contact me. About three days later I received a job offer asking me to start at the beginning of the next week. The entire staff of the restaurant was both impressed and pleased for me.

The medical school was located at Charterhouse Square near to Aldersgate tube station in the grounds of an old monastery dating back to the fourteenth century. Once through the ancient gate there was a large quadrangle with a lawn in the middle. On the immediate right hand side of the gate was the anatomy department housed in a building attributed to Henry VIII. Alongside that building was a modern hostel. Directly opposite to the gate was the modern physiology block, part of which was still under construction. Parts of the original monastery buildings, on the left-hand side of the quadrangle, were still used as the physiology teaching laboratory, the technical preparation rooms and a rest room for the technical staff.

On my first Monday the senior lab technician, who showed me round and introduced me to the rest of the technical staff who welcomed me. I felt very important wandering around in my white lab coat but, by the time it was the morning coffee break, I still did not have a clue about the job. I had no laboratory bench skills whatsoever and the post that I was in was really for a lab auxiliary, that is, someone to wash up and keep the labs tidy. However, before my arrival they had decided to use me as an extra research technician. I was attached to Richard who had been working there since he had left school and was waiting to be called up for National Service. My first job was to help him change some gas cylinders.

Among my new work companions were Ethel and Rose, two spinster ladies who lived together; Pat, an Irishman who was in his early thirties and was in his final year of a part-time degree; John, a forty-year-old bachelor who had survived a Japanese prisoner of war camp and, finally, Miriam a very pretty twenty year old. The team's task was to maintain the physiology teaching labs, to prepare the practical for the medical students, and to assist with research.

By the end of the week I had learned to prepare solutions and to smoke paper and stick it on rotating drums to record frog heart respiratory movements. After a few weeks I was assigned to a Dr. Koffmann who had migrated to England from Austria after the war. She had obtained a degree in Physiology by part-time study at Chelsea Polytechnic and after completing a doctorate, had been appointed as lecturer in Physiology. Her specialty was neurophysiology. As far as I knew, she had never been married. She was temperamental and none of the technicians wanted to work with her, hence I, the newest recruit, was given the task of being her research assistant and was exempted from having to prepare teaching classes. Looking back the department must have felt very pleased as they had, for the same wages as a laboratory assistant (a glorified washer up), acquired a research assistant. After a few weeks I was also expected to assist her when she demonstrated various aspects of physiology to the medical students.

The two best students in physiology at the end of their pre-clinical studies were awarded a scholarship to do a special degree project in physiology and I was also assigned to help them. After preparing for their needs I was used as a guinea pig for some of their experiments.

The reader, Dr. Donald McDonald, was researching the mechanism of how cats always managed to land on their feet. They set out to film using high-speed photography to analyse the movements of a cat during free fall. This was a pre-video slow motion action replay. A high-speed camera driven by a very fast electric motor that consumed a reel of film in a matter of seconds was used. The cat was placed in a large Perspex cylindrical tube suspended about three feet off the ground. The tube could be rotated and, by pulling a lever rapidly, opened to release the animal into the air to fall onto cushions. The idea was to film the whole operation and then to examine the film frame by frame. Both a normal cat and a white, blue-eyed cat (which are genetically deaf) loaned to us by Professor Haldane from University College were used in order to try and find out what signals and clues the cat used to define its position in space. One of the tests involved placing a blindfold over the cat's head. Professor Samson Wright, who at the time had written the definitive textbook on physiology for medical students, also joined us.

The actual experiments did not take long but it took nearly two weeks for the films to be developed and returned. The results showed that once in the air the blindfolded cat first rotated its head and front paws into a position facing down followed by the rotation of the rear part of the body. The back legs were now in the same position as the forelegs so the cat would land on its feet. The rotation of the tail assisted in maintaining the balance of the body in the air. When seen at normal speed, the whole process gave the impression of temporarily defying gravity. However, this was reflex reaction because if the cat were to be released facing downwards, it would nearly always land on its back.

Once the films had been analysed frame by frame, the detail of each aspect of the cats fall was mapped out. I was summoned to the Reader's office and told that I was to make a model cat, which could be used to demonstrate what they had found out. I was instructed to purchase whatever I needed and not worry about the costs. My immediate reaction was to go out and try and purchase a toy cat which I could then dismember and reassemble into the form required. After wandering around all the West End toyshops, I returned empty handed and reported my findings to the Reader. He then told me that he had already been on a sortie and had also found nothing suitable. I was then told to go down to the workshop and make a model cat.

I acquired a ten-inch long piece of four by four wood and used a lathe to convert it into a cylinder and, with a hand rasp, changed it into an oval shape. I then drilled a hole down the centre and found a metal rod that fitted loosely into the hole. I cut the rod in half and made a joint so that the rod could bend through 180 degrees. I cut the wooden body in half and rounded the inner edges. The rod placed through the middle of the body allowed the two halves to rotate, as well as bending left or right while rotating. I made four legs and jointed them into the body so that they could be moved backwards and forwards. I also fitted a tail with a series of joints allowing the tail to swing round while the body was being rotated. I carved a head and attached it to the body with a dumbbell-shaped brass rod. I painted the upper part of the body black and the bottom white - the colours of St. Bartholomew's Hospital. The cat could be made to stand with its tail in the air and when necessary, could be lifted up and manipulated by hand to imitate the movements of a cat falling through the air.

At that year's annual symposium of the Physiological Society, Dr. MacDonald showed his films and used my model to show, for the first time in public, exactly how cats appear to defy gravity when falling. I was told by one of the junior lecturers who attended the meeting that the paper together with the film and the model was one of the highlights of that meeting. About a year later, I heard that my model was used at subsequent meetings in both the UK and the USA. Drawings of my model were also used in published articles.

Chapter 9

I was still living in Swiss Cottage but had found myself much cheaper digs. I was now paying only twenty-one and six per week for a room in South Hampstead. The building was on a slope so from the front my room was on the ground floor but from the back it was actually one floor above ground level. The garden backed onto the main railway lines to Euston and Kings Cross. Those were days of steam trains but somehow or other my sleep patterns were not disrupted.

My landlady, a short rotund grey-haired woman, wore long dresses and had rows of large beads dangling round her neck. She also had a pet bulldog. She made a point of speaking to me more than once a week. I was always terrified that I would upset her because at the blink of an eye she would throw me out. She said that at the price she charged she would easily find another tenant.

My take home wages were four pounds nineteen and six. My rent was one pound one shilling and sixpence. My tube fare for the week was six shillings and seven pence. My food bill was five shillings a day, which left me with about one pound and five shillings to spend. My breakfast consisted of two buttered roles bought at a bakery close to the gate of the medical school. My midday meal was purchased in the staff canteen at the back of the students' refectory. On weekends I ate only snacks or in a café if I could find one open on a Saturday. Concerts, theatre, and the cinema all became very rare excursions. If I did spend money on entertainment it was nearly always an entrance fee into a dance club or dance hall. Smaller West End dance clubs that were open on Sunday nights charged about four to five shillings, and in areas like Swiss Cottage only two and six for entrance. The music in all clubs, big and small, was always live. Disc Jockeys and discos had not yet been thought up. Most of the cheap clubs did not sell alcoholic drinks, only Coke, Pepsi or lemonade - none I could afford. Nearly all the girls and boys without partners were in groups of three to four. I was more often than not the only person on my own, which probably created an air of suspicion round me. Once in a while I would dance with more than one partner and, some nights, end up with an address or telephone number and arrange a date.

One Sunday evening just before I began to work at the Hospital I went to listen to a concert at the Festival Hall conducted by Sir Thomas Beecham. The program included music by Bach, Beethoven and Brahms. At the end of the concert, after all the applause, Beecham silenced the audience and made a speech. After the usual thanks he then said "Now that you have heard the three B's remember there now might be a fourth".

My nightmare fear of a date was always that I wouldn't I remember what she looked like after our initial meeting in the half-light of a cheap nightclub. Most of the dates were on Sunday afternoons and I was always early and, luckily for me, they nearly always recognised me and approached with a big smile. More frequently than not, weather permitting, we strolled down toward the embankment and crossed over the river by way of the Hungerford footbridge stopping half way to look down river and admire the view of St. Paul's Cathedral, which was not surrounded by tall buildings as it is today. There used to be concrete plinths with seats that projected over the side of the river. We sat down and watched the river go by while getting to know one another. After a long chat we strolled off for a cup of tea or coffee or an ice cream. There were, by todays standards, surprisingly few cheap places open on a Sunday afternoon. I knew of a few cheap cafés in Soho I would manoeuvre toward. My poverty must have been obvious as I cannot remember a girlfriend not offering to pay for her share. Some even wanted to pay for me.

If the weather was kind another favourite haunt was a stroll through either Hyde Park or Regents Park, often including spending an hour rowing my date round the lake. On rainy or cloudy days we would go to a gallery or museum. I was quite used to walking everywhere and did not ever consider that my partner was wearing her best non-walking shoes and probably never walked much. They were very polite and never complained about sore feet or that they were starving. Once in a while I would stroll down past the cinema in the Haymarket and, if I was lucky, the doorman on duty would remember me from my coffee bar days.

Among many topics that I would talk about was the fact that I was missing a juicy steak, a luxury item then, which I ate regularly in South Africa. After the date, if the vibes were right, I would wait until midweek to phone her again. Often I would tell some story or other on the phone as part of my chat-up line. One of the girls (Joan), unbeknown to me, had one of the very early devices for recording telephone calls. Joan invited me over the following weekend for a Saturday night meal at her parent's house in Cockfosters. I had not been that far out of central London since I had returned from Scotland. No doubt my desire for a steak had been conveyed to her parents, and as her father owned a butcher shop I was served up a plate size deliciously cooked piece of steak. During the meal conversation it became very obvious that they knew a great deal about me and I soon discovered why. Joan had recorded all of our telephone conversations.

After that meal she invited me to a party at her house. It was then that I discovered that she had a regular boyfriend who owned his own car. I bowed out very quickly. I talked most of the evening to her boyfriend's mate. I saw him again about three weeks later in a coffee bar in Golders Green and went up to speak to him. In front of his crowd he glared at me and told me loudly and aggressively that he did not know who I was and to clear off.

I still continued to patronise the coffee bar in Northumberland Avenue opposite South Africa house on most Saturday mornings hoping to meet someone that I knew or just to strike up a temporary new friendship. One particular morning I met Bill, a Coloured (a person of mixed race in South African parlance) from Johannesburg. He was with some friend's (one lad and two girls) who invited me to become part of their party and when it was time for them to move off, I traipsed along. We wandered off first to the national gallery then ended up in one of the girl's flats eating fish and chips. Before I left Bill and I exchanged telephone numbers and agreed to meet next Saturday in the coffee house.

It turned out that Bill worked in a small embroidery factory in Clerkenwell not far from Charterhouse Square where I was working. From then on, on Saturday morning when he or I had to work, we would meet and have a bacon sandwich in a café next door to his work place. After that we would wander off to the West End.

One Saturday afternoon we were on the South Embankment alongside the Festival Hall strolling past the railway arches occupied by small businesses or craftsmen of sorts. Outside one of the arches, there was a small handwritten notice which said, "Art exhibition, come in." Inside we saw black and white lined drawings of famous and not so famous people hanging all over the walls and scattered about. Some of them were cartoons. In the corner sat a man aged about fifty wearing an old jacket, no tie, and looking very ordinary. He greeted us and invited us to look around and then started up a conversation and offered us a cup of coffee and biscuits. He spoke English with a mid-European accent. He dominated the chat and was very pleased to know that we agreed with his left wing views. Before we left he told his name, which was Felix Topolski, and we each purchased one of his signed post card size drawings. It was a few weeks later that we realised what a well-known artist he was and how many of his illustrations were published in various forms.

One Saturday afternoon I arranged to meet Bill outside the Dominion theatre in Tottenham Court Road. He said that he was going to bring along a friend to join us. I arrived about fifteen minutes early and ten minutes later a gorgeous Diana Dors look alike appeared and stood in the doorway of the theatre. I stood by the exit from the tube station where I had arranged to meet Bill. While I was waiting, I kept looking over my shoulder at the blonde beauty. Finally Bill arrived and, after greeting him, I immediately drew his attention to the lady in the doorway. Bill smiled at me and half ignoring my comments, said let's go meet his friend. I became absolutely speechless as he walked straight over the blonde and greeted her and then introduced me to his friend Sarah. Bill managed to manoeuvre himself to be briefly behind her so that he could witness my surprise, delight and embarrassment. I never found out how or when he had met Sarah but the three of us met up for the next few weekends.

One Saturday Bill invited me to accompany him to a seminar. I met Bill at a tube station in North London. Together, we walked to a large house that belonged to a headmaster friend of Bill's. They had met through a local social group. We drove off to a destination of a large house in Hertfordshire. The topic of the seminar was religious socialism. During the morning sessions Bill and I, for most of the time, were listeners. After lunch we split into small discussion groups and were coerced into giving our views. Ideas and concepts that I had acquired while attending Zionist youth groups in Johannesburg were somehow dragged out of me. Whatever I said must have made an impact as the headmaster told Bill, a few days later, that I had made a good impression during the afternoon sessions.

Chapter 10

That June summer began with a vengeance and for the first time since my arrival in England, I felt hot and experienced bright sunlight again. The new Physiology wing was now completed and we began to move equipment about. The top floor was designated to be the new animal house. Bolts had been set in the walls to attach the metal cage shelves. Three of us were assigned to the job of assembling the shelves. The primitive air conditioning to keep the animals at an even temperature was not yet commissioned. The hot daytime temperature soon heated up the rooms. While working, I changed into a pair of Khaki shorts that I had brought with me from South Africa. Apart from sport, shorts were only worn in the tropics, the Mediterranean and at the seaside. If you dared to wear shorts anywhere else you had to put up with being stared at and hearing a barrage of crude remarks. The first day that I wore them at work, the word got round and no end of people found an excuse to walk through the building to stare at me. The chief technician and the professor actually held a discussion to consider whether or not it was safe to work in shorts. Whatever they decided I wore them for the next two weeks until we had fitted out all the rooms in the new animal house.

As far as I was concerned I had come from a culture where it was considered great to have an opportunity to wear shorts, especially during the week in a work environment. Hence most of the comments and stares did not mean much to me I felt that I was doing the right thing. During the rest of the summer weekends, I wore my shorts wherever possible even though I could feel everyone looking and sniggering.

I was always short of money so I found myself a weekend job in a West End restaurant that catered for weddings and other functions. I worked on either a Saturday or Sunday night in the still room washing glasses. Apart from an hourly wage, I was also given a meal. When we left at the end of the shift we were always searched to ensure that we were not stealing any food or drink. The glasses often contained leftover wine. I had two large jugs handy, one for red and the other for white wine. During the course of the evening I would fill up both jugs and then trade them with the chefs for luxury food such as smoked salmon, steak or beef. The chefs drank the wine straight from the jugs. When it was time for me to have my meal the chefs would hide my luxury items under a layer of mashed potatoes, which was part of the staff meals.

That job only lasted a few weeks and I then worked as a kitchen porter in a restaurant near to Finchley Road tube station. Unfortunately for me, there was a window that overlooked some tennis courts that reminded of my last job in Johannesburg. If I were there now, no way would I be in a hot sweaty kitchen during summer evenings. After two weeks, my emotions got the better of me and I walked out of my evening job.

At the end of the second week in August my pay packet was unusually large. It contained three weeks wages. This was because it was the start of my annual fortnight holiday. Once I realised that I did not have to be at work on Monday I decided do some travelling. On Saturday morning I caught a train to Cambridge then hitch-hiked to St. Ives in Cambridgeshire and stayed the night in a Youth Hostel which was a converted water mill. The river flowed under the dormitories. The next day I made my way to a farm camp at Fridaybridge, the one I stayed at after I had just arrived in England. I managed to slip in unnoticed and wandered around the Nissan huts and found myself a bed and hid my rucksack. I then wandered around and bumped into the camp manager who recognised me. I told him that I had come to do a fortnight's work and he said that I could start Monday.

During that afternoon I joined in a cricket match and while fielding close to the batsman, caught the ball. My delight disguised the pain. Later in the afternoon I was taken to the local hospital where the diagnosis turned out to be a fractured finger and my left hand was encased in plaster. Returning to the camp, now very conspicuous, the camp manager sent a message requesting me to leave the camp the next morning as I would not be allowed to work.

On the Monday morning I hitched to Sherringham and stayed at the local Youth Hostel. From there I moved via several lifts to Yarmouth. I was amazed at the sight of rows of mobile fish and chips vans parked on the promenade. After a night in a hostel, I found myself in Norwich. The local Youth Hostel was full for the night so they sent me to a recommended but cheap bed and breakfast. The landlord, a man in his forties, called me aside and asked me if I would mind sharing what I thought to be a room with other lodgers to which I agreed. I made my way to a large room full of bunk beds and looked for my bed. While I was looking, one of the other visitors asked me had I realised that the landlord had not just asked me to share a room but wanted me to share a bed with him. After catching my breath I went and told him abruptly that I was not sharing a bed with anyone and that I had agreed to share a room with the other hikers only. Once I settled down in the room I was told by the other fellows that he tried it on with all of them.

During breakfast the next day one of the lads called John, persuaded me to travel with him on the back of his 125cc motorbike. I had to keep my rucksack on my back while sitting on the pillion seat. We made our way slowly to the Norfolk Broads and then spent the night in Yarmouth. The next morning, while back on the bike travelling slowly through Yarmouth, we came up to a crossroad. Although the bike slowed down to almost walking pace, we did not stop. A double-decker bus crossed our path. John managed to turn the bike parallel to the slowing bus but the side of the handlebars hit the side of the bus. From the pavements we heard shouts of, look out! We were dragged along for about a yard and then toppled over. I fell off and landed on my rucksack, which cushioned my fall. My main concern at the time was the hand in plaster of Paris and I somehow kept it away from any collision. When the bystanders rushed over to us, they found me with my back on my rucksack and my plastered hand held aloft facing the sky.

Once over the shock we determined neither of us was hurt. The bike was okay but the side panel of the bus was slightly dented. The police arrived and, after some initial questioning, we were asked to go to the local police station. During the process of making statements, I discovered that John was the nephew of the Lord Lieutenant of Norfolk. That impressed the police and, after about an hour, we were allowed to go on our way.

The break lever on the handle bar was slightly damaged and, after travelling for about an hour, we both decided that it was not safe with me on the back so we parted. John rode off back to the Broads and I decided not to push my luck any more and to make my way slowly back to London. I had hoped that I would work for at least ten days and this would help my finances. Instead I now had to face the rest of the holiday living on my vacation wages. My landlady was surprised to see me arrive back on the Sunday and even more horrified when she saw my hand in plaster. The Wisbech hospital had given me x-rays when I told them that I worked at St. Bartholmew's Hospital and told me to report to the outpatients in ten days time. On the following Thursday, I went into work and once again my plaster attracted attention and sympathy and I was sent over to casualty with my x-rays. Being staff I somehow avoided endless queues and was soon examined by a surgeon. He and a colleague looked very carefully at my x-rays and both concluded that the Wisbech doctor must have had very special eyes because neither could see any bone damage and immediately ordered the plaster to be cut off my hand. I was then discharged.

That weekend, the last of my holiday, I started to think about my future and whether to attend evening classes, or try and study full time. I got hold of a copy of the entry requirements to the University of London. Although my South African matriculation was sufficient to gain entry to a South African university, to study at a British university I still had to pass at least two A-levels.

Chapter 11

A few weeks before my holiday I bumped into Mervyn G. in central London who had spent some of his childhood at the same hostel for soldiers' wives and families as I had during the early part of the war. He and I were constantly being compared by our families and, as a result, became friends and rivals. At the age of about five, we were actually made to punch it out wearing a pair of oversized boxing gloves. He had come to England working on a cargo ship and had landed in Cardiff where he stayed for few months until moving down to London. We met up occasionally to go to the theatre or just wander about. One mid-week he phoned me up and asked me to meet him the next evening and said that he would treat me to a meal and visit to the theatre.

During the meal he explained that he could not take it any more in England and that his mother had sent him money for his return fare and told him to contact me and treat me to a night out. I have never heard from or seen Mervyn G. since that evening.

I did consider returning to South Africa to study at Witwatersrand University and wrote to my mother asking if she would pay my fare. She refused saying that I should try and find job on a ship and work my way home. I went down to the docks to see if it was feasible. I reached the dock gates and the atmosphere seemed so foreboding that I crossed the road and caught the next bus, making up my mind to remain in England.

A few days after my return to work I went to see the head of the department and told him about my intentions. I said that I was considering resigning so that I could study full time and work in the evenings and weekends to pay my way. He then told me that my mother had written to him asking his advice about whether or not I had the ability to complete a degree course. He agreed that I should first try studying during the day and working in the evenings and, if it did not work out, then do the reverse. After a positive reply to my mother she agreed to help me financially. To start off she sent me an allowance of five pounds per month and, even at that time it was only enough for about two weeks rent. She made it clear to me that she would have to go without in order to help. (Over the next four years the money slowly crept up to seven pounds ten shillings, to ten pounds, twelve and, the final few months it became twenty pounds.) I always felt guilty about accepting that money but six years later, on my first return visit to Johannesburg, I found out the money was part of the maintenance money my father was sending to her each month. He told me that he only kept up the payments knowing that part of the money was being sent to me.

Chapter 12

The academic term started in September and I enrolled at what was then the Regent's Street Polytechnic. The Chemistry, Botany and Zoology course was full so I enrolled on the Maths, Physics and Chemistry course.

During the previous month I had found the offices of the British Jewish Ort Oze organisation. Their offices were in Swiss Cottage very near to my digs. I had already worked on the South African Ort Oze farm. I was hoping to get some financial help from them but I was up against so much red tape that I gave up. However, they did help to find me a new accommodation with a Jewish family in Hampstead. It was in Finchley Road on the boundary between Hampstead and West Hampstead. It was an NW3 postal address, which made it sound a lot smarter than it actually was. My landlady was an elderly Jewish lady and I had a small room in her rather large flat. She was very different from my previous landlady, speaking with a heavy Austrian accent. She and her family were some of the many thousands who had escaped from Austria in the late thirties. Hampstead, in those days, was populated with refugees who had fled from Nazism. In many ways, it reminded me of my early youth in the Johannesburg suburb of Doornfontein. The main difference was that there were no Afrikaners and almost no Blacks.

Although there were no kosher butchers in Finchley Road (they had moved to Golders Green and North London), there were continental style delicatessens and bakeries such as Grodzinkis. Finchley Road began where St. Johns Street ended and stretched through Swiss Cottage, Finchley Road tube station, the bottom of Heath Drive, through Golders Green, Fortune Green and beyond the North Circular. Travelling by bus toward Swiss Cottage there were empty sites along both sides of the Finchley Road which I assumed to be caused by flying bombs at the end of the war. About halfway between Swiss Cottage and Finchley Road tube station on the left hand side was the old Hampstead baths which, apart from housing a swimming pool, had a gymnasium and a series of public wash houses which were still in use.

At the beginning of the hot weather, while I was still working at St. Barts., I decided to go for a swim one evening. It was my first experience of indoor swimming. As I was leaving, I saw on the notice board that there was a Jewish Swimming Club called Bar Kochba that ran a water polo team and had a gymnastic section, and about a week later I watched them playing water polo. Most of the team were close to or in their thirties and, from their accents I realised they were all refugees. I found out later that in Vienna there were many Jewish sports clubs and the Bar Kochba was one of them. Those members who had survived the war had founded the London version of the club. I also found out that the headquarters of the British Maccabee Association, a body which oversaw all Jewish sports clubs throughout the United Kingdom, was in West Hampstead. Bar Kochba operated as a separate organisation under the umbrella of the Maccabee association. Every Sunday night they held a social at a venue very convenient for me. There was no need for transport or fares and hence I attended as often as possible.

I found myself once again meeting up with Jews but unlike in South Africa, they were not related or old school or neighbourhood peers. In London, when I was in Jewish company, it was always with people near my own age. I never met any of their parents or visited any Jewish homes. I think that I must have been the first contemporary that my English Jewish friends had met that did not live with his parents. I now began to live in world where I took everybody at their face value and their background and religion was not important to me but it did help that there was a common element.

My objective now that I had given up my job was to pass my A-levels and then to proceed on to university to obtain a degree in the sciences. I still had to pay the rent and carry out all of my normal domestic chores such as doing my washing, shopping and cooking.

The first day of study was quite unceremonious. On the notice board outside of the department office was a detailed timetable, a list of groups and names. The first lecture was an introduction to applied mathematics in a room that overlooked upper Regent Street. It seemed so strange. There I was right in the centre of London in a building that, on the outside, looked like any other in that part of the West End. I had grown up with a picture in my mind of a post school University building set in a grand campus. The portal of the building should have been a copy of the Greek Parthenon with the pillars and layers of concrete stairs leading up to the entrance. How was I going to convince all in Johannesburg that I was now actually studying at their equivalent of a 'versity?'

There were about fifteen to twenty of us in the group. There was a Nigerian, a Sikh from Kenya, a Singaporean, a Cypriot and, apart from myself and one Irishman, the rest of the group were from England. Those were the days when anyone who was a citizen of the Commonwealth or British Empire was allowed into England without any fuss or need for special permits, etc. The migration from the West Indies had only just begun. It was still a talking point to see a Black bus conductor or station person on the underground.

My main problem (that was to remain with me for many years to come) was the lack of money. Money to pay the rent, to buy food, books, clothes, etc., was always in short supply. Most of my clothes that I had at the time were those that I had brought with me from South Africa. Another problem was shoes; they seemed to wear out at a much faster rate. I always had to buy cheap and I would spend a long time looking in shoe shop windows finding a pair of shoes that I thought would be hard-wearing but within my price bracket. Looking back, I always wore what could be called plain, sensible, unfashionable shoes. Perhaps I had been brainwashed by my mother or, deep down was trying to impersonate the values I thought to be that of someone who was above fashion and culture.

While I was working in the restaurant in South Kensington I bought a new pair of black shoes. The Italian waiter took them out of the box and held them up and proclaimed to all that only an Englishman would buy and wear such a pair of shoes.

I had imagined that once I was studying again, I would be among contemporaries all the time, not just during the day but evenings and weekends as well. At the end of the day, we left and did not see one another till the next morning class. Once the day finished I seemed to have to face a void of company. Apart from those people I had met at the Jewish youth club (who I only saw on a Sunday night and perhaps one evening a week at swimming or gym) and my landlady, I did not really know anyone else. It was to be many years before I learnt about the important usefulness of pub culture. Of course I should have buried my head in my books, which I did do, but there was still plenty of time to want to socialise.

I did not have radio or any form of record player or access to television so, once in the confines of my room, I sat in silence. The more or less enforced solitude remained with me until the next morning. Breakfast, if any, was a hot drink and a piece of toast. Apart from a morning greeting to the landlady or a familiar neighbour, the first real conversation would be with a fellow student. Even then, most of them had no need for any morning chat and did not always respond to my over-enthusiastic chatter. All the other foreign students lived with either relatives, friends or in hostels, and the locals lived with their parents.

The morning coffee break with a doughnut was my breakfast. Lunch was a hot meal with vegetables and a sweet, my only substantial meal of the day. The canteen opened in the late afternoon to feed the evening students so I usually indulged in an egg on toast or a slice of Welsh rarebit and tea. Most of my fellow students by then had retreated to their lodgings or homes. Afternoon library sessions were, once again, spells of silence. However at the time, I was not really aware of how different my circumstances were I was too preoccupied with my survival and my future.

I joined the rugby club, the one sport I had done reasonably well at school. I had not played since I had left school. Rugby matches were on Saturday afternoons. The Poly playing fields were situated in Chiswick. In those days, to travel anywhere by bus or tube for which the fare cost more than a sixpence was like going on a journey into the country for me. From Swiss Cottage to Chiswick took the best part of an hour that included a long walk from the station to the playing fields.

On the day of the trial games, the only person I knew was one of my classmates. For some reason or other, I had brought a South African rugby shirt that I had 'acquired' from a friend, shorts, socks and a pair of cheap boots. I had not realised at the time that my boots were soccer boots, the wearing of which were frowned upon by the rugby fraternity. After the game we were all treated to tea, sandwiches and cakes. After that, everyone but me retreated to the bar. At that time, I did not know how much beer drinking was part of the rugby culture and, besides I could not afford to drink alcohol. I was still in the South African Jewish frame of mind where drinking in bars (beer halls) was not considered to be the done thing. After that, I became a regular member of the team but never stayed behind for the beer. I did not really benefit, at the time, from the social side of rugby. I would return, after a match, to the cold void of my digs. After being part of a group whether it was in the class, at a social, or on a sports team then having to return to the solitude of my room became the underlying theme of my existence.

On Friday nights there was a group of students who ran a hop. They had a record player and, from five till seven in the evening, played popular music that we could jive to. They charged us nine pence and were probably, in 1955-1956 the first if not the original disc jockeys. Friday night was the only chance there was to really socialise with students from the rest of the institute. I learnt to jive and met my first serious girlfriend. I did not know that after the hops most of the 'hoppers' retreated to a local pub.

No breakfast, a bun at coffee break, a cooked meal at lunch and, then a snack in the evenings was now my routine. I envied those colleagues who lived in hostels or with families and relatives and who talked about their evening meals and Sunday lunches. They had their rooms to study in as well as always having someone on hand to talk to. They had access to radio and television and more money to spend.

My monthly allowance of seven pounds ten shillings was only just enough to keep me going for about a fortnight. I found an evening job in a coffee bar in Golders Green called La Gioconda. Like my job in the South Kensington restaurant, it was owned by a divorcee and managed by an Italian. I was taught to use the latest Italian Gaggia coffee-making machine. I was most likely taken on because I could easily pass for an Italian. I was expected to be at work by six pm. The wages were not brilliant, only two shillings and sixpence an hour. The early part of the evening was always quiet and in addition to time for a welcome meal, there was also time to read. It was difficult to concentrate as there was always music being played from a record player kept under the counter and it was my task to keep it going.

Closing time was near to midnight and after the cinema closed was the busiest time and when I felt most tired. Once I was allowed to leave, it would be a mad rush to catch the last bus to Golders Green station and then hopefully catch the last bus that went up Finchley Road toward Swiss Cottage. I would arrive back in my room exhausted, then have to be up for a nine o'clock lecture. This took care of my activities for four to five nights a week. Somehow I managed at first to avoid working on weekends.

I was flipping in and out of different worlds - my classes, coffee bar, my digs, rugby and the Friday evening hop - without really knowing which I belonged to. To add to the confusion, I was immediately identified as being

South African. Part of me was pleased about it as it made me different but, on the other hand, I wanted to belong and be part of the system.

During my last year in South Africa, while living with the Bornsteins, I had developed a taste for the arts, particularly classical music and fine art and sculpture. Once I had settled in London I went to the Festival Hall or the Albert Hall to listen to a concert whenever I could. Apart from those two halls, there did not seem to be anywhere else to go to listen to live concerts in London at that time.

One Sunday afternoon, I attended my first live Jazz concert at the Festival Hall. The first thing that struck me was the audience – lively, noisy, moving around, constantly applauding and cheering - unlike anything I had experienced before. The bands performing that afternoon were all to become household names - people like Chris Barber and Alex Welsh. Once in a while, I would go the theatre and watch anything from Shakespeare to musicals. I was also a regular visitor to my local library taking out books on everything from Psychology to Tolstoy.

Being informed about the state of the arts was an absolute essential in the Bornstein household and I assumed that, once I was in the company of students, part of our existence would involve debate and discussion about politics, the arts and sport. After my first few weeks, I realised that the likelihood of having such peers in the Maths and Physics department was almost zero. The Biology department had an equal share of males and females and they were mostly local Londoners. I got to know them during coffee and lunch breaks and the Friday hops. They were all studying Chemistry, Physics and Zoology to gain entrance into medical school. They all came from very middle class backgrounds and had attended either grammar or public schools but had decided to do their A-levels in a non-school environment. As I began to socialise with them it became clear that among them were the types of people that, in my ideal world, I would be in contact with as a full-time student. An additional factor that helped me mix with them was that there were at least three Jewish girls from the Golders Green area who had all been to the same school. One was Ada, not a great beauty by any means. She had a stocky build and at first glance most blokes would shy away from her. However, after a closer examination she had very striking eyes and a seductive look about her. I soon found myself during the breaks joining in with them and their classmates. In those days pubs were closed in the afternoons, so we would just hang round in the students lounge or wander off to a Soho coffee bar. I could not stay long as I had to go off to my evening job.

My own classmates took an instant dislike to the Biology group so I had to be very discreet about my meetings. Once again I found myself inhabiting two social worlds.

Ada invited me over to her home for Sunday lunch, the excuse she used was that we would do some Chemistry revision together. I naively thought that she meant academic chemistry but was to soon find out her meaning of the subject. Her parents were from Austria and, like most of the heads of the Jewish families who lived in the Golders Green and Hendon area, had fled from Central or Eastern Europe. Her father was a doctor and had an established practice in the area. They lived very comfortably but did not quite match the opulence of the Johannesburg Bornstiens.

After our meal, Ada invited me up to her bedroom on the pretence that we had work to do. Books and notes were spread out round the room and I was all set for an afternoon of serious Chemistry. At the back of my mind I was hoping that none of my classmates would find out about where I had spent that Sunday. After about a half-hour the conversation wandered off and, while I was lounging on her bed, she came across and kissed me. I did not know quite how to respond. What happened if her parents suddenly entered the room and what would the lads say? I certainly had no intention of getting into a relationship with her and mentally tried to block out the whole episode.

For the next week or two, although I still met up with the Biologists, I tried to keep a friendly distance from Ada. She and her two friends would meet me in the afternoon. The coffee bar that I worked in at the time was not far from their homes; hence, we would all catch the same tube trains. They would actually accompany me all the way and then sit around for about an hour drinking coffee while I set about my job. The Italian manager was polite to me about my friends, but made it obvious that they were not to his taste and hoped that they were also not to mine. The French waitress pointed out to me what striking eyes Ada had. In spite of her attention, (she even came to watch me play rugby) I still tried to keep it all in perspective and just enjoy her companionship. Our relationship became closer when, after one of the games, I discovered that I could not lift my arm and had to have someone to help me get dressed. Ada accompanied me to the casualty department at Middlesex hospital. The X-rays revealed that I had dislocated my shoulder.

In spite of our growing closeness, she kept telling me about a past boyfriend and making me feel quite inadequate. I wanted to break off the relationship, but a stream of passionate letters and long tearful phone calls became the norm. I had neither the courage nor the experience to simply walk away, which I soon came to regret. Just as she had enticed me, she (without me realising it at the time) began to work on a young Israeli lad in our group. One Monday she called me aside during a coffee break and told me quite boldly that our relationship was finished. I was relieved but also very sore about the fact that she, and not I, had ended the relationship. The worst part of it all was that I could not avoid running into them almost every day as well as having been humbled in front of my peers. My confidence took a large blow.

During that relationship, I had met a lot more people than I had previously. I was occupied most of the time and I always seemed to have company. We drifted, mainly on Saturday nights after the coffee bar closed, from large to small parties dancing to 45 rpm records played on 'dancettes'. In every gathering someone had a guitar and during the many singsongs we must have sung the Foggy Dew, John Doolie, the Bandit and every other pseudo folk and pop song of the day at least a hundred times. We jived to Rock Around The Clock, Sydney Bechet's Onions and Louis Armstrong's The Saints until we collapsed into a heap of perspiration. We argued and discussed every left wing topic, talked about the Impressionists and visited the Tate Gallery endless times. We knew all the Goon jokes and mocked suburban culture. We sat on the top balcony of the Albert and Festival Hall and heard numerous versions of the well-known violin and piano concertos.

One of the highlights of the era was attending the live concert given by Louis Armstrong in London; after the musicians union had lifted their ban on American musicians. For some reason or other, at the performance we attended, we were ushered into the front rows instead of the back of the hall and sat no more than ten feet from the great man himself. The end of the relationship did not end my excursions into the arts but they became less frequent.

Chapter 13

My landlady died and her son, who lived in an adjacent four-storeyed building which fronted onto Finchley Road, informed me that I could stay on and all I had to do was pay him the rent from now on.

One of the annual events in Johannesburg was the university students rag day. It was held on a Saturday. A convoy of lorries with decorated 'theme floats' would drive through the centre of the city with the general populace lining the streets while the costumed students collected money for charity. It was considered an essential part of higher education to talk about your rag days. During the spring term the London office of the World University Service held a carnival in Regents Park. The invitations to build floats for the procession was open, not only to the university colleges but, also, to the polytechnics. Posters appeared all round the Poly looking for volunteers to help build a float and to participate. After the Friday night hop all those who were keen enough went down to basement workshop to contribute their labour. Our theme was dragon. The frame was wire and wood and for the outer covering hundreds of egg boxes were used. I felt great actually helping to put the dragon's skin on. While working a group of us from my class decided that we would form another float and called ourselves the chain gang. On the Saturday morning all the floats assembled in the grounds of Bedford College in Regents Park. Luckily it was also a very warm spring day. The procession drove though the streets of Camden Town collecting money. It also happened to be the Rugby League Cup final day and there were lots of people from the North who appreciated our efforts and were quite generous moneywise. The procession returned to the park and when we passed the judging rostrum, the chain gang jumped into the front of the float, hooked a chain onto the front of the lorry and pulled it for a few hundred yards. Much to our surprise, we won one of the trophies that were awarded. I left to go to work in the coffee bar and unfortunately did not join in the celebration that evening.

A few weeks after Ada dumped me I met Paula at one of the Friday night hops. During the first term and the first few weeks of the autumn term she had been watching me jiving. I had acquired a regular partner Dusty, an Anglo Burmese girl, who was very slightly built so I could easily lift her. During the dance we could perform all sorts of acrobatic moves. After asking Paula for a dance, who was also quite slim, we tried the throws with some success. Paula lived at the far end of Hampstead and was within walking distance of where my digs were. One evening she arrived at my digs with her dog. A few hours later while getting dressed, we realised that the dog was missing. My room was on the ground floor and the dog must have climbed out of the window. After searching for about an hour Paula plucked up courage and phoned home only be told by an angry and suspicious mother that the dog had found its own way home.

Apart from studying for her A-levels Paula was also having private singing lessons but throughout our entire relationship, which lasted well into the summer, I never heard her sing. One Saturday night I walked her home after a party. Her parents were asleep, the house quiet, the dog did not bark. Her bedroom was on a lower floor than her parents. At about one in the morning we decided that probably the least disturbing way to part would be through the window and down the drainpipe into the front garden. Luckily for us the dog did not stir. Once in the street I walked away with giant strides only to come across two patrolling policemen who had not seen me climb out of the window. They greeted me and I likewise acknowledged them and they must have decided that I was not a criminal and did not stop me.

Toward the end of the summer term, Lionel (a South African who was living in Israel) suddenly appeared one afternoon in the common room. I vaguely recollect having once met him at a Zionist Youth meeting in Johannesburg. He had no luggage with him and in no time he made himself known to all. He followed me back to my digs and I introduced him to my landlord and landlady Mr and Mrs Kave (the K's). I had to depart to my evening coffee bar job and left him. The next morning I discovered that he successfully chatted them up and they had invited him to spend the next few nights there. Then he disappeared as suddenly as he had arrived only to turn up about six weeks later.

To walk to Paula's house, I had to pass by Belsize Park tube station. Above the station was a small silkscreen printing company. On the first day of the summer vacation a notice appeared on the gate that led up to the print works advertising a temporary job vacancy. I walked straight in and made a verbal application. I was told that the pay was hourly and if I wanted the job I could start immediately, which I did. Silkscreen printing involves stretching a very fine piece of silk over a wooden frame. A stencil is ironed onto the screen which is then hinged onto the rack so that it can be brought down to rest horizontally on a printing table. A sheet of paper is placed on the table, and the screen is brought down to rest over the paper. The printer then pours the appropriate coloured paint onto one end of the upper side of the screen, and with the aid of a squeegee pulls the ink across the screen. In doing so, a small amount of paint penetrates through the screen onto the paper. The screen which, is hinged to a frame and is counterbalanced with weights, is then lifted upwards. A helper then lifts the paper off the table and places it in a drying rack. The drying racks are a series of wooden frames which, when not in use, are folded upwards. The first printed sheet is placed on the bottommost rack, which is on the floor. Once a wet sheet is placed on the frame, the next one is brought down leaving just enough space so as not to touch the wet paper. My job was to remove the newly printed sheet from the table and place it on the rack in one movement so as not to cause any creases or smudges.

Belsize Park Tube Station was one of those stations that were clad in red tiles. There were a series of large arches over the entrances. The printing firm occupied the whole of the upper floor. Two partners owned the printing firm. One was from North London and the other, the more flamboyant of the two, lived in Hampstead. They had one office to themselves and the foreman and two secretaries occupied the other office. There was the 'art' room, then the coffee room. All of those rooms had windows that faced the main road and so all the comings and goings on the street and the station were visible. The actual printing took place at the back of the building.

Among the permanent work staff were Art the chief printer and stencil cutter, Sam the stencil cutter assistant and three other printers. One of them, Reg, was Art's brother. There also was a young apprentice named Joe and the janitor was an old character called George.

Our morning always began with an eight o'clock cup of tea, a read of the morning papers, and then work started at about half-past eight. The morning session was usually quite silent but, after coffee break, conversations that began in the rest room usually continued during the printing. Afternoon chat was permeated with sport, sex, jokes and arguments about whom, when, where, etc., were the best.

After a few days I became skilled enough to be able to do other things during the moments when the printer was lining up the paper and then pulling the squeegee. Lying around the workshop were bits of old hardboard, paint brushes and plenty of left over paint of all colours. I set myself up an 'easel' alongside the drying rack and dabbled in painting designs and masks.

At least once a week we heard one of the foreman's wartime adventures. We all soon knew the ins and outs of how his platoon captured a German Bren gun. George entertained us with his pre war courting days and how he first seduced his missus in a Churchyard and made love on a horizontal tombstone.

Joe the apprentice was a fanatic and devoted fan of the young Elvis Presley. So much so that he one day announced that he was going to have Elvis's portrait tattooed on his forearm. We did our best to talk him out of it. Our argument was that in a few years time Elvis will become a little known has been and he would be marked for life.

Art, who played the violin in the local orchestra, said that although he loved Beethoven's music he would never dream of having him tattooed onto any part of his body. Joe was a rough and tough Teddy boy, yet the teasing and harassing eventually got the better of him and he broke down and cried. A week later a picture of and article about Joe and his Elvis tattoo appeared in that week's edition of 'Titbits'.

Art and his brother Reg had both served their national in the Suez Canal zone and both entertained us with stories of young soldier's misdemeanours. Reg had also been in Kenya at the time of the Mau Mau rebellion. Although he was serving as a paramedic, they all had to undergo riot control training. On one occasion his platoon was playing the role of the rioters. They had been away from home for quite a long time and were like all National Servicemen at the time, counting the days to demobilisation. It was a chance for them to express their feelings. Their mock riot became so realistic that one of the trainee soldiers had to be restrained from firing his rifle. On another occasion, the sergeant was asked what they should do if, in the mob, they noticed a pregnant woman. No problem was the reply. You will get rid of two in one go. The young conscripts were sickened by the reply and their dislike for the army grew deeper.

Chapter 14

One Friday afternoon after a day at the printing, I arrived at my digs to find Lionel having a meal with the K's. He was working for a street trader and had arrived in the firm's large old pantechnicon that was used on weekends as a mobile storehouse. He had made it clear that he was there for the weekend. On the Saturday he and I wandered off to the West End where he had prearranged a meeting with an Israeli girl named Sonia. Sonia came back with us to the K's and they invited her to join them for meal and in the evening Lionel took her back to her digs. The three of us met again on Sunday morning on Hampstead Heath. As the day wore on Sonia took more and more interest in me, and less in Lionel. I tried to play it cool but during the late afternoon she took my hand which I pretended not to want. Lionel then took this as a cue to walk away angrily. Sonia then told me that there was nothing between them and that she had only met him a few days ago. The afternoon then dragged on and I eventually left her at Hampstead Tube Station. As I walked up the Finchley road I saw Lionel speeding along in the van and in the driver's cabin with him was the landlord's son Terry and one of his mates thoroughly enjoying the joy ride.

Once inside it was obvious that I was in the doghouse and no amount of explanation had any effect. Lionel drove off that night. Later on the evening I noticed that my alarm clock was missing and then further investigation revealed that my suit and shirts had also disappeared. I immediately reported it to the K's and, to my surprise, they insisted that I go to the local police station and suggest that Lionel was the chief suspect.

A week later the K's had to leave their late mother's flat and I was offered a room in their house. The house was the last one in a row of Edwardian four-story terrace houses the fronts of which faced onto Finchley Road. The main entrances to all the houses were via a back alley. Shops occupied the ground floors of the buildings. The K's house was above an Off-Licence. Once through the front door there was a steep staircase that led to the kitchen, dining room, and the living room. All the rest of the house consisted of bedrooms and bathrooms. The room they offered me was a small one on a mezzanine floor near the top of the house. The room badly needed decorating; there was hardly any paper on the walls and there was a hole in the ceiling but it did have a wash basin. I was not in a position to refuse because the rent was very reasonable and did include breakfast and weekend meals. One of the good things about the room was the view from the window that overlooked the whole of North London.

The Kave family consisted of Mr and Mrs their teenage son Terry and their eleven-year-old daughter Dianne. There was another lodger John Ware who shared a room with Terry and there was Henry, Mr K's business partner who had a room of his own. Henry, as I was to discover later, was also Mrs K's lover. The K family ran a car hire business from the house, hence, in the kitchen there were nearly always two or three of the drivers sitting around waiting for work. Mr K and Henry also drove.

Chapter 15

I had accumulated quite a few paintings, which I left lying round the printing shop and one day after work I walked round to Paula's house and presented her with what I thought was my best effort. Her mother took one look at it and by her expression it was obvious what her thoughts were- that I should have my head seen to. That summer she developed glandular fever and I received a very curt letter from her mother asking me not to see her again and to break off the relationship. From then on I faded out our friendship but never told Paula about her mother's letter.

Apart from needing money, I also wanted to save up for a late summer trip to the continent before the autumn term started. I booked a trip to a work camp in Holland via the student travel service. I finished at the printing works a week before my departure and spent most of the week either watching the South African cricket team at the Oval or just wandering around the galleries and museums of central London.

I arrived on the Sunday evening at Liverpool Street station to catch the boat train to Harwich. Once I had settled into my reserved seat, I discovered that the rest of the passengers in the compartment were destined for the same work camp in Holland. Apart from a young married couple they were all students, one lad and three girls. We were all in reserved cabins for the overnight crossing. However once the ship left the shelter of the harbour it became very obvious that it was going to be a rough crossing.

While wandering around the ship I met a Jewish girl from New York. Her cabin, like mine, was shared with her fellow travellers so we ended up talking into the early hours of the morning. However, on the train to Harlem, my colleagues did not believe that all we did was talk. At Harlem station we were met by a minibus and were driven to our camp near to Zandvoort near the former Dutch Grand Prix circuit. The first sight of our accommodation did not impress any of us. The camp buildings were old army Nissan huts and inside there were rows of iron beds each next to a small cupboard. The wash rooms and toilets equally resembled war leftovers. There was a reasonable dinning room and common room. The thought of the next two weeks in that environment took some digesting. The other inmates of the camp were from France, Belgium, Germany and Spain. The camp manager told us that our task was to work together with the local workman to prepare the dunes for tree planting. Apart from free board and lodging we would be taken on sight seeing trips. With my knowledge of Afrikaans I could understand basic Dutch and I could have simple conversations with the workmen.

Toward the end of the week the novelty of the work wore off and the blisters, aches and pains began to get the better of us. The camp was situated only a few hundred yards from the beach. One late hot afternoon after work we were messing about on the sands when one of the Belgiam lads produced an inflatable canoe. We all took turns in paddling out into the North Sea breakers and then surfing on the waves back onto the beach. Jean, a French student, and I overdid the paddling. We managed to cross the point where the waves broke and moved out with the swell. The currents then started to push us further out and each time we dipped with the swell we lost sight of the shore. At the same our colleagues on the shore also lost sight of us and went to alert one of the foremen, a Dutch student. Jean and I started to paddle back to the beach but the boat was too light to resist the current and our efforts were in vain. I then dived into the sea and grabbed a piece of rope attached to the front of the canoe and started to swim, towing the canoe behind me and Jean continued to paddle. Gradually we moved toward the shore and when we crossed over the breakers we could just see our colleagues gathered on the beach. The waves now began to push us inwards and at that point a patrolling helicopter appeared and hovered above until we were able to wade ashore. Once we were again on *terra firma* and everybody was relieved we then received a strong rebuke from the Dutch foreman who then forbade the use of the canoe.

That weekend we were taken to the flower market, a trip on one of the Lakes and on the Sunday we spent the day in Amsterdam. On the canal boat ride the commentary was in English, Dutch, German and French. Hence we were told everything about Amsterdam four times over. After the canal trip we were free to do our own thing and once John and I had visited the art galleries and wandered around the streets we caught the train back to Harlem. The Dutch College Jazz Band was playing at the local Konsertgebou. As we passed by we looked into the foyer of the theatre and, while standing in the auditorium, I explained to the doorman in Dutch that we just happened to be passing by on our way back to the camp. Whether he understood me or not I was not certain but he then led us to seats and let us in to listen to the rest of the concert free.

Most of the food we ate in the camp seemed to be served up on bread which we began to get a little bored with. The accommodation and the work started to take its toll on all of us. On the last Thursday afternoon I was holding a garden fork and out of pure frustration threw it into the air like a javelin. To my, and some of the other campers, surprise it landed by a wheelbarrow and one of the prongs pierced through the pneumatic tyre and punctured it with a bang. It brought a big cheer from all the campers and luckily for me none of the Dutch saw me do it.

On our last evening we were treated to a film show and a talk by the camp manager. The married member of our group had decided to tell the management of our discontent. He had told a group of us and we all agreed that on the night of the talk we would vocalise our feelings. When the meeting started he remained silent so I stepped in and listed our discontents and disappointments. Half the campers supported me while the rest sat in silence. We received a half-hearted apology and the meeting then proceeded. Later on two of the English girls went up to the camp manager and made it clear to him that they did not agree with me. What I did not know was that, at some time before the meeting, the married student and the girls had got together and decided not to go ahead with the protest but no one had told me.

On our return journey to the UK we all decided that it was not worth paying the extra for a cabin as we knew that we would be sailing into rough weather and that it would be better to sit it out in the lounge. The ship began to toss and turn as soon as it set sail. I sat down in a comfortable chair and laid back and the next thing I knew was that we had sailed into Harwich. Apparently, much to the annoyance of the others, I had snored loudly all the way.

Chapter 16

The new term was only two weeks old when the departmental secretary interrupted a morning lecture calling me out and then telling me that there was an urgent call from the police for me. It was a detective from the Hampstead CID. They had found Lionel and had held him there in custody but they needed to know there and then whether or not I still wanted to press charges. I had to make an instant decision so that they could detain him or else they would have to let him go. I felt my gut twist as I agreed to press charges and I was then asked to report to the police station as soon as possible.

That afternoon I was shown Lionel through a prison cell door peephole for identification purposes. The detective reassured me that I had done the right thing but could not tell me any more. The only thing that I was told was that he bore no grudges against me. Apparently when I reported the theft I had told the police that one of the addresses that he might go to was that of the Ort Oze, which he did, and they contacted the police.

The next morning in Hampstead Magistrates' Court we had to face each other across the courtroom with Lionel in the accused dock and me in the witness box. Once the proceedings started my suit, shirts and alarm clock were all put on display and I had to identify them. Lionel pleaded guilty and I was asked if I wanted any compensation which I declined. The magistrate and those on the bench with her went into a huddle and then gave him a six months suspended sentence. One of the conditions of his release was that he was to seek help immediately. The detective came over to me and I had to sign for my goods. He then told me that Lionel had been living rough and had fallen into bad company and was close to becoming a down and out. My charging him could almost be considered to be a rescue. The detective told me that he wanted to meet me for chat. After his formal release he came over to see me, outside of the courtroom. We were being discreetly watched in case either of us physically attacked the other. That did not happen and we spent the rest of the morning in a café and he told me that the first decent night's sleep that he had for the last week was last night in the police cell. We walked over to Swiss Cottage where we shook hands and I left him outside of the Ort Oze offices. I never saw Lionel again and the only thing that I did hear about him was that he had returned to Israel. I never did find out why he had not sold off my belongings.

I discovered a small jazz club called the Baker Street Jazz club that only opened on Sundays. The first night there I met Lisa, a student who was studying French and German. By the end of the evening I had managed to get her telephone number. One evening during the following week I phoned her and she answered by saying, "Are you the nice man I met last Sunday." After our next meeting I found out that her father was a Liberal Rabbi. It was about the time that I discovered that Paula's father had once been a lay preacher. We met up every now again. One evening walking from West Hampstead tube station, on our way to jazz club we were, as usual in the midst of a 'philosophical' conversation when she asked me about my future and what governed my life. Without any thought I replied "Let others be your teacher but experience your master." Lisa stopped and looked at me and then remarked about how profound she thought that was and she going to make a note of it. Our friendship lasted for quite some time. Toward the end of September, before the term started, I had spent a weekend at farm camp up in Yorkshire. I hitch hiked back and, as soon as I was back in my digs, I telephoned Lisa. I wondered why they took such a long time about eventually answering. Lisa spoke in a very muffled voice and quickly ended the conversation. Back in my room, while looking at the calendar I discovered that I had phoned the Rabbi's house on the night of Yom Kippur!

The debating society used to meet every fortnight and I became quite an active member. Topics generally centred round student life and one debate, which featured every now and again in one form or another, was premarital sex. Those were the days when no member of the opposite sex was allowed into bedrooms without permission given by the landlord or hostel warden and they had to be seen departing by ten. Contraceptives were only sold in barbershops and pharmacists, never on display. Only in certain male toilets were there condom-dispensing machines. Those debates were always well attended and perhaps it was a sign of the times that motions favouring trial marriages were always defeated. One topic we debated was racism and I was asked to put the case for Apartheid just for debating purposes. To both my surprise and my horror the motion in favour of Apartheid was only narrowly defeated. I had managed to convince most of the 'don't knows,' which appalled me, and I vowed that I would never again speak for a motion that I did not believe in even if it was only for debating purposes.

There was a visit to the UK by the Soviet leaders Bulganin and Kruschev who arrived at Portsmouth aboard a Soviet battleship. One of our colleagues' fathers owned a big black limousine. Two engineering students wearing large dark coats and the appropriate headgear were made up to look like the Russian leaders. All who owned motorcycles were summoned. One afternoon when the two leaders were supposed to be at some meeting or other our spoof motorcade set out across the West End and caused quite lot of fuss until the authorities realised that it was a student prank.

That October was very eventful. The Hungarian uprising began and, when the Soviet tanks began to move, there were student demonstrations in all the major capital cities except London. During the morning coffee break we lamented the lack of any British action. Before long we all decided to meet outside at two o'clock and walk to Kensington Gardens to demonstrate outside the Soviet Embassy. The word spread round the institute like wild fire and a huge crowd of us set off first down Wigmore Street and then onto Kensington Gardens. Someone must have informed the police, because as soon as we set out we were met by a group of policemen. They told us that if this was to be a protest march then we could not march on the pavement but that we could march if we all assembled in the road. In that case, they would escort us. In the brief hours between deciding to protest and marching, banners were hastily produced, then with me at the head of the column we marched chanting and singing. The media appeared from nowhere. Newsreel film crews and journalists kept harassing us and, finally, we arrived at our destination only to be greeted by a barricade of police horses and motorcycles blocking the entrance into Kensington gardens. The biggest police inspector that I had ever seen approached me and politely told me that although they understood our feelings, this was as far as we could go. We stood around for about a half an hour making plenty of noise then drifted off.

At the same time, there was the Israeli invasion of Sinai followed by the British and French invasion of the Suez Canal Zone. The following Sunday a huge anti-war demonstration was held at Trafalgar Square in which I heard Nye Bevan call Antony Eden both a knave and a fool. Following the speeches there was a march down Whitehall toward Downing Street. In Whitehall there were ugly scenes of protestors clashing with the police,

police horses charging into the crowd, and a certain amount of mayhem. Although the pace of everything was fast and furious, there were relatively few casualties compared to what I had seen when the South African police charged a crowd on the Johannesburg City Hall steps in the early fifties. As things calmed down, the demonstrators could be seen stroking the horses and feeding them with their sandwiches.

Chapter 17

I managed to buy a second-hand bicycle and every morning cycled down Finchley Road, then St. Johns Street, through St. Johns Wood, into Regents Park and finally past the BBC to the Poly. The bicycle shed at the time was housed in the basement of a Convent in Cavendish Square. To reach the bike shed you had to pass under an archway on which was mounted a sculpture of the Madonna and Child by Jacob Epstein. Every day I would look and marvel at the work of art.

In the West End there were numerous small Jazz clubs as well as guitar music played in coffee bars. On Monday nights, in a small basement club opposite the Windmill theatre, Cy Laurie and his band used to play. It was cheap, only two shillings and sixpence entrance fee, and only non-alcoholic drinks were sold. They would start playing before eight and played on until just after eleven. I normally did not work in the coffee bar on Monday nights. After classes I would first go to the library and, later, we would meet in the common room and then walk down to the club. Once the music started we would jive almost continuously until closing. By that time we had worked up a good sweat and, to anyone looking in, it must have been smelly and hot. We danced among the Teddy Boys. We all wore drainpipe trousers and they saw us as friendly intruders. In midwinter the outside temperature was close to freezing. Once we left the club the cold fresh air felt marvellous and by the time we reached Piccadilly Circus underground we had cooled off but then we dipped into the warmth of the station.

During the Christmas week I worked in the post office. In those days the volume of Christmas post was such that the post office regularly recruited students and out of work actors to help sort and deliver the Christmas mail. We had to be at our benches by six in the morning. This meant I had to get up very early and cycle through the morning cold. The objective was to clear the mail and to complete the morning delivery by lunchtime.

The sorting office was near to Lord's cricket ground and part of my round was to deliver post to some very smart flats in the St. Johns Wood area. To make deliveries to the flats, I was told to take the lift to the top floor and deliver the letters to the topmost flats first, then walk down. On my first day, as I moved down to the lower floors, I could hear the doors of flats on the floor above opening and the occupants exchanging the letters that I had put through the wrong letter boxes. One of the flats that I delivered to happened to be the home of the Chief Rabbi and it amused me no end to deliver Christmas cards to him. The day before Christmas eve his wife gave me a Christmas box.

Delivering letters to flats invariably meant that you were in and out of the cold December air. No matter how much you prepared yourself, as the morning wore on a visit to a toilet became a necessity. One day walking down the stairs of a tall modern posh block of flats my desperation got the better of me and one of the large potted plants that happened to be on a landing was well watered. My guilty feeling was soon softened when I discovered during a canteen conversation that most of the student male postmen had had a similar experience.

Before I left the Giaconda Coffee Bar, partly sacked and partly voluntary, a Jewish couple in their early thirties suddenly became regular customers. He was over six feet tall and had quite a large, round waist and she was slightly shorter but weighed a lot more than him. I doubt if I could have got my arms around her. How they both managed to sit on the normal sized chairs puzzled all of us. After a few nights they were on speaking terms with the owner, the chef and me. A few weeks after I left the coffee house in Finchley Road and, while wandering down Golders Green Road, I noticed that a new coffee house called the Penguin had just opened. I looked through the door and saw there the huge couple Mr & Mrs S, the rotund customers from the Giaconda in the restaurant. They saw me and called me in to view their new business and offered me a job. Once inside I saw the chef and Italian manager form the Giaconda were working there too. I started the next night.

Mr & Mrs S were quite well known in the Golders Green area and attracted customers of all ages. The early part of the shift was quiet but when the cinemas and pubs closed we became quite busy. I normally finished between half eleven and twelve and if I was lucky, caught the last bus up Finchley Road. While walking home at that time of night carrying my brief case a passing police patrol car would often stop me and question me. It happened so frequently that, as the police approached me, I would open my brief case and have the answers to their questions before they asked me. The first few months in the Penguin all went well; the chef, the manager, the waitress and Mr & Mrs S got on well.

One weekday evening at about ten in the evening three blokes charged into the coffee bar laughing and all on a high. The owners knew them and after a greeting they charged into the kitchen. Once in the kitchen they produced one and five pound notes out of every pocket and, the seldom seen, ten pound notes. Money was everywhere. I had never seen (nor have since) so much money in one place. Giggling and joking, they counted out the money and then divided it out into three lots and then each pocketed their share. I heard one on the telephone telling whoever was at the other end that they had had a big win and he was going to put it all in the building society. The chef whispered to me that they had had a big win at a racetrack. They sat down to a meal and, while eating, they played heads and tails for five pound notes. I looked on enviously as my weekly wage was less than four pounds. A week later they returned but this time were broke.

A few weeks later the manager left. Mr S casually said to me that he had got all that he could out of him and he was now surplus, so he sacked him. The chef called me aside and told me to keep an eye on my wages. Calculate what was due and then count the pay packet before leaving. Two weeks later the chef left suddenly. The friendliness and general bonhomie toward me began to fade and whatever I did was criticised. One Friday evening, I looked at my pay packet and it was short. Mrs. S, as usual, was at the pay desk and as I was leaving I quietly told her that I had not been paid enough. She shouted out loudly in front of all the regular customers that I was accusing them of cheating and not being able to add up. I walked out feeling very embarrassed and then outside by the light of a street lamp carefully recalculated my wages. I was certain that she was wrong. I went back into the coffee bar and was greeted in a mocking fashion but insisted that we both, Mrs S and I, do the calculations together. She then conceded and without an apology opened the till and gave me what was missing. Mr S, in the meantime, stood at the far end but never said a word.

On the following Tuesday I developed a very painful lump on the sole of my foot and next morning went to the casualty department at the Middlesex hospital. I was told to report back that afternoon for a five o-clock 'opening' and not to have anything to eat or drink in the meantime. Late that afternoon I was given a light anaesthetic, and woke up about ten minutes later. The lump had been cut out of my foot. A dressing was inserted deep into the wound so that the wound would heal from the inside out and not leave a cavity. The pain was almost unbearable. I waited for about a half an hour and then started my journey home. I could only just walk. Outside of the hospital I had to rest against the railings. While standing there I noticed Ada, her sister and her husband who were both doctors, on the opposite side of the road. I stood there with half of me hoping that they would see me and the other half hoping that they would not. Whether or not they saw me I will never know, as I then hobbled to a bus stop and managed to get back to my lodgings. Mrs K phoned the coffee bar to tell them that I would not be at work until next week.

I had to attend the hospital each day to have the dressing changed. Each time a nurse pulled out the old gauze and inserted a fresh piece while all the pain returned. A week later I went back to the Penguin coffee bar. As I walked in I was greeted very coldly. The waitress whispered to me to watch my step. Mr S snapped at me and demanded that I make him a black coffee. It was handed straight back to me and I was told that he wanted coffee and not mud. About ten minutes later I decided that enough is enough, money or not I was not going to take that. I walked to the back picked up my jacket and, Mr S. seeing me do that shouted to Mrs S "give him his money, he is going." As I walked past the desk I was handed an already prepared final wage packet.

My next coffee bar was at the far end of Finchley Road in an area known as Temple Fortune. This was the smartest and most comprehensive restaurant that I had worked in yet. Apart from a French chef, it also had an Austrian pastry cook. The bakery was above the restaurant. During the evenings my job was either behind the Gaggia coffee machine or helping in the kitchen. On Saturday mornings I worked in the bakery. The first thing the baker said to me was that whatever cakes we make I can eat as much as I like providing I do so before they were counted. I soon learnt to mix the cream and use a bag to decorate the pastries. In the middle of my first morning he asked me to make some custard. He gave the list of ingredients, which I carefully assembled and measured out. (Milk was then sold and dispensed in pint bottles). I lined up eight bottles on the table alongside a large mixing bowl. After he checked them he told me to mix them and went out of the room. While he was out I placed all the powder into the bowl and then emptied all eight pints into the bowl. He returned a few minutes later looked at the bowl containing the yellowish milk and asked me where the other ingredients were. When I told him that they were at the bottom of the bowl, he blew a fuse. I was supposed to add everything a little at a time while continuously mixing - not all at once. After some shouting, he said to just keep mixing and hope for the best, which I did, and about a half-hour later created a bowl of a type of custard. I then had to layer the custard gently onto pastry slices before placing them in the fridge. Between the two of us we produced a weekend supply of cakes and pastries.

During the weekday evenings I became quite friendly with one of the waitresses, Joan, who lived in a council house in Edgware with her lorry driver husband and three children. She also was very friendly with the French chef. Joan's biggest problem was a baby sitter for her children. She would like to work later during the busy period, as that is when she would earn the most tips. After few weeks she asked me if I would be interested in being a live in baby sitter for which she would give free board and lodging and a small amount of pocket money. After not much thought, I agreed to go to her house meet her husband Alan and get to know the children. He turned out to be huge man who spent quite a few nights away from home. When I told Mr and Mrs K about my offer, all they said to me was be careful and that if things didn't work out I could have my room back.

The week before that offer there was an uneasy atmosphere in the kitchen. The two bosses were in and out, and there were workmen and deliverymen coming and going. The other student washer-up and myself joked about a raid, thinking that any minute something was about to happen to us. When I arrived for the Monday evening shift, there was no chef. He had been arrested that morning. Apparently, over the last few weeks, he had been over-ordering and taking the extras away in his car. The so-called workmen were plainclothes police.

On the first Monday after I moved into Joan's the journey from Edgware to Oxford Circus seemed as if I was travelling from the depths of the country. I had never ventured beyond Golders Green. That Wednesday Joan had a night off. After the children were asleep she invited me into the kitchen to join her for a drink. I retired to bed after listening to a few tales about her being hard up and how the milkman had rescued her on many a occasion by giving her goods on credit. In those days the milkman also sold bread and other basic groceries. Then she told me that shortly after she got married she met who she thought was her dream guy. He had a smart car, was well dressed and always left big tips for her and the other waitresses. A week later he arranged to see her away from work in the afternoons. Then he asked to see her one morning when her husband was away. They met and went for a drive together. A few miles away, he stopped outside a sub-post office. He asked her to go in with him and told her go and browse on the other side of the shop. While looking at the shelves, with her back to the counter, she heard a scream and turned round to see her boyfriend snatch a bag from the woman behind the counter and run out of the shop. Joan followed after him but, before she could get into the car, he drove off. Looking around she saw a tube station, which she hurried toward, somehow not being noticed and made her way home. That night the evening newspapers reported the incident and there were descriptions of her on the front pages. After a sleepless night she confessed to her husband. A big row followed and then he accompanied her to the police station. Once she told her story to the CID they immediately recognized the villain's description and reassured her that she was not his first victim. Within two days he was arrested. She received a suspended sentence and a warning while he was jailed.

On my second Saturday in Edgware I went to a party in Fulham. At about two in the morning, for some reason or other, I had had enough and decided to leave. I was not quite sure where I was and began to walk in the direction of central London. After about an hour I found myself near to Hammersmith. There I saw a trolley bus route to Golders Green via Willesden. Trolley bus routes were easy to follow and I continued my walk. At one point, the road dipped into a poorly lit subway beneath a railway line. As I approached the entrance I could hear footsteps coming toward me from the opposite end. I decided to continue walking, gambling on the fact the other person was probably as frightened of me as I of him. We crossed about half way and both kept going. It seemed an eternity before I reached the safety of the opening. By the time I reached the main road that led to Edgware it was almost daylight. I then tried to hitch a lift. Ten minutes later one of the few cars about at that time of morning stopped. Once in the car, I told the driver where I had come from and where I was going. He felt sorry for me and delivered me to the house in Edgware.

About nine in the morning, Alan woke me up to tell me that Joan had disappeared and had apparently left us. After a long chat, listening to him threatening to kill the guy whoever it was, I was totally bewildered as to my future in that house. I stayed in with the kids while he wandered off to try and find her. He went to the coffee bar and the police. By evening, he found out that she had run off with the French chef who was out on bail.

The following Tuesday Alan was away and during the early part of the evening, after I had put the children to bed, Joan walked in. She had second thoughts and decided not to leave Alan. Besides, the police had warned her of her previous conviction. I phoned Mr & Mrs K and asked if I could have my room back. The next morning I packed and returned to Finchley Road.

During the few weeks that I was away my room had been redecorated, the hole in the roof mended and the walls papered and painted. A young woman named Sarah and her baby had moved in. I was offered a bed in the room occupied by their teenage son Terry and John Ware. I had no choice but to accept. The rent was cheap and I had breakfast with occasional other meals thrown in as well.

The room that I was to inhabit for quite some time was located at the very top of the building. It was a relatively large two bay room the width the building. The windows overlooked the junction of Heath Drive and Finchley Road. The building was the last in a row of large four storeyed terraced houses. Two of the bedroom walls were outside walls. All three beds were placed parallel up against a wall. There was still room for wardrobes at the end of the beds. My bed was in the far corner against the outer wall, under a window. Terry's bed was alongside the wall joining on to the next building in the terrace. John's bed was against the inner wall. With the beds so placed and not jutting into the middle of the room, the centre of the room was free and it contained a small table and chairs.

Sarah, I was told, was married but her husband, who was supposed to be a student, could not live with her for some reason or other. Before work Sarah would drop her baby off at a day nursery. On weekends her husband would show up. He was from Trinidad and of Asian origin. He had tried to persuade Sarah to let him send her and the baby to Trinidad where his parents would look after them but Sarah would not give in. During occasional conversations Sarah told me that, if she could get to work earlier, she could earn more badly needed money. I told her that, if she got the baby ready, I would take the baby to the nursery in the mornings for her. The baby-minders thought that I was the father. One weekend Sarah's husband appeared with another woman wearing a Sari and who was heavily pregnant. She was introduced to me as his cousin. About six weeks later, Sarah left. I later found out that he was also the father of his 'cousin's' baby.

The K family had a maid called Annie who also originated from Austria. She would arrive at about nine in the morning, say nothing and, like a whirlwind attack the whole house-hoovering, dusting and tidying. She seemed to ignore everyone, especially Mr & Mrs K. She would never knock, just barge into the room and you had to stop what you were doing and get out of her way. All the beds in the K's household were large, covered with a continental style featherbed. Annie would change the covers and sheets once a week, make the beds which simply needed a hefty shake, then let the duvet settle over the bed. I used to sleep without pyjamas and, more or less, wrapped the featherbed completely round me. Anyone entering the room would not know whether or not I was in the bed. One morning I was awakened by a scream as Annie had barged into the room and lifted my duvet only to see me lying stark naked on the sheet. From then on, John Ware told me, she always walked to the front of our beds and gave the bedcovers a hefty prod.

The latter part of that February turned very cold and that was long before houses acquired central heating. The only form of heating available was an old fashioned electric heater, and we would have to feed a meter with half crowns to keep warm. One evening, while the three of us were trying to keep warm, the meter ran out. None of us had any ready money. Terry, without a moment's thought, picked up one of the many old chairs we had in the room and broke it up. He then ignited old crumpled copies of the Guardian that had been placed into the fireplace. The chair was then used as firewood. The chair pieces burnt slowly and kept the room and us warm. There were three more chairs in the room that kept us reasonably warm until that cold spell was over.

John Ware, who was about forty, was a born in Canada and as a youth had migrated to Trinidad with his parents. He had returned to Canada to study singing. He was about five foot ten inches tall and had a thick mop of light red hair and bushy eyebrows. His now stocky build covered what must have been a fine athletic body. While back in Canada, in order to pay for his singing lessons he worked in lumber camps. Many an evening he entertained me with tales of life as a lumberjack. I was awestruck when he told me that it was nothing for a lumberman to have a breakfast that contained six to a dozen fried eggs. When he came over to England and must have had a reasonable start to his singing career as the walls of the room were covered with posters advertising his concerts, and one of the venues was the Wigmore Hall. Each morning at about ten, the whole household could hear John going through his vocal exercises before going off to singing lessons. He did not earn very much from his singing and his mother used to send him a regular allowance. He had an old wind-up gramophone and lots of old seventy-eight records, which were still being sold at that time. Folk ballads, the songs of Stephen Foster and Negro spirituals were part of his repertoire. He tried his best, without much success, to teach me to sing some of the more popular songs.

If I was not working on Wednesday nights I would go to the Bar Kochba gym or swimming club where, by now, I knew most of the people. My contact was always restricted to actual gym times as I could not afford to socialise with them afterwards. I also attended free Sunday night socials at the clubhouse in the basement of a house in Fellows Road.

During the height of my relationship with Ada, we used to go to the Spaniards Inn at the top of Hampstead Heath on Sunday mornings. (During the Fifties that pub had become the unofficial meeting place of the Golders Green, Hampstead Garden Suburb and Hendon young Jewish 'wannabees'). There was a relatively large car park and they arrived in droves in their smart cars. Most of the males who were students were studying medicine, dentistry, law or psychology. The girls, if studying, were reading any of the above or modern languages or English literature. They all seemed to have been schooled at one of the Jewish public schools or one of the better known North London grammar schools. Most of those who had been, or were still at university, attended either Oxford or Cambridge. The conversations nearly always centred on what was happening in their committee – to them a euphemism for a local social club. Money seemed to be plentiful and rounds of drinks were bought regularly. I was bought a drink but could not reciprocate the large rounds. Whoever bought me drinks made it seem as though it was not a problem. Somehow, as the morning moved toward closing time and the novelty of meeting someone like me had worn off, I was - by craft - excluded from the drinks round. After closing they all drove off in a manner that attracted the most attention. Once the relationship with Ada ended, I only made rare visits to the Spaniards.

Chapter 18

As the summer approached I was told about an ice cream retailer in Twickenham who was looking for students to work weekends selling ice cream in public places. He had a fleet of three wheeled bicycles each equipped with a large white cool box attached to the side of the bike with a small top opening. The object was to cycle to a park or playing field on Saturdays and establish a prominent site. We were told emphatically not to try to sell ice cream from a shady spot, always pitch in the sunlight. He would load the bike in his van and drive you to where he thought would be good spot, then leave you there. If you required more stock you could contact him by telephone. On occasion, we would cycle from the depot through the suburbs to a sales spot. I acquired a small bell and, as I pedalled along, I rang the bell and every now and again the ringing brought people to their windows and I would call out, "ice cream!" While travelling along, visions of the streets of Johannesburg flashed back. It was quite common to see ice cream vendors cycling round the streets ringing bells. However, most of the vendors were black and I could only speculate about the horror that would be expressed by my ex peers if they saw me now. There were then, in Johburg, also young white ice cream vendors but they were nearly always Afrikaners who we referred to as poor Whites.

One hot Sunday, the boss delivered me to Hampton Court Bridge. He left me near to Bushy Park and I then began to ride toward the bridge. I stopped on the bridge and began to sell but was moved on by the police. The constable suggested that I cross the bridge and set up pitch on the other side of the river where there was a small alcove at the end of the bridge wall. A few yards away there was an elderly peanut vendor. I parked my bike and customers began to arrive. I had a chance to look around and discovered that I was alongside a footpath that led to a riverside café that had a big sign advertising ice cream for sale. About fifteen minutes later, two hefty men walked up to me. One must have been in his forties and the other mid-twenties. The older of the two told me that I had no right to be there and that I was on his land. I replied that a policeman had given me permission to be there. He then shouted at me, "Go away! You cannot stay here." My reply was, "No," and they both came right up to me and, in a more threatening manner shouted at me to go away. I just stood and stared back at them. Next thing I knew he punched me in the face. I was momentarily stunned and, when I recovered my senses, I saw them moving my bicycle. Looking around, I noticed that there was a policeman on the bridge. I ran over to him. He followed me back to my bike and saw the two placing it under a tree. He called the two over and I repeated to the policeman what had happened. They immediately denied it. I look round for the peanut vendor but he had conveniently disappeared. Apparently no one around had seen what had happened. The fellow who had hit me told the policeman that I had been on his property but still denied attacking me. Another policeman on a motorcycle arrived. After they took down some details, they told me that if I wanted to press charges I would have to go the police station the next day. They made my attackers retrieve my bicycle but advised me to move on because I was taking business away from them and the only way I could remain was with police protection. They both told me that I would be better off if I went further down to the river towpath.

I found a new spot where I had been directed and, once again, began to sell ice creams. About a half hour later, another hefty looking fellow who told me that I had no right to be there selling ice creams approached me. I repeated what I had been told by the police, making certain that there was enough distance between us in case I got another fist in my face. He produced a badge indicating that he was acting on behalf of the council and told me to clear off. I stood my ground and he then waved in the direction of some trees, which was a signal to his accomplice. I made a fuss but kept out of their range and then started to pedal back up the towpath. As I pedalled off, I kept being stopped by customers who I defiantly served while the two towpath thugs looked on.

I rode across the bridge and then slowly along the outer walls of Hampton Court. Under an avenue of trees, were numerous strollers. Business was quite brisk and I took my time, always looking around in case of more harassment. I reached the gates of Bushy Park and decided to ride through the park. There was a gatekeeper on patrol who nodded to me and I waved back. About halfway through the park, picnickers hailed me and I stopped to sell to them. While I was serving the third group, a young park official appeared on his bicycle saying that it was an offence to sell anything in a Royal Park. He first wrote down the names of some of the customers and then turned to me, and proceeded to read the riot act to me, warning me that anything that I said could be used as evidence. He also proceeded to loudly say that ignorance of the law was no defence. I then insisted on making a statement and that he must write it down. In front of accumulated spectators, he could not refuse. I stated that I passed by a gatekeeper who did not draw to my attention that there were by-laws governing the park. As in the case of travelling on public transport, unless the issuer of the ticket draws your attention to the by-laws written on the back of the ticket, you cannot then be held responsible for breaking them. He scratched his head with his pencil as I dictated it all much to the amusement of the spectators. One of my matriculation subjects was Mercantile Law and we had dealt with what were called 'ticket-cases'. As I stood there I could see a smile on my old teacher. Once all the paperwork was over, I pedaled off to a rendezvous point with the boss. Sitting in the back of the van I related to him my day's adventures. Naturally, he expressed sympathy and said that if anything arose he would back me. As it turned out the park official had caught three other vendors from the firm that day in Bushy Park. A few weeks later while we were selling ice creams at the Epsom Derby, I learnt that all, except for me, who had been caught in the park selling ice creams were summoned and fined.

Chapter 19

During my first months in London I saw an advertisement for a correspondence course in Journalism. The prospectus invited you to send a few hundred words of copy and they would decide whether or not you could become a writer. The reply to my effort was very favourable. I drew seven pounds ten shillings to pay for my first lessons. I carefully hand wrote what I was asked to do and a week later received the marked assignment. It was very encouraging but I was told in no uncertain terms to watch my spelling and pay attention to the grammatical corrections. I could not afford to pay for the next lesson so I went round to their offices hoping that they would find me journalistic work. Politely, they told me to first finish the course as I needed to try and learn shorthand writing as well as typing. That virtually ended my first attempts at writing.

My desire to write was rekindled by the students' newsletter. The students union used to produce a fortnightly 'magazine,' which consisted of a few duplicated typed A4 sheets of paper. The originals had to be typed onto a waxed master sheet, which was then spread over an inked rotating drum. The individual sheets were collated and it was sold to recover costs. I read each issue religiously and one day in conversation with the editor he suggested that I send an article/letter. I did not need a second invitation. I found my lessons from the journalism course and carefully wrote out my story in longhand. My efforts were not printed in the next issue and, when I eventually met up with the editor, he asked if I always wrote so badly. I felt totally humiliated, bewildered and set back. I knew that I was prone to both spelling and grammatical errors but I thought that what I sent in was a draft and that content would override the errors. I really believed that errors could be mutually corrected before the definitive article went to press.

My desire to write never really died and in odd, inspirational moments I wrote very brief sketches. One of them was about an old man watching a group of youths dancing round a campfire that gets carried away and joins in. As he dances with his head turned toward the heavens, he feels himself floating upwards in state of total contentment and shuts his eyes and falls into a deep sleep. The dancing stops and the youths cover his body up. I used to occasionally read my efforts to colleagues in the coffee room. They always listened attentively and the usual end comment was good. That all came to an abrupt end when one of the girls told me that I was the most romantic person she had ever met. I asked her if that was good or bad and she replied with a sneer. That was the end of that type of writing for many years. However, it did not put me off altogether. I decided to try my hand at writing a play. I based it on the shooting of a dog, an event which took place on the farm in Oogies in South Africa. I managed to get hold of a typewriter and spent many hours writing instead of studying. I delivered the finished product to the Poly drama society who all read it very carefully and were full of praise but could not fit it into their schedule. My writing then remained on hold for the next few years.

Once the blossoms began to appear on the trees, no matter how welcome an event that always was, to me it meant that it was only a matter of weeks before the start of the summer examinations. I was facing two A-levels in Chemistry and Botany. I had only been studying Botany for about six months. A three-hour practical examination and two three hour theory papers was the norm for both subjects. The practical examinations had to be done at special centres. I soon received notification of the dates, times and places which was the old Imperial Institute examination halls, now demolished to make way for new buildings for Imperial College. The examination laboratory was a long room with a corridor running between what seemed to be an endless stretch of peninsula benches. On each peninsula were places for four candidates, two facing up the room and two on the other side facing the entrance. Everything was meticulously laid out while hordes of 18 to 20 year olds strolled nervously looking for the bench with their number, each carrying a pile of books. Most were tense but calm, but there were those who had panic written all over them. As I stood at my bench, I could see all round me through a forest of burettes and reagent bottles, everyone settling down. You were allowed to bring practical notebooks in with you. All I had was a hand written small hard covered pocket book in which I had written almost everything that I had done in chemistry practicals. Besides, I could not afford to buy a printed book. Three hours sped by as I analysed my compound and carried out a titration exercise. I left feeling relieved and, about a week later I returned for a Botany practical exam., which I left without the same confident feeling that I had had after the Chemistry exam. Next, it was time to concentrate on the written exams.

The weekend before my first Chemistry theory exam, I developed a very painful stye on the lower lid of my left eye. On the Sunday Sarah, my current girlfriend, came over to see me. Whenever she arrived, John Ware always politely and conveniently would go out and not return till late evening. Sarah was a Jewish girl from Willesden whose father ran a small business. I had met the parents once and it did not take a psychoanalyst to realise that her father was very wary of me. One evening she told me that her father had tried to stop her going out knowing that she was on her way to visit me and had actually hit her.

The following Monday morning my eye was steadily getting worse. I went to the casualty at a hospital close to Hampstead Tube station. They told me to get hold of a wooden spoon, wrap a cloth round it and dip into a bowl of boiling water and to gently let the steam pass over my eye. As soon as I got back to my digs, Mrs K helped to set my steam treatment which I then did at about two to three hourly intervals while trying to continue my revision. Sarah came round to see me and I just felt more and more miserable. That evening at about eight I walked her down to Finchley Road tube station. At the station entrance I said goodbye and, when she asked me about our next meeting, I thought about her father's hostile reaction to me and realised that I was not serious in the long term about our relations. I remained silent. She then said to me, "So that's it," and turned her back on me to walk into the station. I walked home with the pain in my eye getting worse, feeling emotionally numb about the cruel manner in which I had ended the relationship.

By Tuesday morning the stye had grown and I could not close my eye properly and when open it felt equally uncomfortable. I abandoned my studies for the day and did think about Sarah. I continued with the steam treatment every two hours and kept looking into a hand mirror hoping to see some changes. At four in the afternoon the mirror inspection revealed that there were slight exudates. I pressed the lower eyelid; the pain increased but with that there was gentle pop and out flowed all the rest of the pus. A second press brought even more out and, with that, the pain eased off rapidly. I rushed down for another bowl of steam and Mrs. K. said, "Your eye is looking much better. What have you done?" She continued saying, "I must say I admire your persistence." My thoughts were that I had no choice. My appetite soon returned. I slept undisturbed until morning. When I woke up, my left eyelids were stuck together. A mirror examination revealed that, during the night, the rest of the exudates had poured out and had coagulated. Most important of all was that, apart from a red mark on my lower eyelid, I felt almost normal and spent the day in the library.

The exams came and went and then it was time to find a vacation job. I renewed my association with the printing works and worked there for the next five weeks. It was during mid-August that I learnt that I had passed my Chemistry but had missed my Botany by a few marks. My first thoughts after recovering from my disappointment were what to do when the new term started and how to disguise my failure from my family. I joined (at the Poly) a one-year crash course in Botany and Zoology part of which was taught in conjunction with the first year of an external University of London degrees course. At times, we shared laboratory practical sessions with other groups.

As usual I had to find myself jobs in coffee bars and continued to cycle in each day through Regents Park. The make up of my study group was now quite different from that of my original Maths and Physics course. Firstly, most of the group were female and all were either English or had migrated to England with their families. Besides myself there were two other males. One was filling a year before going on to Medical College and we called him Mac because he was originally from Ireland. His family had settled near St. Albans. One of those who joined in some of our practicals from another group was a West Indian lad named Dan from the Island of Grenada.

When not in lecture rooms we spent endless hours in the laboratory peering down microscopes, drawing or dissecting. The laboratory consisted of a large central wooden bench with the usual gas taps in the middle, and we all sat round facing each other. We tended to accumulate at the blackboard end of the room. Once we had been given our briefing on what to do that session, we would all start out as diligently as possible. There was always one lecturer and one demonstrator in attendance. This was a middle sized lab. There was a larger one for the A-level classes and a smaller one for the third year and specialist students. Quite often the more advanced students would join in with us.

I had no radio or access to a television set. There were only two black and white TV channels, BBC and the new commercial independent television. My personal source of news was The Guardian and the Sunday Observer. My only other source of visual news was via the cinema newsreels but the only picture house that I attended fairly regularly was the Everyman in Hampstead. This was a small, specialised 'art house' cinema where the showing of newsreels was considered to be beneath them and the clientele.

Practical classes nearly always began with the minimum of conversation depending upon how demanding the task was. About halfway through we would stop for a tea/coffee break. After that we would become more talkative.

This was the era of the beginning of the Ban the Bomb campaign, the anti-Apartheid movement was developing roots in England, Kruschev was now in power and the Cold War was in its prime. The Soviets were supporting Nasser's Egypt and the Syrian regime. The Conservative government with Macmillan in charge had a strong grip on the country. It was also the centenary of the Darwin-Wallace theory of evolution.

In our group, the views ranged from the moderate right to the socialist left who were sympathetic to Marxist ideals but not quite communist. The launching of the first Russian sputnik really set us all off into a long, continuing debate. The lecturer would occasionally try and pass on 'informed' impartial comments but generally stayed back only interrupting when needed to help or answer a query. There were times when we all talked noisily over each other, the room temperature rose and any stranger entering the lab could have cut the atmosphere with a knife. The possession of 'the bomb' always roused passion both for and against. (Those for always argued from a deterrent point of view and those against raised the point that simply having a nuclear arsenal gave rise to the possibility of an accidental nuclear explosion). Whoever had recently been to a play or concert would tell us about it. Tastes in music - popular, jazz or classic - books and art were frequently aired and often records and books were lent out or exchanged. Our dress also reflected our differing opinions. The future medical student wore a jacket and tie whereas Mac and Dan (the Irish and West Indian colleagues) wore v-necked shaped sweaters with no tie. I wore a black round necked sweater that had been knitted for me by Ada. The left wings girls were much more casual with a minimum of makeup compared to those who supported the Conservatives.

The merits of the current pop music and the songs - especially Elvis Presley, Tommy Steele, Adam Faith etc. - often came up in our lab discussions. Rock and roll and the Teddy Boys had reached their most popular peak. Personal views of the film actors Marlon Brando, James Dean, and others from the Method were aired as frequently as politics. As I did not have a radio, record player or television, when it came to discussing Pop culture I was often just an attentive listener. Most of the popular music that I had heard was either in coffee bars or at parties.

We all did our share of Christmas postal deliveries and then shared our experiences during the first week of the new term in early January. It was a Friday morning when I happened to tell Mrs K. at breakfast that tomorrow was to be my twenty-first birthday. She asked me what had I planned in the way of a celebration, and suggested that I was welcome to have a party in the house and that I could use their living room. I thanked her but politely refused. However, during the morning coffee, while talking to a group from the language department I mentioned that I was going to be twenty-one on Saturday. All sorts of celebrations were suggested and I told them about my landlady's offer. It took them only a few minutes to persuade me to make a phone call, and Mrs K sounded very pleased about my decision. By midday everyone who knew me had heard about the party. On Saturday the K family, John Ware and myself spent the morning shifting furniture and handling general preparations. At seven p.m. the silence in the house created doubts about whether or not anyone would come. A trickle of guests arrived before eight and then the trickle changed, first, into a stream and then a river of revellers. By nine, the place was crowded. The music soon became inaudible but it did not stop the dancing. There was a piano in the room and a succession of players soon replaced the recorded music. Within a half-hour of the onset of the piano music a clarinet, trumpet, saxophone, double base, guitars and various improvised percussion instruments provided the musical entertainment for the rest of the party. It was the beginning of the era of skiffle music. A tea chest type base and wash board soon appeared and skiffle music alternated with the improvised band.

The room in which the party was happening was above a shop and soon the floor began to move up and down to the rhythm of the heaving revellers but, by then, the drink was flowing and no one seemed to care. Also, despite our morning efforts at vacuum cleaning and dusting, the movements of dozens of feet loosened up years of carpet dust. So much so, that by ten everyone had a ring of brown dust round their nostrils and mouths. The windows were opened and probably every house within a half mile radius could hear us. Private party raves in that part of Hampstead were still quit rare and so we were happily tolerated and no one called the police. Once the crowd had thinned out, John Ware gave a song recital and led a sing-song. The night flew by and about two in the morning the last guests left. The floor had survived but the walls and ceiling were covered in dust.

At coffee break on the Monday after, the party was at the top of every conversation and I was thanked over and over again. Those who had not been there told me that they heard about the party and apologized for missing the event. The fellows who had formed an impromptu skiffle group had met again on the Sunday evening and a few weeks later became one of the many skiffle groups that were performing at concert venues throughout the country. They even made a few records.

Chapter 20

Later, that January, I began to work in a coffee bar near to Finchley Road station, which was only about ten minutes walk from my digs. The K's, by this time, had decided to move most of their business operation to a rented space in a large garage on Finchley Road. Each evening while walking home from the coffee bar, I had to pass by the garage. The night porter Sam was nearly always standing by the entrance and we would exchange greetings.

On one occasion close to midnight, I was walking on the pavement, which was covered with a layer of frozen snow. The icy path slowed me down and, when I reached Sam and was about to greet him, he spoke first saying, "Do you think that there is a fire?" He was pointing to a balcony on the second floor of a block of flats on the opposite side of the road. I looked up and saw flames in the front living room. Sam was quite laid back about it all. I said to him, "Do you know who lives there and the number of the flat?" He answered, telling me the name, the owners and the number of the flat.

"Shall I call the fire brigade" he asked me. I just said follow me and we ran across the road into the building, up the stairs and began to knock as loudly as possible and shouted through the letter box. A few moments later an angry voice from within the flat wanted know what hell we wanted.

I shouted to him "I think there is a fire in your front room!" A few seconds later there was a loud cry "My God, fire!" I asked him to open the door so that we would help him. Sam and I rushed into the room to see the settee and curtains up in flames. The rest of the household members were now up and running around in a panic. Sam and I helped with buckets of water from the kitchen. The owner's wife phoned for the fire brigade then ran round screaming about how much bad luck they'd had recently and how this was going to be the ruin of them. By the time the fire brigade arrived, the worst was over and the family were in such a state that Sam and I decided to leave.

The next morning I told the K's. A few days later Mr K, via his garage contacts, had told the owner about my role in the episode. The owner had told Mr K that he wanted to get in touch with me in order to give me a reward of ten pounds. I knew that Sam went and knocked on the door to collect his reward but my view was that what I did was done out of instinct, and if they wanted to reward me, they knew where and how to get hold of me. No matter how welcome ten pounds would have been, I could not bring myself to call on them.

I had now long since given up playing rugby to be able to work on Saturday afternoons but still went to the Bar Kochba gym and joined the Sunday morning athletic club. One afternoon a week I played basketball, a game I had learnt to play during my first year at the Poly. The Poly also had its own indoor swimming pool so I was able have the occasional swim as well as a game of water polo. I had now experienced quite a few different team games but never performed very well at any of them.

During the coffee breaks and sessions in the students' common room, I had become acquainted with students in the engineering, economics, language, photography and art departments. The art department occupied the top floor of the building and, in general they kept to themselves. They were easily identifiable as in the Fifties any males whose hair was a fraction long (over his ear lobes), wore clothes that were not the norm and had any facial hair were considered to be Bohemians or Beatniks. The female students, likewise, had very long hair and generally wore long flowing dresses or jeans. They, somehow, always contrived to have noticeable paint marks on their clothes. However, there were a few who would occasionally allow themselves to talk to us mortals.

One morning I was sitting with two of the artists, the only other people present in the coffee room at the time. During the conversation I found out the artist Stanley Spencer would be visiting the Art School that day to open a new lithograph facility. After coffee I noticed a small poster in a corridor advertising the artist's visit. At the appropriate time I made my way, into the Art School. I followed a small group of visitors and found myself on the edge of a litho stone almost next to Stanley Spencer who was finishing drawing a girl's face onto a litho stone. Watching closely was the tall Lawrence Dowding, the head of the art school. When the sketch was finished he signed the stone and then chatted to those around him before officially declaring the lithography centre open. At the end of his short speech he noticed an open book on the bench alongside the stone. He looked at it and then said, "I love to see an open book. I always imagine myself lying in the pages of an open book and I try to incorporate that shape into my paintings." He then told us that, in his large resurrection paintings, in one of the bottom corners he painted flat horizontal tombstones in the shape of an open book and drew a figure representing him lying down within the 'pages' of the book. That weekend I went to the Tate gallery to look at the Stanley Spencer paintings depicting the resurrection. They are large canvases bigger than the wall in an average sized living room. In the bottom corner of the painting I saw the little man, wearing a suit and a hat, lying in the centre of two joined tombstones shaped like an open book.

During the breaks I often used to talk to a group of mature West Indians (who came mainly from Trinidad and Barbados and were very friendly with Don) and Polish students. The Poles all spoke English with heavy accents, and spoke Polish among themselves. They were all post-war displaced persons some who been in German, and then Russian, forced-labour camps. One of them told us that once during the depths of winter with snow everywhere, he saw truck loads of naked Jews being driven to the concentration camps. We were told more than once about their hatred of the communists. One day they were going to return to a liberated Poland. They were quite a few years older than the average student and always dressed very conventionally. In spite of their relatively poor spoken English they always created an impression of authority and an attitude that they were in some way superior to the rest of us.

The Poly was located right in the centre of London's West End, hence all of the main attractions and venues of the capital were within easy reach. During my first year I had already become very familiar with London. However, even after two years, I had found it quite exciting to be standing amongst well-known name places I had got to know via films, books and radio. It was exhilarating to know that they were merely a short journey away.

Oxford Street, from Oxford Circus to Tottenham Court Road, had numerous small, male clothing shops. Most of the clothes that I had brought with me from South Africa were now well worn but, as usual, money was in very short supply. I often window-shopped on a free evening or Sunday afternoon looking carefully for clothes that I liked and I could afford. For some reason, the shop I liked most at that time sold very conventional English style men's clothes. My ideal would be to have a pair of cavalry twill trousers with a matching jacket and brown shoes. Perhaps that was what I imagined a cultured, educated, middleclass Englishman would wear. However, those clothes were well out of my price range. If you paused outside one of the Oxford Street shops and looked into the window, you soon found yourself approached by a smart shop assistant asking if you needed help. If you replied, they would entice you into the shop in the blink of an eye and direct you to a particular counter where young so and so would look after you. Most of those shops were Jewish owned. I found out many years later that the street man was known as the 'shleper.' If you walked, without being dragged, into one of those shops and up to the nearest counter the first person you would normally see was the proprietor. He was smart and self-assured, with not a hair out of place and with a hint of aftershave. Having sized you up and decided that you were not a big spender, you were shepherded to a very junior salesman. There were never any Jewish customers as they usually bought their outfits from a wholesaler. Often, in a shop, if they recognised me as a Jew they would not say anything but looked at me almost pathetically as if to say, "Don't you know anyone who can get it for you wholesale?"

Chapter 21

At the Poly during practical classes an outsider could easily have formed the impression that they were amid a talking shop. While working at our tasks, we put the world right. My first attempt at dissecting a dogfish was a disaster. The demonstrators, after an initial briefing, did not really show us what to do. By the time I came round to my second dogfish I had carefully followed instructions from a dissection guidebook. My second attempt was almost perfect but now I had to learn how to draw it. I measured out the animal and placed a series of guide dots on my page. Soon, with practice, I was able accurately record on paper what I had just done and seen. I extended that technique to whatever object I had to draw. Animal sculls held a particular fascination for me. At that time, we only had to draw a dog and frog skull. Comparison of different types of dentition in relation to diet, the articulation of the lower jaw with the main skull, and the position of the eye sockets all kept me occupied for many hours. We also dissected earthworms, crayfish, frogs and rabbits, once again tasks with their own particular challenges, which I tackled with enthusiasm.

As the year moved on the spring blossoms once again heralded a preoccupation with the forthcoming exams. At that level of study one religiously followed the prescribed textbooks. They were like bibles to us. However, we did manage to read articles in the recently created *New Scientist* and the Penguin Science series. In one Penguin book I read what I thought to be a fascinating article on how tapeworms have adapted to their way of life. Little did I know at the time that study of tapeworms was to become a prominent feature of my many years of academic research.

The study of embryology created the biggest challenge. Trying to relate, into the three dimensions, the developmental changes that occur when a fertilised single cell transforms into a multicellular three-layered living form was a preoccupying challenge. Although I was also studying Botany, the plant world (apart from the process of Photosynthesis) did not challenge me, yet. Strangely enough, I had decided to study Botany and not Zoology if and when I reached University. I had been offered a place to study Botany at Imperial College.

Chapter 22

Rose, an aunt of Mrs K, and her daughter Doris became regular visitors to the K household. Rose was a very smartly dressed blue-rinsed widow from North London and had spent her childhood in the East End of London. Doris was in her early twenties, plump, fairly plain and had learning difficulties. Over the next month, their visits became more and more frequent. Then, one weekend, Rose announced that she was flying off to New York to spend some time with her sister and that Doris was to stay in the K household and share the K's daughter's room. The K's, at that stage, took it all in their stride. One more person in the rather crowded house would hardly make any difference.

Doris would go off to work after breakfast and spent the evenings in the front sitting room watching television. After two weeks Doris started to show signs of irritability. Mr & Mrs K tried to find out what was bothering her, as they felt responsible for her wellbeing. A week later, we were all treated to the odd signs of temper and she began to wander off both during the day and at night.

At the time money, began to disappear out of the K's bedroom. I was not aware of the thefts. It was approaching exam time and I did not notice any changed attitudes towards me. Apparently, I was the chief suspect and my every my movement was watched. One morning I noticed a purse on the stairs and picked it up and took it into the kitchen. There was a general surprise at seeing me with the purse with all its contents intact. A few weeks later, after a rowdy confrontation with Doris, the K's contacted her mother and demanded that she return and remove her daughter. Apparently, the final straw was when the K's daughter went into her parent's room to fetch something and came across Doris rifling through a handbag. As I did not know about the thefts or that I was a suspect, I did not notice the change of attitude toward me. The first that I heard about it was only after Mrs K told me about the missing money and then apologetically informed me that I was the first suspect because they knew that I was always short of money.

Two weeks later, at breakfast, in walked an angry Rose - furious with everyone. Apparently Mr K had written to her telling her all about her daughter's misdemeanours and the stolen money, and demanded that she return and take care of Doris. An angry scene followed with lots of accusations flying across the room. By midday, Doris had packed her bags and it was the last we saw of her and Rose.

As the summer and exams approached, I organised my finances so that I needed only to work all day Saturday at a coffee bar in Hampstead Garden Suburb. My mother had increased my allowance to about twelve pounds per month. Apart from my Friday night visit to the Everyman cinema in Hampstead, my only other entertainment was walks across Hampstead Heath. I would walk up Heath Drive through a small lane that led to the top of Holly hill where the old medical research laboratories were located. Then I would either walk down the narrow cobbled roads toward the tube and high street or across to the Horse Pond, which was reputed to be the highest point of London. Once at the pond I would cross the road and stand on the grass slopes of Hampstead Hill and admire the view of the City of London with the dome of St. Paul's Cathedral (then the most dominant feature). I would follow the footpath to a high bridge over the pond. At the back of the bridge, in amongst thick growth, was reputed to be a cave reportedly said to have been the hideout of the highwayman Dick Turpin. Over the short bridge was a steep bank that led down to the pond. I would sit on the grass on the bank and just try and relax and watch the world pass by. I spent, or wasted, many hours on that bank. At infrequent intervals someone I knew would pass by and join me. In those days most of those strolling by must have thought I was the typical Hampstead weirdo. As exams approached the pace of my walks increased in order not to be away from my books for too long.

I received notification of the times and location of my practical examinations and by strange coincidence, my Zoology practical examination was scheduled at St. Bartholomew's Hospital where I had my first job as lab boy. On the day of the exam I arrived early and, once through the gate loads of memories flooded back. I walked over to the Physiology building, which had only just been completed when I left. While walking into the building I was preoccupied with what was to be my dissection. Once I found my place and settled down, I was relived to see a dogfish clearly on display on the dissecting board in front of me. While I was settling down and arranging my instruments a technician came over to make a routine check. I looked up and saw Ethel looking at me she said, "It's our Jack." She quickly called over the academic in charge Dr Dumonier who also said, "Oh, it's our Jack." A few minutes later I had to call them over again to record that there was damage on the upper part of the ventral side of the dogfish. The dissection that I had to do was to expose the Afferent Branchial system, which could only be reached from the ventral side of the dogfish. I knew that it was only really necessary to expose the arteries on one side so the damage might not cause any problems. It so happened that the damage was only superficial. At the end of the exam, once I had completed the dissection drawing, slide drawings and the 'spots' I had time to look back over my work and to see that hours spent in the lab practising drawing and dissection had been worthwhile.

<u>Chapter 23</u>

I was beginning to become restless and was looking for an opportunity move away from the K's. The Saturday after my final written exams Dan and Mike (colleagues from the Poly) turned up unexpectedly at my digs. During the day's conversation, Dan revealed that the he was also unhappy with his accommodation. We decided to look for shared accommodation. An advertisement in a sweet shop window near to Finchley Road tube station gave us an address for a double bed sitting room on the south side of Finchley Road. An Irish landlady who did not flinch at the sight of Dan, a West Indian, and myself, greeted us. There was not an inch of prejudice about her demeanour. It was a room on the top floor overlooking the gardens at the back of a row of a four-storeyed Edwardian house. The rent was reasonable so we accepted. I gave my notice to the K's who were disappointed that I was leaving but understood that I wanted to move on. The following Saturday morning I moved all my belongings.

I had, up till now, always shared accommodation with a person not out of choice but due to circumstances. Now, for the first time, I actually chose my roommate - Dan. He and I were both students studying Biological Sciences. We both received some, but not very much, support from our parents. We had the minimum to live on and had to depend on part-time work. Dan had a slight advantage in that he had a sister who was living and working in London and had an extensive network of West Indian friends.

With my exams over I needed to find a summer job and I also wanted leave London for a while. At the offices of the National Union of Students, I found a job posted. It was on a farm near to Petworth in Sussex. No accommodation was provided so I decided that I could save some money by living in a tent on the farm. I had enough savings to buy myself a small pup tent, a simple cooker, a camping saucepan, plate, knife, fork, spoon and sleeping bag.

I arrived at Petworth station and my instructions were to take a taxi to the farm. The taxi was a late 1940's, large, square Austin driven by a very well-spoken woman, the type of person I imagined living in a large mansion and owning a fleet of saloon cars.

I was driven up an impressive drive past a large smart farmhouse and delivered to a small, modern cottage surrounded by a very substantial fence. The fence, I soon discovered, was to keep in a ferocious little Pekinese-type dog that was determined to bite everyone except its owner. The owner and the farm manager George, was a rotund man who looked every inch the sergeant he had been during his military service. The first thing I was told was that I could not pass through his gate because of the dog which, while talking to me, he held against his chest. The dog barked and growled all the time. Once the dog was safely deposited in a pen, he showed me to a secluded place near to a small wood where I could pitch the tent and left me to it.

Once I had settled in I walked to the nearest village to stock up with provisions. The lady shopkeeper watched my every move and when I went to pay she told me how surprised she was to see a young male who seemed to be such an experienced shopper.

Around the village square were numerous men long past their working age. All had walking sticks. What struck me most all was how many of them had legs that were suffering the effects of arthritis. My immediate thoughts were, is that how a lifetime of agricultural work leaves you? What about how healthy country life is supposed to be!

I spent a restless first night in my tent, then spent the next day helping George with various jobs, preparing the farm for the forthcoming harvest. That afternoon George collected a young Frenchman, Jean, from the station. Jean had decided to stay in a Bed and Breakfast in the village.

For the next three weeks George and I worked (whenever the weather permitted) all the daylight hours on the combine harvester, or in the storage silos, or on one of the tractors harvesting acres and acres of wheat and barley. The farm owner's wife sent over lunch to us and, if it was convenient, we ate ours outside of my tent sitting on improvised seats made out of straw packed into sacks. Jean had just completed his national service. One of his army jobs was the Chauffeur to an army Colonel. He was used to going in and out of large houses via the rear entrance and knew how to wander through without being detected.

One rainy day we were sent to the main mansion to help with some decorating. The owner of the farm spent the week in London but his wife remained behind. During the mid-morning we saw the car drive off and found ourselves alone in the house. Jean was now in his element. He immediately took his shoes off and invited me to do likewise and then said to follow him. We wandered round the lower floor of the house. In the large drawing room was a table full of bottles of all sorts of alcoholic drinks. Jean carefully lifted the half-open bottles and took a quick mouthful straight from the bottle before replacing it. He pointed out to me to only drink from those bottles where any drop in content would be least noticed. After two brandies each we noticed a bowl of some peppermint sweets. We took one each. Jean warned me against more than one sweet because we would breathe out peppermint fumes. The rest of day we spent indifferently painting walls and skirting boards.

Jean had to return to France but before leaving he wanted to visit London. I gave him my address and he introduced himself to Dan and spent two nights in our room.

When I arrived back in London Dan informed me that I had just missed a phone call from the American girl I had met on the ferry going over to Holland. She had managed to get my address and phone number from the National Union of Students offices. She also told Dan that she was leaving for the continent from Liverpool Street station that evening. I went to see if I could find her but never did and I was very disappointed. She had left a vague address, which I followed up but was unable to contact her.

My exam results were mixed. I did well in Zoology but not in Botany and, as a result, I was very disappointed to lose my place at Imperial College. It was now late September and close to the beginning of the new academic year. I managed to enroll at Chelsea College for a degree, surprisingly enough in Botany. Although Chelsea was quite far away from Finchley Road, West Hampstead, I decided not to move as I had only just begun to settle into my shared room with Dan. Dan was now into his second year of an external London degree at the Polytechnic and, besides, we now had quite a few friends in common. Another factor was that it was a fairly simple bicycle ride through Kilburn, Hyde Park and on to South Kensington. Within the first few weeks of the autumn term I was a regular player in the basketball team as well as the occasional water polo and rugby match. My monthly allowance from my mother had now risen to twenty pounds per month but I still needed to do the occasional part-time job. What I did not realise at the time was that I was now eligible to apply for a study grant from the then London County Council.

`At the end of the first month I was invited to attend an evening soiree for overseas students at the Chelsea Town Hall. It was really meant for students who had only just arrived in the country but the organiser persuaded me to attend the meeting that was hosted by the Mayor, John Marsden-Smedley, and his wife Lady Marsden-Smedley, a governor of the college. There were about thirty students in attendance and a group of Chelsea debutantes, each of whom adopted two of us and became our personal host. Entertainment in the form of poetry reading and folk songs followed the speeches. During the evening we were constantly plied with drinks and food. At the end of the evening my host, Fiona (the honourable Lady) whose mother was also present, noted down my telephone number and address.

Most of my fellow students were school leavers; hence I was a few years older than them. Chelsea was then a relatively small college and one of the departments was the then famous Chelsea School of Art which had its share of typical Bohemian types as well as a smattering of South Kensington middle class individuals. In addition to the facilities at Chelsea I could make use of the facilities at ULU, (University of London Students Union) located in the centre of London behind the British Museum. I now had access to a wider range of students and activities. *Sennet* the university newspaper, which I later became involved with, had its offices in ULU.

On the first Saturday of the rugby season I was knocked over from behind during the match. I fell and landed on my head. After that, the only recollection that I had of the rest of the game was hearing the final whistle. It was as if I had woken up from a dream and then drifted off again; I next woke up in the dressing room with a very bad headache. Apparently, according to my team mates I played the rest of the game as if nothing was amiss. That evening and most of the following Sunday I suffered from a thumping headache. I never ever did recall the part of the game that I 'missed'.

In late November, during a basketball game I collided with another player and ended up with a nosebleed. The Saturday after I went to the local hospital near to Hampstead station; the x-ray revealed that I had broken my nose but everything was in the right place and there was no need to worry. During the week I received a letter from the hospital requesting that I go see them the following Saturday. They were not satisfied with my x-ray and I had to have it done again. It turned out that there was something wrong with the original plates and they wanted another look at my injured nose. The healing process was well underway and I was told that I should still protect my nose. I did not dare tell the doctor that that afternoon I was going to play rugby.

It was a typical damp Saturday afternoon and the venue for the match was Merton in South London. I was playing in the pack and was reluctant to get too involved because of my nose. Just after half-time, I broke away and dashed for the line with the ball under my arm. I had only the fullback to beat. I kicked the ball hoping that it would go over his head. Instead it landed in front of him and he dived on it. My momentum was such that I arrived at the ball just as he dived on it and tried to kick it again. However, the full weight of his body was behind the ball as I kicked it. It felt like kicking a wall. I heard a crack fell over and felt a very sharp pain in my ankle. The first thing that my team-mates tried to do was to get me to stand up but I did not even try to put any weight on my injured leg. I lay down again in the mud and asked them to take my boot off before I was carried to the touchline. They told me that help was summoned from the pavilion. They continued on with the game. I sat on the wet grass in agony and after about ten minutes I decided to hop toward the pavilion a few hundred yards away. About half way a young boy came up to me and asked, "Mister would you like to lean on my shoulder?" He helped me to reach the changing rooms where the groundsman told me that he had not received any message and immediately phoned for an ambulance. The ambulance men placed my foot in a temporary splint, which eased the increasing pain.

With me in the back, the ambulance raced through the streets of South London to Merton Hospital with its siren ringing out. I was still covered in mud from the playing field and still wearing a boot on my non-injured leg, however, I was wheeled in and placed, without any hesitation, on top of the clean white sheets of a hospital trolley.

Within minutes the nurse and the doctor carefully removed the sock from my injured foot and the boot and sock from the other foot. The doctor took one look at my ankle and asked me what happened and if I had heard any noise. I told him about the 'crack'. About a half-hour later the radiologist, who originally came from Cape Town, delivered the x-ray plates. I asked her in Afrikaans what was the extent of the damage but she would not tell me. After examining the plates the doctor said to me that that crack I heard 'was real.' He and the sister then told me that if they attended to my injury then they would then expect me to return to that hospital for subsequent treatment. As I lived at the other end of London, they would place my leg in a temporary plaster splint and deliver me to my digs and then collect me on Sunday morning and take me to the nearest hospital.

I was driven across London in an ambulance, without the siren this time. Once we reached my digs the ambulance men looked wearily at the steps that led up to the front door of the three-story Edwardian building. I tried as gently as possible to inform them that I lived on the top floor. I gave the ambulance man my front door key and told him to ring the bell in the hall three times and that should bring Dan down. Dan, a West Indian, went 'pale' when he first saw the ambulance man who then told him that his mate had an accident and that they had brought me back on a stretcher. I would have to be carried up to our room. The landlady then appeared and ran up the stairs with clean sheets and prepared my bed. After a colossal effort by the ambulance men, I was safely deposited on my bed. They told me to be ready at ten the next morning as another ambulance would collect me and deliver me to the hospital in Hampstead and left with me some pain killing tablets that had been prescribed by the doctor.

After a restless night I woke early and managed to hobble to the bathroom to clean myself up and put on some clean clothes. At ten in the morning, an ambulance arrived and much to the relief of everyone I was able, with help, to hobble down the stairs.

The doctor that attended to me was the same one who had seen me the morning before about my nose. All he said was "So you managed to protect your nose then!" He could not understand why Merton had not put a proper plaster on before sending me home. As it was Sunday they decided that they would not do anything until Tuesday when the orthopaedic specialist held a clinic. In the meantime, I would have to lie perfectly still. Before they were about to send me home they asked if I had anyone to look after me. Once I had told them that I lived in digs and only had a roommate the doctor went over to the nearest phone and insisted that they find a bed for me. I was to remain in hospital.

I was wheeled up to the ward and placed next to a young fellow who had broken both of his legs in a climbing accident. A screen was placed round me and some young nurses undressed me, cleaned me up and made certain that I was comfortable. However, the pain was such that I did not really appreciate or enjoy the attention. After a Sunday lunch I slept for the rest of the afternoon.

During the next day I got to know more about my fellow patient. He had been in hospital for the best part of a year and had been told that the likelihood of him walking again was almost zero. Most of the other patients in the ward had damaged their legs in one way or another. On Tuesday I was wheeled away to have my leg covered in a heavy plaster of Paris cast from below my knee to my toes. They embedded into the plaster a steel ring with a protruding strip ending in a piece of solid rubber directly below my ankle. The cast was very heavy and I had to lie still for at least twenty-four hours to allow it to set properly. Coating my leg in the plaster did not stop the continuous pain. A large steel cradle was placed over my leg so as to prevent the bed-clothes from sticking to it, however my toes were left uncovered. It was only after I complained about my freezing toes that a nurse covered them with cotton wool.

Dan visited me in hospital and brought me my library copy of *Endemion,* a novel by Disraeli that I had just started reading the night before the match. Once the plaster was set I was taught to walk, including climbing up and down stairs with the aid of crutches. One of the other patients, who was a tailor, altered my trousers so that I could get them over the plaster.

By the end of the week I was taken home by ambulance. A cheque for my monthly allowance was waiting for me but the only place that I could cash it was at a special branch of Barclays Bank in the City of London. Between Dan and me we scraped together enough money to cover our tube fares to the bank station. The walk to the tube station then escalators, stairs and the walk to the bank from the station, having just come out of hospital, was a living nightmare. Once I cashed the cheque we took a taxi to the nearest tube station.

On the Monday I managed to get on a bus that went from South Hampstead to Chelsea and it was only a short walk from the bus terminus to the college. One of the lecturers who lived in Hampstead offered to collect me in his car each morning. The college was a three storey building without a lift; however, I succeeded in negotiating the stairs and my fellow students were all helpful carrying my books and food trays etc.

That week I received an invitation from Fiona and her mother to join them at their London home for dinner. I informed them about my injury and politely refused, but they insisted, offering to collect me from college and then to take me home.

The meal was a 'mini-posh', with a maid in attendance. Apart from Fiona's parents and a friend, there was her brother and his girlfriend. Fiona's mother spoke to the maid in Italian. My injury, and sojourn in hospital, and the fact that I had acquired it during a rugby match got the conversation off to good start. The atmosphere reminded me very much of my days at Tavrig in Johannesburg. As the evening wore on, I became more of a spectator than a participant as the novelty of my presence wore off. [Many years later I saw a television documentary about the restoration of paintings damaged when floods devastated one of the Northern Italian cities. One of the persons interviewed on the programme was Fiona but I never met her again].

The telephone in our digs was on the ground floor landing and was usually answered by the landlady. If there was a call for either Dan or myself, the internal bell would ring three times. My leg plaster was now about three weeks old. It was a Saturday afternoon and I was in my room reading when three rings summoned me to the phone. It took quite few minutes for me to clamber down the steps on my crutches. As soon as I picked up the phone Roy, one my friends from the Bar Kochba club, said "What's the matter with you? You don't exactly live in a skyscraper. What took you so long? I suppose you're going to tell me that you have busted a leg or something!" As I slowly broke the news about my ankle, I could almost feel his embarrassment creep down the phone line. However, his feelings of guilt paid off because that evening he picked me up in his car and took me to a college dance.

I could not work during that Christmas vacation which made my usual state of poverty even worse. A cousin who was staying in London at the time lent me five pounds, which at least paid for almost two weeks rent.

Chapter 24

All universities and colleges used to have a mascot that was only on display on very special occasions. The rest of the time it was hidden away. Every now and again there would be an attempt by a rival college to 'kidnap' the mascot. The Chelsea mascot was a small ship's anchor called 'Lady Hamilton,' which the year before had been stolen by the Hammersmith School of Building, embedded in a slab of concrete and kept on the fourth floor. Norman S, a first year physics students who had ambitions to become President of the students union, decided that if he could recapture 'Lady Hamilton' it would enhance his chances of being elected.

I was sitting in the common room beside my propped crutches when Norman came over to me. He first asked that whether or not I agreed with his plan, could I please not tell anyone about it. He had been to the Building School several times and had worked out a plan how to recapture 'Lady Hamilton.' He knew her exact position in the student union office and found that at about six in the evening there were not many students about. It would be easy enough for five big lads to be able to lift the anchor plus concrete onto a strong, small skateboard type of trolley. They would then wheel it out to the lift, take it down to the ground floor and out through a side fire escape door into the car park and a waiting vehicle. He told me that five big lads whom he could trust had agreed to participate and that one of the debutants in the art school could get hold of her father's land rover or that several other cars were also available. He had measured the distances the anchor would have to be wheeled and carried where necessary and timed the proposed operation to the nearest second. The only problem was that the lift was kept locked and that students were not allowed to use it and that was where he needed my help. The plan was to take me by car to the building school and drop me at the main entrance. I was to go the main desk and tell the porter that I wanted to attend a class on the sixth floor and ask if I could be allowed to use the lift.

The following Monday evening I was delivered to the front of the Building School. Five minutes before I arrived, the five hefty lads had walked up to the fourth floor and entered the student union office where 'Lady Hamilton' was kept. The porter took one look at me and without any hesitation, unlocked the lift. I proceeded to the sixth floor as a decoy in case the porters watched the lift indicator. I then immediately pressed the button to take me down to the fourth floor. Norman was waiting for the lift on the fourth floor. As it stopped and opened, I kept my finger on the door ajar button. The signal was given; the anchor was wheeled out on the trolley and straight into the lift. I then hopped out to the stairwell and started to hobble down as fast as I could to the ground floor. As I was descending a group of building students rushed past me shouting, "they've taken the anchor!" Approaching the ground floor I was wondering whether the porters and the building students would have realised that I was part of the operation and how they would deal with me. As I walked passed the desk the porter smiled at me and said nothing. I rushed through the side door and, at the car park gate was a car waiting to collect me. By the time we drove off, 'Lady Hamilton' was back in the students union at Chelsea. The whole operation had gone exactly to plan and had taken less than seven minutes to complete.

A few months later, Norman was voted in as President of the students' union. After University he pursued a career in politics. He ended up as one of the non-elected advisers to Margaret Thatcher. It was February before the plaster was removed and replaced with an elastic bandage but I still had to walk with the aid of two walking sticks.

Part 3

Trip to Israel

Chapter 1

While sitting in the library I came across an advertisement for undergraduates to apply for the annual summer vacation scholarship. You had to submit a two-page resumé of a project, in a field of your choice you would like to carry out during the summer vacation. I decided to apply. The theme of my application was to visit various Kibbutzim in Israel where most of the Kibbutzniks were of Anglo-Saxon origin and investigate how they had adapted to a Kibbutz way of life. I wrote out my application on two sides of notepad paper and handed it into the office. A week later a colleague, Ken, told me that he was going to apply and would I help him with his application. I did not tell him that I had already applied and helped and advised him to formulate his submission. About three weeks later we were both invited to attend an interview.

Eight of us sat outside the College Principal's office waiting our turn to be interviewed. I was interviewed second, as there was only one other person whose surname was higher in the alphabet than mine. The interview lasted about twenty minutes and I was told to wait, as they would announce the winner that afternoon. Ken was one of the last to be interviewed and, while waiting, I primed him with the type of questions that they had asked me. Most of the college knew that the interviews were taking place and interested parties kept calling into the waiting room. As the long wait continued, it became obvious by the tone of the callers who the favourite was and it was not me. By the time the last candidate was called I felt blank and hung around in case the person they offered it to decided for some reason or other not to accept and there might be a second choice. I was also curious to know who had won. About a half-hour after the last interview the door opened and the Principal appeared and a few seconds later, I heard him call my name. I stood up and he invited me into his office and then turned around and looked at the others and simply said, "The scholarship has been awarded." I sat in the room alone on one side of a large table with the interviewing panel occupying the opposite side. Each one, in turn, congratulated me.

I received hearty congratulations from some and muted from others and, as I made way home I began to wonder as to what I had let myself in for. Dan and I walked up to the local pub, the North Star, for a celebratory drink. Once I received written conformation of the award I went to the offices of the Jewish Agency for help and advice on travel to Israel by the cheapest method. They booked me in as a temporary helper (so that I could get a reduced fare) to chaperone a party of eighteen-year-olds who were travelling by sea from Marseilles to Haifa. I would have to join the party at

Victoria Station in London and then, once across the Channel, by train via Paris to the south of France.

The appearance of the tree blossoms was the signal that, once again, I would have to face the summer exams. A few weeks later I received a message that Lady Marsden-Smedley, a member of the governing body, wanted to see me. When I finally did meet her she wanted to know if had made my travel arrangements and if I had a camera. I told her that all I had was a small, Kodak Baby Brownie that my father had given me when I was about ten years old. I was hoping that she would help me get something better but unfortunately she did not know anything about cameras and said no more.

My departure date for Israel was not until the middle of August. Once the exams were over I visited the silk-screen printing shop in Belsize Park. Apart from renewing some old acquaintances, they offered me a summer job.

One Friday my printer and I started a new print run and after lunch the boss received a message that the customer needed the posters by Monday. Under normal circumstances it would take us at least until Monday evening to complete the job. The boss asked us to do our best. The two of us continued to work right through the night and eventually finished the job on Saturday afternoon. I hardly remember walking home, and I woke up midday Sunday in my room on top of my bed with my clothes still on. I worked on until the first end of the first week in August. I was due to depart for Israel on the following Monday.

On the Sunday I packed my tent, sleeping bag, my clothes into an army type kitbag and a rucksack, and arrived at Victoria Station at eight on Monday morning. On the train platform were about thirty very excited eighteen-year-olds of both sexes, all with anxious looking accompanying parents. Apart from all being smartly dressed, they had good quality modern luggage. We all had reserved seats and, when I sat down amidst them, both the youngsters and their parents looked me over but resisted asking if I was in the right place. My seat was next to the window and sitting opposite was a young lad clutching his cased violin. I looked out of the window and there were his anxious parents. They appeared to be slightly older and less wealthy than the other parents. They attracted my attention and indicated to me to see that their son (Sydney) should place his violin safely on the luggage rack. Once the train pulled out I learnt that Sydney, a budding violinist, was intending to tour round Israel performing at Kibbutzim in order to gain concert experience. The Jewish Agency had also helped him with his travel arrangements. We soon reached Dover, and Sydney and I became separated. After a rough ferry crossing we boarded the train to Paris. When I found Sydney again he looked very pale and was just recovering from seasickness.

It was my first trip to France and I was fascinated by the French landscape. As we slowly pulled into the Gar du Nord, the Paris that I knew from seeing various French films at the Hampstead Everyman was spread before me. There were five to six storey nineteenth century tenement buildings that I imagined to house an artist's studio on the top floor below the roof, and the cafés with the tables and chairs on the pavement. The station was still heavily marked by more than a century of steam and smoke. The station platforms seemed to be only half as high as those I was familiar with. Disembarking from the carriage with luggage was quite a struggle. A courier escorted us out of the station and loaded us onto a coach. We were then driven across Paris to the Gar du Sud. Noisy fast-moving traffic combined with taxis darting around the single decked, open-backed crowded buses created a certain amount of tension that almost obliterated my delight of actually being in Paris. Seeing people sitting outside at endless restaurants and bars at tables with sunshades was mesmerizing. We had a brief glimpse of the Eiffel Tower and the Seine before we arrived at the station. We had quite some time to pass before our departure and, while standing in the station concourse, I spotted a French student with whom I had worked at the camp in Holland. His English was as bad as my French but after we found a translator, it turned out that he was there to see off relatives who were also travelling to Israel on the same boat.

The train from Paris to Marseilles was almost as crowded as the London underground during the rush hour. The train did not depart until the early evening and we were due in at Marseilles at six the next morning. Each compartment was filled to capacity; every inch of corridor space was filled with people and luggage - and it was hot. Apart from family holidaymakers there were parties of school children, students and soldiers on their way back to North Africa (mainly Algeria). In addition there were handcuffed prisoners and their armed guards. We had reserved seats but, nevertheless, we all had to squeeze up to one another and there was no way you could stretch out. The real nightmare was stepping over bodies trying to make your way to a usable toilet. A large, steam locomotive pulled the train away and slowly fine particles of soot permeated everyone everywhere.

All the members of the party that I was travelling with had brought food parcels for the journey. They had not yet opened them as they had all bought food from the station snack bars. My last meal was a sandwich on the ferry and I did not have any French money with me. I had packed into my rucksack a tin of sardines and a packet of cream crackers. I was now feeling very hungry. I opened my tin of sardines and then used my pocketknife to spread them onto a dry cracker. It was a taste that I was used to and after few mouthfuls I began to feel my blood sugar rise. I looked up and saw all in my compartment staring at me. Their expressions were a combination of amazement, surprise and some disgust. I could not store the open sardines, and besides I was very hungry, so I ate the lot as well as the whole packet of cream crackers. I did not realise that by the time I finished eating, the whole compartment smelt of tinned sardines. With food in me I decided to try and get some sleep.

Listening to the rhythm of the wheels on the track did eventually help some of us to snatch some sleep. As the train pulled into the station at Marseilles, I felt as if I had been travelling for a month.

Chapter 2

We boarded the SS Theodore Hertzel, the new luxury flagship of Israel, at ten in the morning. I was to sleep in a dormitory-type cabin with about twelve bunks. Sydney was in the next cabin and, when I went to look for him, I found him in an empty closet paying his violin. The expression on his face was such that you knew immediately that he was in his element.

We went up on a very hot deck to watch the ship sail out of the dock into the open sea. Once the ship had left the confines of the port, I went back to the cabin to take a shower and change into clean clothes. The bell rang for the midday meal. Since my arrival in England the number of times that I had eaten in a restaurant with table cloths, serviettes, wine glasses and a full set of cutlery could be counted on one hand. Apart from the fact that I was feeling famished, the idea of being served up a three-course meal almost overwhelmed me. I tried not to eat too fast. There must have been something about me because the waiter (without even asking) served me seconds of each course. Until that moment I had not realised how basic my diet had been over the past few years. The ship was comfortably air-conditioned and, after the meal, I returned to my cabin and slept for a few hours.

The ship was a one-class liner and, apart from the sleeping quarters all the facilities were open to all passengers. Most of the passengers were wealthy European Jews who were on a luxury cruise and then a tour of Israel.

In the evening, the lounge and bars were full of men dressed in summer blazers white flannels and cravats round their necks. The women were equally smart in their light summer dresses and many smoked using jewelled cigarette holders. I thought, like on the sea voyage from Cape Town, the duty free drinks would be cheap. My first drink of the night was also my last.

A day later, we docked at Naples at about eleven in the morning. It was very exciting to see from the deck, Capri, the smoke from Vesuvius and the Bay of Naples. The leader of the party that I was travelling with asked me to help his female assistant chaperone about a third of the group round

Naples. One of the other single male passengers, Ben, who was more like an older hitchhiker than one of the smart passengers in the group decided to attach himself to our party. Sydney also decided to join my group. We did not have enough time to visit the ruins of Pompeii so we simply strolled around the city. Near to the docks were narrow streets with washing spread suspended across the roads. The semi-slum condition of the streets was new to us. Wherever we went we stared at lines of apparently unemployed young men. We were crossing one of the roads via a subway in the main part of the town when the leader, Sheila, accidentally dropped her purse. One of the watching Neapolitan men quickly bent down to pick it up. Ben, who was standing next to me, stepped forward at a pace almost too rapid to see. He stamped on the purse, squashing a few fingers at the same time, and did not let off until Sheila got her hands onto it. The Italians just stared in amazement and then teased their colleague.

While we were walking around I kept counting heads worrying that we might lose someone. A few minutes after the purse incident, I noticed that we had lost Sydney. No one had seen him for at least five minutes. A feeling of despair came over me and, as we were boarding the ship, I went straight to the cabin to prepare to break the news to the group leader. As I reached my cabin I heard what to me at the moment was a wonderful sound, that of a violin. The afternoon was getting Sydney down so, without telling anyone, he simply slipped away from us and made his way back to the ship.

The Friday morning after we had sailed out of Marseilles we approached Haifa. I had an early breakfast, packed my bags and went up onto the deck. It was a beautiful clear day and gradually the silhouette of the hills round Haifa bay came into view. Next the sun's rays began to reflect off the golden dome of the B'hai temple. Gradually, as we approached land, more and more detail of the landscape and buildings could be seen. As the ship sailed in closer, numerous small boats came to greet us. Most of the people on the boats were Israeli Arabs greeting one of their leaders who was a passenger on the ship.

The blue skies, the green slopes of the surrounding hills, the gradual sighting of dockside activity as well the circling small boats all created a memorable sight. A deep feeling of welcome and even of return crept over me as the ship tied up in the dock. As the passengers began to disembark and stepped onto Israeli soil, there was a feeling of restraint, as many of them no doubt wanted to kiss the ground.

Once I was ashore I stayed with my party as the leader had told me that there would be a place for me to spend the night. I had to keep convincing myself that everyone I saw, except for those wearing Arab type clothes - the dock workers, the road sweepers, the street vendors and clerical personnel were all Jewish.

The next morning I made my way to the offices of the shipping agent and booked my return passage, as I was not returning with the party I had travelled out with. My first destination was an Anglo-Australian Kibbutz in the North of Israel. My bus journey took me through some moderately hilly country with endless cultivated fields and past Kineret (the Sea of Galilee). What immediately struck me about that journey was how many different languages were spoken among the passengers. Hebrew seemed to be only used to communicate with strangers. It was 1959 and Israel was still a relatively young state and a large percentage of the Jewish citizens were immigrants from all over the world. A great number were survivors of the Second World War.

The driver indicated to me where to get off, as that was the nearest bus stop to the Kibbutz I was travelling to. The blazing heat seemed far hotter than anything I had experienced in South Africa. I went over to a fellow who had been on the same bus and told him the name of the Kibbutz that I was heading for. His reply, in an Australian accent, was to stay with him and he would get me there. I sat with him (Joe) in the shade of a large, wild olive tree after he had made a phone call.

I had already written in advance to the Kibbutz telling them of my reason for requesting permission to stay and work for a week or two. Joe quizzed me as to my reasons for wanting to visit the Kibbutz and, when I told him, he replied that he vaguely recalled my letter being read out at a meeting. A pickup truck arrived about twenty minutes later and as I was climbing onto the back of the truck, he said to the driver, "this is the Pommy who wrote to us."

About twenty minutes later, I arrived at the Kibbutz and met the secretary who welcomed me and explained the basic rules and customs, then allocated me to one of the older original huts. As the Kibbutz was becoming wealthier brick built houses were replacing the huts. It was now lunchtime and I went to the large dining room. I queued up and was given helping of the main course and vegetables. On the table were bowls of tomatoes, olives, onions, raw cucumbers, lettuce and bread. The person seated next to me explained that if I wanted a salad I would have to prepare it myself. I first watched what the others did. In the middle of the tables were bowls to place the uneatable parts of the salad ingredients. As I mentioned earlier Israel was still very much a developing country and the standard of living was basic. This was reflected in the food being served up.

Returning to my hut, I lay down with a full stomach combined with the intense heat. I woke up about two hours later. I spent the rest of the afternoon wandering around and finding out what happens on a Kibbutz. The main activity was agricultural. Apart from the usual features associated with agronomy, such as barn, silos and agricultural machinery, there was also a large dairy herd and chickens. There was also a small furniture factory, a laundry, a crèche, and a junior school.

Chapter 3

In Johannesburg I was a member of the Zionist youth group the Habonim. One of the objectives was to inform us about life in Israel and, in particular, life on a Kibbutz. I had visited the first Hachshara (training farm) at Brits in the Transvaal. Part of the first farm that I worked on after finishing school was let to the Zionist Federation as home to the second Hachshara. Hence, I had a good theoretical knowledge of the origins and functioning of a Kibbutz. Now, for the first time I was actually on a real Kibbutz.

One of most frequently debated issues about Kibbutz life was the raising of the children. As soon as it was practical all babies were housed in a communal crèche and not in the parents' home. Trained babyminders who lived on the premises manned the crèche. The parents (mainly the mother) would then return to the crèche in the morning to feed and dress their child and stay with the child as long as possible. Once the day's work was over the parents would take the child to their house and only return the child at bedtime. This enabled the parents to have an undisturbed nights sleep and did not then disrupt any work patterns.

Apart from very personal possessions all material aspects were communally owned or shared. Kibbutz children grew up knowing that the Kibbutz provided everything and whatever was given to them was automatically shared. Although all the Kibbutzniks accepted that system, I did meet some who were waiting for the time when the Kibbutz would become rich enough to provide them houses that had more than one bedroom so that the children could live with them.

I walked to some of the fields nearby. What struck me immediately was that the non-cultivated land was covered with stones of all sizes. In order to prepare any stretch of land for cultivation the stones had to first be removed. I came across a trailer being loaded with stones by a Kibbutznik, who was also the tractor driver, and two hired Arab workers. The driver, who was in his fifties, told me that when the Kibbutz was first founded everyone who could be spared spent all their working days clearing stones. He pointed out mounds of stone that had not yet been used in any form of construction. Looking across acres and acres of fields, the thought that each one had to first be denuded of rocks of all sizes was mind-boggling to me.

That evening after supper I found the notice board where the details of the next day's work programme were posted. I found my name included in a group that was storing the hay. I spent the next few days helping to build haystacks. I had done some pitch forking on the farms in South Africa and on one of the farms in Cambridgeshire. I enjoyed the work but had to drink pints of cold water because of the intense heat.

The eastern boundary of the Kibbutz was the River Jordan, which was hidden in a very shallow valley. Across the river was the Kingdom of Jordan. The cultivated fields ended about five hundred metres from the river. We were not allowed to walk in toward the river unless accompanied by an armed guard. There were no cultivated fields on the Jordanian side. About half way up the valley a series of huts could just be seen and, I was told, they were barracks housing soldiers of Jordan.

A few days later, a party of English Jewish students who were on an organised tour of Israel arrived at the Kibbutz. Part of their itinerary was to stay and work on a Kibbutz for a short while. They were nearly all assigned to light work in either the kitchen or laundry, or general maintenance tasks. I was taken off the hay work and transferred to a potato planting team on fields in the Hulah area about ten miles north of the Kibbutz. The work was to be done in two shifts, the first started at six in the morning and the second at two in the afternoon. My first shift was the morning one.

The foreman woke me up at five in the morning, and at five-thirty the four of us were driven in a pick-up truck to the fields - a journey that took about twenty minutes. We off-loaded into a small wooden hut a five-gallon milk churn full of ice-cold water, bread, eggs, and salami and salad foods. The fields were situated in the drained Hulah swamps and formed a huge, fertile basin through which streams flowed into the river Jordan - the boundary between Syria, Jordan and Israel. Along the northeast horizon could be seen the Golan Heights. The whole area lies below sea level and once the sun rose, the temperature also rose rapidly.

I was the only non-Kibbutznik on the team. Our leader drove the pick-up to a store and collected a few bags of seed potatoes, then hitched a potato planting machine to the back of the tractor. The machine had a Y-shaped chute with seats on either side. In the front of the machine were two furrow ploughs. We filled the chute with the seed potatoes. The driver started the tractor and the other chap and myself climbed onto the two seats. The leader then drove round the field placing marker sticks for the tractor driver to aim at. The ploughs created two furrows immediately beneath and movement of the wheels started the planting mechanism, which released potatoes into a small trough in front of us. Then a bell rang and, at every ring, we had to drop a single potato down through a tube into the furrow. At the rear of the machine were two blades that closed the furrow and covered the potatoes with soil. While the tractor was moving the bell rang every few seconds. Our job was simply, rhythmically, lifting a potato then dropping it. The noise of the tractor, and the planting machine and the bell made conversation difficult, nevertheless, once our senses had adapted we managed to talk to one another in short spells. After about an hour and a half we stopped for breakfast, which was prepared for us by the foreman.

We had placed our urn of cold water at one end of the field, and after each trip up and back we had to have a drink. The dry heat immediately dried off any perspiration and, if you did not drink regularly, your lips and mouth felt as though they were about to crack wide open. Toward midday a strong, hot wind began to blow across the fields. The strength of the wind was such that if you threw a pebble into the air you could see the wind divert it into the direction of the airflow.

Our shift ended at two in the afternoon. We ate a sumptuous lunch. The food was much better than at the Kibbutz simply because the foreman had managed to accumulate a few luxury items as the kitchen had, on certain days, provided larger rations.

I was in need of a good stretch after all that tractor sitting but once in the shade of the hut and with the aid of food and drink, and no noise, I began to feel normal again. The pickup truck took us back to the kibbutz and I spent the rest of the afternoon sleeping.

At the end of the next day's shift (while doing my stretch walk) I discovered a small fast flowing shallow stream. With the blazing sun on my back, the water looked very cool and inviting. Without any hesitation I stripped off and stepped into the stream, which was only knee deep. I lay down with my feet pointing downstream and wedged against a stone. Water flowed over my head then over my body. A feeling of having momentarily stepped into paradise came over me. However, it did not last long as the water that had originated in the Syrian Mountains and was ice cold. The stream was actually a small tributary of the Jordan. At first the cold water took my breath away and then, after a few minutes, I began to shiver. Once again in the air it was only a matter of minutes before I dried off. I put on my shorts and then returned, refreshed, to the hut for my meal. After the meal Joe (the other planter) and I leaned back against the hut wall with his chair pivoting on the back two legs. Our dream-like state was suddenly shattered by a loud yell of pain from Joe. As he stood up he shook his shirt and out dropped a large centipede. We lifted his shirt and could see two large, red marks where presumably the centipede had stung him. The driver squeezed the rapidly swelling marks straight away and extracted the stings and some of the toxins. Apart from some discomfort, Joe suffered little in the way of after effects.

In Israel the working week begins on Sunday and it seemed to me like a Monday. On the next Sunday my team was transferred to the afternoon/evening shift, which began at two in the afternoon. At one o-clock, the three of us collected our food rations and water supply and were driven to the main road to a bus stop. At the stop while waiting in the queue, one or two people asked us for a drink of water. The tractor driver was very reluctant to part with our ice-cold water but finally did. We boarded a full bus with our five-gallon water churn and food packets. After alighting from the bus we still had about a mile to walk to the hut.

We started to work in what seemed like the hottest time of the day. In the next field I noticed about a dozen large vulture-type birds on the ground with their wings spread out. Only in flight would I be able see how large they were and, perhaps, identify them more positively. At the end of the row I jumped off the tractor and threw a small stone at them. They watched the stone almost hovering in the strong wind and only when the stone began its descent toward them did they take to flight. Their heads and almost featherless necks suggested that they were carrion eaters.

We ate just before sunset and the started our final session. It was dark now so, apart from the tractor headlights, our only light was a lamp over the planting machine. Once we started working I noticed that the driver had alongside him a loaded Uzi machine gun and a spare round of bullets. He told me that we were only about five hundred metres from the river and the border, which was a common point of infiltration, hence the need for some protection. As the evening wore on I realised that, in the darkness, the tractor noise and lights, along with our slow movements, made us sitting targets. There was no way we could defend ourselves from an attack. The gun was used on only two occasions, which resulted in the death of a porcupine and a wild pig.

Chapter 4

On my first Saturday, a non-working day I walked over to a small Arab village. I walked up to a group of men who were playing chess under a shelter. They greeted me and invited me to join them, and offered me some traditional coffee. It was served in a very small cup and was quite strong. One of the chess players could speak some English and nearly all the men could speak Hebrew. In fact, most them actually worked on the Kibbutz. I wandered around and was invited into some of the houses, which seemed quite poor and reminded me very much of the homes of the African workers I had visited when working on the farm. When it was time to leave they all shook hands with me and invited me back. The following Saturday Rita, one of the student party, asked me if I would go with her to the Arab village. This time, as I approached, they came down the road to greet us. We once again were invited into the shelter for coffee. The Arab women apart from their faces, were completely clothed from head to toe. In contrast, Rita wore a sleeveless tee-shirt and very short almost revealing shorts. No comment was made, but the impression we made can only be speculated upon.

At the end of the week the party of students moved off and I cadged a lift on their coach to Jerusalem. Buses and coaches were not air-conditioned then. To keep cool either all the windows were permanently open or the glass was removed from the top half of all the windows. In spite of the continuous airflow, after about fifteen minutes, most passengers fell asleep. Falling asleep in a sitting position often leads to heads flopping all over into most undignified positions. Rita was sitting next to me and her head flopped onto my shoulder, then I fell asleep. I woke up to a completely wet shoulder where she had dribbled over me in her sleep. Needless to say she was even more embarrassed than I was.

I moved with the party into their hostel in Jerusalem. The leader of the party simply booked in the number so there was no name check. Jerusalem in 1959 was still a divided city with the old city in Jordanian control and out of bounds to Israelis. One of the border crossings were then at the Mandelbaum gate in an area known as Maya Shirim (a thousand gates) the home of most of the *chasidim* (ultra orthodox Jews). The area was home to numerous Yeshivas (religious seminaries) and there were large notices in the streets asking the daughters of Jerusalem to dress modestly - not to wear shorts and to cover their arms. No requests were made to men.

I wandered around wearing my usual short shorts, which were the fashion then, and a tee-shirt and white Kibbutz-style hat. The Chassidim speak Yiddish among themselves, not Hebrew, although I am certain that most could speak Modern Hebrew. I had a working knowledge of Yiddish from speaking to my grandmother (my Bobe) who did not speak any English. All the doors and windows of the Yeshivas were open, and as I walked round, I looked in. In one, a group was chatting over a cup of tea and saw me peep. They invited me to join them. I was given a glass of lemon tea and then they asked me the usual questions. Where was I from? How long had I been in Israel? Then they probed me to find out not only how religious I was, but whether I observed any of the religious rituals. When I informed them that I was totally *areligious* they uttered a few snorts of disgust. Their leader then informed me, in a sad tone of voice, of the low percentage of Jews who are religious and, as far as he was concerned that was cause for despair. I replied that, like them, I was alive and so were all the non-Jews. I wanted to know from them how it would affect my life if I practised all their rituals. I had noticed, before entering the *Yeshiva,* a couple of very young teenage boys smoking. I also saw one young boy standing on a first floor balcony peeing down onto the cobbled street. No one said a word to him or the smokers. I asked those who I was debating with as to why no one took any notice of what I considered to be anti-social behaviour. After all, they had been trying to tell me that being religious was good for discipline. They simply shrugged their shoulders and said that they were children and we must be tolerant toward them.

Although they were all totally against me the atmosphere was generally good-natured and, when I left, they all shook hands with me and invited me back. I walked off toward the Mandel Baum gate. The border was marked with barbed wire and the gate very securely closed. There were notices in Hebrew, Arabic, English and French saying beware enemy territory and that it was mined.

Back at the hostel, I told the group of my discussions and some were amazed that I actually emerged in one piece and even more astonished that I had been invited back. The next day Rita walked round with me. She was wearing shorts and a short-sleeved blouse. During the afternoon we found ourselves in Maya Shirim. We had heard how the *Chassidim* had chased women out of the area who did not observe their dress code and were expecting to be stopped. We slowly made our way toward the *Yeshiva* and no one took any notice of us. I was welcomed in again but pointed out to them that I was with Rita. Their reply was not to worry and they invited her in as well.

The next day I caught a bus to Kibbutz Tzorah, only a short ride from Jerusalem. Tzorah is supposedly the birthplace of Samson. I went there because most of the founders of the Kibbutz were South African and it was a chance for me to meet up with one or two of my old Habonim leaders. I was given various tasks to do but nothing specific. Once again in the evenings I got into deep discussion about Kibbutz life and Israel in general.

Staying on that Kibbutz was Zwi who had lived in a small house in Derby Road, Bertrams, Johannesburg, which was only a five-minute walk from where I had lived. Their house was one of those where the front wall of the house formed the inner edge of the pavement. The bedroom window opened over the kerb. The front door was in a slight recess, which formed a mini veranda. Zwi arrived in South Africa at about the age of three with his mother who was from Lithuania. Somehow his mother had managed to ship all of her belongings, including furniture, with her. Once inside her Johannesburg house it was difficult to realise that you were in a city on the African Highveld and not in Eastern Europe. I was walking to my room on the Kibbutz when I passed a small, two bedroom house and sitting outside was Zwi's elderly mother. Once I told her who I was she invited me in. As soon as I had entered I was back in the same house that I remembered in Derby Road, only this time it was situated close to the hills of Judea. She had never really mastered English and still spoke with a strong East European accent. With a certain amount of hesitation she told me about how Zwi had brought her to Israel and how she now occupied her days. There were no local shops, or trams that passed by the front door to take her to town. Although there were people all round there was no, in the urban sense, neighbourhood. There she was for the second time in her life having to endure a major migration and resettlement.

Chapter 5

I returned to Jerusalem and made my way by bus to Kibbutz Hasolalim near to Nazareth. It was a scenic but hot bus ride to Nazareth where I arrived about midday. In order to get to the Kibbutz I had to catch a bus operated by an Arab bus company. The bus station consisted of a small building and a huge light sandstone archway through which the buses drove in and out. I had about an hour to wait for my bus. I lay down under the arch out the way of buses and rested my head on my rucksack and fell asleep. I woke up to find that a heavily laden camel was standing over me. I was immediately under its stomach with its front legs on my right and its hind legs to my left. For few seconds I lay there frozen, then carefully slithered out from under the camel before I stood up, only to notice that I was being watched by a very amused group of locals.

When my bus arrived I was the first passenger on board and went to find a seat in the middle of the bus. No sooner had I sat down when the driver came over to me and insisted that I move to the front of the bus to the seat next to him. By the time the bus moved off it was full and I was the only non-Arab. About half of the male passengers wore western style clothes and the rest wore variations of Arab dress. Some wore what I would describe as Bedouin dress. It was a slow and bumpy journey. As we drove along, a group of passengers became first very noisy then argumentative. I turned round to see a Bedouin squaring up to one of the other passengers. All the rest, including the women, joined in the shouting - trying to calm them down and to prevent a fight. The adversaries grabbed each other, a scuffle started and the noise level rose. The Bedouin lost his headdress and exposed his entire long, pitch-black hair. He looked very Christ-like. Fists were flying and then a knife appeared in the non-Bedouin's hand, which was grabbed by the other passengers. The driver stopped the bus and took a large baton from behind his seat then charged into the scuffle cursing loudly in Arabic. After a few strikes order was quickly restored and the opponents were threatened with eviction from the bus. I was mesmerized by the entire goings on and did not move from my seat. The driver sat down again, looked at me and winked.

His expression said, "Now you know why I told you to sit by me." We drove off in total silence.

The reason for wanting to visit that particular Kibbutz was that I had heard some of my school friends from Johannesburg were staying and working there. One in particular was Jackie G. Apart from the fact I had known him since early childhood we were also in Habonim together.

I asked the first person I met as I walked through the gates for the whereabouts of Jackie G. He pointed to a group of people standing outside the dining room and there was the unmistakable bright red hair that could belong only to Jackie. He did not recognise me at first as I had grown a beard. He took me into the dining room and we spent the rest of his dinner hour reminiscing. He then took me to his house and left me there. After a shower I sat down in a comfortable chair and soon fell asleep. Next I heard a voice and stood up to greet Helene who introduced herself as Jackie's wife. Although I stood up, I was not properly awake and all I could see through half closed eyes were her feet. I sat down again and only really woke up after I was offered a drink. Then Jackie returned and showed me to a hut, empty except for a bed and a wardrobe, where I could stay.

The next morning I reported for work. I was assigned to work in one of the large chicken houses. They had several and one was kept empty for cleaning. My task was (together with a local Arab worker) to clean out all the chicken manure. A tractor-trailer was driven in and placed between the rows of chicken cages. The chicken droppings had fallen into long, concrete troughs. All the cages had to be first removed. We stepped onto a layer of chicken manure nearly two foot deep. We, including the driver, stood on the crusty surface and then began to shovel the manure into the trailer. The top few inches was dry but underneath that there was a dark, soft, smelly mass. Once the lower layer was reached it exposed a myriad of small black coprophilic insects to daylight. They rushed all over the place and crawled over our boots and up our legs. Luckily they were negatively phototropic and once they had reached the level of the top our gumboots they darted down again. Nevertheless some did climb up my legs and at the first feeling of crawling over me, I tried to brush them off with my hands. After a while I began to ignore the insects running over my skin. The roof was made of corrugated zinc and soon heated up. The heat together with the increasing smell made it a really unpleasant task.

At the end of the first day, I spent a long time in the shower trying to scrub away the effects of the smell and the insects that I still felt crawling over me. After a few days, the three of us were able to carry out quite intensive conversations despite the working conditions. Each evening I would make notes about what I had learnt about Kibbutz life from the driver.

On the first Saturday, a day off, I caught the bus to Nazareth. I spent the morning wandering around the tourist sights. At the Cave of the annunciation, there were some monks supervising archaeological digging. They were wearing their traditional brown robes and, as one of then stepped down into the pit I noticed that he had shaved the crown of his head, I suppose to fit the image we have of monks.

After a snack I wandered into a bookshop and was surprised to see how many bookshelves were lined with classical English literature. After about ten minutes of browsing I began talking to the proprietor about the merits of various English authors. Once the conversation began, others, who appeared from the back of the shop, and customers joined us. I became the centre of attention and all was going well, in fact I was even offered a cup of tea. Then the proprietor said to me, "You are not Jewish are you?" When I replied that I was Jewish, the whole atmosphere suddenly cooled right down almost to silence. I shook hands with all of them and left.

I spent that evening talking to some of the younger single males in the Kibbutz lounge. I recalled my bookshop experience and the majority responded that I shouldn't expect anything else. During the evening we discussed the status and role of the Israeli Arabs. All, like me, were originally from South Africa and I supposed I should not have been surprised how they had carried with them to Israel many of their anti-African attitudes. I was almost alone in speaking up for total equal and social rights of the Arabs. The evening ended rather abruptly when I was asked how long I had been in Israel. When I replied nearly three weeks all but Jackie G and his wife stood up and walked out.

I moved on to Tel Aviv where I went to the South African Embassy and collected my mail. A letter from Dan told me that I had passed my exams and there was also a cheque from my mother. A girl friend had given me the address of her aunt who lived in Tel Aviv. I managed to find out what bus to catch. What had struck me again when travelling on public transport in Israel was how many different languages you heard being spoken. Hebrew seemed only to be used to communicate with strangers. The other aspect was that the bus radio was nearly always tuned to a radio station that played classical music. The bus in Tel Aviv was no exception. I showed the address of where I wanted to go to the driver and, in a mixture of broken Hebrew and Yiddish asked him to call me when I reached my stop - a practice quite common in England. It was the rush hour and I was till on the bus when most of the passengers had disembarked and no passengers travelling back to the city were getting on. The driver came over to me and loudly scolded me for not paying enough fare and asked if I intended to spend the whole day travelling backwards and forwards. Once I understood what he was on about, I spoke back loudly asking why he had not called me. I told him that in all the other countries that I had visited, drivers were helpful. I then offered to pay more fare at which stage all the passengers joined in on my side and told the driver not to accept my money. At the appropriate stop, passing it on my way back, the driver called me and one of the passengers then walked with me to my address. I was made welcome by the family and spent the night there.

The next morning I caught a bus to Ber Sheba, a town on the northern edge of the Negev desert. In those days it was considered by the Israelis to be remote and had a touch of the Wild West about it. After finding accommodation for the night in the local youth hostel I went out that evening. I had a meal in a bar located in a back street. The bar seats were all parts of small, temple-type pillars that had been obtained from a local archaeological site.

The following morning I travelled by bus to an American Kibbutz that had been established in the Negev close to Gaza and the Egyptian border. At the bus stop in Ber Sheba there was an orderly queue and I was at the front. As soon as the bus arrived, there was a mighty forward rush and I was wedged into the entrance to the bus. I shouted out in English, "What's the matter! Can't you control yourselves and be civilised." My outburst was followed by almost total silence. They stood back and I climbed onto the bus, paid the driver and sat down. As soon as I sat down the noise and crush started up again.

The Kibbutzim on the edge of the desert were supplied with water from a pipeline that originated in the north of the country. All the settlements from the north southwards pumped their excess water into the pipeline. The water was used for irrigation by the settlements in the arid regions; hence, huge tracts of lands had been opened up to cultivation. The kibbutz that I was staying on had citrus orchards, vineyards and cereal crops. On that particular Kibbutz was stationed a platoon of soldiers that had chosen to do most of their military service working on a Kibbutz and also serving as border guards. Apart from the members of the Kibbutz being of Anglo Saxon and North American origin, the Nachal (the border platoon) were all, apart from the officers, South Africans. The type of irrigation used was based on a sprinkler system. The sprinklers were fed by long aluminium water pipes. In spite of the length of the pipes provided, you picked them up in the middle and you could carry several on your shoulders at a time. My first day's work was to help lay out pipes in fields where a cereal crop had been sown. The pipes were joined end to end by a simple clasping mechanism and the water was sprayed out from the end nozzle in a circular motion. While the water was being sprayed out into the air we set out the next few rows of pipes almost parallel to the first. Once the ground was saturated, which took a few hours, we then would connect the next row to the water supply. The not too waterproof joints combined with the uneven ground led to leaks and, after a few hours large puddles were created in the original desert-type sandy soil. The next morning when we went out to move the pipes, I noticed that in nearly all the larger puddles there were dozens of tadpoles. No doubt some of the desert toads had become adapted to taking advantage of this regular bonanza of water in an area where rain and water was scarce throughout the year.

Another of my jobs was weeding in a vineyard. I worked with a young American student who went into a panic every time a large wasp came close. He would not believe me that if you ignored them they mostly ignored you and would yell out in amazement every time he saw a wasp flying round my face, which I ignored. It was extremely hot and, to cool himself, my colleague would fill his hat with water and then rapidly put it on his head and the water would run down over him.

At first I slept in the soldiers' quarters. However, as they were on duty and part of their training was done at night, I soon got fed up with being woken up at all hours and found myself sleeping accommodation in the Kibbutz proper. Some of the soldiers had fermented a fruit mixture in a large milk churn. They had also rigged up a simple distilling plant and slowly accumulated bottles of a very strong alcoholic liquid. On one particular evening we had stayed up late and, after a few beers started on the 'white liquid'. The alcohol soon took over and behaviour became more and more reckless and finally ended with one of the soldiers firing off a round of bullets from his Uzi into the walls and ceiling. The noise attracted a lot of attention and before long the officers and Kibbutzniks restored order. The next morning after an enquiry the distillery was dismantled and the 'white liquid' poured down the drain. Luckily for me none of the officials knew that I was there, hence, I was not asked to give evidence.

The Israeli born soldiers were able to go home, when on leave, to their families and their families subsidized their wages. However the South Africans in the army on leave, apart from the occasional excursion, remained in the camp and had little money to spend.

Chapter 6

After about ten days I felt that I had enough information for my purposes and travelled back to Ber Sheba and decided to try and hitchhike to Eilat, Israel's most southerly port on the Red Sea. It took me only a few hours and two lifts to reach a large motorway type stop on the edge of the Northern Negev, the last bit of civilisation before the desert proper. Fleets of lorries were parked there while the drivers refreshed themselves. All goods to Eilat and Timna, the copper mines, were transported by road on huge lorries. There were very few cars about. It was now a matter of finding a lorry driver who was prepared to give me lift. I came across a driver who had a flat tyre. The wheels on those trucks were enormous and the driver was a small Yemini and was having quite a struggle. Without saying anything I began to help him and between us we changed the wheel in almost total silence. The heat was intense and we both had to move to some shade and quench our thirst. He did not speak any English and the Jews from Yemen don't speak Yiddish, however, in my stilted Hebrew I managed to ask him for a lift. He replied that he was only going to Timna about ten miles from Eilat and, if he did give me lift I must not fall asleep. I agreed to his conditions. Before we departed we returned to the café for a meal.

We set out about mid-morning. The cab of the lorry was high off the ground and I had a good view of the countryside. The small driver could barely see above the steering wheel and I doubt if there was power steering. There were two gear levers. Driving the truck kept the driver very busy and it was at least a half-hour before we started any conversation. As the journey progressed I felt more and more sleepy and he kept talking to me keep me awake. Somehow I managed to stay awake and make myself understood.

We had to drive up over a ridge of mountains. The road wound up and down and the most hair-raising moments were while passing another truck travelling in the opposite direction. Those were the days before one purchased bottled water and my mouth began to crack with thirst. Once we crossed the mountains and the road flattened, a hut, which seemed to be in the middle of nowhere, came into sight and we stopped there. It turned out to be a transport café for the lorry drivers. It was run by one man who had quite an armoury of weapons which he said he had to use quite regularly because of raiders from the nearby Jordanian and Egyptian borders. On the road again, it was getting dark and we passed by small herds of wild camels as well as the occasional lone jackal.

It was dark when we reached the turn-off to Timna and the driver said that he was not allowed to take me with him into the mine compound. I pleaded with him and when we did reach the gate, the guard insisted that I get out and return to the road.

It was pitch dark and the only sounds were from movement in the scrub bushes. It was now about 7.00 pm and I could not contemplate spending a night in the open where both the Jordanian and Egyptian borders were only a few miles away, let alone the wild life. I decided that if I was still there at ten I would have another go at pleading with the guard or I would sleep as close to his hut as possible.

I was lying in the road with my head on my rucksack looking up at the stars when in the distance I saw a pair of headlights approaching from the North. I got up and stood in the middle of the road, determined not to let the vehicle pass by without stopping. As the vehicle approached it began to slow down and when it finally reached me it turned out to be the regular bus from Ber Sheba. My whole body seemed to revive as I paid the driver my fare. I settled down and as the bus drove on, I saw that close to where I had been were at least three jackals. It was only a short ride to Eilat and once there, I soon found the local youth hostel.

Eilat, a Southern Israeli outpost on the Northern most point of the Gulf of Eilat part of the Red Sea, is squeezed in between Jordan and Egypt. The Jordanian port of Amman, like Eilat, had only a few miles of seafront and was squeezed between Israel and Saudi Arabia. It was strange to be in an area so close to three countries - all of them potential enemies. Yet, in spite of its locality, Eilat gave the impression of a calm, small urban oasis. Unlike the rest of Israel, some of the buses ran on Saturday. The place did not entirely shut down for the Sabbath. There were two hotels close to a small airport. The flight path of the planes was very tight, flying down a narrowing strip of Israel and then turning sharply over the sea. The climate was far hotter than the rest of the country and the only cool time was during the early morning.

At the hostel I acquired a snorkel mask and a pair of 'frog feet' and, together with Joe, (who was from England and, like myself, had only arrived the day before), caught a bus to a beach very close to the Egyptian border. On the beach was a small hut, which sold refreshments and few large open shelters. These consisted of a straw roof attached to four poles. From the beach you could see, across the gulf, the rugged treeless mountains of Saudi Arabia, the port of Amman and the small hotel complex of Eilat. Looking inland, just visible, were the bare hills and mountains of the Sinai desert. Apart from the odd human voice and bird sounds, there was silence and stillness. It was a perfect place to relax and reflect. The tensions of the world did not appear to exist. Was this what the world was like before man? It was hard to believe that a few hours away lived millions of people!

Living in a shelter just off the beach was an American, Sam, who was studying at the Hebrew University in Jerusalem. He decided to spend his summer vacation in this splendid isolation. He was equipped with underwater swimming gear and spent his morning spear fishing, then sold the fish to local restaurants. Joe and I struck up a friendship with Sam. He taught us how use our snorkels and then swam with us over and among the corals.

The first time I submerged it was quite frightening. The whole perspective changes dramatically. Looking straight down at the sea floor was not so forbidding. Looking around into a blue mass with light beams streaking through forming alternating dark and light pillars and a very limited horizon as if you were looking into a blue abyss was scary. It was as if some large creature was suddenly going to appear. After only a few seconds under water, I rapidly surfaced relieved at seeing a familiar world. However, the beauty of the sea floor covered in rows of coral growth and a multitude of fish and sea creatures soon had me submerging again and again, each time for a longer period. Slowly the lack of a horizon substituted by a blue infinity became the norm. To begin with we only swam in relatively shallow waters.

One morning I persuaded Sam to let me go out with him into deeper water on one of his spear fishing trips. He warned me of the danger of sharks and barracuda and instructed me on how to communicate under water using hand signals (in particular what to do if we came across any of the large sea predators). He gave me a belt with a series of hooks on it. We swam out with our heads just below the surface, breathing through our snorkels. The seabed, coral and fishes became more and more exciting to look at the further out we went. Sam suddenly dived down and speared a fish and then hooked the bleeding fish to my belt. After a short while I had a row of bleeding dead fish round my waist. It then occurred to me that if any predator picked up the scent of the dead fish, I would be a sitting target. Nevertheless I decided to remain close to Sam, relying on him for protection. After about an hour, in spite of the water temperature being well above twenty degrees centigrade, I began to shiver with cold. Sam then gave me the signal to return to the shore. I swam as fast as I could, not daring to look behind in case I was being chased.

After about eleven in the morning it became almost impossible for us not seek the shelter of shade. The upper part of the beach was stony rather than fine sand. After a midday drink and snack we lay down on the hard surface and slept for at least an hour. While not sleeping all I could think about was drinking a pint of cold beer.

Chapter 7

A few mornings later I stood for about two hours at the roadside hitchhiking before I got the lift that took me to Tel Aviv. The next morning I made my way to Haifa to board the ship to Marseilles. I had arrived, several weeks earlier, at Haifa on board the Theodore Hertzel - the newest and flagship of the Israeli shipping lines. I was now returning on the Artza, the oldest ship in the fleet, which was originally a submarine supply ship for the wartime German navy. Once on board, it seemed like having just climbed into a large rusting tub. The only consolation was that I was now with the party of students that I met up with on the first Kibbutz that I had worked on. I had met up with them quite a few times in various parts of Israel and they adopted me. One of the girls, Rachel, was good looking with long dark hair. As the voyage progressed we became friendly. However, she came from a very orthodox family and was engaged to a fellow who was working on a religious kibbutz. [A few years later I heard that she had returned to Israel to get married and after their first child was born he had been killed by lightning].

As we sailed through the gulf of the Adriatic, the weather took a turn for the worse. We sailed for nearly a day and a half through a huge swell. The ship was tossed about violently. Slowly, one by one, the passengers became ill and you could not walk more than a few feet without seeing a sick bucket. I had been alright for most of the morning but then I needed to go below deck to put on a light jumper. As I walked down the stairs my legs felt as if they were being stretched beyond breaking point and then, suddenly, my feet came rushing toward my head. As I tried to walk along the lower deck I was thrown about quite violently and by the time I reached my cabin I was, like everybody else, heaving into an old oil barrel. I lay on my bunk feeling that my end had come but, after an hour, managed to make my way back onto the open deck. As I surfaced I saw Rachel who commented that I was probably the first real green man she had ever seen. I found my way to the middle of the ship and climbed into a life boat, lay down, and never moved till the next morning.

As we sailed through the Straits of Sicily the ship rounded the Island of Stromboli and provided a spectacular view of the active volcano, especially in the early evening. The ship docked for half a day in the port of Genoa and then we sailed on to Marseilles.

We docked in Marseilles in the morning. There were buses waiting to take us to the railway station. Apart from the party I was with, there were other ships passengers on the bus. As the bus approached the station a silence settled over all of us. It was as if, suddenly, it dawned on us all that this would be the last time we would experience a totally Jewish environment. As the bus drove into the station yard everyone simultaneously began to sing *Hatikvah*, the Jewish national anthem.

Among the passengers were a family of Yemeni Jews who had lived in Aden. They had British passports and were making their way to England. They had with them all their worldly possessions including a collection of religious silverware. They hardly spoke Hebrew, let alone any English, and we were all concerned about how they would fare.

The train that we were booked on was due to leave that evening so we had the rest of the day to spend in Marseilles. I wandered around with Dave, a medical student. We visited the harbour and then walked through the town. We lunched at a small café. After the meal the proprietor started up a conversation with us and told us that he collected coins. We gave him the few Israeli coins we still had, then dug up some English coins. Our small gifts pleased him and his wife so much so that he gave us free tots of whisky.

Dave and I made our way to the station. We were both dreading the night journey to Paris. Once at the station we rejoined the rest of the group. We did not have booked seats so it was matter of walking up down the train to look for a seat. The second-class carriages of the train were full and the Yemeni family was left in the corridor. Dave and I ended up having an argument with the guard trying get him to allow the family into one of the empty first class compartments. He threatened to stop the train and call the police if we did not back off. We moved away and found a compartment with only one person and we settled into it. Next morning in Paris we discovered that once we had backed off the guard had moved the family into an empty first-class compartment. We travelled across Paris by bus to the Gar du Nord and then on to the boat train. It was now late September and the weather was remarkably warm for that time of year. We sat on the deck of the cross channel ferry with a sense of relief knowing that we were returning to a familiar environment. It was made even more reassuring hearing all the announcements in English. I had only enough money left to pay for my tube fare from Victoria station to my digs in Hampstead.

Chapter 8

A few days after my return the autumn term began at Chelsea. I now had to settle down to the second year of my course and start to write up my report. It took quite a while to make some sense of my notes and then I started to write my first draft in long hand. One of the girls at the Bar Kochba gym club offered to type it out for me. I showed the typed draft to the head of the Liberal Studies department who edited it for me. His secretary typed out the final draft, which I handed in. As far as I know it is still in the Chelsea College library.

The end of the autumn term was concert or review time. A couple of the second and third year students wrote a sketch making fun of the staff and students. That particular year the theme was cave man society. No one volunteered to participate, however people like me were eventually coaxed and bribed with beer to take part. A series of short sketches were written and one of them required a few colleagues and me to dress up as cavemen. We acquired the necessary artificial fur skins and plastic clubs and my contribution was to receive a blow to my head and then make a spectacular dive across the stage. My fall was supposed to be funny but it did make the audience squirm on my behalf. I also did a spell as a compere and one of the acts that I had to introduce was two big lads in ballet dress performing a pas de deux. As I stood in front of the stage curtains, one fellow held up the other so that it appeared that he was standing on his toes. I did a circus ring master type of introduction and when it came to mentioning the names of the dancers my mind went blank. So I prolonged my announcement but still I could not recall the names. I suddenly felt a punch in my back followed by a loud whisper of "get on with it." I then announced loudly that I had forgotten their names, the audience responded with laughter and a round of applause. Everybody thought that it was part of the act. One of the 'dancers' was a post graduate student, David Bellamy, who later became a professor of botany as well as a well-known television personality.

The term soon went by and, once again, I was helping to deliver the Christmas mail. Dan, my roommate, was also working in the post office but at a different branch. Both of us were getting up at five in the morning and starting work at six o'clock. On Christmas Eve I went to a party and at about ten o'clock, when it was noisy and swinging, I sat down in a comfortable chair with everybody dancing in front of me. The next thing I knew it was four in the morning and I was alone in an empty room. On Christmas Day Dan and I walked over to Camden Town to have a meal with his sister. Then the three of us called in at one of Dan's West Indian friends and we had another meal and more drink. After that we moved off to another house and so on. All I remember is waking up in a very large bed with Dan at one end and his sister between the two of us. After a breakfast Dan and I made our way home. We recovered just in time for the New Year celebrations, which saw out the Fifties and welcomed the new decade of the Sixties.

Kibbutz Kfar Hanasi

The neighbouring Arab village

Part 4

HITCH-HIKING

It was the beginning of the school summer holidays and I had just completed my first two terms as a teacher in a local comprehensive school. Now with some earned money I had an opportunity to travel. I decided to cross over to France and try my luck at hitch hiking. South Africa had just left the Commonwealth and all those who wanted to could apply to adopt British nationality within the next six months. There was not much paper work involved. I simply had to fill in a few forms and then obtain a signed affidavit. In Bloomsbury Square I passed by an office and on the outside brass plate under the name of a solicitor were the words Commissioner of Oaths. I went in with my forms, but the receptionist was not at her desk. I rang a bell and a very smart but slightly pompous looking man came out. I showed him my form and he signed it then asked for a fee of seven shillings and sixpence.

I had to surrender my South African passport to South Africa house then filled in a British passport application form and delivered it to the passport office at Petit France in Victoria. After my forms had been checked, I paid the appropriate fee and the elderly man behind the desk informed me that my passport would be ready in ten days time. It was now Tuesday and I had planned to start my journey by Thursday at the latest. I looked at him and said that I needed a passport urgently because I was going to the Student Games in Bulgaria. He looked at me and said, "Ooh you'll need a visa. Can you come back in an hour's time?" An hour and a half later I walked out of the building with a British passport valid for the next ten years.

On the Thursday morning I packed my rucksack. Most of my luggage consisted of my sleeping bag, a small tent, a meths burning cooker, and the minimum amount of clothes. As I walked up to the Finchley Road tube station, one of my sandal straps became detached from the bottom layer. I stopped and bought a box of pins and, using a sidewalk stone, bent two of them into a kind of staple, which fixed the strap onto the lower part of my sandal.

On the tube I met my former room mate Dan, who was engaged to Fern, an Italian girl who had just returned to Milan to visit her parents. He gave me her address. I caught a train to the outskirts of southwest London and, at about eleven o'clock, began to thumb a lift. I arrived at Dover via Canterbury in the late afternoon.

While buying a foot passenger ferry ticket I met up with Joe. Once onboard I bought a plate of sandwiches and beers for Joe and myself. Joe made no effort to buy anything and said very little for most of the crossing. When we arrived at Calais it was dark and Joe stayed close to me. We walked out of the town. About a hundred yards from a roadside café, all I could make out in the dark was a field. I decided that it was good place to spend the night and unrolled my sleeping bag. Joe simply lay down about a yard away. The passing night traffic seemed to be very close to our heads and the music from the local café lasted until almost dawn.

Daylight revealed that we had been sleeping on a narrow stretch of grass between the road and a canal. We started on an aimless walk away from Calais. During our conversation Joe revealed that he had never been abroad before. He claimed not to have any money and was hoping to find work. At the next crossroads I politely told him that I had only enough money to keep myself and we shook hands and went our separate ways.

About an hour later, still waiting for my first lift, two English lads came walking up the road. Neither had any luggage and they both had an air of nervous excitement about them. I told them that for the past hour every car that had passed was full of holidaymakers and that the chances of a lift were very slim.

They invited me to join them for a coffee. They were very well spoken and on their way to Paris. They maintained an air of nervous excitement and I got the impression that they were on the run. We decided to catch a train to Arras to get away and to give ourselves more of a chance of getting a lift. On the train, the ticket inspector demanded more money telling us that we had caught an express non-stopping train.

We walked to the main road and within a few minutes a car stopped and offered us a lift down south. They wanted only to go to Paris but I accepted. Alongside the driver sat his colleague who was introduced to me by the driver as his brother. After about an hour's drive they stopped to pick up a young Irish couple. The car was now full and we drove for hours along pleasant tree-lined roads as most of the major French motorways were still under construction. We had to stop to change a wheel. At about ten that night the spare tyre that had replaced the punctured one developed a slow leak. In addition, the engine did not sound too healthy. We decided to spend the night by the roadside.

The next morning a local farmer sent out a mechanic from the nearest village who arrived with a second hand replacement tyre. He could not mend the car engine at the roadside. We all sat in his truck, which towed the car to his garage. Two hours later we were on our way again.

Just before Lyon the Irish couple left us and we drove off toward the Alps. As we began to ascend the mountains we were stopped at a police roadblock. After examining the papers of the driver and his companion, they took my passport and we were instructed to follow their vehicle. They stopped in the next village. We were ordered out of the car and locked in a room at the back of a small café. About an hour later they came back and started a long heated conversation with the driver and his brother. I stood by not understanding a word of what was going on. Suddenly the senior policeman turned to me and told me to take my luggage out of the car gave me back my passport and told me to go. In a small French Alpine village there was nowhere for me to go so I stood by while the argument continued.

A local person who spoke some English pointed out to me that car I was travelling had Algerian number plates and the drivers were Algerian. At that time the war in Algeria was only just reaching a conclusion, however the haggle with the police turned out to be about an unpaid traffic fine that had been detected while we were locked up. The police asked me if I had any money to help them. I pretended not to understand and also pleaded poverty. Eventually they were allowed to leave on the understanding that they would report the next morning and pay their fine. I was allowed back in the car and we drove off in the direction of Annecy. We stopped for petrol and they asked me for some money and I gave them enough to pay half the price of the fuel.

We arrived at a campsite on the shores of Lake Annecy. There was quite a long discussion with the persons at the gate before were allowed in and my passport was taken from me. Once the sun set the temperature began to drop and I decided to pitch my tent.

The early morning was very cold but, as soon as the sun appeared from behind a mountain, it was as if an electric heater had suddenly been switched on. Within a half hour it was back to summer heat. Before we set out the driver and his friend thanked me for staying with them and gave me a pair of 'gold' earrings for the money I had given them. I never did find out if they were valuable.

I drove out of the campsite with them and once I had collected my passport we went our separate ways. They drove back toward the Alpine village and I took the road toward the Alps to cross over to Italy.

I walked along a road on the shores of the lake. The scenery was quite spectacular with huge mountains casting shadows across the water. My first lift took me to the beginning of the pass that crosses over the Alps into Italy. The morning became hotter and I decided that walking was going to get me nowhere. I stood at the roadside with my thumb permanently raised to attract the attention of passing motorists.

A convertible American Chevrolet, driven by a mature male with a companion, came by. They both looked at me laughed, the passenger gave me rude hand signal, and the driver hooted and accelerated up the pass.

A view of Annecy

About ten minutes later a 2CV Citroen chugged along and then stopped. The driver and his female companion looked at me and smiled and then said, "We go slowly but if you don't mind you're welcome to come with us." Without any hesitation I climbed into the back and placed my luggage on the seat beside me. The canvass roof was rolled back and my head was almost protruding out of the back of the car.

Off we went and, as the road became steeper and the bends sharper, our speed slowed right down. The air rapidly cooled down. We were now travelling at a little more than running pace and round each bend the air-cooled engine had to try harder. We were nearing the summit of the pass and, while engaging the final bend, we had to move into the middle of the road to avoid the convertible Chevrolet with its bonnet up and steam hissing out the radiator. The driver and his mate were standing helplessly alongside their vehicle. The three of us could not contain a chuckle and smile. As we drove on up the mountain I glanced back at the two miserable looking, once macho, blokes but resisted giving them a rude hand signal.

We soon reached the frontier post and crossed over into Italy. As the car coasted down, the air rapidly warmed. I left them in the middle of Turin and caught a bus to the nearest campsite.

The next morning I woke up to find that I had camped alongside a French family who were already up and preparing their breakfast. As I emerged from my tent each member of the family including the two young children came and greeted me and asked, in French, if I had slept well.

I made my way by bus to the tollgates at the start of the Autostrada to Milan. I had only been there about ten minutes when a medium sized lorry pulled up and the driver asked in Italian where I was going. I replied 'Milano' and he immediately gestured to me to get into the cab. Once through the tollgates the driver started to talk to me. Both my window and that of the driver were open so we had quite a lot of wind noise to contend with. My knowledge of Italian was almost non-existent yet, while driving, he mimed everything and somehow we managed a basic conversation. As we approached Milan he asked where in the city I was heading. I produced the address that Dan had scribbled out for me on the London tube the day I started my trip. He looked at the paper in silence and gave it back to me.

We left the autostrada and were now driving through the suburbs of Milan. While driving along a smart avenue he drew my attention to the street name, which was *Via California*. He was looking for the building numbers and I looked again at the address Dan had given to me, 52 *Via California*. He dropped me right outside the house and called over to the porter at the entrance to the building telling him that he had a delivery for him. He then insisted that I take a photo of him alongside his truck, shook hands with me, refused a tip and drove off.

I walked over to the entrance to the building (a seven storey block of flats) and was greeted by the porter. As soon as I mentioned Fern's family name Gorni, he walked into the courtyard looked up and yelled Gorni. Fern and her mother looked down at us from their fifth storey balcony. Once inside their flat Fern introduced me to her father and mother and a meal was then prepared for me. Then came the welcome offer staying a few days with them.

The next morning I was shown round the centre of Milan. In the middle of the famous arcade the floor is covered with a large mosaic. The central feature of the mosaic is a black bull. The Milanese considers it lucky if, while walking along, you tread on the bulls testicles. I went over to place my foot on the appropriate part of the bull's anatomy. As I looked up I saw numerous pairs of eyes staring at me. Apparently, the treading on the bulls testicles must be accidental not deliberate.

Milan

Later that afternoon, Fern took me to a convent to see the mural of The Last Supper. It was in the process of being restored. The original paint had faded and there were small areas where the plaster seemed to have no paint on it at all. However the masterpiece was still breathtaking.

That evening Fern's sister and brother-in-law came over to visit. During the course of the evening we all became involved in a political discussion. Fern, who took a different point of view to mine had the task of translating for both sides as well as her own arguments into Italian. Fern's father, who worked in publishing and was once an active trade union member, was keen to join in but found the process of waiting for the translation tiresome and gave up and departed to his nightly card game.

After about two days I felt rested, my clothes were now clean again and I had seen most of Milan. It was time to move on. Fern's father gave me four rolls of colour film and, after a large breakfast, I caught a bus to the beginning of the autostrada.

I stood as close to the toll booths as I was permitted. Two of the officials came out to greet me and, once again, I became involved in a broken English and mime conversation. I told them that I was heading for Trieste. A car with German number plates approached and, as the driver was fiddling around for money to pay the tolls, one of the officials called me over and then asked the driver to give me a lift. He looked at his wife and then his two little girls on the back seat who all gave shrug of indifference. After more pleading the driver nodded to me and before anyone could change his or her minds I was sitting on the back seat with my rucksack on my lap.

I have a working knowledge of Afrikaans and Yiddish - two Germanic languages - and after about ten minutes I began a conversation with the two little girls. Both parents then asked where I had learned to speak German to which I replied at school. For the first time I was in the presence of Germans and my German was actually better than their English. As we drove along I felt their attitude toward me soften and they offered me a drink and a sandwich. They were on their way to Verona and dropped me and then left the autostrada. My next lift dropped me on the actual motorway. The cars approached me at high speed and all I could do once a vehicle came into sight was to wave furiously hoping that they would stop. A fellow in a Fiat sports car pulled up abruptly and encouraged me to get in the car as quickly as possible. We had only driven about a half a kilometre when a police motorcycle came rushing by. The driver then explained that they were actually looking for me. A motorist had reported that there was a pedestrian on the autostrada and the police had come to collect me. He (the driver) had overheard the conversation at the toll booth and was anxious to get me off the road.

My next stop was Venice. I walked toward the Grand Canal where all the passenger boats were moored. A porter came up to me and said, "Camping?" to which I replied, "Si," and he then pointed to a boat and said, "Lido." He even went with me to buy a ticket. I had arrived in Venice during the latter part of August at the height of the tourist season and at the hottest time of the year. People everywhere, but somehow the lack of roads and traffic gave the impression of a place in a superior carnival atmosphere. The boat sailed down the Grand Canal. I felt overwhelmed by the sights that I was very familiar with via paintings, photos and films and, now, I could see that scenes so familiar actually did exist. The pace of travel was such that I seemed to have plenty of time to absorb it all. Eventually the boat reached the Lido, an island in the Venice lagoon. I disembarked, caught a trolley bus to a campsite and pitched my tent. This was followed by a swim in the sea.

Before dark I caught the boat to San Marco Square. I walked around admiring the sites and looked for somewhere cheap to eat. I looked enviously at those who could afford to have a ride on a gondola. While standing on the banks of the Grand Canal, I noticed that the local Venetians were all getting on a plain looking gondola, and when it was near full, the gondolier then took off and deposited his passengers on the opposite bank. Another similar gondola was arriving and, as the passengers disembarked they dropped a few coins into a tray. It was a local ferry service. It then occurred to me that now was an opportunity for me to experience a ride in a gondola. I crossed over and walked about on the opposite shore for about ten minutes and then returned feeling that I had had a ride, albeit a brief one, on a genuine gondola.

I returned to the Lido on the last boat and bus. The next morning I met up with a young American named, Alan, who invited me to have coffee with him and his German wife Sonja. We all went for a swim and before I left I was invited to join them that evening for a glass of wine. After walking what seemed to be the length and breadth of Venice and taking in as many sites as I could, I returned to the campsite.

Alan and I opened a large bottle of Italian red wine and between the two of us, with a little help from Sonja, we finished the bottle and then cracked open another. While drinking, all we consumed were packets of salted dried biscuits. It was a marvellously hot evening, which went by very quickly. Shortly after midnight I got up to leave. As I walked toward my tent all of the guy ropes of every other tent seemed to get in my way. I frequently had to pick myself up off the ground. Eventually I found my small pub tent. I took one look at it and wondered how on earth I was going get inside. Then, suddenly, my stomach heaved and I managed to reach some bushes on the edge of the campsite and was violently sick. Luckily there was no one about to see me with my head in the branches and backside facing skywards. After minutes of heaving with nothing more to throw up I crawled back to my tent. This time I did manage to get inside and as soon as I lay down on my back the roof of the tent start to spin round and round and I waited for it to take off.

When I woke up the sun was already quite high in the sky, the tent was baking hot and I felt as if I had an axe lodged into the back of my head. My whole body shuddered as I tried to get up. Once out of my tent it took a few minutes before I could stand upright without falling over. My feelings were that I was going to die and that this was the end of my voyage. I had planned to leave for Trieste but I did not think that I would survive the day nor did I care. Eventually I made it to the showers. Despute cleaning myself up I felt no better. For some reason I remembered that someone had once told me that you should drink milk to counteract any poison. With that in mind I walked over to the café and bought a small carton of milk. I foolishly drank it all down in one go and then had to run as fast as possible to the toilet block to be sick at both ends.

I went back to the café and told a woman that I was *male,* which I believed to be Italian for ill. Whether or not she understood my predicament she sold me a small bottle of very bitter tasting medicine, which made me shudder from head to toe once it was down my throat. I returned to my tent.

There was no shade near to my tent so I put on my swimming trunks and walked down to the beach. The sea in the Venice lagoon is very calm and there are only minute waves. I lay down and wedged myself between two smooth boulders making certain that my head was well above the water line. I spent the rest of the day in that position occasionally splashing my face.

Toward the middle of the afternoon I noticed a family (mother, father and daughter) picnicking about fifty yards away. They kept giving me very concerned looks. I was by now very suntanned and as dark as any native Italian. My hair at that time, 1960, was quite long, but my hair is not heavy and as it grew it tended to protrude outwards and stand up rather than hang down. In addition I had a full beard that had not been trimmed for many weeks.

During the late afternoon, the mother, who was quite dowdy looking, approached me and said clearly and slowly, "Are you alright?" She repeated the question several times and even began to mime it. I replied, "I think so but I am feeling rather fragile after too much wine." "Oh you can speak English," was her reply. I then told her that I can't speak much else and that I was from England. She then said, "You don't look very well, would you like a cup of tea?" They then invited me over to their tent.

I was made the largest mug of tea I had ever seen and had ever had and it tasted marvellous. Gradually I felt my body returning to me. I began to realise that I was going to live after all.

Venice

I decided that I would spend that night in Venice. On my way out of the camp I passed by Alan. He had spent the day feeling sorry for himself but, worse still, had fallen asleep in the sun. He was very fair skinned and his body was now bright pink and stinging. In Venice I passed by a bar and the smell of red wine made me shudder all over and feel like throwing up again. (In fact, that reaction to red wine remained in my system for the next two years).

The next morning, although I still felt fragile, I decided to move on. Once back in Venice proper, I caught a bus to the beginning of the road to Trieste. It was a slow day in terms of lifts. I was standing beside a canal and a small rowing boat came by. There was an old man sitting looking forwards and in the back a young lad of about fourteen was standing and propelling the boat with a single oar protruding from the rear of the boat. They were hardly moving faster than walking pace and there a few yards away, on the road, were motorised vehicles travelling at forty plus miles per hour. All the lifts were short runs and it took me all day to reach my destination. I booked into the local youth hostel. While I was eating in the canteen two English girls came over to me and said, "So you made it. We never thought that you would." They then explained that they passed me standing by the roadside just a few miles out of Venice. They had just been picked up and their driver took one look at me and said no one is ever going to risk picking him up! I just looked blank and thought that I had better find a mirror before I set out again.

Trieste is only a short distance from the then Yugoslav frontier (the original Yugoslavia Federation before the country split up into several independent states) and had been disputed territory just after the Second World War. There were still signs, now faded, on walls and buildings declaring that Trieste is Italian. Yugoslavia was then ruled by Tito and was still very much a Communist state although not a Soviet satellite.

That night in the youth hostel I met Ahmed, an Algerian student studying in Zagreb. I was able to converse with him using my very limited knowledge of French. He, too, was hitch hiking and was on his way back for the start of the new term. He gave me his address in Zagreb and told me to look him up if I should get there.

After breakfast I caught the bus to the frontier. I already had a visa and hence without much trouble I walked through into Yugoslavia. I was surprised to see that almost everybody on the bus walked through the border post and that there were as many people crossing back into Italy. The impression that I had brought with me was that crossing over into any Communist country could only be achieved with difficulty.

Without trying too hard I got lift with a local driver who took me to the outskirts of a local village. I was taking a shortcut across a field to get to the centre of the village. Just as I reached the road, two young English lads each with a rucksack on their backs appeared from nowhere. After our initial greeting they seemed to be very down. I told them that I was going to find somewhere to eat and asked would they like to join me. We found a local café, which after conversing with the waitress in German, was to me very cheap. They were hesitant ordering as they said that they did not have much money left. I offered to pay for them and they accepted without any hesitation. Once the food arrived they ate quickly. It was obvious that they had missed out on a few meals. After they had eaten while drinking coffee they told me what had happened to them.

They had been hitch-hiking through Italy, and had left Rome and were making their way down South. They were passing through a small town and stopped at roadside café for a drink. Two smooth looking men who could speak some English sat at the next table. Before long they chatted to the two lads and after ten minutes produced a gold watch and told them that it cost them an arm and a leg and even had receipt to prove it. They offered to sell to the lads an identical one at a very much-reduced price. After a lot of sales talk one of the lads went to the bank and changed most of his sterling into lira. One of the men left them saying that he was going to his home to collect the watch for them. While they were waiting for him return his friend took his watch from his wrist and offered it to the lads at a reduced price telling them they would be then able to sell it back, for a greater profit to his friend. They handed over the money he gave them the watch and that was the last they saw of either of them. After waiting at the café for about half an hour they went over to the local jewellery shop who informed them that they had been tricked. They had been cheated out of nearly all of their money. They were at the beginning of their holiday and now only had enough to last them for a few more days. They reported the incident to the local police who suggested that they go to the nearest British Consul, which was in Naples.

They managed to get to Naples and went straight to the British Consul. After telling their tale of woe to a consular official, saying they were now broke, he replied, "Oh not another couple of suckers." He took their passports from them and wrote "Valid only for return to England". They were each given a train ticket back to London and then escorted to the station and put on a train. On the train, they felt sick about first being robbed and then the unsympathetic treatment. When they reached Rome they got off the train and decided to make for Yugoslavia where they reckoned that what money they had left would last them about a week. They hitch-hiked to Trieste but, with their passports no longer valid, they thought it would be best to walk over the frontier during the dark.

They walked during daylight to be as close as possible to where they guessed the frontier to be. After midnight they started their walk and stumbled into a thin wire, which they crawled under. A few minutes later armed guards surrounded them. They raised their hands above their heads and stood still. They were marched at gunpoint to a hut. An officer asked them for their passports. They watched him and when he turned past the page that said that their passports were no longer valid they guessed that he could not read English. They had intended to visit Yugoslavia and each had a valid visa, obtained in London, stuck into their passports. Once he saw the valid visa he gave them their passports back and offered them each cup of coffee. They remained in the hut until daylight and then were allowed to go and when I met them they had been walking for about an hour. After I paid the bill I gave them some left over Italian money and we then went our separate ways.

Back on the road my next lift was with a young French woman. My apparent wild appearance did not prevent the young lady from stopping to give me lift. We first went to Ljubljana where we stopped for a while and then on to Zagreb where we arrived just before nightfall. I was dropped on the outskirts of the city, found a policeman and showed him the address that Ahmed had given me. I was placed on a bus to the town centre. He also instructed the bus driver to tell me how to get to my destination from the town centre.

I knocked at the front door of Ahmed's address. All I could say to the woman who opened the door was Ahmed. She looked very surprised, replied in Serbo-Croat and gestured to me to go inside, sat me down in her living room and then disappeared out of the house. She returned a few minutes later with a neighbour who could speak fluent English. She explained to me that Ahmed was not yet back and they were expecting him anytime. After telling them that I was looking for accommodation they showed me to Ahmed's room, which had two single beds in it, and said I could stay there if I wanted. I was also offered a meal. The neighbour, who it turned out taught English in the local school, remained with us most of the evening, glad of the opportunity to practise her English.

The next morning I woke up to find Ahmed asleep in the other bed. He had arrived in the early hours of the morning. Ahmed spoke very little English so the conversations were at first limited to what I could understand of his French. However, somehow or other, we got on quite well. After breakfast the landlady informed me that I could stay as long as I liked for what I regarded as a very cheap rate.

Later that morning we walked over to the University. The term had not yet started and most of the students congregated in the large students centre. There were quite a large number of foreign students, most of them from what was then described as the neutral 'third world countries.'

After morning coffee we wandered around the town. We sat around a fountain and joined an informal gathering of local youths. They were mostly smart and trendy and some had motor scooters or even small cars. Not what I had expected to see. I had not thought that I would see people of my age group with all the trappings of capitalism in a socialist country. Ahmed then explained to me that they were mostly actors and pop musicians.

It was a very hot day and we decided to spend the rest of the afternoon at an open-air swimming pool. During the course of the afternoon we chatted up two girls who were both wearing the briefest of bikinis. I was attracted to one of them whose name was Lujbista (Violet). We met them again the following day at the pool and we all wandered over to the students' union that evening. Ahmed mentioned to me that he knew that our landlady was going out that evening and would probably not return until late. We persuaded both girls to go back with us. Once we were certain that we had the place to ourselves we took them up to our room. About ten that evening we crept out of the house. Just as we reached the road we came across the landlady returning home. We walked on in silence. The following morning she had plenty to say, but, as I could not understand, poor Ahmed had to take most of the flack while I just nodded in sympathy.

By now Ahmed and I could understand each other well enough to be able to conduct quite a serious conversation. I remarked to him how Tito's presence was everywhere in the form of photos, posters and his name in places in neon lights. I asked if he was really liked that much. Ahmed replied that he was very popular and it was he who was unifying the country. I had not realised that Yugoslavia really was a federation of different states, a truly composite country. Memories of the Second World War were still quite vivid. Who sided with the Nazis and who had fought with Tito's partisans against the occupying German army still caused bitter rifts. Ahmed mentioned that in his view, without Tito, the country would fragment into separate nation states. What a true prophecy that turned out to be.

Another morning wandering around and then we met the girls again in the afternoon at the student centre. To me it seemed as if all eyes were staring at us. I felt as if it was me and my closeness to Lujbista that was the cause of the imagined gossip. That night Ahmed told me that he had overheard the girls saying that Lujbista's parents were coming to Zagreb the next day. He then explained that they were country folk and that if they were introduced to me the inference would be that I wanted to marry her. I then had two choices either to marry her or leave town as soon as possible. Early the next morning I was standing on the road thumbing a lift to Belgrade.

About mid-morning two men driving a Russian Moskvich picked me up. The man in the front passenger seat (Jan) spoke to me in mixture of broken German and English. He managed to get over to me that they were on their way to Belgrade but had to first go to Osijek a town on the River Drava close to both the Hungarian and Romanian borders. This meant that they would not reach Belgrade until the next day. I had no timetable to follow and agreed to go with them. After an hour's drive we turned left off the main road and proceeded along a rough dirt road. The rate of travel slowed right down and I was reminded of the roads on the South African Highveld. Every time we passed a group of farm workers they opened the windows and began to throw out leaflets in Serbo-Croat. What type of people had I now landed with? My mind flashed back to the penniless fellow on the ferry, the chaps on the run and my brief arrest in France.

A few miles further on they stopped in a small, drab village and took me to visit the local church. It was built during the time when the area was part of the Austrian Hapsburg Empire. The interior of the church was decorated with huge paintings. It was like an oasis of art and culture in the midst of a flat agricultural landscape.

Back on the road and few miles further on, we came across two local girls thumbing a lift. Jan told the driver to stop and then made me sit in the middle of the back seat and invited the girls to sit on either side of me. A very animated conversation ensued and all I could do was sit and enjoy the fact that I could not but also did not want to, join in. Every now and again Jan would turn and wink at me as if to say don't worry we are looking after you. We dropped the girls on the outskirts of Osijek. They departed laughing. In the town we drove to one of the hotels. Jan and the driver took me up to their room where I had the chance to shower and change. They told me that later on they would take the car to a local campsite and I could then sleep in the car. After we were all refreshed and changed they treated me to a meal in the hotel.

During the early part of the evening we went for a walk down the main street. As we left the hotel we walked into a mass of evening strollers. There was no traffic. On the pavements and roads were people of all ages. They just seemed to be parading up down greeting everyone in sight. Groups of boys shouting over to the girls and vice versa, it was no doubt the evening watering hole for the town. No sooner had they reached a certain point they would turn and go back the way they had just come. There was almost a carnival atmosphere. Jan told me that it happened regularly but only on certain nights, the weekend attracting the biggest crowds. He pointed out to me that they all arrive and depart at approximately the same time. We sat at a prominent café and watched it all go by. At ten o'clock it was as if a bell had been rung. Within about ten minutes the streets were clear and silent.

The three of us then strolled across the town and, for a small entrance fee, found ourselves in a large open-air nightclub that overlooked the river. Most of the tables and chairs were on a lawn that sloped toward a small stage and dance floor backing onto the riverbank. We sat down, ordered some beer and listened to live music performed by a local dance/jazz band.

The small dance floor soon filled up. It was the era when you still danced with a specific partner. Like dance halls anywhere, there were those who could dance, those who tried to and, of course, the posers. We had hardly finished our beer when the two girl hitch-hikers we had given a lift to that afternoon showed up and sat with us. About ten minutes later without much persuasion, I was on the dance floor showing the girls my version of jive and rock and roll steps, which I had acquired, attending numerous Friday night student hops. We all sat down to watch a cabaret act. An Indian performer stood before a lamp, projecting a light beam on to a screen. He held his hands in front of the light and with fingers and the palm of his hands was able to create figures in silhouette on the screen. Some of the images were animals and others were celebrities of the day.

After the act, the music and dancing began again. As we were walking back to our table, during a pause in the music, we found two young lads there. Angry verbal exchanges followed between Jan and the driver with the two lads. The girls joined in and, at one point, I thought it was going to end up in a fight. The girls then stood up and walked away followed by the two lads. It was then explained to me that they were the girls' regular boyfriends and neither had told the other party that they were going out that night.

Jan, the driver and myself left soon afterwards. They went to their hotel room and I to the campsite to spend the night in the car. After a relatively uncomfortable night, they came to collect me and we set off to Belgrade. The episode with the girls was soon mentioned. They explained to me that girls were very annoyed and were going to end the relationship with their boyfriends. I could not help think about why I had made a hasty departure from Zagreb. As we approached Belgrade Jan asked me where I intended to stay. I told him that I would try and find a hostel or a campsite of some sort as I had a tent with me. We arrived in Belgrade during the late afternoon and drove straight to a very large government building. Jan disappeared into the building and I got out of the car to stretch my legs. I walked over to the main entrance and, from what I could make out, the place was the equivalent of the ministry of agriculture.

The driver then delivered Jan and myself to Jan's flat fairly close to the centre of the city. His wife, Sonja, and his sister-in-law greeted us in a very traditional manner. Sonja held a tray, which contained a small dish of jam, a loaf of bread and jug of hot water. Standing behind Sonja was his sister-in-law. Jan swallowed a very small spoonful of the jam, followed by a bite of the bread and drink of the hot water. Sonja then came over to me and offered me the contents of the tray. My first instinct was to politely refuse but

Jan said that I must accept. I took a larger spoonful of the jam, which was very thick sweet and syrupy followed by a bite of the bread and then the hot water.

It was a one-room flat plus a small kitchen, a bathroom and an entrance hall. In the main room was a large settee and a table. Within a half hour of our arrival a meal was served up. Where I was going to stay that night was then discussed. Jan phoned the hostel for me and after a heated conversation banged down the phone, turned to me and said you can stay in my 'park'. The flat was on the ground floor and he had a tiny garden, which he called his park.

About 10pm there was a sudden very heavy thunderstorm which put an end to my camping. However nothing seemed to worry them about where I was going to end up that night. At about eleven the dining room table was moved and folded away, then the large settee was moved to the side wall, the cushions removed and Jan pulled at a lever and there, before us, was a massive bed. While they were making the bed there was a knock at door and in walked Jan's father-in-law wearing a thick sheepskin coat and looking like someone more at home in the country than in a city. Once the bed was laid out the sleeping arrangements were explained to me. At the far end was his wife's sister, then his wife, then Jan, the father-in-law and finally me. It took quite bit of pleading before they let me sleep in my sleeping bag on the floor. Somehow or other we all got changed without causing any embarrassment. I fell asleep rather quickly only to be woken up by the father-in-law's loud snoring. Next thing it was about six am, the father-in-law had already left and Jan and his wife were having breakfast. Only the sister and myself were still in our respective beds. Just before Jan and his wife left for work he came over to me and gestured that when he left I should jump into bed with the sister-in-law whose name was Alexandra.

I felt that I was guest in their house taken in on trust and, besides, if I did go over to her and she objected or made a fuss, what would I do then? Ten minutes later I had showered and got dressed. Alexandra was up in the kitchen, wearing only a flimsy nightie, preparing breakfast for us. I looked for any come-on signs but only saw what I interpreted as none. Conversation was limited to gestures and continuous referral to a dictionary and phrase book. After we finished breakfast Jan phoned, I guessed to find out what state our relationship had reached and she giggled very shyly.

Later on we went downtown, first to the Bulgarian embassy to get a visa (which as it turned out I never needed) and then we met up with a group of her friends. While we were all drinking coffee they must have been teasing me because suddenly Alexandra, who was sitting next to me, took my arm and smiled sympathetically. That afternoon I wandered off on my own down to the banks of the Danube. I was very surprised to see how fast the river flowed and the banks were mainly sandy. Back at Jan's flat that evening his father-in-law did not turn up, so I was persuaded to give up sleeping on the floor.

In Belgrade at that time the first meeting of the heads of state of third world or non-aligned states was being held. The centre of the city had been spruced up for the occasion. All the streets were bedecked with flags and slogans in English, French and Serbo-Croat. In attendance at the meeting was Pandiht Nehru, the prime minister of India, President Sukharno of Indonesia and Kwasi Nkrumah of Ghana. Every now and again a cavalcade of cars preceded by sirens sounding and a posse of police motor cycle outriders would appear conveying one or other of the leaders across the city. As the day wore on it became such a common sight that no one in the street took much notice.

The next day Alexandra had to go home. I had by now learnt that she was a teacher and the new school term was about to begin. She did invite to me her parent's home but my excuse was that I had to move on. I stayed for another two nights and then managed to convince Jan that it was time for me to depart. Early next morning I caught a bus to the southern outskirts of Belgrade.

My first lift was with a man in a large smart black car. Without asking, he took me down a bumpy side road to visit a factory that made parts for power stations. I was told that the location, in a wooded valley, was mainly for camouflage purposes. My first thoughts were why, then, was he showing me the place? He must have been some high up official as we were waved through the security gate and greeted by everyone very respectfully. He ordered me a coffee and then disappeared into an office. Twenty minutes later we returned to the main road.

We were delayed in the next town. A farmer was walking in front of an ox cart. He was holding a leather rope tied to the yolk that kept the animals apart and attached to the boom of the cart. Suddenly both oxen stopped and lowered their heads with their noses touching the ground. They froze in that position, became rigid and refused to move. The man pulled shouted and whipped but nothing he could do could coax any movement out of the animals. As they lodged their protest right in the middle of road the traffic in both directions was held up. Before long the bystanders all joined in with a cacophony of yells, hooters and other noises but nothing moved the oxen. The exhausted owner of the cart stood erect and loosened his grip and tried to calm all of his now unwelcome helpers and also paused to wipe his brow. Then suddenly the oxen lifted their heads, lunged forward for a few steps and then proceeded to walk on in a leisurely stroll. The onlookers cheered and jeered and all the traffic started to move again.

I was dropped a short way out of town as he turned to leave the main road presumably to visit another 'secret' site. He told me that he could not take me with him this time. Another official car, this time driven by a woman in her fifties, pulled up to offer me a lift. We had travelled for about twenty minutes when she, too, turned off the main road. We drove along a dirt road for about a mile and then came across an open stretch of ground. There were workmen levelling the ground presumably to be turned into a large public garden. An old fifty yard three stranded barbed wire fence occupied the centre of a level piece of ground about half the size of a football pitch. A few elderly workmen were busy raking over the soil. My host, the lady driver, came up to me and pointing to the far end of the field said, "The Nazis lined them up over there, the machine guns were on this side and they were made to run up against the wire where they were trapped and shot."

I asked, "Were they captured partisans?" She replied, "Mostly Jews".

I had my camera in my hand and managed to take a photo when one of the workmen came over to us shaking his head and waving his hand shouting, "No photo!" She then told me to quickly put my camera away and said they were still very sensitive about this place. We returned to the car and she dropped me about twenty miles further on.

The main tar road to the south came to an abrupt end. The road was now of a type that would have been more in place in Africa rather than Southeast Europe. I soon got covered over in red dust as numerous lorries and the odd car came by.

About lunchtime, an English Norton motorcycle with a large box replacing the normal passenger type of sidecar came by. The machine stopped about a hundred yards further on and the rider casually started to study a road map. He seemed to be in no hurry as I walked over to him. After the initial greeting, I could tell by his accent that he came from the North of England. He asked me where I was heading and I simply replied "Wherever!"

"Well if you don't mind a rough, bumpy ride on the back pillion seat you're welcome to come with me. I am on my way to Turkey and beyond." I did not need a second invitation and after strapping my rucksack on to the box, off we drove. He introduced himself to me. He was Colin, a toolmaker from Burrow-in-Furness who worked in the ship building trade. It was the beginning of both a friendship and a partnership that took me all the way to Istanbul and the Black Sea.

The road was bad enough for a four-wheeled vehicle but for a motor-cycle (albeit one with three wheels) it was really rough. We could hardly travel faster than thirty miles per hour and we still had a very long way to go. A new highway was being built alongside the one we were travelling on.

Yugoslavia by European standards was a poor country and the labour used to construct the road was mainly students and young volunteers from all over. There seemed to be a scarcity of road construction machinery.

The road we were on was very neglected and we bounced from one rut to the next pothole. As evening approached we drove into a village and bought some freshly baked bread, filled our water bottles and had a meal in a café with half the village staring at our machine and us. While we sat at an outside table we watched a wrestling match between two equally matched youths in the street. They rolled about in the dust with all the village men looking on and no one made any effort to stop them. It lasted about ten minutes by which time they were both thoroughly exhausted and, only then, were they dragged apart by two women. We drove out of the village and found an open spot to pitch Colin's tent. He had a bell tent, which could easily accommodate up to four persons. We cooked a meal from freeze dried packets and enjoyed our freshly baked bread. Before we fell asleep Colin told me that his wife was originally with him and that they had been hoping to travel to India over land. However she had taken ill in Vienna and returned to England. She had persuaded Colin to go it alone as they had spent a year preparing for the trip.

I woke up during the early hours of the morning to the sound of footsteps prowling round the outside of our tent. Colin seemed to be fast asleep. I thought that it would be best not to venture out into the dark but wait. However I fell asleep again and woke up just as the sun began to rise. I went out of the tent and checked everything. Nothing had been disturbed, everything was intact and, apart from a few footprints, there was nothing to indicate that someone had been there. Colin, like me, had also been woken by the same noises and had followed the same pattern of behaviour as I had.

While we were preparing breakfast we noticed sitting, at about twenty yards away, a small shabbily dressed elderly man. He had a stick resting against his shoulder and, by his side, an untidy dog. We heard the sound of bells and there in the distance was a flock of sheep. We surmised he was a local shepherd who must have had to spend day and night with his flock. We presumed he must have been the night prowler. He just sat and watched all our movements. We offered him some coffee. He shook his head in a manner that suggested no. While we were drinking our coffee he kept up his staring and then it dawned on us that in Eastern Europe head signs are reversed. What we take as no actually means yes. I walked over to him with a mug of hot coffee and for the first time his face broke into a smile. He watched us pack up, shook hands with us and waved goodbye as we set off.

Luckily for me, while I was in Belgrade, I had managed to visit a barbershop. Hence, my hair was relatively short but my beard had not been trimmed. Riding along we both soon became covered in red dust. The temperature rose very rapidly and after about a half-hour we were both shirtless but wore dust goggles and I covered my shoulders with an Arab type headscarf, which I had bought during a visit to Israel. Colin had spent his time during national service in Aden and he too had a similar type of headdress only the top was covered by his crash helmet. Progress was slow and as we passed through numerous villages we attracted quite a bit of attention. At midday we arrived in a small town in southern Serbia. The main road went right through the town centre and town square. There was no traffic and crowds of people, lining the outer perimeter of the square, blocked our way.

We parked the bike and walked over to see what was happening. In the centre of the square there were crowds of men and women, young and old, dressed in folk costumes dancing in circles to sounds of a local folk band. The band was made up of a variety of percussion instruments, small and large home made drums, tambourines, primitive clarinets, trumpets violins and mandolins. To me, the music sounded very reminiscent of what I knew to be Gypsy music.

They sang as they danced and the atmosphere was carnival-like. Many of the men carried homemade skin flasks providing schnapps for all who wanted to partake. A woman produced two small glasses and poured out one tot for Colin and one for me. We were encouraged to down it in one, which we did. Our throats burnt, eyes watered while they all cheered. What we had just drunk was home brewed Slibovic, a plum brandy. Once we recovered our senses we were invited to join in the dances and to have some food. An hour later we were on our way again only to drive into another celebrating village and once more we were indulged with food and drink. In the third village not only was there dancing, but we also noticed a bride and bridegroom. A wedding celebration had been tagged onto the folk festival.

The Slibovic had its affect. The road suddenly became less bumpy and we were able to drive much faster. At about six o'clock we stopped, bought our supply of bread and milk and whatever else we needed, drove along and found a spot to spend the night. Once we had pitched the tent and eaten, we sat around for about an hour before the total darkness of the night sent us to an early sleep. Again, footsteps in the night, but this time they were accompanied by the sound of sheep bells. Back to sleep and the next thing I knew the sun was rising. We both emerged out of the tent about the same time and walked around to the back of the tent. There, sitting wrapped against the night cold with a stick propped against his shoulder and with his dog with its head on his lap, was a shepherd. He looked so similar to the one we saw the morning before that it felt as if we had not travelled at all. Once the kettle had boiled I walked over to him with a hot mug of coffee which he accepted with the same confusing head shrug.

Studying the map before we set off, we realised that we were now deep into Macedonia and that we should arrive at the Greek border in the early afternoon. During the morning we stopped beside a river. A large steel-constructed bridge spanned the river. A path from the road led down to it. We pushed the bike under the shade of an arch. Colin had decided that his bike needed some attention. While he was working on the engine I took a stroll down the river and came across some women standing ankle deep in the water. Beside them in the water were bundles of what at first looked to me like reeds. They lifted a single bundle above their heads and then thrashed it down into the water and kept repeating this action. Every now and again they would put the bundle back into the water and then continued the thrashing using a different bundle. I managed via sign language to find out that the plants were being prepared so that the stems could eventually be woven into a fabric. The bundles were wreaths of flax plants harvested from a nearby field.

While we were beside the water, we took the opportunity to mend a puncture. Earlier that day one of the wheels was punctured and we were now riding on the spare wheel. Not far from the road bridge was a rail bridge. A crowded train came by with passengers standing on the footplates. One of the passengers was holding on to the door handle with one hand and in the other he held a great big fish which, no doubt, he had caught that day somewhere in the river. By the time we were ready to move, it was late afternoon so we decided that we would spend the night nearby and then make for Greece the next day.

We reached the Greek border about mid-morning. Once in Greece, we were back on tarred roads and it felt like riding on cushions. We stopped at a small village for lunch. Neither of us could read the menu. The chefs invited us both into the kitchen and showed us all the dishes he had prepared and then let us make a choice. In the café a musician was playing a clarinet-type reed instrument. At the end of each tune someone would bring him a glass of Ouzo which he downed in one. Occasionally he would dip his reed into the Ouzo.

Sitting at our table was a young American couple who looked like a pair of hippies. They were Greek Americans and could converse with the locals. During our conversation it turned out that they were collectors of folk music and dances. They told us that they had found that in most of the villages they had visited they knew more about the local folk dances than the villagers. When we described the folk festivals that we had come across in lower Serbia they were quite envious. American citizens at the time had problems getting visas to tour Yugoslavia, then officially a non-aligned Communist state.

Early that afternoon, we drove through the northern Greek city of Thessaloniki and made our way to the northern Greek coast road. We drove along the coast toward Kevalla. Once through the town, on one side of the road was an endless sandy beach and on the other mostly tobacco fields. The last building on the outskirts of the town was a small café with its back to the road and its front opening onto the beach. We stopped for a meal and once more the chef took us on a tour of the kitchen to help choose our meal.

A few hundred yards further along was an old derelict building on the edge of a field. We decided to pitch our tent just beyond the building on a piece of land that appeared to have never been cultivated. From our camp, looking westwards we could see the back of the old building and the town in the distance. In the other direction we could see the road disappearing through a small group of rocky cliffs.

The next morning we were awakened to the usual sound of sheep bells plus the ever-present shepherd. We worked out that it was Sunday. During the morning we noticed women in black walking along the road toward the cliffs. Most were carrying flowers. Our curiosity was satisfied after a stroll down the road took us to a cemetery about a half mile further along.

Colin decided to take the bike engine apart. I was sunning myself beside the tent. From where I sat I could see the back of the building. Every now and again one of the women on her way to the cemetery would suddenly dart behind the building where presumably she could not be seen from the road. She lifted her dress, to squat down, and then relieved herself before rejoining her companions on their walk. Whether they saw me or not I was never to know. After the first two I moved to the other side of the tent. Colin, in the meantime, carried on working on the bike and never once looked up.

Early the next morning we walked over to the cliffs and swam among the rocks. I ended up with the end of a sea urchin spine in my knee. Trying to extract the point was quite painful. I found out later on that although I managed to get most of it out a tiny fragment remained beneath my skin which never emerged until I was back in England. Back at the tent Colin told me that one of the engine valves needed replacing and the other regrinding. He caught a bus into the town while I stayed behind to mind the campsite. A couple of hitch-hikers came by and joined me for coffee. They were returning from Turkey. They told me that before leaving Greece we should try and get hold of as much Turkish money as possible because the official rate of exchange in Turkey was ridiculously low. I was told that near to the border roadside moneychangers would approach us. Deal with them, but with caution. Count all the money out on the road to avoid sleight of-hand tricks. The other point to bear in mind was that it was not legal to take Turkish currency into Turkey.

Colin returned that afternoon with a new valve and a reground one. I helped him to re-install them. It took a lot of coaxing and pushing before the engine burst into life again. After that we persuaded a couple of local students we had met in the café to join us for a late swim by the cliffs. When we arrived there we found a group of men sitting on the rocks. Every now and again one of them would dive into the sea. Colin and I wasted no time in diving into the sea. The students however were very reluctant to follow us in. They did not speak to any of the other men. They called us both to follow them to the top of the cliff. Once at the top we saw why they were reluctant to swim there. We stood overlooking the town's garbage dump, which almost reached down to the sea. The men on the rocks were the local dustbin men. We returned to the town beach where there was a fresh water shower and scrubbed ourselves down.

That evening, sitting on the beach, we watched the local fishermen operating from large rowing boats. There were two persons per boat. At the back end of the boat a lantern hung over the water. One person did the rowing while the other kept banging the water with an oar. Presumably, the light attracted the fish and the banging was to drive them into a net.

The next morning we set off toward Alexandropoulus, a town on the Greece-Turkey border. Once through town, two men speaking broken English stopped us. It soon became obvious that they were the moneychangers. We disposed of most of our Greek money and then hid some of the Turkish money in the side-car and the rest on ourselves. We passed through Greek customs without any problem then across no-man's land into Turkey. Two, machine-gun carrying, customs officials, stopped us. They asked if we had any Turkish money, which we denied and they then proceeded to look through the side-car asking if we had any radios or tape recorders. Having not found anything they frisked us for weapons and then stamped our passports and let us go. We were now in that small area of Turkey on the European mainland and on our way to Istanbul. The road was flat and the village skylines dominated by minarets. By sunset we were halfway. We stopped at a village, bought a fresh loaf of bread and found a quiet site to camp. Like in Yugoslavia and Greece, we heard the sound of sheep bells during the night and in the morning a silent shepherd was sitting there to greet us.

We reached Istanbul about midmorning. After spending so much time travelling long country roads the speed and noise of city traffic was, to say the least, hair raising. We made our way to the central YMCA hostel in the old city and booked in. The accommodation was a series of large rooms lined with bunk beds. The hostel was close to the famous Blue Mosque or to give it its proper name The Sultan Ahmed Mosque and opposite one of the main city museums.

A military government, which had overthrown the previous civilian government, ruled Turkey at that time. Armed soldiers as well as civilian police were everywhere. From our room we had a view across one of the main squares and one of the features of the square was a public gallows. Thankfully during my stay in Turkey I never saw it being used.

Most of the side streets in the old city were still cobbled. From the hostel it was short walk to the main post office in front of which was a kind of traffic junction. Vehicles of all description raced through seemingly only using their hooters as brakes. From there it was a short walk to the Golden Horn and the ferry ports on the Bosphorous. The bridge across the Bosphorous was then still only in its planning stages.

Once we had settled down and parked the bike in a safe place we went out for a meal. Once again the chefs were only too keen let us into the kitchen so that we could choose what we wanted to eat. Numerous small teashops lined the streets. You could purchase a small glass of black tea for a few pence and sit and watch the world go by. All the customers were male many of whom were playing chess, draughts or smoking hubbly-bubbly pipes. We wandered through the large market and two new sights greeted us.

Firstly we saw men of all ages carrying large loads on their backs. All sorts of goods - fridges, stoves, small desks, packed tea chests, rolls of cloth, etc. Some were bent double and struggled to walk along the uneven kerb and cobble stones. The second sight was that of a man sitting on a low chair with a portable typewriter on his lap. He was a scribe with his illiterate clients squatting beside him whispering whatever they wanted to be written on their behalf.

Besides stalls selling anything and everything there were workshops of all descriptions. In one sat a man operating a wood turning lathe. It was powered by a string bow held in one hand, which he pushed backwards and forwards to rotate a short length of timber. In the other hand he held a chisel steadied by his toes and fashioned the piece of wood into the shape of a round table leg. The work looked hard and tiring. In another stall only about ten yards further along was a similar workshop but the lathe was driven by an electric motor. The whole market was very noisy due to music from radios and record players, vendors shouting out, loud conversations and everywhere the hammering of metal into all sorts of shapes, objects and patterns.

The first morning in the hostel I was awakened by a loud conversation conducted in English by other lodgers while lying on their bunks. There were those who were telling someone what they had done the night before or where they were going to or coming from. It soon became obvious that the hostel was a major staging post for those who were venturing into the Asian subcontinent and those who had just returned. The route was across Turkey into Iran, then Afghanistan, Pakistan and finally

India. Those who returned had journeyed via lifts, local buses and, where possible, trains. There were also those who were travelling in various forms of vehicles, or on motorbikes or pedal bicycles. One group had fitted out an old van with beds; others had old jeeps or land rovers.

I was on the top bunk and Colin was below me. He and I joined in the general discussion. Suddenly someone shouted out, "I know that voice," and called out my first name followed by "We met during at a water polo tournament at the London University students union."

There was a communal kitchen of sorts mostly used to boil water for a hot drink. It was there that we met Bill, a young American who had been cycling round the Middle East and had sold his cycle and was preparing to return home. The kitchen was also the place where the inmates exchanged information about what to see where to go, and where not to go. We kept being asked whether or not we had been to the street on the hill to see the cluster of brothels. The emphasis was on the naked women on view through the doorways and windows. The other sites to see were the Blue Mosque, the Church of St. Sophia, the museum, the Dolmarbachi Palace and a ferry trip up the Bosphorous to the entrance to the Black sea.

Bill joined Colin and me as we set out on our tour that morning. The museum was only across the road from the hostel and that was our first stop. The labelling of most of the exhibits was in Turkish and French. The museum, a poor version of the British Museum, housed a great variety of exhibits - many from ancient Egypt and Greece. Next stop was the magnificent Blue Mosque. The road outside was hot and as noisy as ever but once you removed your shoes and entered through the portals an atmosphere of peace, tranquillity and coolness prevailed. We found a window ledge where the three of us sat in silence and admired what we saw around us. We had another look around the market and then crossed the Golden Horn Bridge toward the new town. After a meal we sat on the shoreline looking across the Bosphorous toward Asia Minor. The Soviet navy and commercial fleet had the right to sail through to and from the Black Sea. It was strange to see warships flying the Hammer and Sickle in the midst of the then Cold War.

Somehow we did not find the street of the brothels. We had a vague idea what the area was called in Turkish. After some discussion we decided to ask a passing group of lads. As soon as we mentioned the place name they all smiled and then gave us directions. We were sent down to the ferry port. The buying of our tickets also lit up a few faces in the booking office.

Once on board the ferry, three jet fighter planes flew over performing aerobatics. It was apparently in celebration of Turkey's national day. The aircraft returned flying low over the water front, up into the sky and then returned flying even lower. So low in fact that the shock waves caused all the ferries to sway as if they had been suddenly struck by a large wave. The sound and the shock was so intense that everybody on the boat ducked and some yelled out in both fear and fury. Anyone who was not holding on would have been tossed out into the water.

While crossing over to Isikidar on the opposite side we were puzzled. We thought that our supposed destination was in Istanbul proper. From the ferry we were directed (with smiles) to a tram that wound its way up a steep hill and ended its journey in an open area. The conductor laughingly (after once again asking directions) showed us the footpath to follow. We ended up at a restaurant on the very summit of a hill. Once we saw the name of the restaurant we realised what had happened. Our version of the Turkish pronunciation of where we wanted to go was very similar to the name of the restaurant. The place had a commanding view. From there you could see the entrance to the Black Sea and in the opposite direction the Sea of Marmara. In addition looking across the Bosphorous was a panoramic view of both the old and new city of Istanbul. This was a place visited regularly by the locals but at that time hardly known to the tourists. Visitors asking to go there was probably the cause of the smiles. We stayed to watch the sun set behind the old city.

We caught the tram down the hill and then onto the ferry. A ticket inspector looked at our tickets and insisted that we had not paid the right fare. That made Bill quite angry and when we arrived at the quayside in Istanbul he went straight over to the office. A stream of officials came out, examined our tickets and walked with us back to the ferry. After a heated exchange with the ferry ticket man, telephone calls and us listening on without understanding, we were invited back into the office, given an apology and offered a refund of the extra we were asked to pay. Apparently they had been waiting to catch out the inspector who had already extracted money from several other tourists.

Walking along the quayside we bumped into another hostel inmate. After telling him where we had been and why we ended up there he directed us to the street of the brothels. It turned out to be only a few hundred yards from where we had initially asked the first group of lads directions. The houses were in a side street on the hill that led up toward the new city. Outside on the street were crowds of men, all staring into the houses where the prostitutes in various states of undress were standing and sitting around. Some were staring out at the men and trying to entice them in, others looking blank, smoking and some were even reading. There were several houses in a cul-de-sac. One rather large woman, wearing nothing but a G-string which was hardly visible beneath the folds of skin on her lower abdomen tried to grab hold of any bloke who approached too close to the threshold of her door. A young Turk, egged on by his mates, walked into one of the houses, handed over a roll of notes to the madam at the desk and then turned round to select his purchase. The woman he chose was one of the younger and more attractive females on display. She stood and gave him a hard look as if to say, "So you think you can handle me."

The following day we caught a ferry that slowly made its way up the Bosphorous to the Black Sea. A steam-powered ferryboat zigzagged in and out of the many stops along the way. We passed close by to a splendid large mansion. Sitting on benches on the shoreline were a group of Arab men, women and children. The women wore gold trimmed garments. The men with their Arab robes and headdresses looked very distinguished. They, too, had gold braiding around their headgear. They all waved up at the passengers on the ferry. A passenger standing alongside us told us that the building was one of summer palaces belonging to the Saudi Royal Family. The man with the goatee beard in the middle was either the King himself or one of his brothers and the women were all his wives and children. In attendance were both male and female servants. There was not a bodyguard in sight. We went ashore at the terminus on the Black Sea, had a meal then sailed back to Istanbul.

The next morning we made an early start. Once again we caught the ferry to Isikidar. At the bus station we found the bus with a named destination that matched the name we had been given the night before in the hostel. This was a trip that we were told we should attempt. The crowded windowless bus shook and bounced over potholed roads on into the interior. We drove up along narrow passes and through valleys. Some hills were quite wooded and others almost bare with only small shrubs. Three hours later we arrived at a village on the shores of the Black Sea.

Lovely endless stretches of white sandy beaches merged with short grass banks a few hundred yards wide, eventually disappearing into the hilly scrub. A stone turret, the remains of small fortress, stood on a patch of high ground overlooking the calm dark blue sea. The grass banks in places ended on to small cliffs that overlooked a beach below. Apart from a few local picnickers there were about a dozen local youths gathered round a few mature men. They had a shotgun and were shooting at sea birds. Eventually they bagged one and they all rushed toward their trophy. The noise of excitement and triumph sounded as if they had shot a tiger. From what we saw all they had killed the bird for was for some of its feathers. Colin told us that they would be used to attach to fishhooks to act as lures. After that they all moved on and the quiet returned.

We caught the return bus late in the afternoon. Once again it was crowded. All sorts of goods from cases to mattresses were tied to the roof. Almost everyone had a parcel of sorts on their laps, which included live fish, vegetables and even a live chicken. No one was inhibited about forcing you to move over so that everyone sat shoulder to shoulder. The three of us were split up and Bill kept shouting over to us that the smell of the man next to him was going to knock him out.

About halfway into the journey it became dark. As the bus shook and bounced, most people fell asleep. Suddenly the bus came to an abrupt halt. The driver shouted to the passengers who immediately started to disembark. As we stepped off the bus we walked through a line of armed soldiers. Each passenger was made to stand with his or her back to the bus. They then aggressively questioned each passenger. We did not understand them but they still demanded to see our passports. All the passengers except us three were searched. Some of the soldiers went all through the empty bus and the contents of the roof. After a lot more shouting and questioning we were all allowed back on the bus and to proceed on our way. Two hours later we were safely back in Istanbul.

That evening, back in the hostel, we discussed what we should do next. Bill told us that the next day he was going his own way. Colin decided that he was ready to continue on his quest to try and reach India. I decided to start my return to England the next day. I needed to renew my visa for entry to Yugoslavia.

Early the next morning I went over to the Yugoslavian embassy. In the main waiting room was a long queue of mostly young travellers. While waiting two Swedish girls came out of the office asking in English if anyone would like to change or buy some Yugoslavian currency off them. Apparently you could not pay for a visa in the currency of the country you were hoping to travel to. I still had plenty of Turkish money. I called them over and much to my embarrassment they gave me all of their Yugoslavian money just to have enough Turkish money to pay for their visa. They seemed to be only too pleased to be rid of the money.

I caught a bus from Istanbul back to Erdine, the last town before the Greek border. I spent some of my Turkish currency on a meal and a few souvenirs at the border town. It was now mid-afternoon. I walked toward the frontier and through the Turkish customs without being questioned. A small river separates the two countries and in the river were some buffalo. They must have belonged in either Turkey or Greece. How were they retrieved if they strayed on to the wrong side? The Greek customs agent glanced at my passport and waved me through.

There was no traffic in either direction and I started to walk. At first the road passed through an area of thick bush. I was hoping that I would come across a suitable clearing to pitch my tent for the night. While walking along, a young couple came along on a motor scooter travelling toward Turkey. I stopped them. They turned out to be from New Zealand. Luckily for me they did not have any Turkish currency. They had resisted the overtures of the moneychangers they had met early on. I managed to persuade them to buy my Turkish currency. I ended up with a mixture of Greek, Yugoslavian and Italian money. Although they did not change their money with men on the street they were aware of the rates of exchange. We both parted pleased. I at having got rid of my excess Turkish money and they at having received a generous rate.

A half hour later, with dark approaching, I came across some open fields that had been recently harvested. I left the road and found a level spot. As I was about to unpack, I heard someone calling over to me. I looked up and at the other end of the field a young farmer was beckoning to me to come over to him. I picked up my belongings and walked over to him. He led me to mini shelter in the shape of a tent made out of straw. He gestured to me that I could sleep in there. I accepted his invitation and got my sleeping bag out and made the most of what light there was left.

I was about to boil up some water when the farmer came over and led me to his house. He and his wife and small child were about to start their evening meal and they invited me to share it with them. Somehow or other we managed an elementary conversation. It was a hot night and I slept well in the straw shelter under the stars. I woke up early, packed up and set off. The farmer was already in the field and we waved our farewells to each other.

My first lift of the day took me to Alexandropolous. Once out of the town, there was far more traffic about. Hitching now suddenly became much easier. The police stopped a lorry and more or less told the driver to give me lift. I climbed up on to the back of a large uncovered truck and lay on top of a load of grain sacks. I was not alone as there were five others who the driver had to pick up. The sacks were easily moulded into our body shapes and with a breeze and the sun shining down out of a blue sky nothing could have felt, better at the time. It soon came to an end about twenty miles on. As we climbed off the truck a policeman called over to us and told us to climb into the back of a covered lorry. At the cab end of the lorry was a stack of gas cylinders and lying in front of them was young Greek boy fast asleep. As we drove along the cylinders began to shake loose. One of my fellow hitch-hikers was a tall blond German in his thirties who had just come back from the hippie trail to India. He seemed very streetwise and full of advice to the rest of us. We all became concerned about the fact that one of the cylinders was working its way out and could land on the head of the sleeping boy. The German who knew some Greek moved over and tried to wake him by calling to him. Eventually he was only woken up after being rolled over and, even then, he had been in such a deep sleep that he was reluctant to move. We made him sit up then moved him and propped him up. A minute later a cylinder came crashing down and had he not moved it would have landed on his head.

About midday, after several more lifts, we approached the border. Slowly the group dispersed, and I was the only person who actually crossed over back into Yugoslavia. A short lift took me a few miles along and then the traffic just seemed to vanish. While waiting and hoping, a young blond lad of about twenty appeared out of nowhere. He reminded me very much of a white Afrikaner. He beckoned me to follow him and ten minutes later together we arrived at his very small village. All the houses were basic, similar to the better quality homes that I had associated with African farm workers. I was introduced to his family and was offered some watermelon. The last few days my stomach had felt rough and at the best of times too much fruit upsets me. I felt that I could not refuse so I ate a slice as slowly as I could. His mother then produced a large bowl of thick soup and a few slices of bread. By now the entire village stared at me. After the meal he took me through the village to a small rail station. It was nothing more than a siding. There was quite a crowd waiting for the train. It seemed to be the event of the day. Among those waiting was a group of students who could speak some English. A train pulled by a steam engine arrived and, amidst much noise and excitement, the students and myself boarded. Once on board I learnt that our destination was Skopje.

The train stopped at every siding let alone station. The carriage was basic with hard seats but clean and almost full to capacity. I sat with a group of students who were making their way back to college for the start of the new term. At each stop the train became more and more crowded. Everybody squashed together and soon people had to sit on the floor. As on the journey out, I saw a man hanging onto the footplate with one hand and a large fish in the other. Someone produced a guitar and a sing-song helped us all forget the discomfort. I had learned some Italian/Sicilian songs during my days working in coffee bars and my attempt at singing went down well.

We reached Skopje in the middle of the evening. After a meal I walked to what I thought to be the outskirts of the town and pitched my tent. Before I fell asleep I started to count what money I had left. Once I had calculated the various rates of exchange I realised that I had made small profit of ten shillings. I had had a free stay in Turkey.

I was woken in the dawn by the sound of shunting steam engines. Looking out of my tent I saw that I had camped close by to a railway yard. I made an early start and the first lift took me about ten miles up country.

I now stood beside what could only be described as nothing but a cart tract which was the main highway to Belgrade and beyond. What on earth was I doing there in the middle of nowhere and would I ever get away from it? A bullock cart came by and the driver invited me to climb on. I sat with my feet dangling as the two-wheeled animal drawn vehicle plodded on. There was no way I would get anywhere at that rate. Every now and again I would jump off and walk behind. The road now began to ascend a gentle incline and I had a good view of the road behind. When I saw a lorry approaching I would jump off raise my thumb and then as the lorry passed by jump back on the cart. I was beginning to give up and took my eyes off the road. The cart jolted, I looked up and there only a few yards behind was a Peugeot saloon with Austrian number plates. I jumped off and waved at them and they stopped and they asked me in German if I wanted a lift. They said that they could only take me as far as Belgrade as they were planning to stop there for the night. Within a minute I was sitting on the back seat with my rucksack along side of me.

The fellow who drove the car was in his twenties and alongside of him was his father and on the back seat with me was his mother. At first, the luxury of a car compared to a motor-cycle, lorries and an ox cart was beyond belief. However the rough road soon made its presence felt as we slowly made our way. We arrived in Belgrade at nine in the evening. They dropped me in the centre of the city. I then proceeded to make my way to Jan's flat. By the time I got there it was past ten and, without a moment of hesitation, I knocked on the door. I had to identify myself through the letterbox. When I think back I still feel embarrassed at my sheer chutzpah. They welcomed me back and fed me. This time Jan slept in the middle of the bed. However with only three of us and me hugging the end of the bed it did not seem such an intrusion as during my first stay there.

The next morning I found a calendar and realised that I had been away for more than six weeks and that I should have been back at my temporary teaching post the day before. I decided to return to England by train. I walked down to the rail station and paid for my ticket in pounds sterling, as it was cheaper that way. I then found a bank and changed all my remaining currency into pounds.

The train left Belgrade just after midnight and, unlike my journey to Skopje, this was a modern fast train - part of the Orient Express. I arrived in Paris the next morning and decided to catch the late afternoon boat train in order to be able to spend a few hours wandering around Paris. At midday I sat on a bench near to the Arch de Triomphe. Sitting next to me was a group of young English tourists. By this time my beard was quite overgrown and my hair desperately needed attention. I was still wearing the same sandals only with more repair pins and apart from my stop in Milan and my first visit to Belgrade I had hardly washed any of my clothes. I also was very brown and probably looked more like a Mediterranean tramp than someone from England. One of the persons on the bench tried to discreetly point me out to his companions and said quietly, "If you think we are untidy get a load of him." I pretended that I did not understand English.

Later on that evening on the boat train I was sitting in the bar and who should I see but one of the chaps from the Paris bench. He became even more sheepish when I offered to buy him a drink.